QUE Bee

From Doubts to **Distinction**

Your ICSE 2026 Exams Partner

GIST OF THE TEXTBOOK

Crisp & Complete Theory - No need to go back to bulky textbooks!

ALL TYPES OF LATEST PATTERN QUESTIONS

MCQs | Case-based | Assertion-Reason; All in one place!

KEYWORDS HIGHLIGHTED

Important points and keywords are neatly Underlined; Never miss what matters

10 YEARS' PYQS ANSWERS

Previous Year Questions with solutions

COUNCIL-STYLE ANSWERS

Write responses like an examiner expects

SAMPLE & SPECIMEN PAPER

Practice in real-exam mode. Perfect your timing, strategy, and confidence.

arihant
SUCCESS AND NOTHING LESS

ARIHANT PRAKASHAN
(School Division Series)

ADMINISTRATIVE & PRODUCTION OFFICES

Regd. Office
'Ramchhaya' 4577/15, Agarwal Road, Darya Ganj, New Delhi -110002
Tele: 011- 47630600, 43518550; Fax: 011- 23280316

Head Office
Kalindi, TP Nagar, Meerut (UP) - 250002, Tel: 0121-7156203, 7156204

SALES & SUPPORT OFFICES
Agra, Ahmedabad, Bengaluru, Bareilly, Chennai, Delhi, Guwahati, Hyderabad, Jaipur, Jhansi, Kolkata, Lucknow, Nagpur & Pune.

PO No : TXT-XX-XXXXXXX-X-XX

Published By Arihant Publications (India) Ltd.

For further information about the books published by Arihant, log on to www.arihantbooks.com or e-mail at info@arihantbooks.com

Follow us on

PRICE ₹ 225.00

PRODUCTION TEAM

Publishing Manager
Keshav Mohan

Project Head
Shivam Gupta

Cover Designer
Bilal Hashmi

Inner Designer
Ankit Tyagi

Page Layouting
Jashoda

Proof Reader
Ayushi Sharma

QUE Bee

ICSE
GEOGRAPHY
Class 10

Types of Questions & their Respective Number

Type of Questions	Total Number
Multiple Choice Questions (MCQs)	271
Assertion-Reason (A-R)	46
Short Answer Type Questions (SA)	208
Long Answer Type Questions (LA)	143
Structured Questions	28
Map Based Questions	22
TOTAL NO. OF QUESTIONS	**718**

Created by

Manisha Rana
M.A. (History & Geography), M.Ed.
30 Yrs. Experienced
PGT (Geography)

Contributor
Akshat Sharma

From Learner to Leader

Step-Into the Spotlight

QUE Bee is more than just a book - it's a platform for young achievers like you to guide future toppers. If you've cracked the code to smart study or have insights that can make learning easier for others, this is your moment to shine!

What Can You Share?

- Your study techniques, time management tips, or motivation hacks
- Feedback or suggestions to make QUE Bee even better
- Real experiences that can guide other students through the exam maze

What's in It for You?

- Your name will be featured in our exclusive Student Panel in the next edition
- Win exciting & surprise rewards for impactful suggestions
- **Get published** - your photo, Ideas-or even interviews can be featured in the book
- **Become a student icon** - recognized and followed by peers across schools

Let your learning become someone else's ladder.
Be remembered. Be featured. Be the guide.

SCAN TO SHARE YOUR IDEA

QUE Bee

Index

Part I Map Work

1. Interpretation of Topographical Maps 1-14

Part II Geography of India

2. Location, Extent and Physical Features of India 15-30
3. Climate 31-45
4. Soil Resources 46-57
5. Natural Vegetation 58-71
6. Water Resources 72-85
7. Mineral and Energy Resources 86-102
8. Agriculture 103-122
9. Manufacturing Industries 123-140
10. Transport 141-151
11. Waste Management 152-162

ICSE Solved Paper 2025 **165-178**

ICSE Latest Specimen Paper **181-194**

Sample Question Paper **195-200**

Latest Course Structure

There will be one paper of two hours duration carrying 80 marks and Internal Assessment of 20 marks.

PART I MAP WORK

1. *Interpretation of Topographical Maps*

a. Locating features with the help of a four-figure or a six-figure grid reference.

b. Definition of contour and contour interval. Identification of landforms marked by contours (steep slope, gentle slope, hill, valley, ridge / water divide, escarpment), triangulated height, spot height, bench mark, relative height/ depth.

c. Interpretation of colour tints and conventional symbols used on a topographical survey of India map.

d. Identification and definition of types of scale given on the map.
Measuring distances and calculating area using the scale given therein.

e. Marking directions between different locations, using eight cardinal points.

f. Identify: Site of prominent villages and/or towns, types of land use / land cover and means of communication with the help of the index given at the bottom of the sheet.

g. Identification of drainage (direction of flow and pattern) and settlement patterns.

h. Identification of natural and man-made features.

2. *Map of India*

On an outline map of India, candidates will be required to locate, mark and name the following

Mountains, Peaks and Plateaus: Himalayas, Karakoram, Aravali, Vindhyas, Satpura, Western and Eastern Ghats, Nilgiris, Garo, Khasi, Jaintia, Mount Godwin Austin (K2), Mount Kanchenjunga. Deccan Plateau, Chota Nagpur Plateau.

Plains: Gangetic Plains and Coastal plains – (Konkan, Kanara, Malabar, Coromandel, Northern Circars).

Desert: Thar (The Great Indian Desert)

Rivers: Indus, Ravi, Beas, Chenab, Jhelum, Satluj, Ganga, Yamuna, Ghaghra, Gomti, Gandak, Kosi, Chambal, Betwa, Son, Damodar, Brahmaputra, Narmada, Tapti, Mahanadi, Godavari, Krishna, Cauveri, Tungabhadra.

Water Bodies : Gulf of Kutch, Gulf of Khambhat, Gulf of Mannar, Palk Strait, Andaman Sea, Chilika Lake, Wular Lake.

Passes: Karakoram, Nathu-La Passes.

Latitude and Longitudes: Tropic of Cancer, Standard Meridian (82° 30′E).

Direction of Winds: South-West Monsoons (Arabian Sea and Bay of Bengal Branches), North-East Monsoons and Western Disturbances.

Distribution of Minerals: Oil-Mumbai High (Offshore Oil Field) and Digboi. Iron – Singhbhum, Coal – Jharia.

Soil Distribution : Alluvial, Laterite, Black and Red Soil.

Cities : Delhi, Mumbai, Kolkata, Chennai, Hyderabad, Bengaluru, Kochi, Chandigarh, Srinagar, Visakhapatnam, Allahabad.

Population : Distribution of Population (Dense and sparse).

PART II GEOGRAPHY OF INDIA

3. *Location, Extent and Physical features*

- Position and Extent of India. (through Map only).
- The physical features of India – mountains, plateaus, plains and rivers (through Map only).

4. *Climate*

- Distribution of Temperature, Rainfall, Winds in Summer and Winter and factors affecting the climate of the area.
- Monsoon and its mechanism. Seasons –March to May – Summer; June to September – Monsoon; October to November - Retreating Monsoon. December to February –Winter.

5. *Soil Resources*

- Types of soil (alluvial, black, red and laterite) distribution, composition and characteristics such as colour, texture, minerals and crops associated.
- Soil Erosion – causes, prevention and conservation.

6. *Natural Vegetation*

- Importance of forests.
- Types of vegetation (tropical evergreen, tropical deciduous, tropical desert, littoral and mountain), distribution and correlation with their environment.
- Forest conservation.

7. *Water Resources*

- Sources (Surface water and ground water).
- Need for conservation and conservation practices
  (Rain water harvesting and its importance).
- Irrigation: Importance and methods.

8. *Mineral and Energy Resources*

- Iron ore, Manganese, Copper, Bauxite – uses and their distribution.
- Conventional Sources: Coal, Petroleum, Natural gas (distribution, advantages and disadvantages).
  Hydel power (Bhakra Nangal Dam and Hirakud).
- Non-conventional Sources: Solar, wind, tidal, geo-thermal, nuclear and bio-gas (generation and advantages).

9. *Agriculture*

- Indian Agriculture – importance, problems and reforms.
- Types of farming in India: Subsistence and commercial: shifting, intensive, extensive, plantation and mixed.
- Agricultural seasons (rabi, kharif, zaid).

- Climatic conditions, soil requirements, methods of cultivation, processing and distribution of the following crops
  - rice, wheat, millets and pulses.
  - sugarcane, oilseeds (groundnut, mustard and soybean).
  - cotton, jute, tea and coffee.

10. Manufacturing Industries

- Importance and classification.
- Agro-based Industry - Sugar, Textile (Cotton and Silk).
- Mineral-based Industry – Iron & Steel (TISCO, Bhilai, Rourkela, Visakhapatnam) Petro-Chemical and Electronics.

11. Transport

- Importance and Modes – Roadways, Railways, Airways and Waterways – Advantages and disadvantages.

12. Waste Management

- Impact of waste accumulation - spoilage of landscape, pollution, health hazards, effect on terrestrial, aquatic (fresh water and marine) life.
- Need for waste management.
- Methods of safe disposal - segregation, dumping and composting.
- Need and methods for reducing, reusing and recycling waste.

INTERPRETATION OF TOPOGRAPHICAL MAPS

Topographical Map

- A Topographical map is a detailed graphic representation of natural and man-made features within a specific geographical area.
- In the UK, topographical maps are also known as Ordnance Survey Maps. These maps serve as essential tools for planning, executing projects, navigation and Understanding terrain features.
- Topographical maps are divided into a grid of square, with each side representing 1 km on the ground.
- The grid has a network of intersecting horizontal (latitude) and vertical (longitude) parallel lines. This is identified as grid reference.
- Vertical lines are called Eastings and horizontal lines are called Northings.

Four-Figure Grid Reference

- In this method, first two digits refer to the Eastings (vertical lines),and the last two digits refer to the Northings (horizontal lines).
- The origin, where counting begins, is located at the South-West corner of the map.
- Eastings are numbered and read from West to East, and Northings are read from South to North, both starting from the origin.
- Eastings are always stated first, followed by Northings.
- For example in the figure given below, the four-figure grid reference of the school (marked as S) is in the square with its centre at the Easting marked 17 and again its centre at the Northing marked 03.
- Thus, the four-figure grid reference will be 1703. The first two digits represent the Easting, and the last two digits represent the Northing.

Six-Figure Grid Reference

- A six-figure grid reference is used to precisely locate a specific point, such as a temple, school, railway station, or spot height, on a topographical map. It can be understood by the image given below
- The first three figures are the Eastings and the last three are the Northings.
- To find the six-figure grid reference of a triangulated height, start by identifying its location within the square marked by a four-figure grid reference. On a 1:50,000 scale map, each grid square is 2 cm by 2 cm, representing an area of 1 km^2 on the ground.
- In this example, the four-figure grid reference of the triangulated height is 7212, meaning it lies within the square where Easting 72 and Northing 12 intersect.
- To determine the six-figure grid reference, divide the 1 km^2 square into a 10 × 10 grid, where each smaller square represents 100 meters on the ground.

- Locate the 5th division along Easting 72 and the 5th division along Northing 12. Their intersection marks the precise point where the triangulated height is situated.

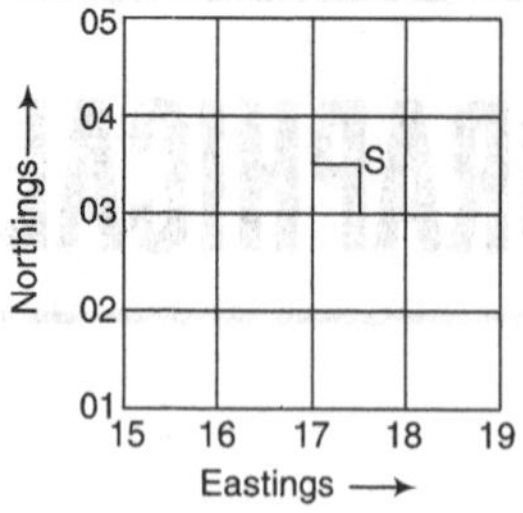

Four-Figure Grid

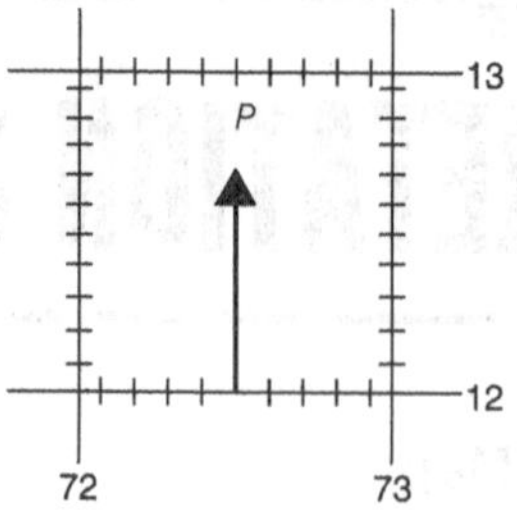

Six-Figure Grid

- Therefore the six-figure grid reference of point *P* is 725125.

Contours

- Contours are imaginary lines on a map that join points having the same elevation above mean sea level (MSL). They depict the terrain's relief and topography.
- Contours are drawn at fixed vertical intervals, representing the difference in elevation between two successive contour lines on a map.
- The contour interval is of 20 metres.
- Contour interval is the difference of height between the two successive contours.

Identification of Landforms marked by Contours

- The spacing of the contour lines indicates the nature of slope.
- **Steep Slope** In such a slope, the land suddenly slopes up or down. The contours of this slope are drawn close to one another.
- **Gentle slope** In gentle slopes, the elevation increases gradually. This is represented by widely spaced contour lines on a map.
- **Hill** A hill with a uniform slope and narrow top is represented by concentric contours spaced almost at regular intervals.
- **Valley** Valley are areas of low ground which penetrate into highlands. The types of valleys are - V-shaped valley, U-shaped valley, hanging valley, cirques, Gorge canyons.
- **Ridge/Water Divide** It is a naturally elevated area, such as a mountain range or hill, that separates the flow of water into different directions. On maps, it is typically represented by contour lines that form a 'V' or 'U' shape, with the point of the 'V' indicating the direction of water flow.
- **Escarpment Chiff** It is abrupt, comparatively long and regular, steep face of any hill or a plateau. It has a narrow top with a steep slope on one side and a gentle slope on the other. It is represented by sudden merging of several contours at one point.
- **Triangulated Height** When a point is accurately surveyed and shown with a triangle is called 'triangulated' height, e.g. Δ340. It is determined trigonometrically denoting height of that point above mean sea level.
- **Spot Height** It is a height of a point above the mean sea level. It is indicated by a 'dot' followed by a number on the map, e.g. • 300.
- **Bench Mark** These are surveyed marks or permanent marks on a stone or a building to indicate the accurate height of that object above mean sea level. It is written on survey maps as BM 200, BM 300 and so on.
- **Relative Height/Depth** Relative height or depth indicates the difference in elevation between the highest and lowest points in an area. It is often denoted by '*r*' on maps, especially in steep terrain as 30r.

Interpretation of Colour Tints

Six colours are used in a survey map to show various features as follows

- **Black** All names, heights and their numbering, latitude and longitude lines, railway lines, telephone or telegraph lines, dry streams and river banks, surveyed trees and broken ground.
- **Yellow** Cultivated areas or lands.

- **Green** All forested areas, orchards, scattered trees and scrubs.
- **Brown** It is used to depict contour lines (along with their height numbers), sand dunes, sand hills, and other landforms that show relief features.
- **Blue** Perennial rivers, ponds, lakes, tanks, wells and other water bodies.
- **Red** Grid lines (Eastings and Northings with their numbering), roads and tracks, all buildings and settlements with specific symbols being shown for buildings with specific functions, permanent huts.
- **Orange** Plateau

Sometimes white patches are there, to show barren lands.

Conventional Signs and Symbols Used on a Topographical Map

Man-made Features

Settlements

■ ■	Permanent hut
□ □	Temporary hut
	Settlement type
	Nucleated Settlements
	Linear Settlements
	Scattered or **Dispersed** Settlements

Structural Features

	Tower
	Antiquities
	Fort
	Boundary Pillars
■	Surveyed
□	Unsurveyed
	Chhatri
	Mandir (temple)
	Church

	Tomb
	Graves
	Mosque
	Idgah
	Police Station
....	Telegraph Lines
PO	Post Office
Red ⊕	(Ayurvedic) Hospital
Red +	Dispensary
Blue ⊕	(Veternary) Hospital pylons
o-o-o	Powerline (Unsurveyed)
•-•-•	Powerline (Pylons surveyed)
Aqueduct	Printed on sheet (An artificial channel for conveying water).
TO	Telegraph Office
PTO	Post and Telegraph Office (combined)
	Rest House or Inspection bungalow
CG	Camping Ground
	Circuit House

Political Boundaries

	Boundaries
	International boundaries
	State boundaries (demarcated)
—x—x	State boundaries (undemarcated)
– – –	Districts (sub-divisions)
• • • •	Teshil/taluka dots
	Boundary pillars
•• ••	Forest boundary
	Boundary Pillars
□	Unlocated
■	Surveyed

Transport and Communication

	Roads
	Metalled (Pucca) Roads
	Unmetalled (Kutch) Roads
	Cart Track
---x---	Pack Track (Pagdandi)
	Footpath with a Bridge

	Railways
	Broad Gauge
	Metre Gauge
	Narrow Gauge
	Railway line with a station.
	Light railway or tramway.
	Cutting with a Tunnel
	Level Gossing

	Bridges
	A bridges is a structure constructed across a road, river or railway to carry the traffic.
	A ridge without a causeway
	Bridge with Piers
	Tunnel
	Ford or Ferry
	Causeway

Natural Features

Drainage System

	Seasonal Stream
	River
	Stream with track in bed.
	Stream Undefined
	River, dry with water channel shown in blue
	River with Island and Rocks
	Disappearing Stream
	Seasonal Streams
C	Confluence
	Meander (bend formed by river in its middle age)
	Broken Ground
	This sign in blue shows river bank selving
3r	River bank steep (3 to 6 metres)
6r	River bank (over 6 metres)
Dep	Depression (hollow formed by wind in sandy region)

Means of Irrigation and Other Water Features

	Canal
□	Perennial tank
	A dry tank
	Tank with embankment

Symbol	Meaning
	Perennial lined well (shown as a blue dot)
	Unlined well (shown as a blue circle)
(Brackish)	Brackish water
	Shoal (submerged rock)
	Swamp
	Dam (masonry)
	Aqueduct
	Reservoir (talao/table)
	Earthen dam
	Weir (a low dam across a river.)
	Island (If an island is uncultivable it is shown in white colour)
	Overhead tank
	Causeway

Vegetation Cover

Symbol	Meaning
	Vine on trellis
open scrub	Open Scrub
	Plantain
	Palmyra
	Grass
	Bamboos
	Surveyed tree (Shown in black colours)
PF	Protected Forest
	Deciduous forest
Fire line	Fire line

Other Important Features

Symbol	Meaning
Stony waste	Stony Waste (Shown as a whitte)
Sheet rock	Sheet Rock
Rock out crop	Rock Out Crop
	Sand Dunes
Brick kiln	Kiln (bricks)
Lime kiln	Kiln (lime)
Stone quarry	Stone Quarry
	Powerline with poles surveyed
	Powerline with poles un-surveyed

Legend

Diggi	Tank used for collecting water.
Siphon	Bend pipe taken from a canal/aquaduct for supplying water.
Sluice	A movable gate allowing water to flow under it.
8	Roads, metalled with distance stone
	Roads unmetalled
	Cart track Pack track and Pass. Footpath with bridge....
	Bridges; with piers, without causeway. Ford or Ferry.....
	Streams with track in bed; undefined. Canal.....
	Dams: masonry or rock-filled; Earth work, Weir......
	River banks shelvings: steep 3 to 6 meters; over 6 meters....
	River dry with water channel: with island and rocks. .Tidal river....
	Submerged rocks. Shoal, Swamp, Reeds....
	Wells lined unlined. Tube-well. Spring Tanks: pernnial:dry
2r 4r	Embankments: road or rail tank. Broken ground.....
RS	Railways, broad gauge: double: single with station:under construction.
	Railways other gauges double single, distance stone, under construction..

REVISION NOTES

	Light railway or tramway, Telegraph line, Cutting with tunnel.
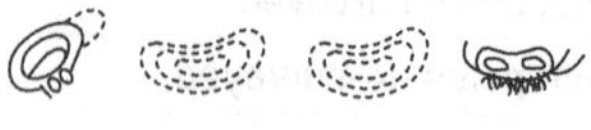	Contours with sub-features, from-line, Rocky slopes, Cliffs.
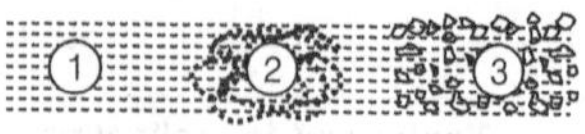	Sand features : (1) Flat, (2) Sand-hills (permanent), (3) Dunes (shifting)...
	Towns or villages: inhabited; deserted, Fort....
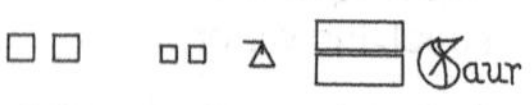	Huts: Permanent temporary, Tower, Antiquities
	Temple, Chhatri, Church, Mosque, Idgah, Tomb, Graves
	Lighthouse
	Mine, Vine on trellis, Grass, Scrub....
	Palms palmyra; other, Plantain: Conifer, Bamboo, Other trees
—·—·—·—·—·—·—·—	Boundary international.....

-·-·-·-·- —×—×—×—×	Boundary state: demarcated; undemarcated...
——— •••• ••—••—•• •••	Boundary district; sub-divn, tashil or taluk, village, forest....
■ □	Boundary pillars: surveyed; unlocated; village ....
△200 •200 •63	Heights, triangulated: station: point......
BM 63.3 BM63.3 .63	Bench-mark geodetic: tertiary: canal.....
PO TO PTO PS	Post Office, Telegraph Office, Combined Office, Police Station....
DB IB (Canal) RH (Forest)	Bungalows Dak or travellers: inspection Rest-House.....
CH CG RF PF	Circuit house, Camping Ground, Forest Reserved, protected....
KIKRI DUAR NAGA	Spaced names administrative; locality: tribal....

Scale

Scale of a map is the ratio of the distance on the map to the corresponding distance on the ground. Connecting two points, represented by the same unit.

Types of Scale

- **Simple Statement or Verbal Scale** It expresses the units of the map as well as the ground e.g. 1 centimetre = 10 kilometres.
- **The Representative Fraction (RF)** It is the numerical scale of a map which indicates the relationship between the distance measured on a map and the corresponding distance on the ground. It can be measured by the following

  RF = Distance on the map / Distance on the ground. RF 1:50,000 means 1 unit on the map represents 50,000 units on the ground. It is also called universal scale.

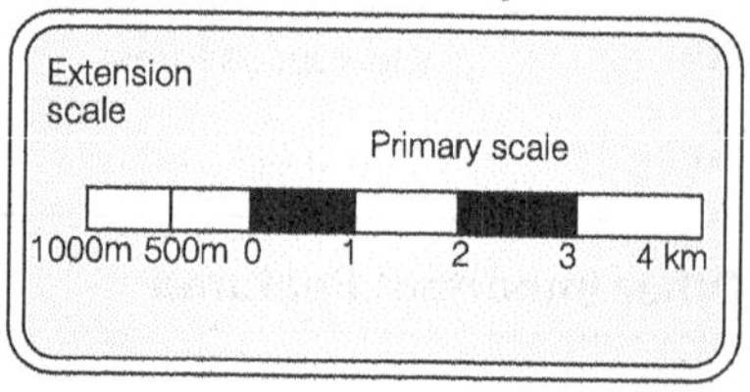

- **Linear or Graphic Scale** In this, scale is represented by a straight line divided into equal parts (primary and secondary). Primary division are major division from left to right. Secondary divisions are smaller units graduated from right to left. It is used to measure the distance between two points on the map.

Measuring Distances using the Scale

Measurement of Straight Distances (as crow flies)

To determine the straight-line distance between two points on a map, we can use a scale or a piece of paper and follow the steps below

1. It can be used by using the scale or a divider.

2. Place the two legs of the divider on the two points and then place the divider on Linear scale.
3. For example the distance between *A* and *B* is 2 km.

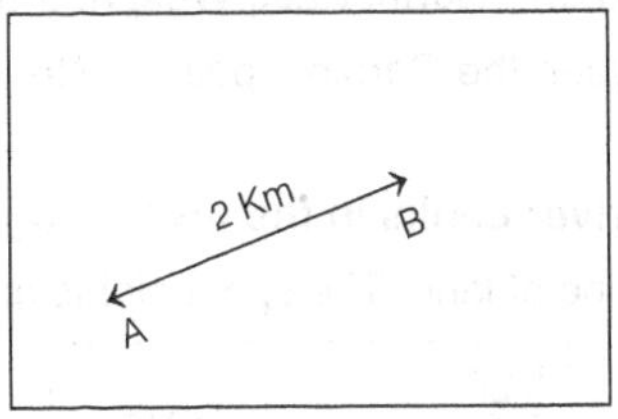

Measurement of an Indirect or Curved Distance

To measure the curved distance (such as a river or winding road) between two points on a map, we use the following steps

With the help of thread

(i) Take a piece of thread and put a mark with dot on one end. Place the mark at the starting point and move it along the curve of river.

(ii) Mark the end point with an ink dot.

(iii) Now stretch the thread along the linear scale till the marked end and calculate the distance.

(iv) Distance is always calculated in km or metres.

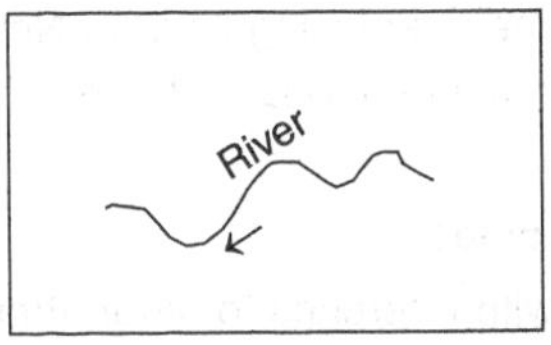

Measurement of Area by Grid Square Method

In topographical maps, each grid square measures 2 sq. cms (2 cm × 2 cm) or
(1 km × 1 km). Since, 2 cm is equal to 1 km. Hence, the area of each square is 1 sq km. To calculate a certain area of topographical map, we need to follow some steps

(i) Count the number of complete grid squares within the area.

(ii) The number of remaining squares which cover more than half, take them as 2/3.

(iii) If some squares covered half, take them as 1/2.

(iv) If the squares covered are less than half, take them as 1/3 squares and count (shown in figure below). Now, all these estimated squares are added together and then the sum is multiplied by the scale of the map.

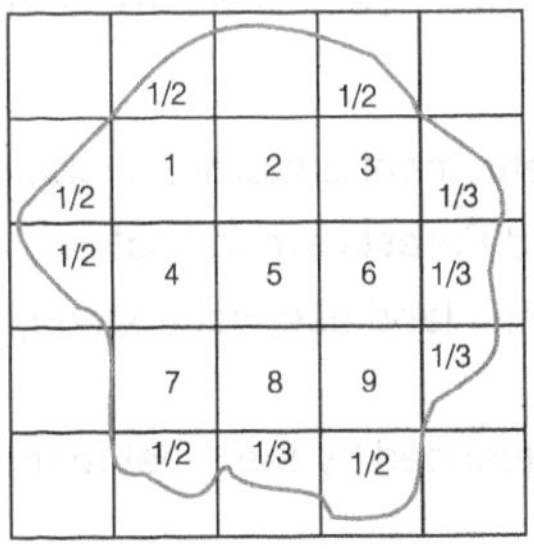

Marking Directions between Different Locations

There are four main directions (Cardinal points) - North, East, West and South.

There is another set of four directions between the Cardinal points - North-East (NE), North-West (NW), South-East (SE) and South-West (SW).

(a) Direction with reference to river and river banks in the given diagram

- First look at the spot heights to find the slope of land. The spot heights are receding from North-East to South-West.

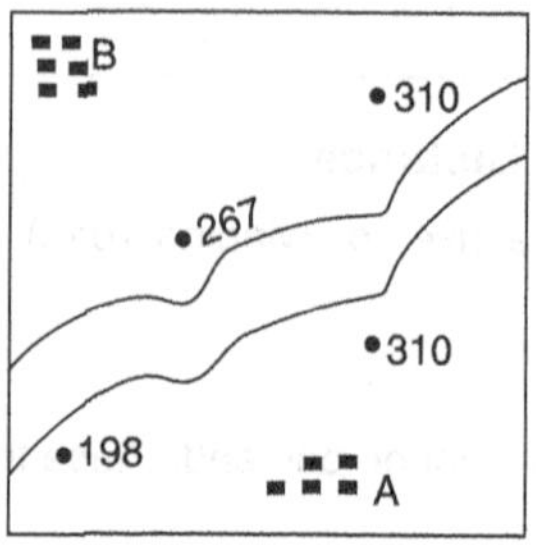

- Thus, in the given diagram the slope of the land is from North-East to South-West, hence the river is flowing from North-East to South-West.
- To know which side/bank of river a particular settlement is located, one has to locate the source of the river. Then imagine yourself standing at the source of the river facing its flow. Now your right hand is right bank and your left hand is the left bank of the river. For e.g., settlement B is on the right bank of the river and settlement A is located on the left bank.

(b) Directions with reference to the Urban cities

- To find out the direction of one settlement with reference to other attention should be paid 'of' and 'from'.
- As in the above diagram settlement 'B' is located to the North-West of 'A'.

Identifying Site of Prominent Villages and/or Towns

- Most of the information regarding the map is given on the margins of a topo-sheet and that's why it is also called marginal information.
- To identify the site of prominent villages or towns. The following information must contain
  - (i) Number of the sheet e.g. G43S7, G43S10, etc.
  - (ii) Latitudinal and Longitudinal Extent
    - Eastings and Northings
    - Contour Interval
    - Legend
    - The Scale of the Map
    - Direction of True North and Magnetic North
    - Year of Survey and Publication

Types of Land Use

- These include means of communication, settlement patterns, rivers, means of irrigation etc.
- In forested land the Reserved and Protected Forests are indicated by green bands around them.
- In the Indian topographical maps, settlements, land use, occupation, trade routes and patterns of population are shown in Chinese vermilion colour.
- The distribution of settlements is greatly influenced by the relief features - like highland areas, lowland areas, rivers, drainage patterns, etc.

- The evidence of land use is shown by various symbols as follows

Symbol	Land Use	Symbol	Land Use
Open Scrub	Sheep and Goat rearing	Stony waste	Uncultivable land
Tanks, wells, canals, etc.	Agriculture	Yellow coloured area	Agriculture
Rock outcrop	Uncultivable land	Green coloured area	Forest area
Sheet rocks	Uncultivable land	Broken ground	Uncultivable land

- Presence of broken ground, causeway, dry stream indicates scanty rainfall.

Means of Transport in relation to Relief

- These include national or state highways, cart tracks, pack tracks, causeways, metalled roads, unmetalled roads, footpaths with bridges, railway lines, telephone lines, post offices, dak bungalow, telegraph line and other utilities/facilities like dispensary, police chowki etc.
- The size of a town may be estimated by the size of the cluster and the presence of special buildings like post office, railway station etc.
- If the town is shown as connected by a metalled road and/or railway line with other towns, it indicates that it is well developed economically.
- A larger town indicates the varied occupations of the residents, including business, trade, agriculture, government, public services, etc.
- Causeways are raised platform build across a dry stream.
- Presence of many causeways shows that the area gets seasonal or scanty rainfall.

Identification of Drainage and Settlement Patterns

The drainage pattern means the 'form' of the drainage systems and the spatial arrangement of streams in a particular locality or region. The drainage patterns are divided into the following types

- **Trellis Drainage Pattern** It is like a rectangular drainage pattern where all the streams flow parallel to each other and join the main consequent stream at right angles.
- It develops in a region of alternate belt of hard and soft rocks.
- **Dendritic Drainage Pattern** In this pattern, the tributaries come from all directions, to meet the main river. The trunk or master stream resembles the branches and roots of a tree. It is generally found over homogeneous and flat lands.
- **Radial Drainage Pattern** It is formed by the streams which diverge from a central higher point of a dome mountain in all directions. It forms a pattern like the spokes of wheel.

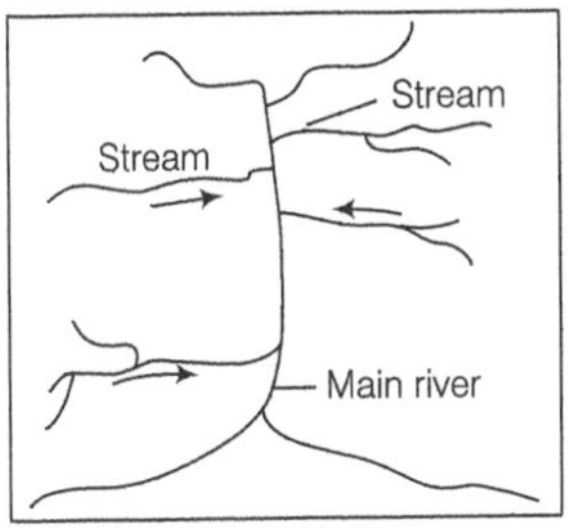

Trellis Drainage

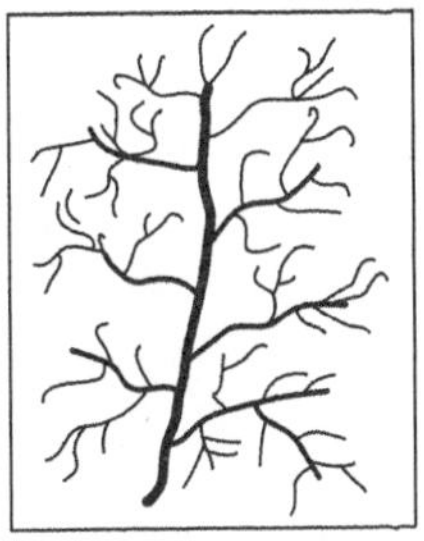

Dendriic Drainage

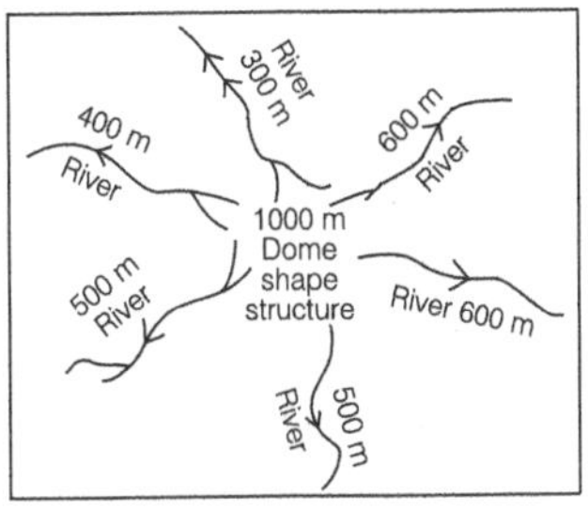

Radial Drainage

- **The Inland or Disappearing Drainage Pattern** When rivers or streams do not have enough water, they dry up or disappear into the sand. This is known as disappearing drainage pattern. Sometimes, due to scanty rainfall, the streams disappear and flow underground. This is called the inland drainage pattern.

Identification of Settlement Patterns

A settlement is an area where a group of families live together. Settlements generally follow some simple patterns such as

- **Nucleated Settlements** Nucleated or clustered settlements often form at crossroads or clusters with post office schools, temples, etc. These settlements are shown in red colour.
- **Dispersed or Scattered Settlements** These settlements have no obvious centre and are often hamlets spread over in fertile farmland. These settlements are shown in red squares on the toposheet map.
- **Linear Settlements** These settlements are also known as Ribbon-Patterned settlements. These settlements grow along a road or river i.e. in a narrow valley or along the coast. These facilities include post office, police station, inspection bungalow, hotel, temple, church, etc.

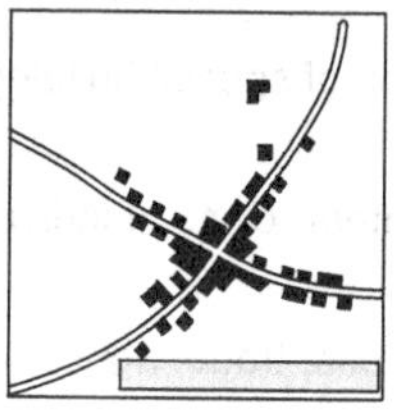
Nucleated Settlement

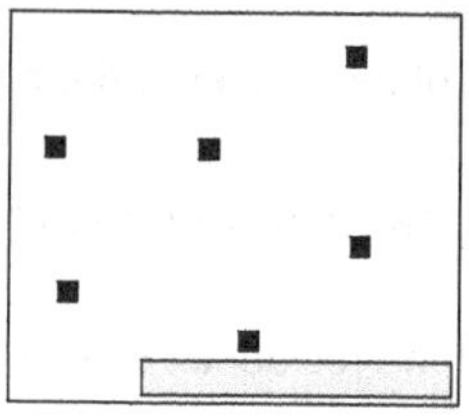
Dispersed Settlement

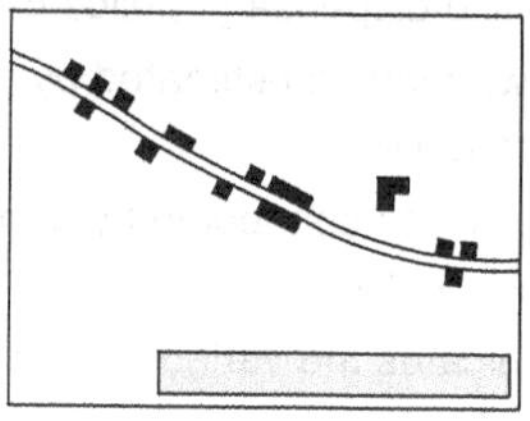
Linear Settlement

Identification of Natural and Man-Made Features

- **Natural Physical Features** These include various landforms, relief features i.e. plains, plateaus, hills, mountains, waterfalls, passes by streams, broken ground, etc. These are depicted by various techniques like, contour, hachures, hill shading, layer tinting/colouring, etc.
- **Man-Made or Cultural Features** These are villages, towns, types of land use, means of communication, settlement patterns, canals, bridges, etc. These are depicted by symbols called 'Conventional sign'.

EXAM ORIENTED QUESTIONS

Q.1 Study the extract of the Survey of India Map Sheet No. G43S7 (Map 1 given at the end), Eastings 25-35 and Northings 89-99 and answer the following questions.

(i) (a) Give the four-figure grid reference of spot height .224 **(2)**

(b) Give the six-figure grid reference of the covered tank near Ramsida settlement.

(ii) (a) In which direction does the river in the map extract flow? **(2)**

(b) On which bank of the river, the settlement Dantiwada (2992) located?

(iii) (a) What does 14r in 3189 indicate? **(2)**

(b) How does the drainage pattern in grid square .3397 and 2698 differ?

(iv) (a) What is the general pattern of human habitation in the map extract? **(2)**

(b)What is the area in square kilometres enclosed by the vertical grid 30 to 35 and horizontal grid lines 96-99.

(v) (a) What does the black vertical line running along Easting 33 indicate? **(2)**

(b) What do you mean by 'dep' written in the South-East corner of the map?

Ans. (i) (a) 3396 (b) 312908

(ii) (a) River flows in Westward direction from East-West.

(b) Left Bank

(iii) (a) 14r indicates that the relative height of the sand dune is 14 meters.

(b) 3397-Dendritic 2698-Trellis

(iv) (a) The general pattern of the human habitation is Nucleated

(b) 30 – 35 = – 5

96 – 99 = – 3

2 cm = 1 km

Area = L × B

5 km × 3 km = 15 sq km

(v) (a) The black vertical line is the line of longitude.

(b) 'Dep' means depression found in sandy regions at the top of a mound or dune where the wind easily blows the sand away leaving a hollow.

Q.2 Study the extract of the Survey of India Map Sheet No. G43S10 (Map 2 given at the end) Eastings 61-71 and Northings 13-23 and answer the following questions.

(i) Give the four-figure grid reference of the

(a) hospital near Abu

(b) surveyed tree 277 **(2)**

(ii) Give six figure grid reference of

(a) Gautam Maharshi Mandir

(b) Triangulated height 1327 **(2)**

(iii) (a) What is the scale of the given map extract?

(b) What does it mean? **(2)**

(iv) (a) What do you mean by 12r written in grid. 6913?

(b) Calculate the distance in km between the causeway in grid square 6213 till the end of the metalled road in grid square 6712. **(2)**

(v) What do you mean by the terms used on the map extract?

(a) Causeway (6213)

(b) Falls 15 m (6718) **(2)**

Ans. (i) (a) 6821 (b) 6316

(ii) (a) 654183 (b) 673216

(iii) (a) 1:50,000

(b) It means 1 unit (1 cm) on the map is equal to the 50,000 unit (50,000 cm) on the ground.

(iv) (a) 12r means relative depth of the perennial lined well is 12 metres.

(b) The distance in 5.5 km.

(v) (a) Causeway is a raised metalled road across a minor stream.

(b) Falls 15 m indicates a waterfall of height 15 metres.

Q.3 Study the extract of the Survey of India Map Sheet No. G43S10 (Map 3 given at the end), Easting 47-57 and Northing 13-23 and answer the following questions.

(i) Give the six-figure grid reference of

(a) Post office near Dattani settlement **(2)**

(b) Temple near Bherugarh

(ii) (a) What is the distance in kilometres along the metalled road from the Eastern edge of the map to where the East track crosses the metal road at Pipliya (5418)? **(2)**

(b) Name a feature of the relief that can be seen in grid square 5516.

(iii) (a) What does 3r in 5419 mean? **(2)**

(b) What is the drainage pattern of the grid 5213?

(iv) (a) What is the compass direction of Dolpura from Dhavli? **(2)**

(b) On which bank of river Sipu, river Sukli join it.

(v) (a) Identify one natural and one man made feature in 5321. **(2)**

(b) Give two reasons to show that the rainfall in the region shown on the map extract is seasonal.

Ans. (i) (a) 558150 (b) 473179

(ii) (a) 4.2 km

(b) Conical Hill

(iii) (a) 3r means the relative height of the dry tank embankment is 3 metres.

(b) Radial

(iv) (a) The compass direction of Dolpura from Dhavli is North-West.

(b) Left

(v) (a) **Natural** Seasonal stream, broken ground

Man made Metalled road, Post-office Surveyed and unsurveyed pylons, Settlement, Temple.

(b) Reasons are-seasonal, dry stream and broken ground.

Q.4 Study the extract of the Survey of India Map Sheet No. G43S10 (Map 4 given at the end), Easting 47-57 Northing 24-34 and answer the following questions.

(i) Give six figure grid reference of

(a) Veterinary hospital in grid square 4924 **(2)**

(b) Brick Klin near Serua

(ii) (a) Calculate the length of N.H 168 from grid square 4925 to grid square 5222 in km. **(2)**

(b) What do the tiny curved black lines in grid square 4932 indicate?

(iii) (a) What kind of road connect Revdar to Warka and Selwara to Jolpur? **(2)**

(b) Give two reasons to show that the area in the map experiences seasonal rainfall.

(iv) (a) What could be the occupation of the people in the settlement of Revdar? **(2)**

(b) What does 3r in 5630 indicate?

(v) (a) What is the settlement pattern in grid square 5230? **(2)**

(b) Give four figure grid reference of the marble stone querries.

Ans. (i) (a) 491246 (b) 544244

(ii) (a) 4.8 km (b) Broken ground

(iii) (a) **Metalled Road** Revdar to warka

Cart track Selwara to Jolpur

(b) Two reasons are-Dry tank dry/seasonal streams/Broken ground.

(iv) (a) Agriculture, working in PWD and veterinary hospital.

(b) 3r indicates the relative height of the dry tank embankment in 3 meters.

(v) (a) Scattered (b) 5427/5527

Q.5 Study the extract of the Survey of India Map Sheet No. G43S10 (Map 5 given at the end), Easting 60-70 Northing 26-36 and answer the following questions.

(i) (a) Give the six-figure grid reference of the police station near Pamera settlement. **(2)**

(b) Give the meaning of fire line written or shown in the South-East corner of the map extract.

(ii) (a) What do the double dots on green given in 6726 indicate? **(2)**

(b) Name the different types of forest seen in the given map extract.

(iii) (a) What is the general flow of direction of the Sipu river in the given map extract. **(2)**

(b) On which bank of the river Sipu, the settlement Sirori located?

(iv) (a) What do you mean by sluice written in grid square 6832? **(2)**

(b) What does 10r in grid square 6832 mean?

(v) (a) What is the area of the region enclosed by Easting 63-69 and Northing 29-36? **(2)**

(b) What is contour interval? What is the contour interval of the given map extract?

Ans. (i) (a) 627338

(b) Fireline is clearing made between two forests to check the spread of fire.

(ii) (a) Forest boundary

(b) Open mixed jungle, fairly dense mixed jungle, reserved forest, open scrub.

(iii) (a) Sipu river flows in Westward direction.

(b) Right bank

(iv) (a) Sluice is a water channel controlled at its head by a gate. It is a movable gate allowing water to flow under it.

(b) 10 r is the relative height of the embankment is 10 m.

(v) (a) Area = L × B 2 cm = 1 km

6 × 7 = 42 sq km

(b) Contour interval is the difference in height between the two successive contour lines. The contour interval of the given map extract is 20 m.

Q.6 Study the extract of the Survey of India Map Sheet No. G43S7 (Map 6 given at the end), Easting 21-31 Northing 92-02 and answer the following questions.

(i) Give four figure grid reference of the following

(a) Circuit house near Dantiwada **(2)**

(b) Triangulated height 166 near Godh.

(ii) (a) Which is the most prominent settlement in the given map extract? Give reason to support your answer. **(2)**

(b) In what way does the pattern of settlement in grid square 2792 differ from that in grid square 2296?

(iii) (a) On which bank of river Sipu the settlement Jorapura is located? **(2)**

(b) Name a feature of the relief the can be seen in grid square 3096.

(iv) (a) Give in kilometres the length of the entire region depicted on the map from North to South. **(2)**

(b) What is the direction of Agdol from Jorapura?

(v) (a) What type of rainfall is experienced in the region shown in the map extract? Justify your answer. **(2)**

(b) What do you mean by 6 written in grid square 2699.

Ans. (i) (a) 2992, 2792 (b) 2294

(ii) (a) Dantiwada is the most prominent settlement in the given map extract. The reason is that it is well connected with the metallic road, it has temple, circuit house, overhead tank, earthern dam aslo near to it.

(b) 2792- Permanent/Nucleated

2296- Temporary/Scattered

(iii) (a) Left Bank (b) Conical Hill

(iv) (a) 10 km

(b) Agdol lies to the North-West of Jorapura

(v) (a) The region experiences seasonal rainfall. The different evidences are broken ground, dry streams.

(b) 6 is the distance stone of 6 km.

Q.7 Study the extract of the Survey of India Map Sheet No. G43S7 (Map 7 given at the end), Easting 28-38 Northing 02-12 and answer the following questions.

(i) (a) Give four figure grid reference of the triangulated height Δ277. **(2)**

(b) Give six figure grid reference of the surveyed tree 181 near Ganodara.

(ii) (a) What is 200 written in 3203 indicate? **(2)**

(b) What is the contour interval of the given map extract?

(iii) (a) Calculate the area between the Eastings 29-35 and Northings 06-11. **(2)**

(b) What do you mean by the term causeway written in 3407? What do they indicate?

(iv) (a) What could be the occupation of the people in grid square 3604? **(2)**

(b) What is the drainage pattern of grid 3106?

(v) (a) What is the common mode of transportation in the given map? **(2)**

(b) What is the meaning of 1 : 50,000 printed below the map extract?

Ans. (i) (a) 3410 (b) 281043

(ii) (a) 200 written in grid 3203 is the contour of 200 joining places of height 200 m above the mean sea level.

(b) The contour interval is 20 metres.

(iii) (a) Area = L × B

6 × 5

Area = 30 sq km

(b) Causeway is a raised platform built across a stream. They indicate that the region receives scanty or seasonal rainfall.

(iv) (a) The people could be involved in cattle rearing as it has open scrub.

(b) The drainage pattern is Dendritic.

(v) (a) The general mode of transportation is by pack track, cart tract and metalled roads.

(b) 1 : 50,000 printed on the map means that one unit on the map is equal to 50,000 units on the ground.

Q.8 Study the extract of the Survey of India Map Sheet No. G43S7 (Map 8 given at the end), Easting 36-46 Northing 85-95 and answer the following questions.

(i) (a) Give the four-figure grid reference of triangulated height Δ217 **(2)**

(b) Given the six-figure grid reference of chhatri near the settlement Juyal.

(ii) (a) What does the black curved lines in 4487 indicate? **(2)**

(b) What is 10r in 4186?

(iii) (a) Identify two landforms shown in 4388 and 4294. **(2)**

(b) What does the black horizontal line near northing 89 indicate?

(iv) What you understand by?

(a) The black broken lines in 3887 **(2)**

(b) Blue line in Balaram Nadi

(v) (a) What is the area of the region enclosed by Easting 39-45 and Northing 89-94. **(2)**

(b) How does the drainage pattern in grid 4294 and 4488 differ from each other?

Ans. (i) (a) 3890 (b) 374945

(ii) (a) They indicate broken ground or broken land.

(b) It is the relative height of the sand dune that is 10 metres.

(iii) (a) Landform in 4388-Conical hills, ridge steep slope, watershed or water divide.

Landform in 4294-Conical hill

(b) It is the line of latitude.

(iv) (a) The black broken lines are undefined streams or disappearing streams.

(b) It is a dry river with a narrow water channel.

(v) (a) The area enclosed by the Eastings 39 and 45 and Northings 89-94 is

Area = Length × Width

6 × 5 = 30 sq km

(b) The drainage pattern of the grid 4294 is Radial and 4488 is Trellis.

Q.9 Study the extract of the Survey of India Map Sheet No. G43S7 (Map 9 given at the end) and answer the following questions. **(ICSE Specimen 2025)**

(i) (a) Give the six-figure grid reference for .201 in the Eastern part of the map extract. **(2)**

(b) What are the brown patches in the North-East quarter of the map extract?

(ii) Mohan goes on a bicycle from 02 Northing to 12 Northing in a straight line. If he moves at a speed of 10 kilometers per hour, how much time will he take to reach his destination? **(2)**

(iii) (a) What is the compass direction of Rampura (2709) from Kotda (3005)? **(2)**

(b) If you are moving along the left bank of the Sipu River, which settlement will you come across?

(iv) (a) Ramesh returned to his native place Mahudi Moti (2404) after a gap of ten years and was happy to see the development around his village. What according to you shows that the area around his village has developed? **(2)**

(b) What is the black vertical line made between the Easting 25 and 26?

(v) Mention two man-made and two natural features in the grid square 2508. **(2)**

Ans. (i) (a) 301074

(b) Sand Dunes

(ii) One Hour

(iii) (a) North-West

(b) Jhat Bhadli

(iv) (a) Powerline showing that the village now has electricity.

(b) Longitude of 17′30″

(v) **Natural features** Sand dunes, Broken ground

Man-made features Cart track / Pack track / Permanent hut/temple, covered tank

LOCATION, EXTENT AND PHYSICAL FEATURES OF INDIA

Location

- India is a vast country and located in the Northern hemisphere.
- It lies on the Western edge of the Indian Ocean and in the middle of South-East and South-West Asia.
- Its mainland extends between latitudes 8°4′N and 37°6′N and longitudes 68°7′E and 97°25′E.
- It is divided into almost two equal parts by the Tropic of Cancer (23°30′N) i.e., sub-tropical in the North and tropical zone in the South.
- Tropic of Cancer passes through 8 states of India i.e., Gujarat, Rajasthan, Madhya Pradesh, Chhattisgarh, Jharkhand, West Bengal, Tripura and Mizoram.

Size and Extent

- India is the 7th largest country in the world. Its landmass has an area of 3.287 million sq km. It occupies 2.4% of the total geographical area of the world.
- India has a land boundary that extends over 15,200 km and a coastline of 7.516.6 km, including the mainland and island and territories.
- India has 28 States and 8 Union Territories. It shares its land boundaries with Pakistan and Afghanistan in the North-West, China, Nepal and Bhutan in the North-East and Myanmar and Bangladesh in the East.
- Two island countries i.e., Sri Lanka (separated by Palk Strait and Gulf of Mannar) and the Maldives, lie to the South of India across the Indian Ocean.

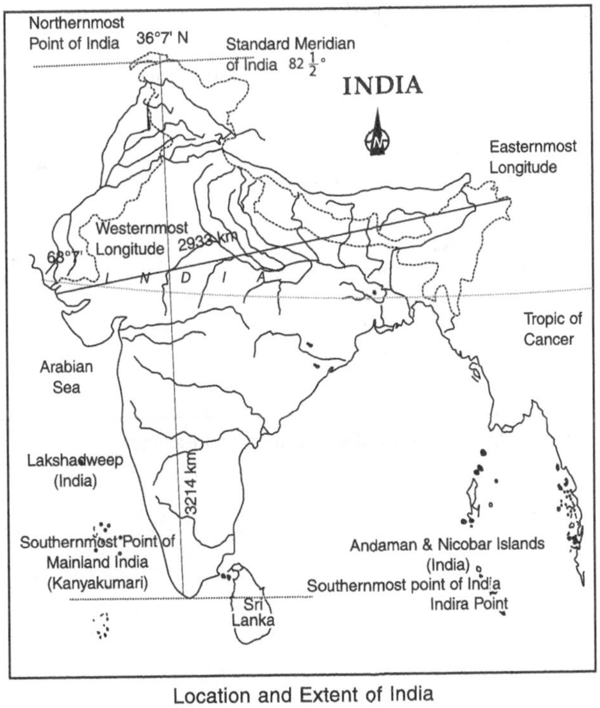

Location and Extent of India

REVISION NOTES

Physical Features of India

Mountains, Peaks, Plateaus and Passes

- The important mountain ranges in India are the Himalayas, the Karakoram, the Aravali, the Vindhyas, the Satpura, the Western and the Eastern Ghats, the Nilgiris, Garo, Khasi, Jaintia.
- The important mountains in India are Mount Godwin Austin (K2), Mount Kanchenjunga.
- The important plateaus in India are Deccan Plateau, Chota Nagpur Plateau.

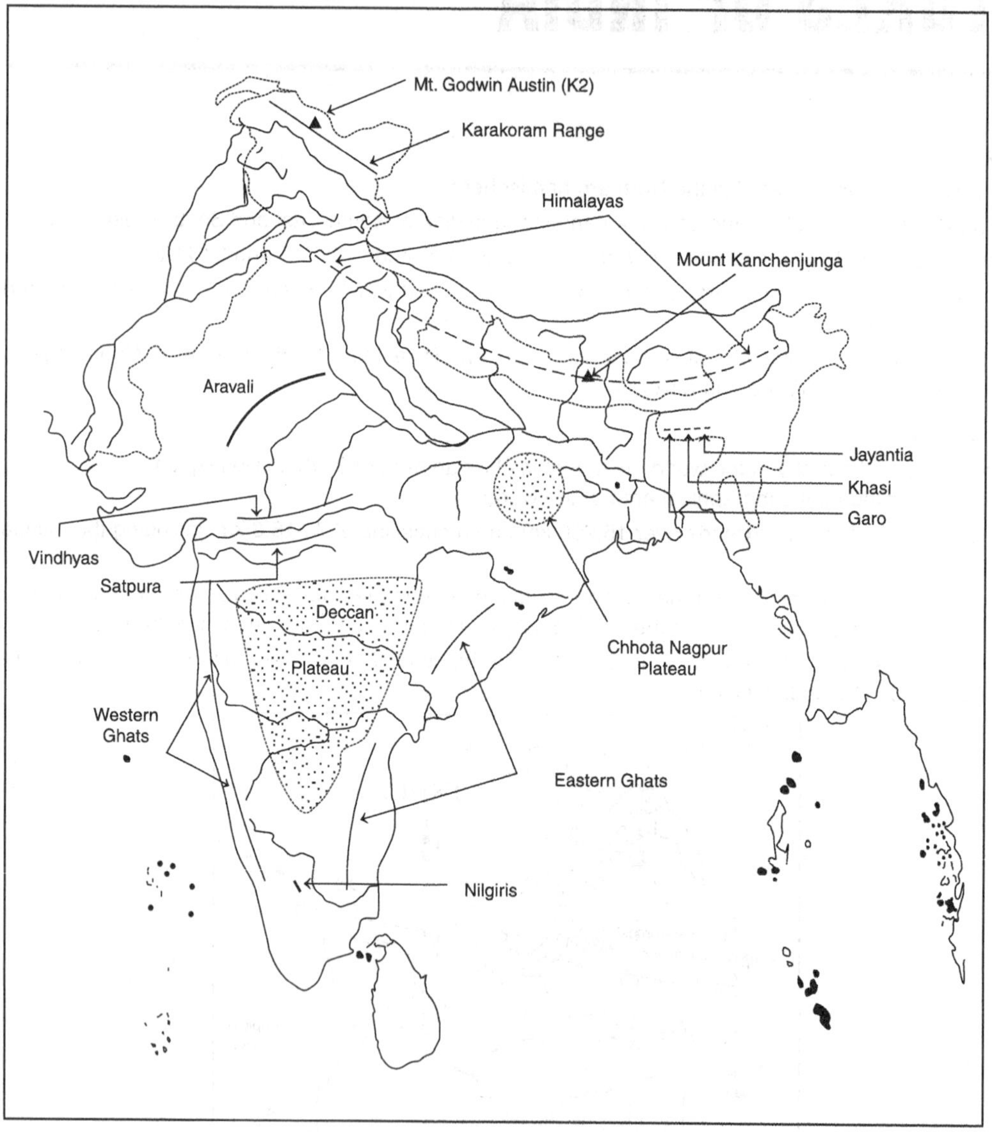

Mountains, Peaks, Plateaus and Passes

Plains and Deserts

- The important plains in India are Gangetic Plains and Coastal Plains - Konkan, Kanara, Malabar, Coromandel, Northern Circars.
- The important desert is Thar (The Great Indian Desert).

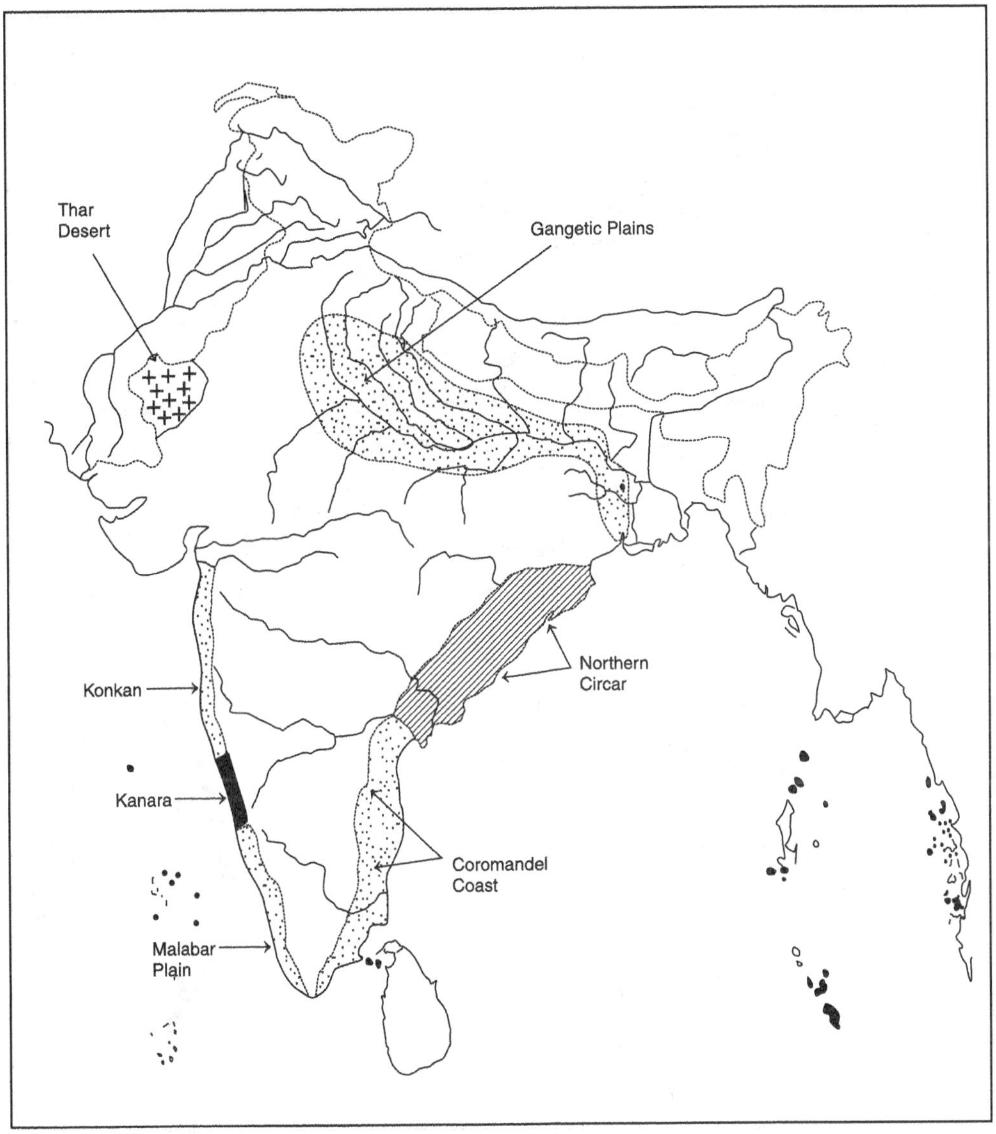

Plains and Deserts

Rivers

- The important rivers in India are - Indus, Ravi, Beas, Chenab, Jhelum, Sutlej, Ganga, Yamuna, Ghaghra, Gomti, Gandak, Kosi, Chambal, Betwa, Son, Damodar, Brahmaputra, Narmada, Tapti, Mahanadi, Godavari, Krishna, Cauvery, Tungabhadra.

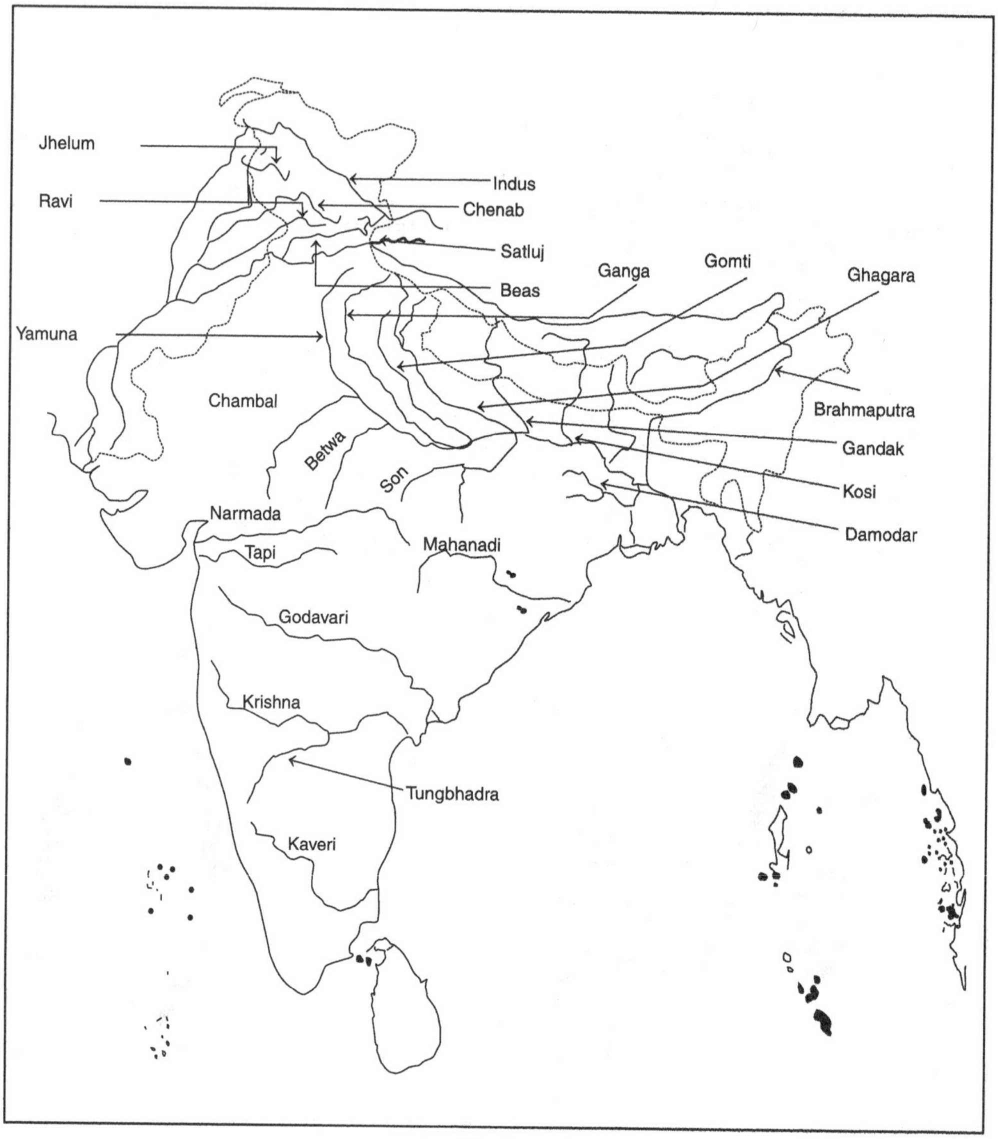

Rivers

Water Bodies

- The important water bodies in India are Gulf of Kutch, Gulf of Khambhat, Gulf of Mannar, Palk Strait, Andaman Sea, Chilka Lake and Wular Lake.

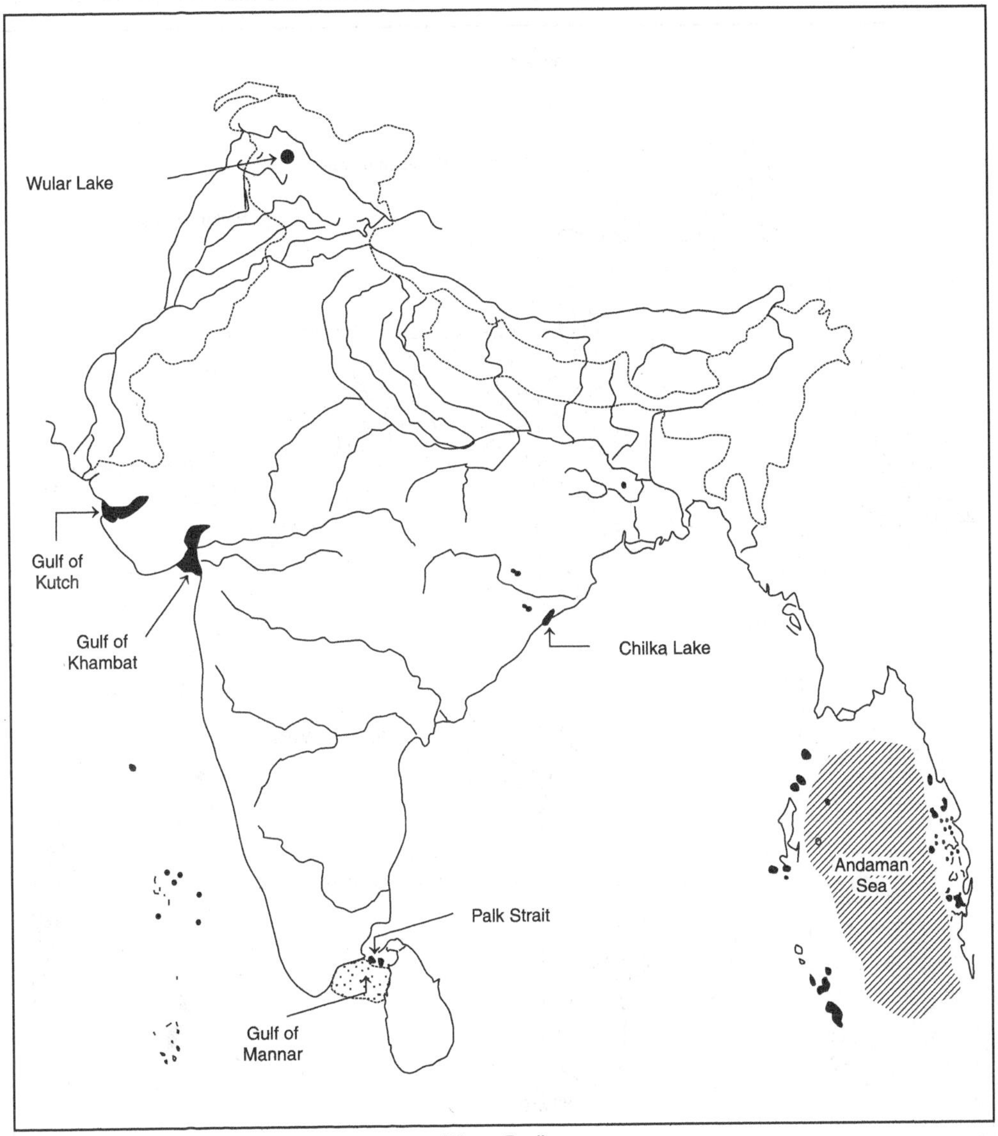

Water Bodies

Major Passes, Latitudes and Longitudes, and North-East Moonsoon

- The important passes in India are Karakoram, Nathu-La Pass.
- The important latitudes and longitudes in India are- Tropic of Cancer, Standard Meridian (82°30′E).

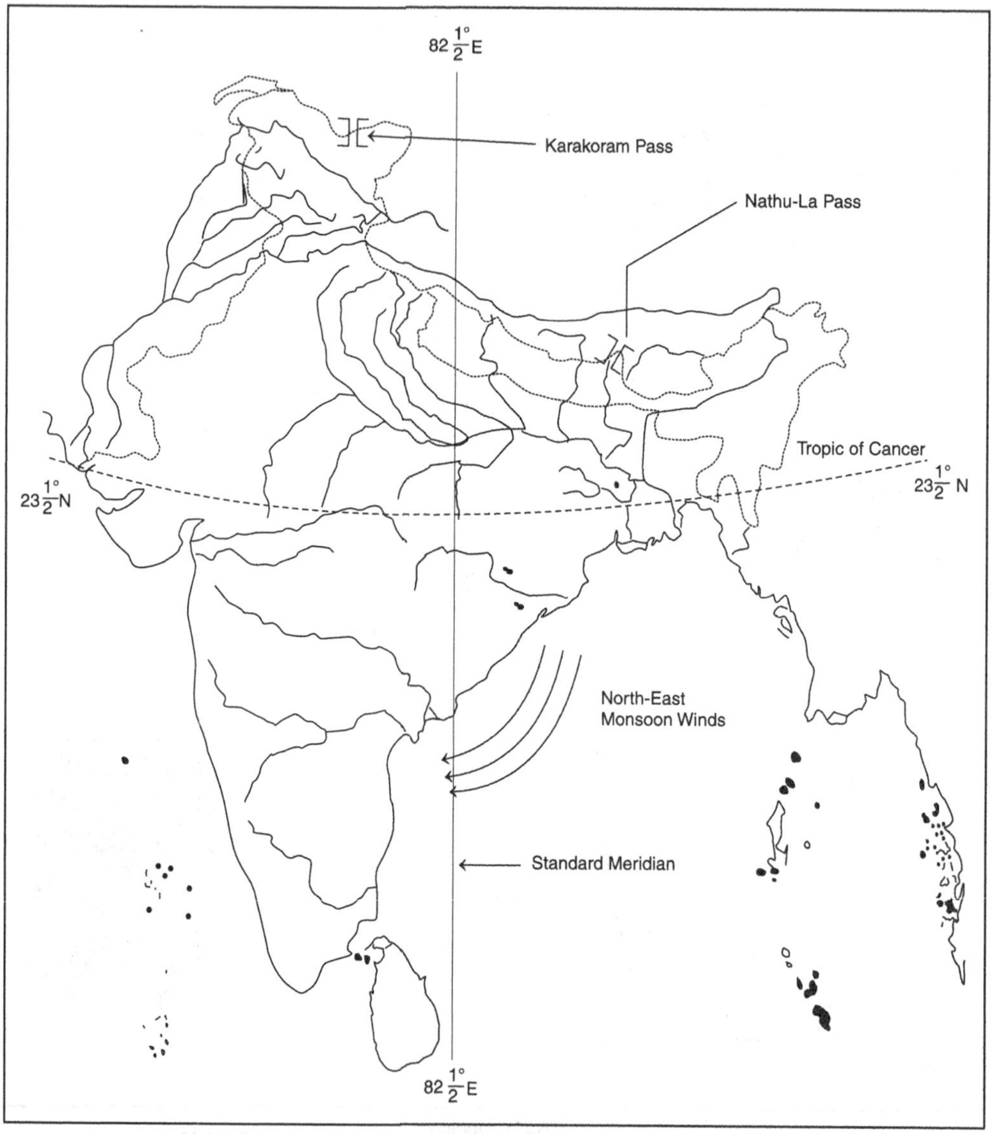

Major Passes, Latitudes and Longitudes, and North-East Moonsoon

REVISION NOTES

South-West Monsoon (Arabian Sea and Bay of Bengal Branches) and Western Disturbances

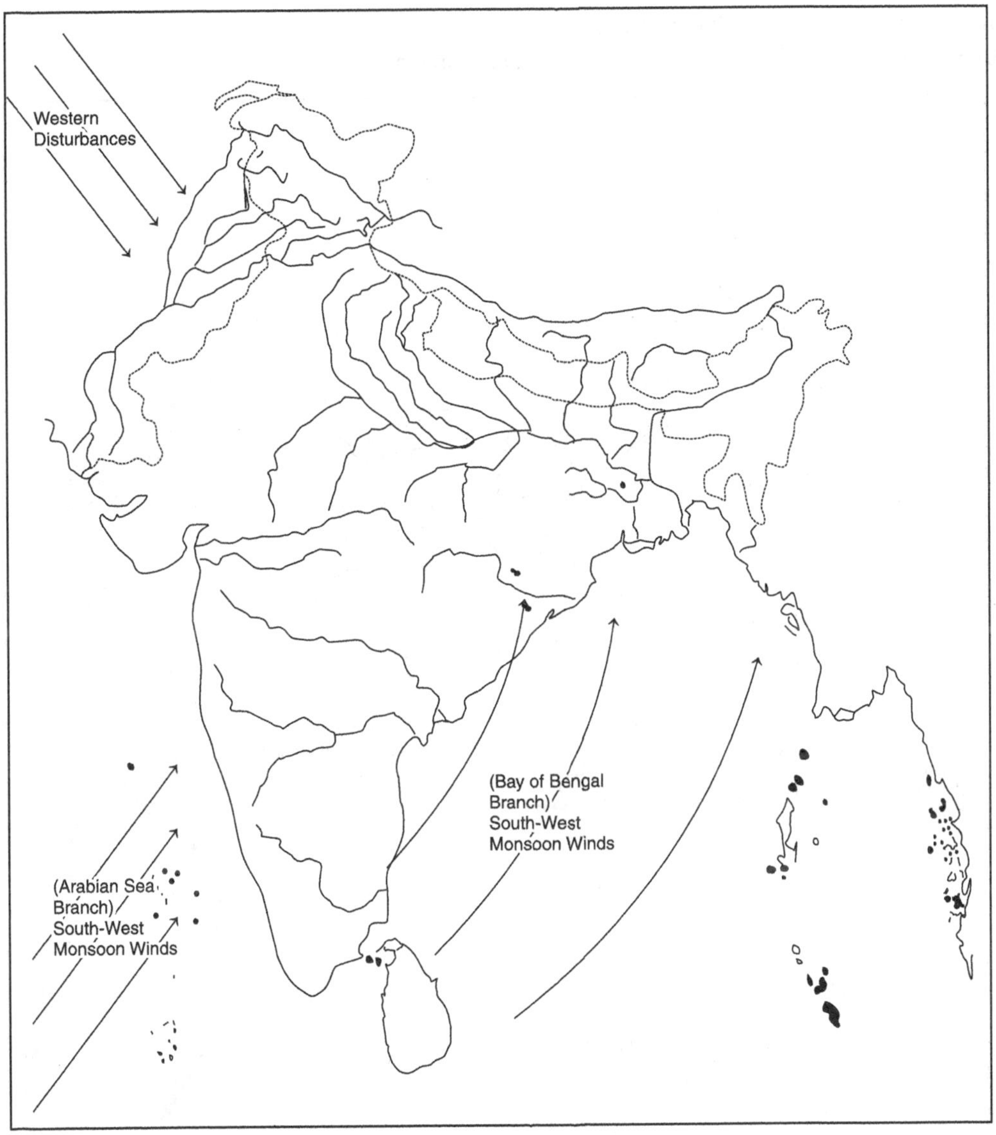

South-West Monsoon and Western Disturbances

Distribution of Minerals

The distribution of minerals in India are

- Oil - Mumbai High (offshore oil field) and Digboi.
- Iron - Singhbhum
- Coal - Jharia.

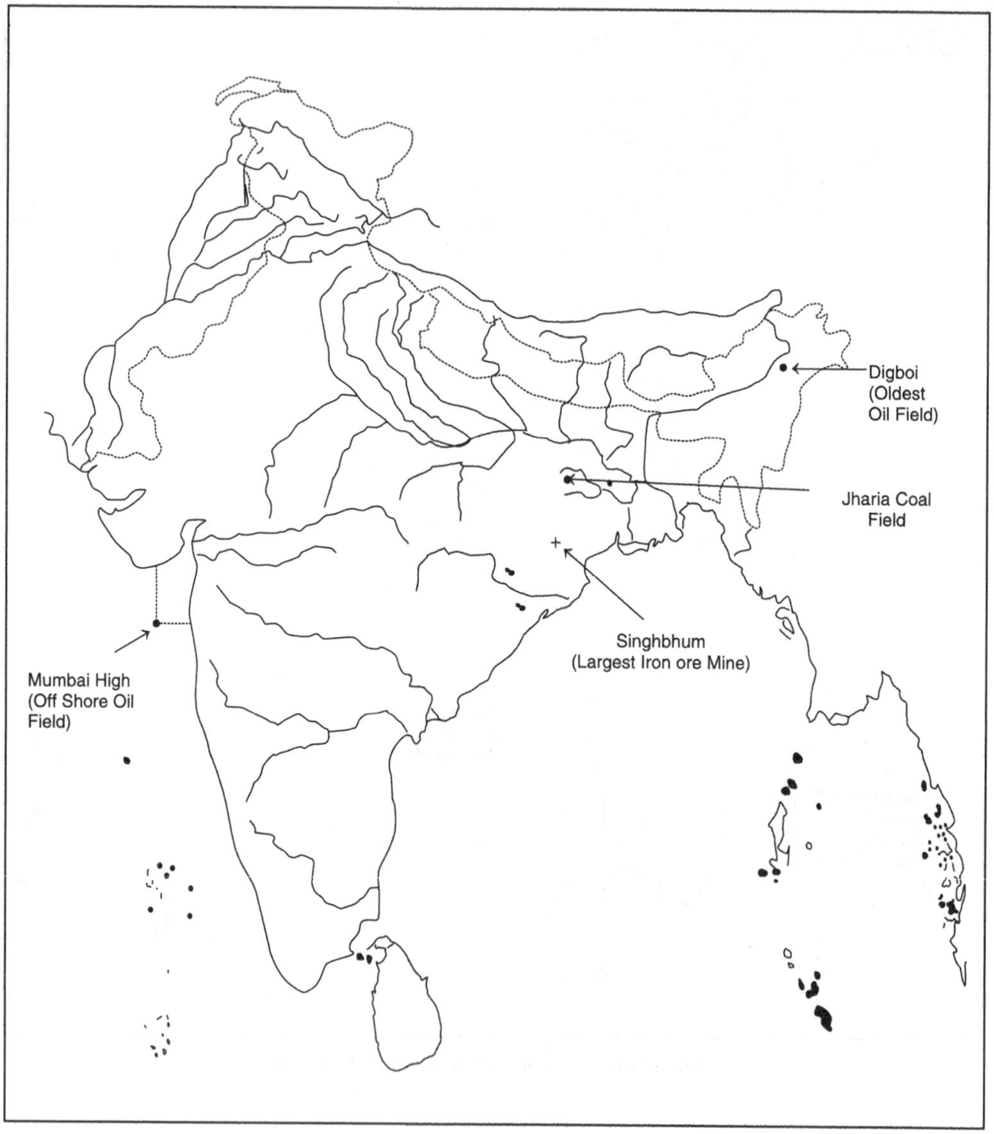

Distribution of Minerals

REVISION NOTES

Soil Distribution

There are mainly four types of soil found in India which are alluvial, laterite, black and red soil.

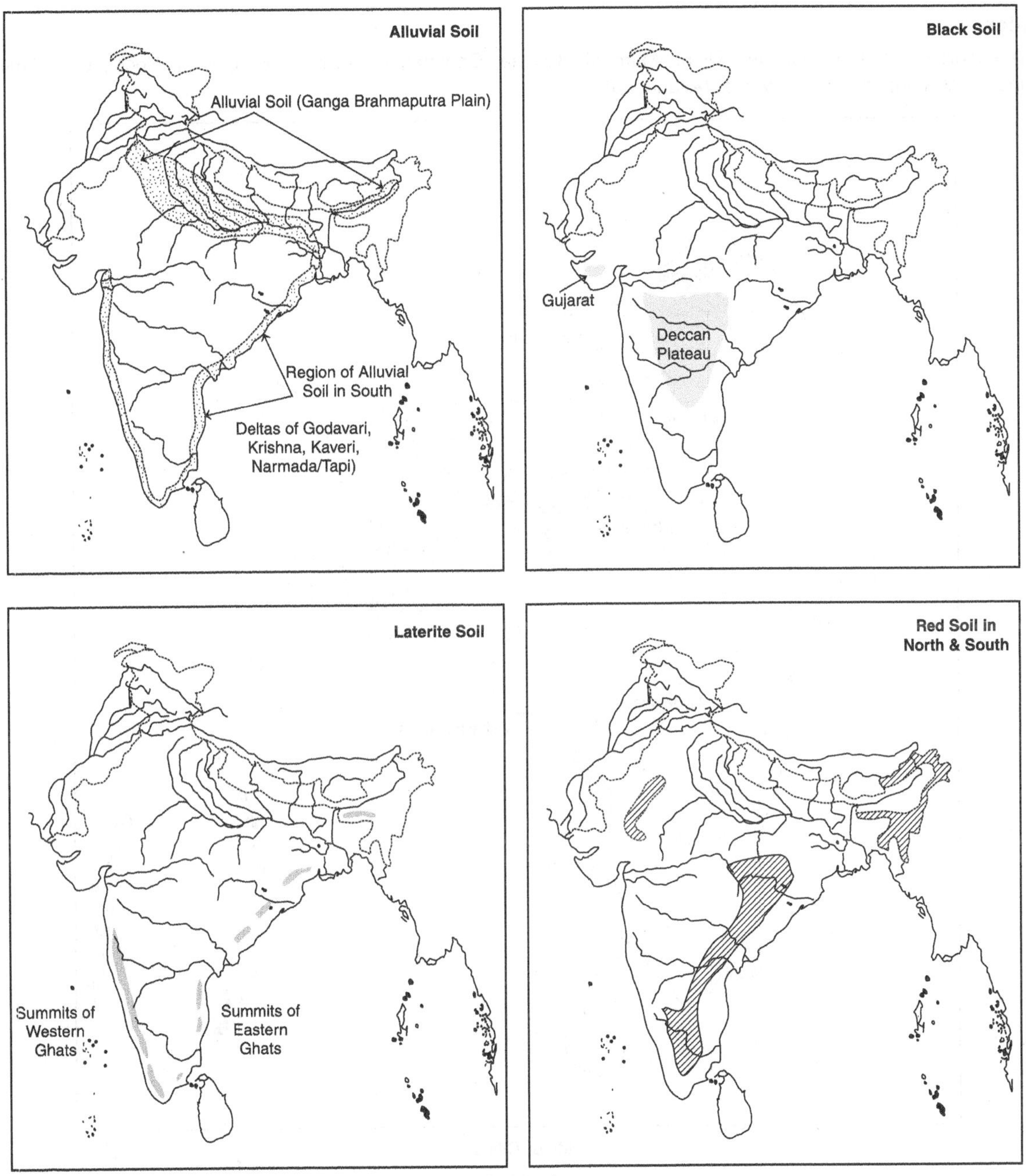

Soil Distribution

Cities

The important cities in India are Delhi, Mumbai, Kolkata, Chennai, Hyderabad, Bengaluru, Kochi, Chandigarh, Srinagar, Visakhapatnam, Prayagraj (Allahabad).

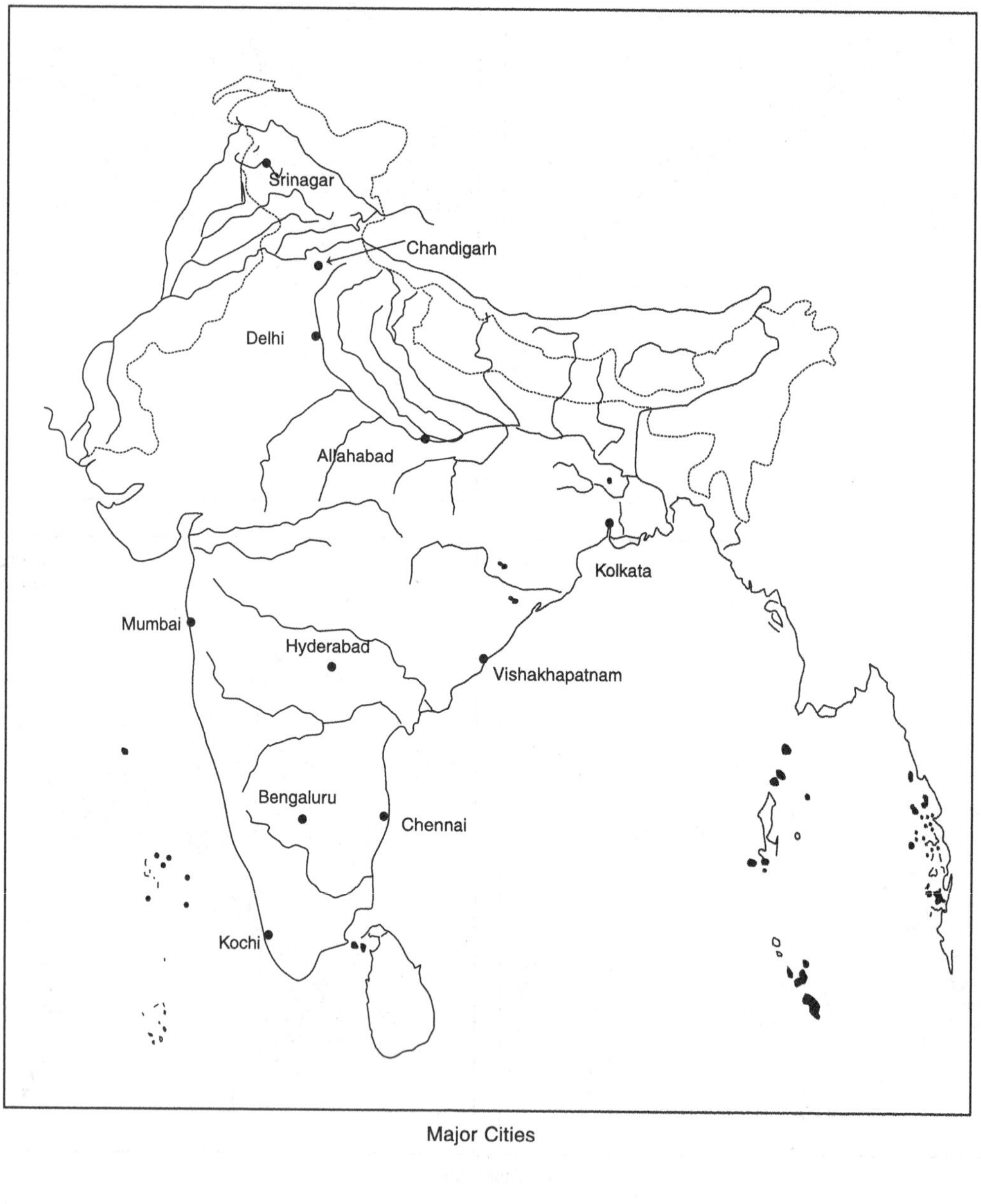

Major Cities

Distribution of Population (Census 2011)

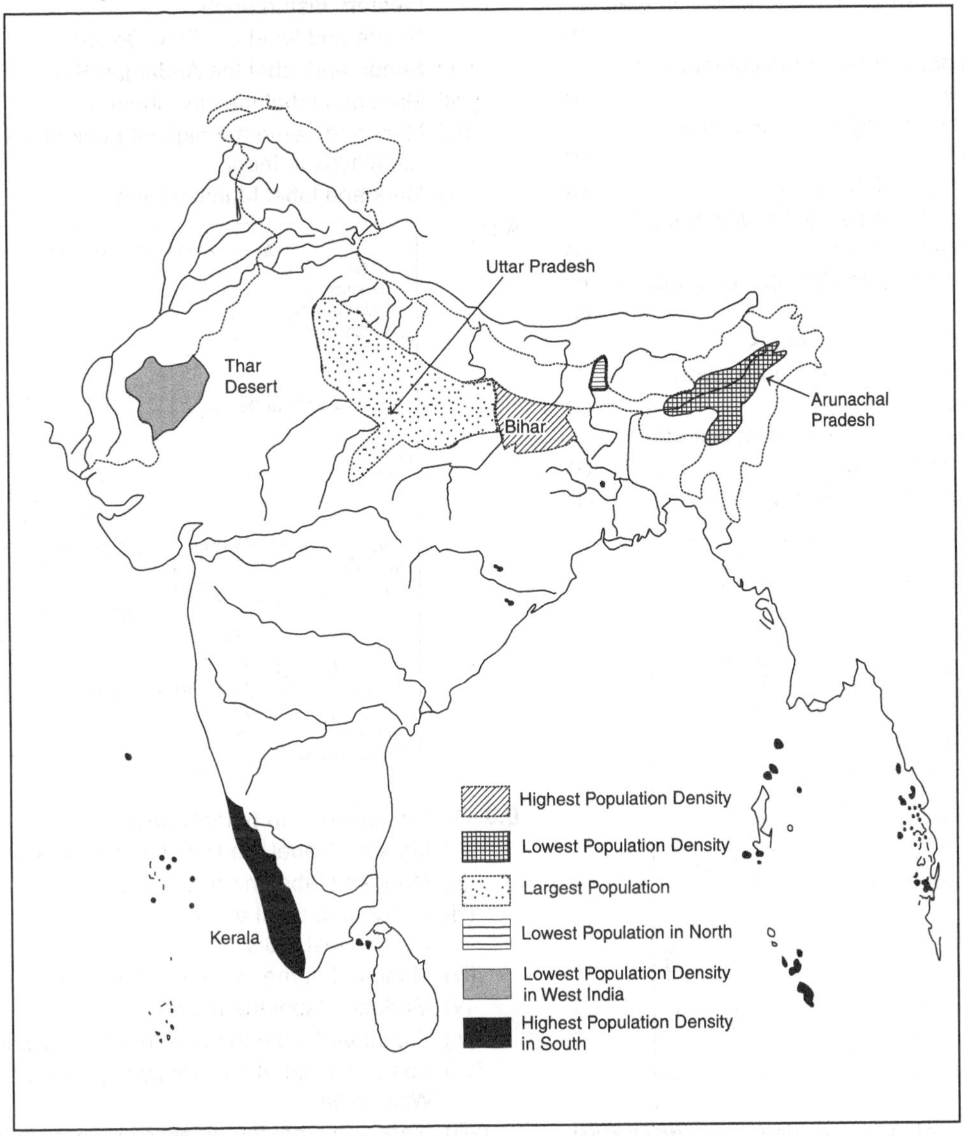

Distribution of Population

EXAM ORIENTED QUESTIONS

Q.1 On the outline map of India provided **(ICSE Specimen 2024, 2025)**

(i) Shade and label an area of alluvial soil in the North-East **(1)**

(ii) Mark using a dot and name the commercial capital of India **(1)**

(iii) Mark and name the highest peak of the Himalayas in India **(1)**

(iv) Shade and label Gulf of Kutch **(1)**

(v) Mark with arrows and name the wind bringing rainfall to Punjab in winter **(1)**

(vi) Shade and label a sparsely populated area in the West **(1)**

(vii) Mark and label the Eastern ghats **(1)**

(viii) Mark and name a tributary of an important peninsular river **(1)**

(ix) Mark and label the most important latitude passing through the country **(1)**

(x) Mark and label Coromandel Coast **(1)**

Ans.

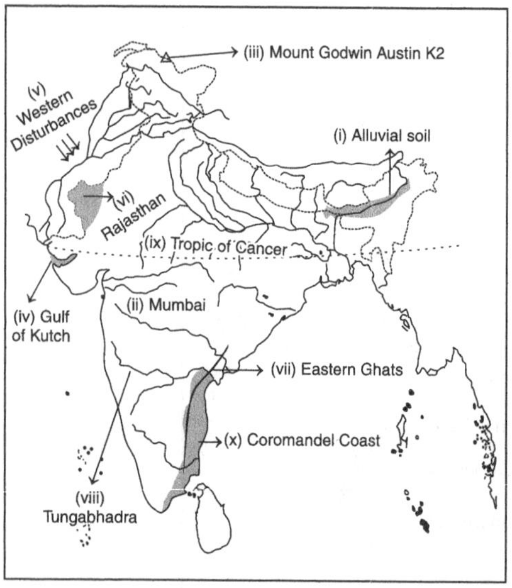

Q.2 On the outline map of India provided **(ICSE 2024)**

(i) Mark and label the river Krishna **(1)**

(ii) Mark and label the Eastern ghats **(1)**

(iii) Shade and label a densely populated area in the Southern part of India **(1)**

(iv) Shade and label the Konkan coastal plain **(1)**

(v) Mark with an arrow and label the direction of the Western disturbance **(1)**

(vi) Shade and label the Thar Desert **(1)**

(vii) Shade and label the Andaman Sea **(1)**

(viii) Mark and label the city Chennai **(1)**

(ix) Mark and name the highest peak of the Himalayas in India **(1)**

(x) Mark and label Mumbai High **(1)**

Ans.

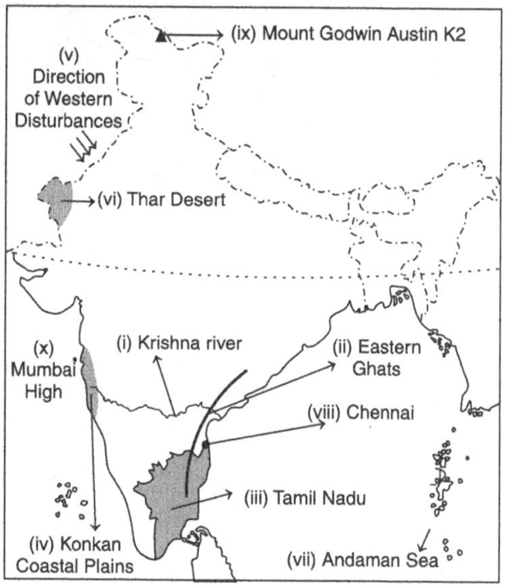

Q.3 On the outline map of India provided

(i) Mark and label the Himalayan mountain range **(1)**

(ii) Mark and label the river Indus **(1)**

(iii) Shade and label an area of laterite soil in South-West India **(1)**

(iv) Mark and name the national capital of India **(1)**

(v) Mark and label the river Ravi **(1)**

(vi) Shade and label the area of Gulf of Khambhat **(1)**

(vii) Shade and label a sparsely populated area of West India **(1)**

(viii) Mark and label the oldest oil refinery in India **(1)**

(ix) Mark and label the Cauvery river **(1)**

(x) Shade and label an area of black soil in West Gujarat **(1)**

Ans.

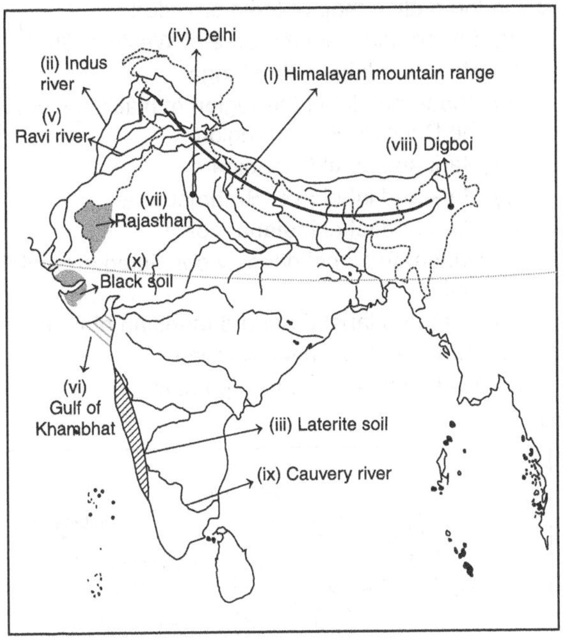

Q.4 On the outline map of India provided

(i) Mark and label Karakoram range **(1)**

(ii) Mark and label river Beas **(1)**

(iii) Shade and label an area of alluvial soil in North India **(1)**

(iv) Mark and label Kolkata **(1)**

(v) Mark and label river Chambal **(1)**

(vi) Mark and label Gulf of Mannar **(1)**

(vii) Shade and label a sparsely populated area of North-East India **(1)**

(viii) Mark and label Jharia coal field **(1)**

(ix) Mark and label Godavari **(1)**

(x) Mark and label Hyderabad **(1)**

Ans.

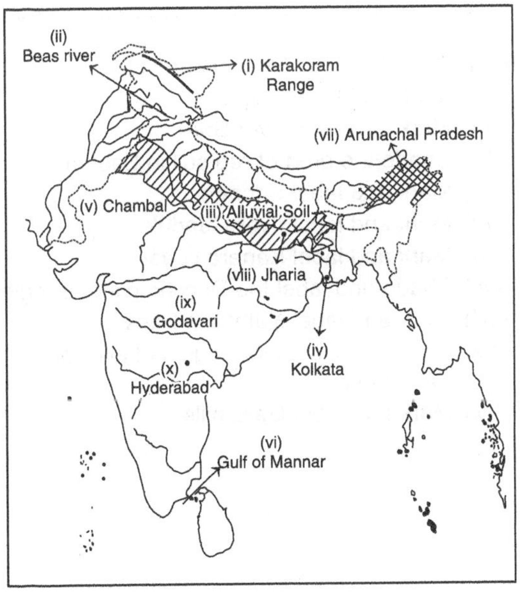

Q.5 On the outline map of India provided

(i) Mark and label Aravali range **(1)**

(ii) Mark and label Chenab river **(1)**

(iii) Shade and label the area of red soil in South-West India **(1)**

(iv) Mark and label Allahabad **(1)**

(v) Mark and label Mahanadi river **(1)**

(vi) Mark and label Palk strait **(1)**

(vii) Shade and label a densely populated area of North India **(1)**

(viii) Mark and label Singhbhum iron city **(1)**

(ix) Mark and label Tapti river **(1)**

(x) Shade and label the area of Chota Nagpur Plateau **(1)**

Ans.

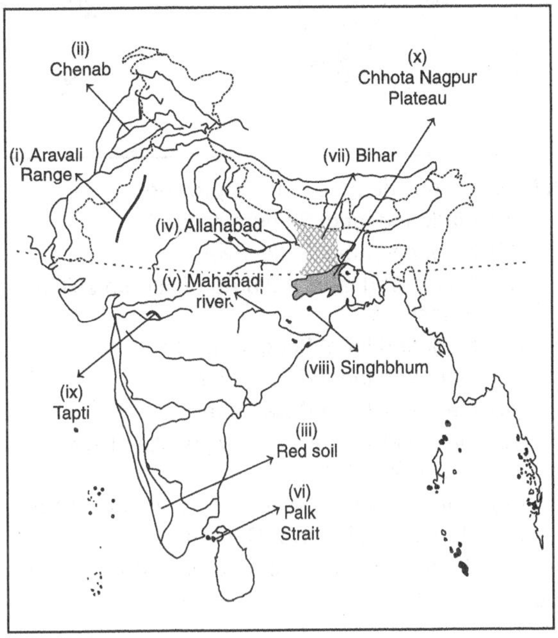

Q.6 On the outline map of India provided

(i) Mark and label Vindhya mountain range **(1)**

(ii) Mark and label Jhelum river **(1)**

(iii) Shade and label the area of alluvial soil in Gujarat **(1)**

(iv) Mark and label Kochi city **(1)**

(v) Mark and label Narmada river **(1)**

(vi) Mark and label Chilika lake **(1)**

(vii) Mark and label densely populated area of South India **(1)**

(viii) Mark and label the direction of South-West monsoon winds **(1)**

(ix) Mark and label Kosi river **(1)**

(x) Mark and label Karakoram pass **(1)**

Ans.

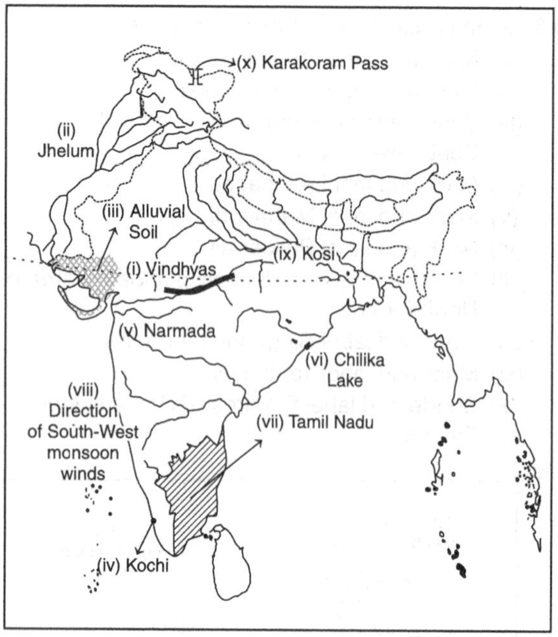

Q.7 On the outline map of India provided

(i) Mark and label Satpura range **(1)**
(ii) Mark and label Sutlej river **(1)**
(iii) Shade and label the area of laterite soil in Rajasthan **(1)**
(iv) Mark and label Bengaluru city **(1)**
(v) Mark and label Gomti river **(1)**
(vi) Mark and label Wular lake **(1)**
(vii) Mark and label a sparsely populated area of South-West India **(1)**
(viii) Mark and label North-East monsoon winds **(1)**
(ix) Mark and label river Damodar **(1)**
(x) Shade and label the area of Northern circars **(1)**

Ans.

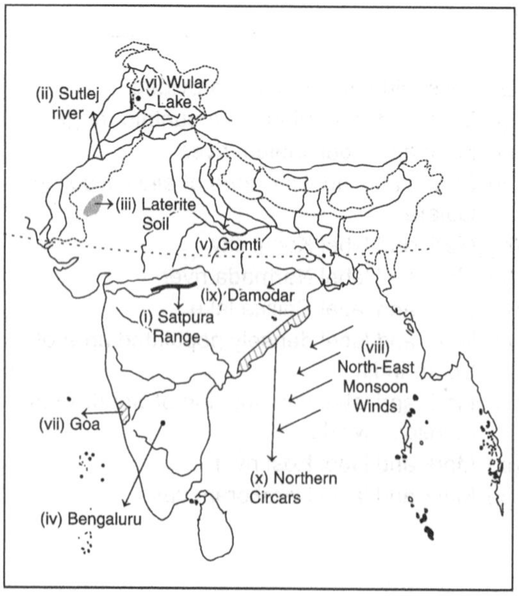

Q.8 On the outline map of India provided

(i) Shade and label the area of Western Ghats **(1)**
(ii) Mark and label river Ganga **(1)**
(iii) Shade and label the region of black soil around the Deccan Plateau region **(1)**
(iv) Mark and label Chandigarh **(1)**
(v) Mark and label river Brahmaputra **(1)**
(vi) Mark and label Malabar coast **(1)**
(vii) Shade and label densely populated area of East India **(1)**
(viii) Mark and label Standard Meridian of India **(1)**
(ix) Mark and label river Yamuna **(1)**
(x) Mark and label Visakhapatnam **(1)**

Ans.

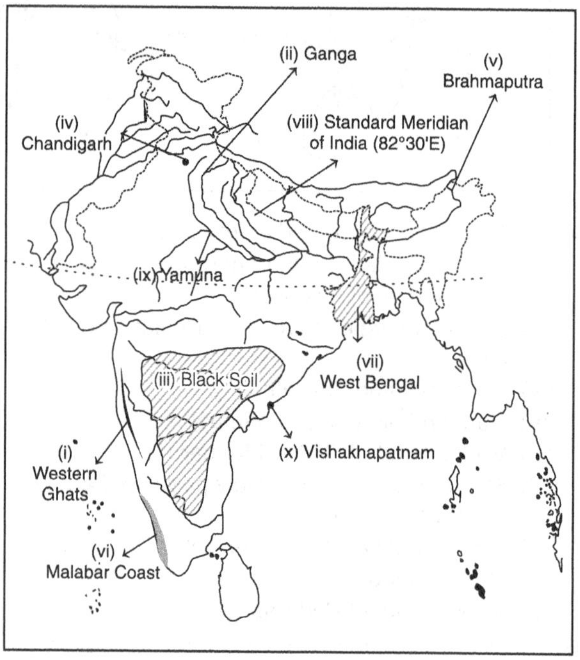

Q.9 On the outline map of India provided

(i) Mark and label Nilgiris **(1)**
(ii) Mark and label river Son **(1)**
(iii) Shade the area of red soil in East India **(1)**
(iv) Mark and label Srinagar **(1)**
(v) Mark and label river Gandak **(1)**
(vi) Mark and label Kanara coast **(1)**
(vii) Shade and label the Deccan plateau region **(1)**
(viii) Mark and label Nathu-La Pass **(1)**
(ix) Shade and label the region of alluvial soil in East India **(1)**
(x) Mark and label Garo hills **(1)**

Ans.

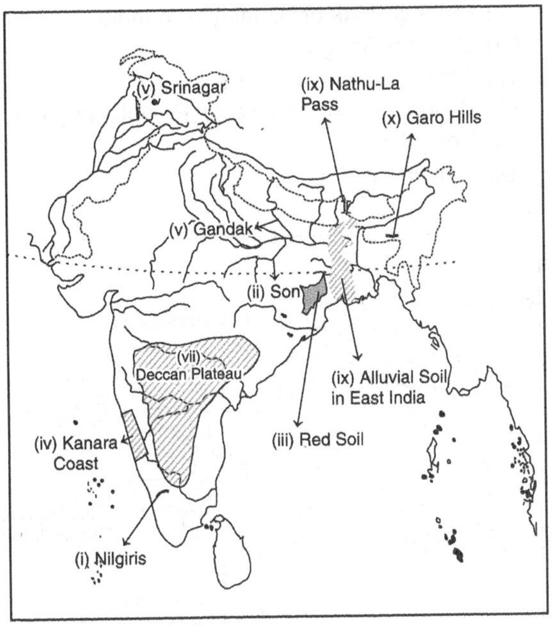

Q.10 On the outline map of India provided

(i) Mark and label Ghaghara river **(1)**

(ii) Shade and label red soil in the North-East **(1)**

(iii) Shade and label the area of laterite soil in North-East India **(1)**

(iv) Mark and label the Tungabhadra river **(1)**

(v) Mark and label Khasi hills **(1)**

(vi) Shade and label the area of Thar desert **(1)**

(vii) Mark and label the latitude which divides India into two equal halves **(1)**

(viii) Mark and label Jaintia hills **(1)**

(ix) Mark and label mount Kanchenjunga **(1)**

(x) Shade and label Gangetic plains **(1)**

Ans.

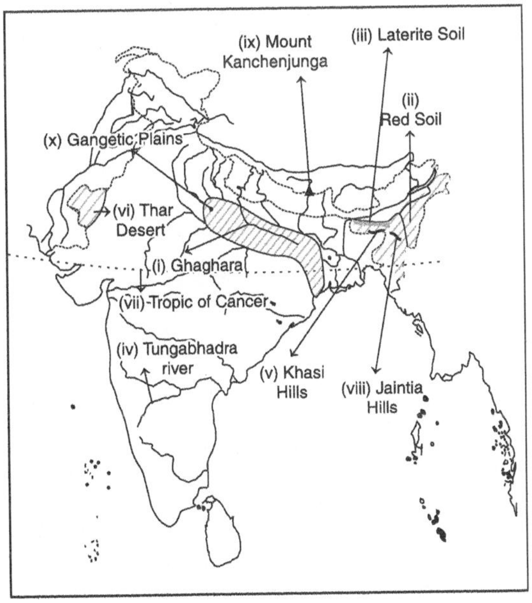

Q.11 On the outline map of India provided mark and label

(i) Plateau rich in mineral **(1)**

(ii) Largest fresh water lake in India **(1)**

(iii) Chenab **(1)**

(iv) Yamuna **(1)**

(v) Gulf of Khambhat **(1)**

(vi) Pass connecting Ladakh with China **(1)**

(vii) Financial capital of India **(1)**

(viii) A region of red soil in East **(1)**

(ix) Coromandel Coast **(1)**

(x) Arabian Sea Branch of South-West Monsoon **(1)**

Ans.

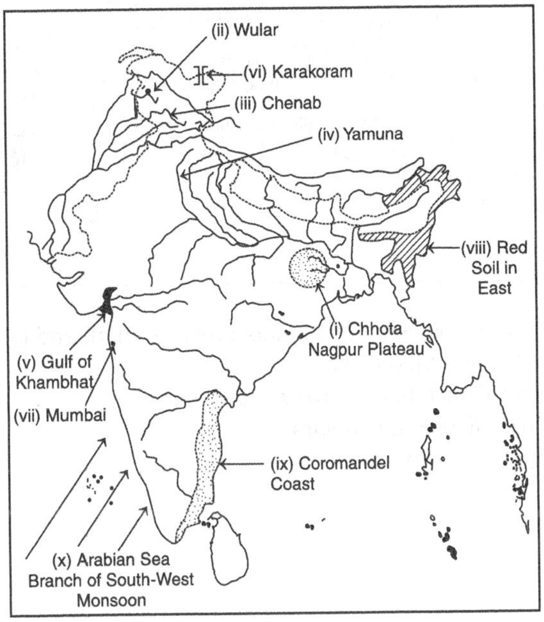

Q.12 On the outline map of India provided mark and label

(i) Old fold mountains-Aravalli **(1)**

(ii) River Beas **(1)**

(iii) I.T. capital of India **(1)**

(iv) Highest Peak in India **(1)**

(v) Gulf of Kutch **(1)**

(vi) Chilika Lake **(1)**

(vii) Riverine Port of India **(1)**

(viii) River Tungabhadra **(1)**

(ix) A region of black soil in South **(1)**

(x) Malabar Coast **(1)**

Ans.

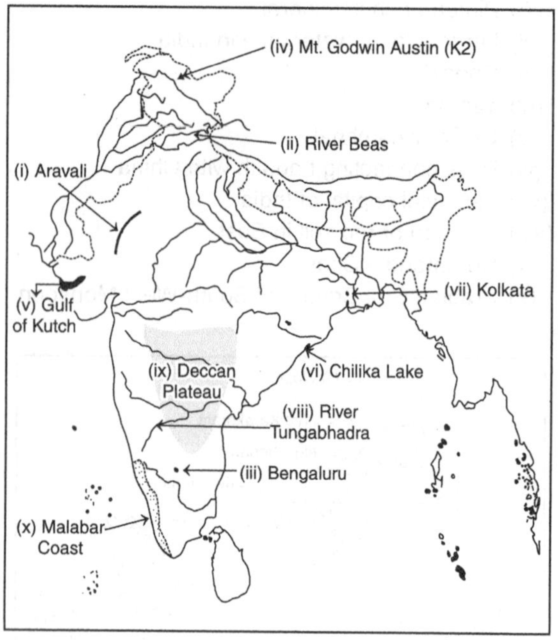

Q.13 On the outline map of India provided mark and label

(i) Blue Mountains **(1)**

(ii) Coast that receive winter rainfall **(1)**

(iii) River Brahmaputra **(1)**

(iv) Tropic of Cancer **(1)**

(v) Highest Peak of Himalayas in India **(1)**

(vi) Dakshin Ganga **(1)**

(vii) Oldest oil field in India **(1)**

(viii) Winds that bring rainfall in Punjab Haryana **(1)**

(ix) Bengaluru **(1)**

(x) Prayagraj **(1)**

Ans.

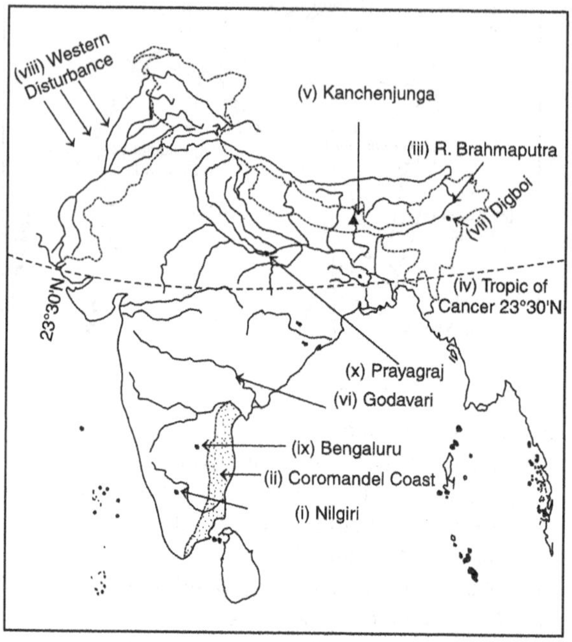

3

CLIMATE

The term **climate** refers to the atmospheric conditions, which prevails in a large area over a long period of time.

Temperature Distribution in India

India has a Tropical monsoon type of climate but regional variations occur due to differences in temperature, rainfall, wind patterns, seasonal fluctuations and the levels of moisture. The Northern part of India experiences continental type of climate and Southern part experiences moderate climate.

Some Regional Variations in Temperature

- The Annual range of temperature is 3°C along the Malabar Coast and more than 20°C in the interiors.
- The regions nearer to the equator (coastal areas) have a range of 25-27°C average temperature during the entire year due to the moderating effect of the sea, e.g. Bengaluru, Mumbai, Chennai, etc.
- In Kargil in the month of December, temperature goes down to as low as - 40°C, whereas Kerala records 20°C or 22°C in the same month.
- The variation between day and night temperatures in the Andaman and Nicobar Islands and Kerala is 7 to 8°C, whereas the same goes up to 25°C to 30 °C in the Thar desert.

Factors Affecting the Climate of India

- **Latitude** It is the measurement of distance of a point on the Earth's surface in North or South of the equator. At the equator, the Sun's rays fall directly thus, temperatures are highest here. But when the distance of a place increases from the equator, the Sun's rays become more slanting and cover large areas thus, the temperaure reduces.

  It influences India's climate by causing higher temperature near the equator in the South, while the North experiences greater temperature variation due to its distance from the equator.
- **Altitude** Temperature decreases with increase in altitude. For every 166 m rise in altitude, there is a decrease of 1°C in temperature. That is why hilly areas are cooler than the plains because of high altitude.
- **Himalayan Mountains** The Himalayas prevent the cold winds of Central Asia from entering into India. It also traps the monsoon winds, forcing them to shed their moisture within the sub-continent.
- **Western Disturbances** These cyclones are caused by weather conditions during winter which are influenced by the distribution pattern of pressure in Central Asia and West Asia. These cyclones give rains to Northern Plains and snowfall in Jammu & Kashmir.
- **The Monsoon Winds** The summer rains over India are caused due to the South-West monsoon winds and the winter rains are caused due to the North-East monsoon winds.
- **Distance from the Sea** The Peninsular India is surrounded by sea from three sides. Due to this, the Southern region experiences moderate climate in summers as well as in winters.

  North India situated far away from these seas, has an extreme type of climate with very hot summers and very cold winters.
- **Relief features** The presence of mountains, plateaus, etc. also affect the climate of India. For example, the Aravalli hills do not block the way of rain bearing winds, hence Western Rajasthan is dry.

Seasons

India observes four seasons in a year, which are summer, monsoon, retreating monsoon and winter. Temperature range of each season varies greatly from each other.

Hot and Dry Season (March to May)

- In these months, the Sun moves from over the equator towards the Tropic of Cancer and the Inter Tropical Convergence Zone (ITCZ) shifts Northward.
- Northern plains experience intense heat with temperatures 45-48°C. This high temperature leads to low pressure conditions in North India.

Local Winds in Summer

- **Loo** It is a hot, dusty and dry wind blowing over the North and North-Western India in the months of May and June.
- **Mango-Showers** They bring little rainfall in South and help in early ripening of mango, hence are called mango shower. They are called cherry blossom in Karnataka, and are considered good for coffee plantation there.
- **Kaal Baisakhi** These are the local winds in West Bengal. These winds are accompanied by thunder storms and bring rainfall in the months of April-May. This rain is good for the cultivation of tea in Assam and rice and jute in West Bengal and are called Bardoli Chheerha in Assam.

The Rainy or the Season of South-West Monsoon Season (June to September)

- During this season, low pressure areas over the Northern plains intensifies by mid-June and attracts the trade winds.
- These winds blow from the South-West to North-East entering peninsula as monsoon winds and cover the entire Indian Subcontinent and bring abundant rainfall.
- These winds are erratic, unpredictable, irregular and unevenly distributed.
- The onset of the South-West monsoon leads to significant fall in temperature. For example, in Mumbai, the temperature drops by 10°C after a rain of just 1 week.
- It is also known as Orographic/relief rainfall.
- South-West monsoon winds bring heavy rainfall as well as violent thunder and lightning. This rainfall is termed as the **burst of monsoon**.
- When these winds fail to bring rainfall for two or more weeks, then this dry period is termed as break of monsoon.

The Season of Retreating Monsoon (October to November)

- This season is also known as the Retreating South-West Monsoon season. During this season, the Sun starts shifting towards the South. The South-West monsoon winds become weak and start retreating.
- Winds blow from North-East to South-West Direction.
- Winds during this season pick up moisture from the Bay of Bengal and cause rainfall in Coromandel Coast.
- High temperature and humid conditions prevail in the Northern plains during this season. This weather is known as October heat.
- The temperature during this season is high being 25°C in the beginning of October and then it gradually decreases in November.
- Tropical cyclone are common over Bay of Bengal during this season and cause heavy loss of life and property.

The Cold Season or the Season of the North-East Monsoon (December to February)

- This season experiences clear skies, low temperature, humidity and feeble (weak) winds.
- Frost occurs in the Northern plains and snowfall occurs in the mountainous regions of Himalayas.
- The average temperature lies between 20°C to 25°C in Peninsular India with warm days and cold nights.
- During this season, the inflow of Western Disturbances or temperate cyclones is observed which originate over the Mediterranean Sea and Western Asia. These disturbances cause a small amount of rainfall to Punjab, Haryana and Utttar Pradesh which is highly beneficial to rabi crops. (Wheat and barley).

Winds in Winter

- **Jet Streams** These are narrow belts of high altitude Westerly winds in the troposphere, which help in determining the arrival of monsoon.
- **El Nino** It has significant impact on global weather patterns. In India El-Nino can influence the Indian monsoon.

Monsoon and its Mechanism

The word 'Monsoon' is derived from the Arabic word 'Mausim' which means season.

In India, Monsoon season remains from June to September and is known as South-West monsoon. It is divided into two branches which are

1. The Arabian Sea Branch (The South-West Monsoon/Summer Monsoon)
2. The Bay of Bengal Branch (The Retreating Monsoon/Winter Monsoon)

Mechanism of Monsoon in Summer Season

- During the summer, low pressure is developed due to intense heat in northern plains which causes winds to blow from the Indian Ocean towards North and North-West.
- These winds carry moisture and bring heavy rainfall. This is called the South-West Monsoon.

Mechanism of Monsoon in Winter Season

- During winters, a low pressure zone develops in the Indian Ocean which causes winds to blow from the northern plains to the Indian Ocean.
- These winds bring some rainfall to the Coromandel coast from winter monsoons. This monsoon is known as the North-East Winter Monsoon/Retreating Monsoon .

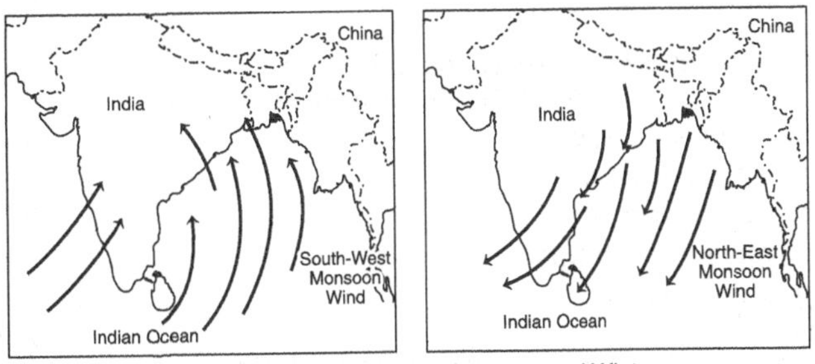

Mechanism of Monsoon in Summer and Winter

Distribution of Rainfall in India

The distribution of rainfall is uneven due to the pressure conditions, direction of relief features and winds bearing moisture and cyclonic depressions. The variations in rainfall can be categorised as

- **Areas of Heavy Rainfall** These areas receive more than 200 cm of rainfall. These include Western Ghats, Assam, Arunachal Pradesh, West Bengal and Meghalaya.
- **Areas of Moderate Rainfall** These areas receive 100-200 cm of rainfall. These include the North middle Ganga Valley, the Southern parts and North-Eastern Peninsula covering Odisha and Eastern Madhya Pradesh.
- **Areas of Low Rainfall** These areas receive 50 to 100 cm of rainfall. These include Western Uttar Pradesh, Eastern Rajasthan and Gujarat, Delhi, Haryana, Punjab and Jammu & Kashmir and Deccan region.
- **Areas of Scanty Rainfal** These areas receive less than 50 cm of rainfall. These areas include Western Rajasthan, Southern Punjab and North-East Kashmir.

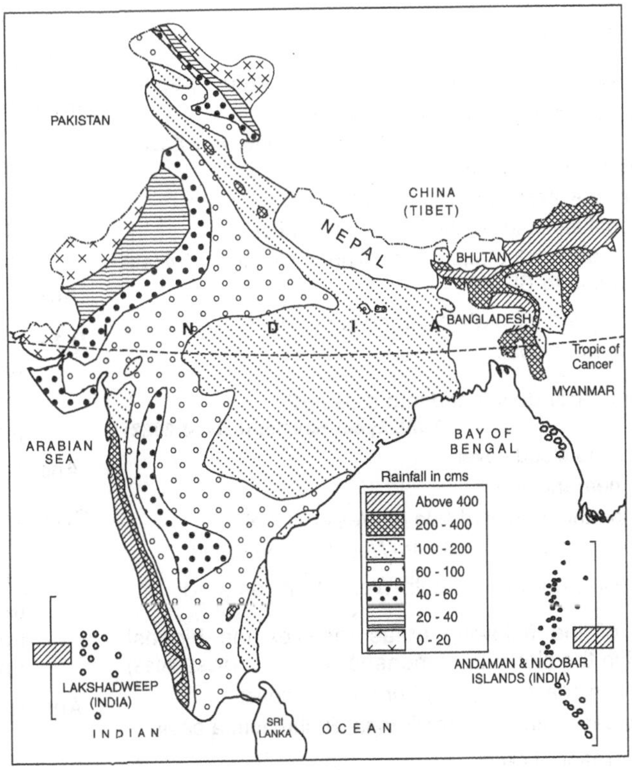

Distribution of Rainfall in India

EXAM ORIENTED QUESTIONS

TYPE - 1 — 1 Mark

Multiple Choice Questions

Q.1 Chennai: East Coast
(a) Delhi: Northern Plains
(b) Mumbai: East Coast
(c) Meghalaya: Malabar Coast
(d) Kochi: Coromandel Coast

Ans. (a) Delhi: Northern Plains

Q.2 Name the type of climate experienced in India. **(ICSE Specimen Semester I 2022)**
(a) Tropical monsoon type
(b) Tropical cyclonic type
(c) Subtropical monsoon
(d) Temperate monsoon type

Ans. (a) Tropical monsoon type

Q.3 The places to the North of the Tropic of Cancer experience............ type of climate.
(a) continental (b) moderate
(c) oceanic (d) Equatorial

Ans. (a) continental

Q.4 Read the statement and identify the incorrect option.
In June, Bhopal is warmer than Kolkata. **(ICSE Specimen Semester-I 2022)**
(a) Due to its continental location.
(b) Due to Kolkata's proximity to the sea.
(c) Bhopal is closer to the Tropic of Cancer.
(d) Himalayan hill station Darjeeling is closer to Kolkata than it is to Bhopal.

Ans. (d) Himalayan hill station Darjeeling is closer to Kolkata than it is to Bhopal.

Q.5 Why has Thar developed into a desert? **(ICSE Specimen Semester-I 2022)**
(a) It has no cloud cover.
(b) It is near the sea.
(c) It is on the windward side of Western Ghats.
(d) Aravalli is parallel to South-West Monsoon wind.

Ans. (d) Aravalli is parallel to South-West Monsoon wind.

Q.6 Which of the following areas receives the highest rainfall in the North-East monsoon? **(ICSE 2023)**
(a) Konkan coast (b) Coromandel coast
(c) Malabar coast (d) Ganga- Brahmaputra basin

Ans. (b) Coromandel coast

Exp. Retreating monsoon winds blow from North-East to South-West and pick up moisture from Bay of Bengal and carries rainfall in coromandel coast.

Q.7 The Western coast gets its heaviest rainfall during .... by South-West monsoon winds.
(a) August (b) September (c) June (d) July

Ans. (c) June

Q.8 Why does the Deccan Plateau get less rainfall than the Western Ghats?
(a) The Deccan Plateau is located at a higher altitude than the Western Ghats.
(b) The Western Ghats act as a barrier to monsoon winds, causing heavy rainfall on their windward side.
(c) The Deccan Plateau is surrounded by large bodies of water that cause more evaporation.
(d) The Western Ghats receive more rainfall due to the presence of dense forests that attract moisture.

Ans. (b) The Western Ghats act as a barrier to monsoon winds, causing heavy rainfall on their windward side.

Q.9 The Eastern coast gets its maximum rainfall during ....
(a) summer season (b) rainy season
(c) autumn season (d) winter season

Ans. (d) winter season

Q.10 In May-June each year, the monsoon winds approach the Southern part of India from
(a) North direction
(b) South-Easterly direction
(c) North-Westerly direction
(d) South-Westerly direction

Ans. (d) South-Westerly direction

Q.11 .... is a hot and dry local wind that blows in North India during the pre-monsoon period.
(a) Western Disturbance (b) Loo
(c) Kaal Baisakhi (d) Cherry Blossom

Ans. (b) Loo

Q.12 The pre-monsoon mango showers occur predominantly in
(a) West Bengal and Assam
(b) Deccan Plateau
(c) Gujarat and Maharashtra
(d) Kerala and Karnataka

Ans. (d) Kerala and Karnataka

Q.13 Among the given options, which of the following is important for tea and jute cultivation?

(a) Kaal Baisakhi (b) Loo
(c) Western Disturbance (d) Monsoon Showers

Ans. (a) Kaal Baisakhi

Q.14 Which of the following coasts of India is most affected by extreme tropical cyclones?

(a) Malabar (b) Coromandel (c) Konkan (d) Kanara

Ans. (b) Coromandel

Q.15 Which monsoon causes rainfall on the windward side of the Eastern Ghats as given in the image marked with 'A'?

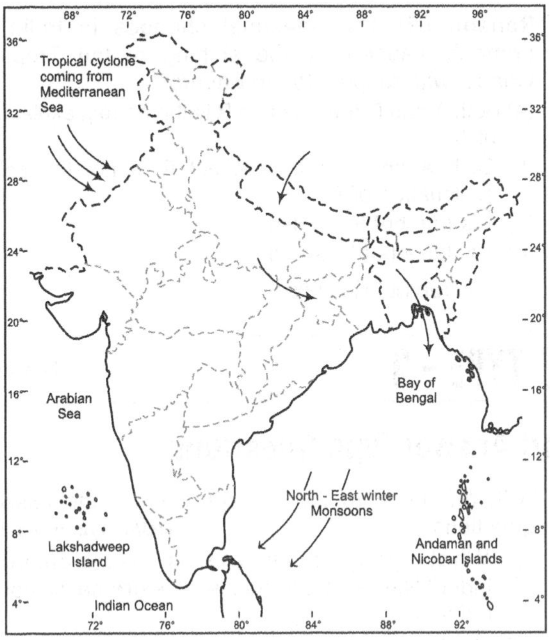

(a) South-West Monsoon (b) North-East Monsoon
(c) Winter Monsoon (d) Summer Monsoon

Ans. (b) North-East Monsoon

Q.16 Himalayas have a significant impact on the climate of India as they **(ICSE Specimen 2025)**

(a) block the North-East monsoon winds
(b) causes rainfall in the Gangetic plains
(c) create a rain shadow area in the Deccan plateau
(d) cause cyclonic disturbance in the Bay of Bengal

Ans. (a) block the North-East monsoon winds

Q.17 Give reason for the following.

The extreme temperature between summer and winter is quite low in the Southern part of peninsular India mainly because

(a) the adjoining oceans moderate the temperature.
(b) the sky is generally cloudy.
(c) the Sun's rays are almost vertical throughout the year.
(d) the strong winds flow throughout the year.

Ans. (a) the adjoining oceans moderate the temperature.

Q.18 What causes snowfall in Kashmir during winter? **(ICSE 2024)**

(a) Tropical cyclone
(b) North-East Monsoon wind
(c) South-West Monsoon wind
(d) Temperate cyclone

Ans. (b) North-East Monsoon wind

Q.19 Westerly depression is active in India during which of the following months?

(a) Between September and November
(b) Between December and January
(c) Between June and September
(d) Between March and May

Ans. (b) Between December and January

Q.20 Western disturbances provide rain to which of the following states? **(ICSE Semester I 2021)**

(a) Punjab (b) West Bengal
(c) Sikkim (d) Maharashtra

Ans. (a) Punjab

Q.21 Read the table and identify the pair that is correctly matched

	Type of Monsoon	Months
P.	South-West monsoon	August - November
Q.	Winter season	December - March
R.	North-East monsoon	December - April
S.	Summer season	March - June

Codes

(a) P (b) Q (c) R (d) S

Ans. (d) S

Q.22 If a farmer in Northern India relies on monsoon rains, how would their cropping pattern differ from a farmer in Tamil Nadu?

(a) North Indian farmers depend on North-East monsoon, while Tamil Nadu farmers depend on South-West monsoon.
(b) North Indian farmers depend on South-West monsoon rains, while Tamil Nadu farmers depend on North-East/Retreating monsoon.
(c) North Indian farmers depend on Western Disturbances, while Tamil Nadu farmers depend on South-East monsoon.
(d) North Indian farmers depend on Mango Showers, while Tamil Nadu farmers depend on South-West monsoon.

Ans. (b) North Indian farmers depend on South-West monsoon rains, while Tamil Nadu farmers depend on North-East/Retreating monsoon.

Exp. The South-West monsoon winds come from the South-West and bring heavy rainfall to most of the parts of North India. So, the farmers in North India depend on the South-West monsoon. The state of Tamil Nadu receives most of the rainfall by the North-East monsoon which is beneficial for the crops grown there.

Q.23 Which of the following is the cause of 'October Heat'?
(a) Low temperature and Heavy rainfall
(b) High temperature and High humidity
(c) Low temperature and High humidity
(d) High temperature and Heavy rainfall

Ans. (b) High temperature and High humidity

TYPE - 2 1 Mark

Assertion-Reason Questions

Q.1 Assertion (A) The Indian sub-continent experiences milder winters as compared to Central Asia.
Reason (R) The Himalayas prevent the cold winds of Central Asia from entering the sub-continent.
(a) Both A and R are true and R is the correct explanation of A
(b) Both A and R are true, but R is not the correct explanation of A
(c) A is true but R is false
(d) A is false but R is true

Ans. (a) Both A and R are true and R is the correct explanation of A

Q.2 Assertion (A) The coastal areas of India experience a moderate climate throughout the year.
Reason (R) The sea has a high heat capacity, which helps in maintaining a moderate temperature in coastal areas.
(a) Both A and R are true and R is the correct explanation of A
(b) Both A and R are true but R is not the correct explanation of A
(c) A is true but R is false
(d) A is false but R is true

Ans. (a) Both A and R are true and R is the correct explanation of A

Q.3 Choose the correct answers to the questions from the given options. **(ICSE 2025)**
Assertion (A) Mumbai receives more rainfall than Pune.
Reason (R) Mumbai gets rain from Arabian Sea branch of South-West monsoon.
(a) Both A and R are true and R is the correct explanation of A
(b) Both A and R are true but R is not the correct explanation of A
(c) A is true and R is false
(d) A is false and R is true

Ans. (a) Both A and R are true and R is the correct explanation of A

Q.4 Assertion (A) The retreating monsoon occurs during the months of October and November.
Reason (R) During this period, the South-West winds lose their moisture due to the decrease in temperature and change direction.
(a) Both A and R are true and R is the correct explanation of A
(b) Both A and R are true but R is not the correct explanation of A
(c) A is true but R is false
(d) A is false but R is true

Ans. (a) Both A and R are true and R is the correct explanation of A

Q.5 Assertion (A) The climate of India is characterised by seasonal changes.
Reason (R) The seasonal changes in India are primarily caused by the shifting of the Tropic of Cancer with respect to the Equator.
(a) Both A and R are true and R is the correct explanation of A
(b) Both A and R are true, but R is not the correct explanation of A
(c) A is true but R is false
(d) A is false but R is true

Ans. (c) A is true but R is false

TYPE - 3 2 Marks

Short Answer Type Questions

Q.1 With reference to the climate, answer the following questions. **(ICSE Specimen 2023)**
(i) What type of climate is experienced in India? Name three places of extreme climate in India.
(ii) Mention any two factors responsible for it.

Ans. (i) Tropical monsoon type of climate is experienced in India. Delhi, Lucknow and Jodhpur are three places that experience extreme types of climate.
(ii) Two factors responsible for such a type of climate are
(a) India lies in the tropical belt.
(b) Its climate is deeply influenced by the monsoon winds.

Q.2 Explain the various factors that influence the climate of India or South Asia.

Ans. The climate of India and South Asia is influenced by several factors, which include

- **Latitude** India is located between 8°N and 37°N latitudes, placing it in the tropical zone. The Indian sub-continent is divided into two parts by the Tropic of Cancer. The Northern part lies in the temperate zone while the Southern in the tropical zone.

- **Altitude** Higher altitudes lead to cooler temperatures especially in the Northern regions. The mountains also influence the monsoon winds creating different weather patterns in the plains and along the coast.
- **Distance from the sea** Areas in the interiors of India have extreme types of climate whereas coastal areas have equable climate.
- **Relief features** Relief features play an important role in the climatic conditions of India. The Western Ghats receive substantial rainfall on the Western side because they block the South-West monsoon.

Q.3 Give reasons for the following.

(i) **Northern Plains do not experience snowfall in winters.**

(ii) **Kochi has a lesser annual range of temperature than Agra.**

Ans. (i) The Northern Plains do not experience snowfall because Himalayas do not allow the cold polar winds to enter India.

(ii) Kochi is located on the Western coast due to which it experiences a maritime climate and has low range of temperature. On the other hand, Agra lies in the interior as it is far away from the sea so it experiences continental type of climate and has a greater range of temperature.

Q.4 'Severe cyclonic storms are often formed over the Bay of Bengal during the retreating monsoon season.' **(ICSE 2025)**

(i) **Name two states that are affected by tropical cyclones on the Eastern coast of India.**

(ii) **The temperate cyclones cause less damage than the tropical cyclones. Give any two points to support this statement.**

Ans. (i) Two states that are affected by tropical cyclones on the Eastern coast of India are West Bengal and Odisha.

(ii) The temperate cyclones cause less damage than the tropical cyclones due to the following reasons

- **Lower Wind Speeds** Temperate cyclones have weaker winds than tropical cyclones, causing less damage.
- **Wider Area of Influence** Temperate cyclones affect a larger area with less intensity, while tropical cyclones are more concentrated and destructive.

Q.5 Give reasons for the following. **(ICSE 2014)**

(i) **Western Rajasthan receives no rain from the Arabian Sea branch of the South-West monsoon winds.**

(ii) **Mangalore is not cold even in the month of December.**

Ans. (i) Western Rajasthan receives no rain from the Arabian Sea branch because these winds run parallel to the Aravalli ranges and do not cross it to give rainfall in Western Rajasthan. Also, the temperature is so high that monsoon winds become dry and do not shed any moisture there.

(ii) Mangalore is not cold even in the month of December because it lies on the Western coast of India and therefore has the moderating influence of the sea.

Q.6 Western coastal plains receive more rainfall than Eastern coastal plains. Give a reason.

Ans. Western coastal plains receive more rainfall because they lie in the windward side of the Western Ghats that block the way of rain bearing winds coming from the Arabian sea. While the Eastern coastal plains lie on the leeward side of the Western Ghats and receives less rainfall.

Q.7 Give a reason for each of the following.

(i) **West Bengal gets rainfall from South-West monsoon much before Uttar Pradesh.**

(ii) **Mawsynram is the rainiest place in the world**

Ans. (i) Due to its closer proximity to the Bay of Bengal which enables moist winds to reach the state sooner, West Bengal receives rainfall from the South-West monsoon far earlier than Uttar Pradesh.

(ii) Mawsynram is regarded as the world's rainiest place because it is situated in the Khasi hills of Meghalaya where the rocky terrain forces the wet monsoon winds from the Bay of Bengal to rise rapidly, resulting in heavy condensation.

Q.8 Give a geographical reason for the following

(i) **Kolkata gets more rain than Delhi during the rainy season.** **(ICSE 2024)**

(ii) **Though both are hill stations, Shimla experiences snowfall during the winters but Ooty does not.**

Ans. (i) Kolkata receives heavier rain than Delhi because Kolkata is closer to the Bay of Bengal. Being near the coast, it directly receives the moisture-containing air which results in more rainfall.

(ii) Shimla experiences snowfall due to its higher altitude and colder temperatures while Ooty, being at a lower elevation and in a subtropical climate, does not receive snowfall.

Q.9 Give reasons for the following.

(i) **The annual rainfall of Rajasthan is less than 25 cm.**

(ii) **The Coromandel coast gets most of its rain during the Winter season.**

Ans. (i) Rajasthan gets less than 25 cm of rainfall or very little rainfall as it lies parallel to the direction of South-West monsoon winds and do not form any barrier.

(ii) Coromandel coast gets most of its rainfall from the North-East monsoon winds that travel from land to sea.

On the way, these winds pick moisture from the Bay of Bengal and cause rainfall in Coromandel coast that includes parts of Andhra Pradesh and Chennai.

Q.10 (i) **Name the local wind that causes rainfall in the states of Assam and West Bengal in the month of April.** **(ICSE 2025)**

(ii) **How is this rainfall beneficial for the states mentioned above?**

Ans. (i) The local wind that causes rainfall in the states of Assam and West Bengal in the month of April is the 'Norwesters' or 'Kalbaisakhi'.

(ii) This rainfall benefits Assam and West Bengal by aiding crop growth and cooling down temperatures, providing relief from the heat.

Q.11 Name the source of winter rain in Tamil Nadu. How does the state of Tamil Nadu benefit from it?

Ans. North-East monsoon or Retreating monsoon is the major source of winter rainfall in Tamil Nadu. During the months of October to December, North-East monsoon winds pick up moisture from the Bay of Bengal and bring it over the Eastern coastal regions.

This rainfall replenishes the soil moisture, which is crucial for many crops like pulses, groundnut, sugarcane and vegetables. The rain also helps fill up important reservoirs in the area.

Q.12 Name the following.

(i) **The winds bring heavy rain in Cherrapunji.**

(ii) **The local winds that bring a light rainfall to South India and are good for mango, tea and coffee crops.**

Ans. (i) Kaal Baisakhi winds of South-West monsoon.

(ii) Mango Showers.

Q.13 Define Jet Streams. Also explain how they affect the climate of India?

Ans. Jet streams are Westerly winds which blow in the upper layers of the atmosphere. These winds blow at a speed of 110 kmph in summers and 184 kmph in winters. These winds are air currents and greatly help in determining the arrival of monsoons in India.

Q.14 What is the direction of South-West monsoon? Why?

Ans. The South-West monsoon winds blow over the Arabian Sea from the South-West because during the summer season in the Northern hemisphere, the Indian subcontinent landmass gets heated up and develops low pressure.

As a result of this, the South-East trade winds are attracted towards the Indian sub-continent and become the South-West monsoon winds in the Indian sub-continent due to Coriolis force.

Q.15 Name two types of cyclonic systems that affect India and two areas that receive rainfall from these systems.

Ans. Two cyclonic systems that affect India are

(i) **Temperate Cyclones** Two areas that receive rainfall from these cyclones are Punjab and Haryana.

(ii) **Tropical Cyclones** Areas which receive rainfall from these cyclones are Andhra Pradesh, Tamil Nadu, Odisha and West Bengal.

Q.16 Mention the different sources of rain in Punjab and Tamil Nadu during the winter season. **(ICSE 2014)**

Ans. The different sources of rain in Punjab and Tamil Nadu during the winter season are

(i) Punjab receives rainfall due to the cyclonic disturbances (Westerly disturbances) that originate over the Eastern Mediterranean sea during the winter season.

(ii) Tamil Nadu receives rainfall from North-East monsoon wind during the winter season.

Q.17 Mention two differences between South-West monsoon and retreating monsoon.

Ans. The two difference between South-West monsoon and retreating monsoon are

South-West Monsoon Winds	Retreating Monsoon Winds
Winds blow from June-September.	Winds blow during October-November.
The direction of these winds is from South-West to North-East.	The direction of these winds is from North-East to South-West
They bring heavy rainfall as winds blow from sea to land.	They bring less rainfall as winds blow from land to sea

Q.18 Give two reasons as to why the entire Indian sub-continent has the Tropical Monsoon climate.

Ans. The entire Indian sub-continent experiences the Tropical Monsoon climate due to two reasons

(i) **Geographical Location and Latitude** The Indian sub-continent lies between the Tropic of Cancer and the Equator. This positioning places the majority of the area in the tropical zone, which is characterised by high temperatures throughout the year. Due to the closeness to the Equator, the entire region receives a significant amount of solar energy, which influences temperature and seasonal weather patterns.

(ii) **Influence of the Indian Ocean and Monsoon Winds** The Indian sub-continent is bordered by the Indian ocean to the South, which plays a crucial role in shaping its monsoon climate.

The ocean acts as a moisture reservoir, and the seasonal winds (South-West monsoon winds) bring moisture-laden air from the Indian ocean. As a result, they bring heavy rainfall, which results in the Monsoon season.

Q.19 With reference to the monsoon, answer the following questions. **(ICSE 2018)**

(i) Name a state that is the first to experience the onset of the monsoon.

(ii) How does the 'Mango Showers' influence the state of Karnataka?

Ans. (i) **Kerala** is the first state in India to experience the onset of the monsoon from the Arabian branch of monsoon.

(ii) Mango shower influences the state of Karnataka as it helps in **early ripening** of **mangoes** in Karnataka and parts of Kerala.

Q.20 Explain the term 'Burst of Monsoon' ? Name the state that experiences the 'Burst of Monsoon'.

Ans. Around the time of the arrival of the monsoons, the sudden violent onset of rainfall in first week of June is known as the 'Burst of Monsoon'. Meghalaya experiences the burst of monsoon.

Q.21 Mention some most important features of the tropical monsoon type of climate.

Ans. Some important features of the tropical monsoon type of climate are

- Temperatures remain high throughout the year, generally between 25°C to 30°C.
- The monsoon season brings a lot of rain, often more than 2000 mm a year. This is caused by the South-West monsoon winds that carry moisture from the oceans.

Q.22 Mention two characteristics of the South-West monsoon.

Ans. Two characteristics of the South-West monsoon are

(i) South-West monsoon winds are periodic. These winds are erratic, unpredictable, irregular and unevenly distributed.

(ii) Orographic in nature and does not cause uniform rainfall in the country.

Q.23 With reference to the summer season in India, answer the following questions. **(ICSE 2019)**

(i) Mention the duration of the summer season In India.

(ii) What is the atmospheric pressure condition during summer season over the central part of India?

Ans. (i) The months of March, April and May are the summer months in India when the Sun moves from the Equator towards the Tropic of Cancer (Northward movement) and the global heat belt shifts Northward. By 21st June, it is directly overhead the Tropic of Cancer.

(ii) The atmospheric pressure conditions in Central India is low in summer as the region experiences high temperature and heat waves during summer.

Q.24 Give a reason for each of the following. **(ICSE 2020)**

(i) Rainy season in India comes after the summer season.

(ii) Tamil Nadu has more rainy months than Kerala, yet, Kerala receives more rainfall than Tamil Nadu.

Ans. (i) Rainy season always comes after summer because during summer, there is a lot of water loss due to excessive heat. This increases the amount of moisture and humidity in the atmosphere which ultimately results in rainfall.

(ii) Tamil Nadu has more rainy months than Kerala because it receives rainfall from both-South-West monsoon winds and North-West monsoon winds (during winters), but Kerala receives rainfall only from South-West monsoon winds. The South-West monsoon winds first strike Kerala and give abundant rainfall there. Thus, Kerala gets more rainfall than Tamil Nadu.

Q.25 Give two important characteristics of the hot and dry summer in India.

Ans. Two characteristics of the hot and dry summer in India are

(i) It is a dry season with high temperature and low humidity.

(ii) The tornado-like dust storms, hot winds (loo) and the Norwesters occur during this season.

Q.26 Explain the role of Western Disturbances in the occurrence of winter rainfall in Northern India.

Ans. Western Disturbances are the weather systems that originate in the Mediterranean sea and travel towards Central Asia Northern India. During winter, these disturbances bring moisture causing rainfall and snowfall in the Western Himalayan region. This winter rainfall is crucial for replenishing water resources and Rabi crops.

Q.27 'The summer and winter seasons impact agriculture and daily life in India'. Explain

Ans. In summer, high temperatures and water scarcity can stress crops, reducing agricultural production. In summers, demand for water and energy increases which makes daily life more difficult. In the winter season, lesser temperatures benefit Rabi crops like wheat and mustard, with less strain on resources like water and energy but the cold winds and frost in Northern India makes daily life more difficult.

TYPE - 4   3 Marks

Long Answer Type Questions

Q.1 Give a geographical reason for each of the following. **(ICSE 2016)**

(i) Kanpur has extreme temperature conditions.

(ii) Kochi is warmer than Mumbai even though both lie on the Western coast of India.

(iii) The Ganga plain gets the monsoon rain much later than the West coast of India.

Ans. (i) Kanpur has extreme temperature condition as it is located in the interiors and has no moderating influence of the sea. Therefore, it is very hot in summers and very cold in winters.

(ii) Although Kochi and Mumbai lie on the West coast of India, yet Kochi is warmer because it is situated closer to the Equator and gets adequate sunshine throughout the year.

(iii) The West coast of India gets monsoon rains first as the Arabian sea branch of the South-West monsoon enters India from there. Then, it moves upwards from the Deccan plateau in Central India towards Ganga plains in North. So, the Ganga plain gets monsoon rain later than the West coast.

Q.2 Give a reason for each of the following. **(ICSE 2017)**

(i) Kolkata receives heavier rain than Lucknow.

(ii) The summer monsoon winds blow over the Arabian sea from the South-West.

(iii) Thar is a desert.

Ans. (i) Kolkata receives heavier rain than Lucknow because Kolkata lies in the lower Ganga plain and lies first on the way of Bay of Bengal branch of South-West monsoons, and by the time it reaches Lucknow, their moisture holding capacity decreases, therefore it sheds less rainfall.

(ii) The summer monsoon winds blow over the Arabian sea from the South-West because during the summer season in the Northern hemisphere, the Indian sub-continent landmass gets heated up and develops low pressure. As a result of this, the South-East trade winds are attracted towards the Indian sub-continent and become the South-West monsoon winds in the Indian sub-continent due to Coriolis force.

(iii) The Arabian sea branch of the South-West monsoon blow parallel to Aravali hills, so they do not intercept winds, therefore Thar is a desert.

Q.3 Give a reason for each of the following. **(ICSE 2018)**

(i) Kanyakumari experiences an equable climate.

(ii) Central Maharashtra gets less rainfall than coastal areas of Maharashtra.

(iii) Jaipur has a higher annual range of temperature than Mumbai.

Ans. (i) Kanyakumari experiences an equable climate because it is located near the coast and there is not much difference between the temperatures during the summer and winter due to the sea effect.

(ii) Central Maharashtra gets less rainfall than coastal areas of Maharashtra because Central Maharashtra lies in the rain shadow area of the Western Ghats.

On the other hand, the coastal area of Maharashtra lie in the windward side of Western Ghats.

(iii) Jaipur lies in the interior far away from the sea, so it experiences extreme temperature, whereas Mumbai lies on the Western coast, so it experiences moderate type of temperature.

Q.4. Distinguish between cold dry winters and hot dry summers. **(ICSE 2025)**

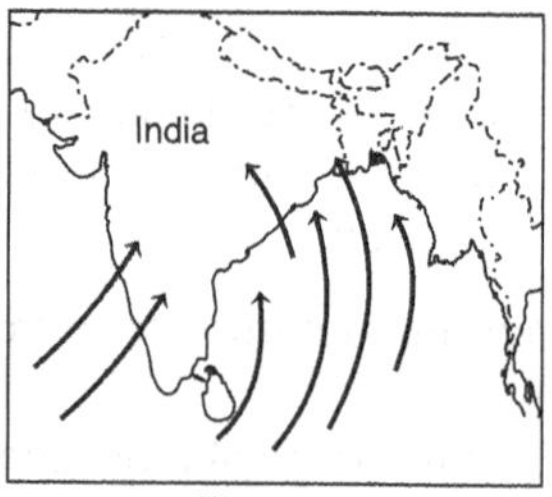

Figure A

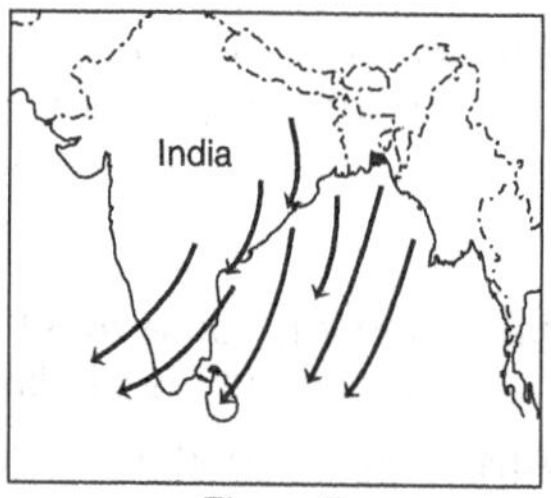

Figure B

(i) Name the winds shown by arrows in figure A and figure B.

(ii) How is the wind shown in Figure A different from the one shown in Figure B?

Ans. (i) The winds shown by arrows in Figure A represent the South-West monsoon Winds. The winds shown by arrows in Figure B represent the North-East monsoon Winds.

(ii) The wind shown in Figure A is different from the one shown in Figure B in the following ways

- South-West monsoon Winds (Figure A) These winds blow from the Indian Ocean towards the Indian subcontinent during the summer season (June to September), bringing heavy rainfall to most parts of India.
- North-East monsoon Winds (Figure B) These winds blow from the land (India) towards the Indian Ocean during the winter season (October to December), bringing rainfall mainly to the southeastern coast of India (Tamil Nadu, Andhra Pradesh, etc.).

Q.5 Study the climatic data given below and answer the questions that follow. **(ICSE 2017)**

Month	Jan	Feb	Mar	Apr	May	Jun	July	Aug	Sep	Oct	Nov	Dec
Temp (°C)	12.0	25.5	26.3	27.1	30.0	36.2	36.0	35.9	30.3	28.4	21.0	16.6
Rainfall (cm)	1.5	0.1	0.0	14	1.1	21.0	25.3	27.2	24.0	9.4	1.5	0.4

(i) What is the annual range of temperature of the station?
(ii) What is the total annual rainfall experienced by the station?
(iii) Why would it be correct to presume that the station lies in the interior and not on the coast?

Ans. (i) The annual range of temperature of the station is 36.2°C - 12°C = 24.2 °C

(ii) The total annual rainfall is 1.5 + 0.1 + 0.0 + 1.4
+ 1.1 + 21.0 + 25.3 + 27.2 + 24.0 + 9.4 + 1.5 + 0.4 = 112.9 cm.

(iii) The station is located in the interior because the annual range is high and experiences continental type of climate i.e., very hot during summers and very cold in winters.

Q.6 Study the climatic data of station X given below and answer the questions that follow. **(ICSE 2016)**

Month	Jan	Feb	Mar	Apr	May	Jun	July	Aug	Sep	Oct	Nov	Dec
Temp (°C)	24.5	25.7	27.7	28.4	30.0	32.5	31.0	30.2	29.8	28.0	25.9	24.7
Rainfall (cm)	4.3	1.6	1.7	2.4	2.8	4.6	8.6	11.4	11.8	30.6	35.0	13.9

(i) Calculate the total annual rainfall experienced by the station.
(ii) What is the annual range of temperature?
(iii) On which coast of India does the station lie?
Give a reason for your answer.

Ans. (i) The annual rainfall is 4.3 + 1.6 + 1.7 + 2.4 + 2.8
+ 4.6 + 8.6 + 11.4 + 11.8 + 30.6 + 35.0 + 13.9
= 128.7 cm.

(ii) The annual range of temperature is 32.5°C - 24.5° C = 8° C.

(iii) The station lies on the East coast as maximum rainfall is in the months of October-November i.e. in the retreating monsoon season.

Q.7 Study the climatic data given below and answer the questions that follow. **(ICSE 2015)**

Month	Jan	Feb	Mar	Apr	May	Jun	July	Aug	Sep	Oct	Nov	Dec
Temp (°C)	21.0	21.9	24.3	27.2	28.0	26.4	26.1	25.4	25.0	26.0	23.8	21.2
Rainfall (cm)	5.1	2.8	1.2	1.7	3.9	4.6	8.4	11.4	11.9	31.6	34.5	14.8

(i) Identify the hottest month.
(ii) Calculate the annual rainfall.
(iii) Name the winds that bring the maximum rainfall to this city.

Ans. (i) Hottest month is May.

(ii) Total annual rainfall is 5.1 + 2.8 + 1.2 + 1.7 + 3.9
+ 4.6 + 8.4 + 11.4 + 11.9 + 31. 6 + 34.5 + 14.8
= 131.9 cm.

(iii) The winds of retreating monsoon bring maximum rainfall to this city as the maximum amount of rainfall is received during the months of October and November.

Q.8 Study the climatic data given below and answer the questions that follow. **(ICSE 2014)**

Month	Jan	Feb	Mar	Apr	May	Jun	July	Aug	Sep	Oct	Nov	Dec
Temp (°C)	25.0	25.5	26.3	27.1	30.0	36.2	36.0	35.9	30.3	28.4	27.0	24.6
Rainfall (cm)	24.5	23.1	15.0	2.4	0.1	11.0	9.3	7.2	4.0	9.4	14.5	20.4

(i) Calculate the annual range of temperature.
(ii) What is the total annual rainfall?
(iii) Presuming that the station is located in India, give a reason for its location being on the East coast or the West coast of India.

Ans. (i) Annual range of temperature is 36.2° C - 24.6°C = 11.6°C

(ii) Total annual rainfall is 24.5 + 23.1 + 15.0 + 2.4
+ 0.1 + 11.0 + 9.3 + 7.2 + 4.0 + 9.4 + 14.5 + 20.4
= 140.9 cm

(iii) The station is located on the Eastern coast of India, because heavy rainfall is observed in the winter season.

Q.9 Study the climate data of station X and answer the following questions. **(ICSE 2025)**

Month	Jan	Feb	Mar	Apr	May	Jun	July	Aug	Sep	Oct	Nov	Dec
Temp (°C)	24.0	25.4	26.7	28.3	30.0	28.9	27.4	27.4	27.3	27.1	27.0	25.0
Rainfall (cm)	0.25	0.25	-	-	1.75	50.2	61.0	37.0	27.0	4.75	1.50	-

(i) What is the annual range of temperature for station X?
(ii) Which is the wettest month?
(iii) Name the wind which brings rainfall for station X during the rainy season.

Ans. (i) Annual range of temperature = Highest temperature - Lowest temperature
= 30.0°C (May) - 24.0°C (January)
= 6.0°C

(ii) July is the wettest month.

(iii) The wind that brings rainfall to station X during the rainy season is the South-West.

Q.10 Study the climatic data given below and answer the questions that follow.

Month	Jan	Feb	Mar	Apr	May	Jun	July	Aug	Sep	Oct	Nov	Dec
Temp (°C)	23.8	25.0	27.7	28.3	30.2	30.3	30.4	33.4	30.0	30.3	25.5	24.2
Rainfall (cm)	0	0	1.1	1.5	2.1	45.3	46.5	45.4	43.3	20.1	3.0	0.1

(i) Calculate the mean annual temperature.
(ii) What is the total rainfall during the monsoon season?
(iii) Does the station have a maritime or a continental climate? Give a reason for your answer.

Ans. (i) The mean annual temperature
Sum of all observations / No. of observations
339/12 = 28.25° C

(ii) The total rainfall during the monsoon season (June to October) is 200.6 cm.

(iii) The station has a maritime type of climate because it has less temperature variation (from 30.4°C to 23.8°C).

Q.11 Study the climatic data given below and answer the questions that follow.

Month	Jan	Feb	Mar	Apr	May	Jun	July	Aug	Sep	Oct	Nov	Dec
Temp (°C)	24.5	25.7	27.7	20.4	30.0	32.5	31.0	30.2	29.8	28.0	25.9	24.7
Rainfall (cm)	4.6	1.8	1.3	1.8	3.8	4.5	8.7	11.3	11.9	30.6	35.0	13.9

(i) Name the driest month.
(ii) Calculate the annual rainfall experienced by the station.
(iii) What is the annual range of temperature?

Ans. (i) The driest month is March (1.3 cm).

(ii) The annual rainfall experienced by the station is 4.6 + 1.8 + 1.3 + 1.8 + 3.8 + 4.5 + 8.7 + 11.3 + 11.9 + 30.6 + 35.0 + 13.9 = 129.2 cm.

(iii) The annual range of temperature is 20.4 to 32.5°C - 20.4°C = 12.1°C.

Q.12 Study the climate data of Station X and answer the questions that follow. **(ICSE 2024)**

Month	Jan	Feb	Mar	Apr	May	Jun	July	Aug	Sep	Oct	Nov	Dec
Temp (°C)	8.4	11.5	21.6	28.3	35.1	38.5	41.0	38.0	30.8	29.2	15.6	11.2
Rainfall (cm)	1.5	0.9	0.5	-	-	12.5	17.8	18.5	12.5	12.5	6.2	2.1

(i) Calculate the annual range of temperature of Station X.
(ii) Name the rainiest month of Station X.
(iii) Is Station X located in the coastal area or in the continental interior?

Ans. (i) The annual range of temperature of temperature experience by the station X is 41.0 - 8.4 = 32.6

(ii) The rainiest month of station X is August.

(iii) Station X is located in the continental interior as the variation in temperature is large.

Q.13 Give a geographical reason for each of the following. **(ICSE 2023)**

(i) The Malabar coast receives heavy rainfall in the month of July but the Coromandel coast during this time remains comparatively dry.
(ii) Punjab receives rainfall in the winter season.
(iii) Mumbai is warmer than Delhi in the month of December.

Ans. (i) Malabar coast receives heavy rainfall from the Arabian sea branch of South-West monsoon during June to October as it lies in the windward side of Western Ghats. On the other hand, Coromandel coast gets very low rainfall from South-West monsoon as it lies in the leeward side of Western Ghats.

(ii) The cyclones originating in the Mediterranean sea during the winter gradually shifts towards the East and reach India. This causes winter rainfall in Northern plains, especially in the Punjab region.

(iii) Mumbai is warmer than Delhi in the month of December because it has an equable climate due to coastal location, while Delhi lies in the interior away from the coast and experiences extreme climate.

Q.14 How do the Himalayas act as a 'climate divide'?

Ans. The Himalayas act as a climate divide by creating distinct climatic conditions. This is due to their large height, their influence on air currents and the geographical positioning of the mountain range which separates the Indian sub-continent from the Tibetan Plateau and Central Asia.

Himalayas intercept the rain-bearing South-West monsoon winds, forcing them to shed their moisture resulting in heavy rainfall in the North-East and Indo Gangetic Plain.

Q.15 Give three important characteristics of the hot and dry summer in India.

Ans. Three characteristics of the hot and dry summer in India are as follows

(i) It is a dry season with high temperature and low humidity.

(ii) Tornadoes like dust storms, hot wind (loo) and the Norwesters are the characteristics of summer season.

(iii) The hot summer in India is often characterised by dry conditions with very low humidity levels, particularly in the Northern regions. This results in a dry weather with limited rainfall during the pre-monsoon season.

TYPE - 5 Structured Questions

10 Marks

Q.1 (i) India Meteorological Department (IMD) brings a ray of hope for India's agricultural sector and weather patterns in the upcoming year. After grappling with 'below normal' rains and dry conditions in 2023, the forecast suggested above-normal rainfall in certain regions, including the Southernmost parts of Peninsular India, North-West India, and several parts of East-Central, East, and North-East India. *Investing.com (1st November, 2023)*

(a) As a student of Geography, what according to you may be the possible reason for the 'below normal' rains in 2023? **(ICSE Specimen 2025) (2)**

(b) During which months of the year does most of India receive a major amount of its rainfall?

(ii) What is the source of winter rainfall in each of the following areas? **(2)**

(a) Punjab (b) Tamil Nadu

(iii) Give a reason for each of the following **(3)**

(a) Kerala gets rainfall from the summer monsoons much before Uttar Pradesh.

(b) Visakhapatnam records a low annual range of temperature.

(c) Winds are mostly offshore during the cold season.

(iv) Study the climatic data of station X and answer the following questions. **(3)**

Month	Jan	Feb	Mar	Apr	May	Jun	July	Aug	Sep	Oct	Nov	Dec
Temp (°C)	23.1	24.8	26.5	29.3	32	32.8	33.1	32.1	30.5	29.3	28.7	26.1
Rainfall (cm)	7.3	1.1	0.3	0.1	1.3	4.5	6.1	8.2	8.5	20.1	20.8	9.0

(a) What is the annual range of temperature of station X?

(b) Which is the driest month?

(c) Name the wind that brings maximum rainfall to this season.

Ans. (i) (a) The possible reasons for the 'below normal' rains in 2023 could be Global warming or El Nino effect.

(b) Most of India receive major amount of its rainfall during June to September.

(ii) (a) Western disturbances originating in the Mediterranean region/Temperate cyclones is the source of winter rainfall in Punjab.

(b) North-East winter monsoon wind/retreating monsoon is the source of winter rainfall in Tamil Nadu.

(iii) (a) Kerala lies in the South-West of the country where the South-West monsoon wind strikes first. The wind then advances to the North and reaches Uttar Pradesh.

(b) Visakhapatnam has a coastal location and experiences the moderating\influence of the sea.

(c) Land loses heat fast and high pressure develops over it during the cold season. The surrounding seas remain warm and have low pressure during this time. Thus, winds blow from land to sea and are offshore.

(iv) (a) 10 (b) April

(c) Tropical Cyclones / Retreating Monsoon winds/ North-East Winter Monsoon wind bring maximum rainfall to this season.

Q.2 (i) Mention two characteristics of the Indian Monsoon. **(2)**

(ii) Tamil Nadu has more rainy months than Kerala, yet, Kerala receives more rainfall than Tamil Nadu. Give a reason. **(2)**

(iii) (a) What is the difference between weather and climate? **(3)**

(b) Name a region in India which receives rainfall both in summer and winter.

(iv) India's climate is influenced by the location of the Himalayas, the Thar desert, and the Indian ocean. The Himalayas block cold winds from the North, and the Thar desert heats the air, while the Indian ocean provides moisture, contributing to monsoons. **(3)**

(a) How do the Himalayas affect India's climate?

(b) Name the three key factors influencing India's climate?

Ans. (i) Two characteristics of monsoon in India are

- A large part of the country receives rainfall mainly in the summer from the South-West monsoon winds. Very little rain is caused in winter from the written carlier also North-East winter monsoons.
- Erratic and unpredictable nature of the monsoon causes heavy or very little rainfall in some years.

(ii) Tamil Nadu has more rainy months than Kerala because it receives rainfall from both South-West monsoon winds and North-West monsoon winds (during winters), but Kerala receives rainfall only from South-West monsoon winds. The South-West monsoon winds first strike Kerala and give abundant rainfall there. Thus, Kerala gets more rainfall than Tamil Nadu.

(iii) (a) Difference between weather and climate

Weather	Climate
Weather refers to the atmospheric conditions at a specific time and place.	Climate refers to the average weather conditions over a long period.
Weather can vary day to day.	Climate remains relatively stable over long periods.
It Includes elements like temperature, humidity, precipitation and wind.	It Includes long-term patterns of temperature, rainfall and wind over a region.

(b) Kerala receives rainfall both in Summer and Winter.

(iv) (a) The Himalayas act as a climate divide by creating distinct climatic conditions. This is due to their large height, their influence on air currents and the geographical positioning of the mountain range which separates the Indian sub-continent from the Tibetan Plateau and Central Asia.

(b) Three key factors influencing India's climate are

- **Latitude** These are the horizontal lines that indicate the distance North or South of the Equator.
- **Altitude** Refers to the height of a location above sea level.
- **Pressure and Winds** Air pressure or atmospheric pressure is the weight of the air, and wind is the velocity of the air. Both of these are interconnected with each other and undermine the climate of the particular region.

Q.3 (i) Name the following. **(2)**

(a) Name the factors affecting the climate of a region.

(b) The local winds that bring a light rainfall to South India and are good for tea and coffee crops.

(ii) **(a) Name one state in the North-Western part of India that receives rainfall during winter. (2)**

(b) What is the source of this rainfall?

(iii) **(a) Why has Mawsynram become the place that receives the highest rainfall in the world? (3)**

(b) Define 'October heat'.

(iv) **(3)**

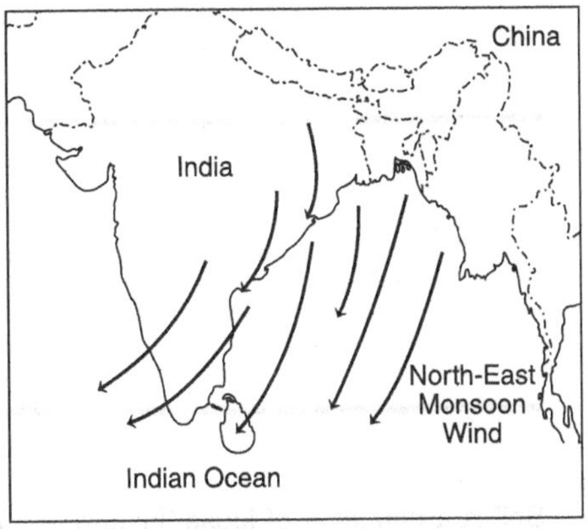

(a) Identify the type of monsoon season depicted in the above picture of map.

(b) When does this monsoon occur?

(c) Mention the main features of this monsoon.

Ans. (i) (a) The climate of a region is influenced by several factors, namely Latitude, Altitude, Distance from the Sea, Relief features, The Himalayas, The monsoon winds, Western disturbances, Jet streams, El-Nino effect, etc.

(b) Mango Showers

(ii) (a) Punjab/Haryana (b) Western Disturbances

(iii) (a) Mawsynram receives the highest rainfall due to its location in the Khasi hills, where moist monsoon winds from the Bay of Bengal are forced to rise, causing intense orographic rainfall. The region's topography and monsoon winds create this phenomenon.

(b) The withdrawal of monsoon leads to clear cloudless sky, high temperature and high humidity during the month of October. This oppressive weather is often referred to October heat.

(iv) (a) Retreating monsoon season

(b) The retreating monsoon occurs from October to December when the South-West monsoon winds weaken and reverse direction, shifting moisture away from the Indian sub-continent, leading to dry weather in most regions.

(c) The retreating monsoon features include decreasing rainfall, shifting winds from South-West to North-East, clear skies, cooler temperatures and dry conditions across most of India, during the months of October to December.

SOIL RESOURCES

Soil is a thin layer of loose mixture of small rock particles and decomposing organic matter that covers the Earth's surface.

- Climate, parent rock, humans, plants, animals are important factors that affect the formation of soil.
- The organic matter in soil is called humus. It is formed by decomposition of plant remains, animal waste and dead animals.
- The process of soil formation is called **pedogenesis**.

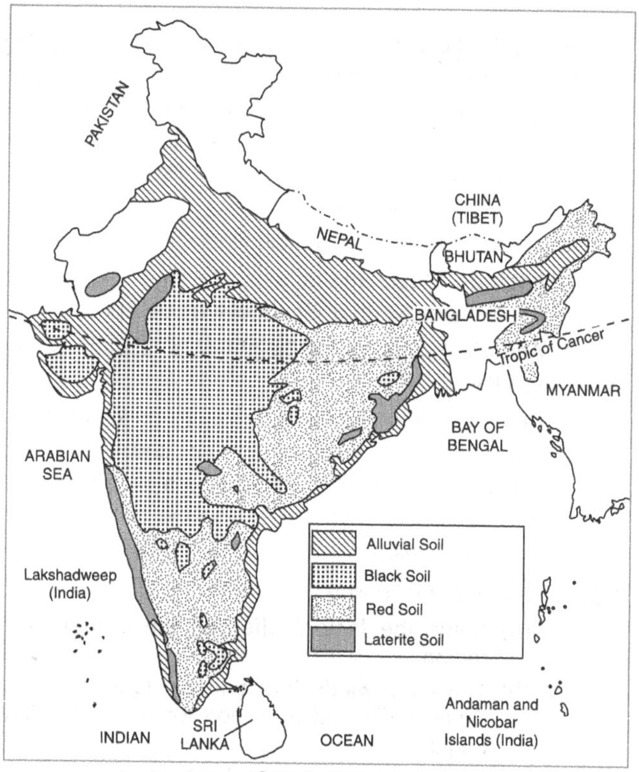

Soils in India

Classification of Soil

The Indian Council of Agricultural Research (ICAR) has classified the soils found in India into different types

Alluvial Soil

- **Origin** It is formed by deposition of sediments brought by rivers.
- **Distribution** It is primarily found in the river basins of the Indus, the Ganga and the Brahmaputra.
- **Composition** It is rich in minerals like potassium and lime but deficient in nitrogen and humus.
- **Colour** It is light to dark grey in colour.
- **Texture** It is coarsest in the upper section, medium in the middle section and finest in the delta region.
- **Crops Grown** Kharif and Rabi crops like rice, wheat, sugarcane, cotton, jute, oilseeds, pulses, etc.
- **Characteristics** Alluvial Soil is classified into two types on the basis of their age
  (i) Bhangar (Old alluvium)
  (ii) Khadar (New alluvium)

Alluvial Soil of North India	Alluvial Soil of South India
Formed by River Indus, Ganga	Formed by River Godavari, Krishna, Narmada, Tapi
Porous in nature	Non-porous in nature
Consist of clay and organic matter	Dark in colour as these flow over black soil.

Black Soil (Regur/Residual/Cotton Soil)

- **Origin** It is formed after solidification of molten lava during volcanic activity.
- **Distribution** It is found in the Deccan region and areas of Gujarat, Maharashtra, Malwa region of Madhya Pradesh.
- **Composition** It is rich in minerals like lime, potash, iron and magnesium.
- **Colour** It is black in colour.
- **Texture** It is finely grained in texture.
- **Crops Grown** Cotton, sugarcane, groundnut, millets, tobacco, fruits and vegetables, etc.
- **Characteristics** It retains moisture and becomes sticky when wet.

Red Soil

- **Origin** It is formed due to weathering of igneous and metamorphic rocks.
- **Distribution** It is found in low rainfall areas of Tamil Nadu, Odisha, Madhya Pradesh, Karnataka, Maharashtra, Andhra Pradesh, the Chota Nagpur plateau areas of Chhattisgarh, Jharkhand and in some parts of North-East India.
- **Composition** It is rich in potash and iron but it lacks nitrogen, phosphoric acid and humus.
- **Colour** It is red in colour due to high iron content.
- **Texture** It is porous and friable (dry) in texture.
- **Crops Grown** Wheat, rice, millets, gram, groundnut, coconut, ragi, oilseeds, pulses and cotton.
- **Characteristics** It is suitable for dry farming as it does not require much moisture. It is infertile but crops can be grown with the help of fertiliser and irrigation.

Laterite Soil (Leached Soil)

- **Origin** It is formed under conditions of high temperature and heavy rainfall with alternate wet and dry period.
- **Distribution** The word 'Laterite' is derived from the Latin word 'Later', meaning 'Brick'. It is found primarily in the summits of Eastern and Western Ghats.
- **Composition** It is rich in iron but lacks potassium, magnesium and lime.
- **Colour** It is red in colour due to presence of iron oxide.
- **Texture** It is coarse in texture, friable and porous.
- **Characteristics** It is also known as leached soil as it is found in the areas of heavy rainfall. It has a unique property of providing valuable building material as it becomes hard like iron when exposed to air.
- **Crops Grown** Tea, coffee, cashew nuts, rubber, coconut, rice, ragi, etc.

Soil Erosion

Soil erosion is the removal of the top layer of soil by natural forces (wind, water, etc.) or human intervention. When this top layer is removed, soil becomes less fertile.

Erosion by Water

Water erosion is the removal of soil by the action of rain, rivers, or waves. It takes place in different forms

- **Sheet Erosion** It happens when water flows over large areas and washes away the top soil e.g. Nilgiri Hills and hilly regions of Himalayas.
- **Rill Erosion** Rills are created when water forms small channels, creating finger-shaped grooves on the land. These rills are made after sheet erosion happens for a long time.
- **Gully Erosion** During heavy downpours, water runoff creates deep gullies which is known as gully erosion. It is commonly seen in the Chambal valley region.

Gully Erosion

- **Splash Erosion** It happens when the soil is pulverised by impact of heavy drops and hailstones, e.g. erosion in Uttar Pradesh and Madhya Pradesh.
- **Leaching** It is the process in which the top mineral nutrients of the soil are washed away, making it infertile. This often happens when farmers leave soil bare after harvest.

Erosion by Human Intervention

Human interferences lead to soil erosion in a variety of ways which are

- **Faulty Practices of Farming** These include practices like shifting agriculture, lack of rotation and wrong ploughing methods.
- **Overgrazing** The continuous grazing by animals on the same area of land without sufficient recovery periods is known as overgrazing. It leads to the removal of plant cover on a large-scale and becomes open to erosion by wind and water.
- **Deforestation** The cutting down of forests on a large scale which leaves an open and exposed landscape is known as deforestation. It is mainly caused due to the constructional and developmental activities.

Prevention and Conservation of Soil

Soil conservation is the practice of protecting soil from erosion and degradation to maintain its health and productivity.

Methods for Prevention of Soil Erosion

- **Strip Farming** Under this, fields are divided into grass strips which helps in reducing wind impact and slowing water runoff.
- **Contour ploughing** It involves ploughing along hillsides in curved rows, creating ridges and furrows that slow the flow of water and improve soil absorption.
- **Shelter Belts** In this method, rows of trees are planted between the fields which slow down the wind and reduce wind erosion.
- **Terrace Farming** In this farming method, step-like terraces are built on slopes. They prevent the soil from being washed away by running water.
- **Stone Walls or Bunds** In this method, low stone walls are built along the contour of a hill. These walls hold water and allow it to reach into the soil rather than flowing downhill.
- **Crop Rotation** It is a farming method in which a systematic succession of different crops is grown on the same piece of land. This improves soil fertility.
- **Plugging Gullies** It refers to the process of filling up eroded gullies with soil, rocks, or other materials to prevent further erosion and restore the land's structure. This helps in controlling water flow and reducing soil loss.
- **Construction of Dams** Dams are built in the upper course of rivers to control the flow of water thereby reducing soil erosion.

EXAM ORIENTED QUESTIONS

TYPE - 1
1 Mark

Multiple Choice Questions

Q.1 Feel and consistency of the soil is called .... of the soil. **(ICSE Specimen 2024, 2025)**
(a) Profile (b) Parent rock
(c) Texture (d) Density

Ans. (c) Texture

Q.2 Which is the most widespread soil of India? **(ICSE 2023)**
(a) Red soil (b) Alluvial soil
(c) Laterite soil (d) Black soil

Ans. (b) Alluvial soil

Q.3 Khadar and Bhangar are the types of which of the following soil?
(a) Black (b) Laterite
(c) Red (d) Alluvial

Ans. (d) Alluvial

Exp. Khadar is younger, fertile and found near the riverbanks while Bhangar is older, less fertile and found on higher/hilly areas.

Q.4 Which soil type is found in the shaded region as given in the image below?

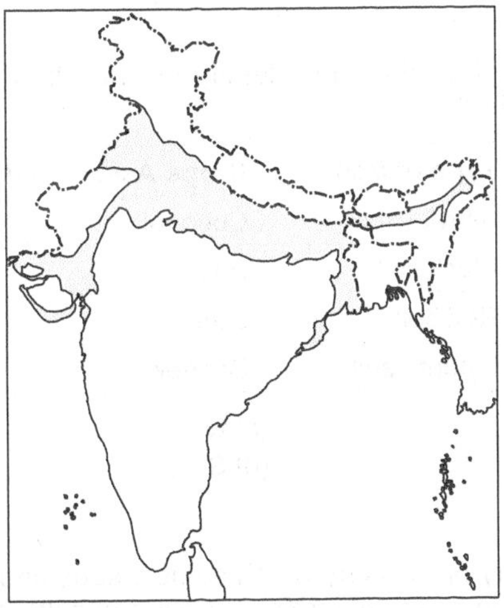

(a) Black soil
(b) Alluvial soil
(c) Laterite soil
(d) Red soil

Ans. (b) Alluvial soil

Q.5 Soil, also known as riverine soil :
(a) Red soil (b) Black soil
(c) Alluvial soil (d) Laterite soil

Ans. (c) Alluvial soil

Q.6 Black Soil: Maharashtra
(a) Alluvial Soil: Uttar Pradesh
(b) Laterite Soil: Punjab
(c) Black Soil: Arunachal Pradesh
(d) Red Soil: Himachal Pradesh

Ans. (a) Alluvial Soil: Uttar Pradesh

Q.7 If a farmer wants to grow cotton, which soil type would be the most suitable?
(a) Black (b) Laterite
(c) Red (d) Alluvial

Ans. (a) Black

Exp. Black soil has good moisture retention capacity; it is rich in nutrients like calcium, magnesium and has a slightly alkaline nature due to which it is considered a good soil for cotton cultivation.

Q.8 Which of the following soils need to be tilled after first rain?
(a) Black soil (b) Red soil
(c) Laterite soil (d) Alluvial soil

Ans. (a) Black soil

Q.9 What is the main reason for the red colour of red soil? **(ICSE Specimen Semester-I 2022)**
(a) Abundance of magnesium
(b) Accumulated humus
(c) Presence of ferric oxides
(d) Abundance of phosphates

Ans. (c) Presence of ferric oxides

Q.10 Red soil is generally poor in ....
(a) phosphorus (b) humus
(c) nitrogen (d) All of these

Ans. (d) All of these

Q.11 Which of the following factors is responsible for the acidic nature of laterite soil? **(ICSE Specimen Semester-I 2022)**
(a) As it is friable in nature.
(b) As it can retain moisture.
(c) As the bases leached down from the top soil.
(d) All of the above

Ans. (c) As the bases leached down from the top soil.

Q.12 Why is laterite soil used in Goa and Kerala for the construction of houses?

(ICSE Specimen Semester-I 2022)

(a) It become hard when dry.
(b) This soil is generally coarse in texture and poor in nature.
(c) It has more clay content in it.
(d) It looks beautiful when used in buildings.

Ans. (a) It become hard when dry.

Q.13 Which of the following pairs of soils displays similar characteristics in terms of their colour and texture?

(ICSE 2025)

(a) Alluvial soil and laterite soil
(b) Black soil and red soil
(c) Red soil and laterite soil
(d) Alluvial soil and black soil

Ans. (c) Red soil and laterite soil

Q.14 Name the process of removal of soluble mineral salts, especially the bases and silica from horizon A or the top soil by percolating rainwater.

(ICSE Specimen Semester-I 2022)

(a) Pedogenesis
(b) Leaching
(c) Lithification
(d) Conglomeration

Ans. (b) Leaching

Q.15 Afforestation prevents soil erosion because

(ICSE Specimen Semester-I 2022)

(a) it reduces pollution.
(b) it protects the soil from being exposed.
(c) the roots of the trees bind the soil particles.
(d) trees produce fruits.

Ans. (c) the roots of the trees bind the soil particles.

Q.16 Which of the following is a consequence of soil erosion?

(a) Increased soil fertility
(b) Decreased risk of flooding
(c) Loss of top soil, reducing agricultural productivity
(d) Improved soil structure

Ans. (c) Loss of top soil, reducing agricultural productivity

Q.17 What is 'Sheet erosion'?

(a) Erosion caused by small, concentrated water flows forming gullies.
(b) Erosion that removes thin layers of top soil uniformly across large areas.
(c) Erosion caused by wind lifting fine particles of soil.
(d) Erosion due to volcanic activity.

Ans. (b) Erosion that removes thin layers of top soil uniformly across large areas.

Q.18 Which of the following is not a type of soil erosion?

(a) Rill erosion (b) Plugging gullies
(c) Leaching (d) Stream bank erosion

Ans. (b) Plugging gullies

Q.19 Gully erosion is common in the ....

(ICSE Specimen 2023)

(a) Chambal basin (b) Ganga basin
(c) Rajasthan (d) Hilly region

Ans. (c) Rajasthan

Exp. Gully erosion is common in Rajasthan where it occurs due to intense rainfall, loose soil, deforestation, overgrazing, and improper farming practices, especially in sloped areas with little vegetation.

Q.20 Which is the most important factor of soil erosion?

(a) Wind
(b) Overgrazing
(c) Running water
(d) Faulty methods of cultivation

Ans. (c) Running water

Q.21 Advantages of organic manure are

(a) It binds the soil.
(b) It improves the water-holding capacity of soil.
(c) Both (a) and (b)
(d) It binds the soil but decreases its water retention capacity.

Ans. (c) Both (a) and (b)

Q.22 Which of the following helps in soil conservation?

(ICSE 2024)

(a) Afforestation (b) Overgrazing
(c) Mining (d) Shifting agriculture

Ans. (a) Afforestation

Exp. It helps in soil conservation by stabilising the soil with tree roots, reducing erosion, improving water retention.

Q.23 Read the table and identify the pair that is correctly matched.

	Type of Soil	Crops Associated
P.	Alluvial soil	Coconut
Q.	Black soil	Pulses
R.	Red soil	Jute
S.	Laterite soil	Cashew

(a) P (b) Q
(c) R (d) S

Ans. (d) S

Q.24 Identify process by which soluble substances such as organic basic minerals and mineral salts are washed out.

(a) Soil conservation
(b) Pedogenesis
(c) Soil erosion
(d) Leaching

Ans. (d) Leaching

TYPE - 2
1 Mark

Assertion-Reason Questions

Q.1 **Assertion** (A) The state of Maharashtra is emerging as the largest sugar-producing state in India.

Reason (R) The black soil of Maharashtra is more fertile and well-drained.

(a) Both A and R are true and R is the correct explanation of A
(b) Both A and R are true, but R is not the correct explanation of A
(c) A is true, but R is false
(d) A is false, but R is true

Ans. (a) Both A and R are true and R is the correct explanation of A

Q.2 **Assertion** (A) Red soil is mainly found in regions with moderate rainfall and high temperatures.

Reason (R) The reddish colour of the soil is due to the presence of high amounts of iron oxide, which are a result of high temperature and weathering of metamorphic rocks.

(a) Both A and R are true, and R is the correct explanation of A
(b) Both A and R are true but R is not the correct explanation of A
(c) A is true, but R is false
(d) A is false, but R is true

Ans. (a) Both A and R are true, and R is the correct explanation of A

Q.3 **Assertion** (A) Overgrazing by livestock is one of the major causes of soil degradation.

Reason (R) Overgrazing leads to the depletion of vegetation cover, which exposes the soil to wind and water erosion.

(a) Both A and R are true and R is the correct explanation of A
(b) Both A and R are true, but R is not the correct explanation of A
(c) A is true, but R is false
(d) A is false, but R is true

Ans. (a) Both A and R are true and R is the correct explanation of A

Q.4 **Assertion** (A) Terrace farming is an effective method of soil conservation popular in the Northern plains.

Reason (R) Terrace farming prevents soil erosion by reducing the velocity of water flowing down the slopes.

(a) Both A and R are true and R is the correct explanation of A
(b) Both A and R are true, but R is not the correct explanation of A
(c) A is true, but R is false
(d) A is false, but R is true

Ans. (d) A is false, but R is true

Q.5 **Assertion** (A) Afforestation leads to soil erosion and degradation.

Reason (R) Tree roots hold the soil particles together, preventing the soil from being washed away by rainwater.

(a) Both A and R are true and R is the correct explanation of A
(b) Both A and R are true, but R is not the correct explanation of A
(c) A is true, but R is false
(d) A is false, but R is true

Ans. (d) A is false, but R is true

TYPE - 3
2 Marks

Short Answer Type Questions

Q.1 With reference to the alluvial soil, answer the following questions. **(ICSE 2018)**

(i) Why does alluvial soil differ in texture?
(ii) State two cash crops that grow well in Alluvial soil.

Ans. (i) Alluvial soil differs in texture, as it is formed by the deposition of sediments by rivers. The Alluvial soil that gets deposited in the upper reaches of the river is coarse and dry, while extremely fine and moist Alluvial soil is deposited in the lower reaches of the river.

(ii) Sugarcane and jute are the two major cash crops that grow well in Alluvial soil.

Q.2 State two differences between Bhangar and Khadar. **(ICSE 2023)**

Ans. The differences between Bhangar and Khadar are

Bhangar	Khadar
This is old Alluvial soil.	This is new Alluvial soil.
It is fine and sandy in texture.	It is coarser and more clayey in nature .
It gets replenished.	It does not get replenished.

Q.3 The Ganga Plain is known for its fertile soil. It is often referred to as the food bowl of india. This region suppons a variety of crops such as rice, wheat, pulses, jute and sugarcane. **(ICSE 2025)**

(i) Name the soil that is found in large pans of Ganga plain.
(ii) Give two properties of this soil which helps it to produce a variety of crops.

Ans. (i) The soil found in large parts of the Ganga Plain is Alluvial Soil.

(ii) Two properties of alluvial soil that help in producing a variety of crops:

- **High fertility** It is rich in nutrients like potash, phosphoric acid, and lime, which support the growth of crops like rice, wheat and sugarcane.
- **Good moisture retention** This soil has the ability to retain water, making it suitable for both rain-fed and irrigated agriculture.

Q.4 Distinguish between alluvial and laterite soil. **(ICSE Specimen 2024)**

Ans. Alluvial and laterite soil can be differentiated as follows

Alluvial Soil	Laterite Soil
It is formed by the deposition of river silt and alluvium in floodplains.	It is formed by weathering of rocks in tropical climates with heavy rainfall.
It is highly fertile, ideal for growing crops like rice, wheat and sugarcane.	It is less fertile, often requires fertilisers and is suitable for crops like tea and coffee.

Q.5 Mention any two characteristics of black soil. **(ICSE 2023)**

Ans. The two characteristics of Black soil are

(i) It has been formed by weathering of the parent rock material found in the Deccan Plateau i.e. igneous rocks are called Regur soil.

(ii) It is made up of extremely fine particles i.e. clayey material.

Q.6 Name the following. **(ICSE 2020)**

(i) A soil that occurs in situ and is good for cotton crops due to high temperatures and heavy rainfall.

(ii) Soil that is formed with reference to Alluvial soil.

Ans. (i) Black soil is the soil that occurs in situ and is good for cotton crops. It is due to high temperatures and heavy rainfall.

(ii) Khadar soil is formed with reference to alluvial soil.

Q.7 Distinguish between alluvial soil and black cotton soil. **(Specimen 2018), (ICSE 2017)**

Ans. Two differences between alluvial soil and black soil are

Alluvial Soil	Black Soil
Alluvial soil is coarse in nature and contains kankar, pebbles and gravels.	Black cotton soil is fine-grained in texture with more than 60% clay. They do not contain gravel or sand.
Alluvial soil is very fertile.	Black soil is less fertile in the uplands.

Q.8 With reference to black soil, answer the following. **(ICSE 2018)**

(i) Name one important crop which grows in this soil.

(ii) Give one chemical property of this soil.

Ans. (i) The important crop which grows in Black soil is cotton.

(ii) The chemical property of the Black soil is that it is rich in calcium, potassium and magnesium.

Q.9 Answer the following. **(ICSE 2020)**

(i) Name the parent rock that contributes to the formation of red soil.

(ii) How does this soil get its 'red' colour?

Ans. (i) Metamorphic rocks and old crystalline rocks are the most common parent materials that contribute to the formation of Red soil.

(ii) The colour of the soil is red due to the abundance of iron oxide in it.

Q.10 Mention two main characteristics of laterite soil.

Ans. The two main characteristics of Laterite soil are

(i) The soil is compact, reddish, or yellowish-red in colour and turns black on exposure to the Sun.

(ii) It is rich in iron and aluminium.

(iii) Leached soil.

(iv) Provide building material. (any two)

Q.11 State the characteristic of each of the soils named below that makes them most suitable for crop cultivation. **(ICSE 2015)**

(i) Black Soil (ii) Red Soil

Ans. (i) **Black Soil** It is suitable for the cultivation of cotton as it is rich in calcium carbonate, magnesium carbonate, sodium carbonate, potash and lime.

(ii) **Red Soil** It is suitable for the cultivation of wheat, rice, cotton and sugarcane as it is rich in iron and potash.

Q.12 Name the following. **(ICSE Specimen 2023)**

(i) This soil is sticky when wet and cracks when dry.

(ii) This soil is mainly used for making bricks.

(iii) This soil is classified into Khadar and Bhangar.

(iv) When heavy rainfall washes away the topmost layer of the soil.

Ans. (i) Black soil becomes sticky when wet and cracks when dry.

(ii) Laterite soil is mainly used for making bricks.

(iii) Alluvial soil is classified into Khadar and Bhangar.

(iv) Leaching is the washing away of the topmost layer of the soil.

Q.13 Define the following. **(ICSE 2016)**

(i) Sheet erosion (ii) In-situ soils

Ans. (i) Sheet erosion is the gradual removal of thin layers of soil by rainfall and runoff which leads to soil degradation.

(ii) In-situ soils refer to the soil that is found in its natural, undisturbed state where it has formed and is located without being moved or altered by human activity. eg. black soil.

Q.14 (i) What is meant by soil erosion? **(ICSE 2025)**

(ii) Name any two agents of soil erosion.

Ans. (i) Soil erosion is the removal of the top fertile layer of soil by natural forces such as wind and water, leading to the loss of nutrients and reduced soil fertility.

(ii) Two agents of soil erosion are wind and water.

Q.15 Study the given picture below and answer the following questions.

(i) Identify the type of erosion given in the above picture.

(ii) In which area of India is it commonly seen?

Ans. (i) Gully erosion

(ii) It is commonly seen in the Chambal Valley region.

Q.16 State the geographic term for each of the following processes. **(ICSE 2015)**

(i) The process by which soluble minerals dissolve in rainwater and percolate to the bottom, leaving the top soil infertile.

(ii) The process by which rainwater, flowing in definite paths, removes the top soil, thus causing deep cuts to the surface of the land.

Ans. (i) Leaching (ii) Gully erosion

Q.17 Name two major causes of erosion and mention one method to control the erosion caused by each.

Ans. Two major causes of erosion are running water and wind.

(i) **Running Water** It can be controlled through techniques such as contour ploughing, terracing, filling gullies, and tree planting.

(ii) **Wind** It can be controlled through methods like strip cropping to reduce wind impact and planting shelterbelts around fields or farm borders.

Q.18 Explain two points to show that human intervention cause massive Soil erosion.

Ans. The two points that shows the human actions cause massive soil erosion are

(i) Faulty farming practices which lead to the removal of top soil.

(ii) Cutting of trees for Shifting Cultivation which leads to soil erosion.

Q.19 Distinguish between sheet and gully erosion.

Ans. The differences between the sheet and the gully erosion are as follows

Sheet Erosion	Gully Erosion
It involves the removal of thin layers of soil over a large area.	It involves the formation of deep channels or gullies due to concentrated water flow.
It affects large, flat areas and gradually depletes top soil.	It affects localised regions and creates deep, visible channels, leading to more severe soil loss.

Q.20 With reference to crop rotation, answer the following questions.

(i) Define Crop rotation.

(ii) How crop rotation is beneficial for the soil?

Ans. (i) Crop rotation is an agricultural practice where different crops are planted in a specific sequence on the same land over several seasons.

(ii) Crop rotation is beneficial for the soil as it helps improve soil fertility, reduce soil erosion, control pests and diseases and maintain balanced nutrient levels, ultimately promoting sustainable farming.

TYPE - 4 3 Marks

Long Answer Type Questions

Q.1 With reference to the alluvial soil, explain the following.

(i) Distribution (ii) Composition

(iii) Characteristics

Ans. Alluvial soil can be defined as follows

(i) **Distribution** Alluvial soil is distributed along the river valleys of Satluj, Ganga, Brahmaputra, in the delta region of Mahanadi, Godavari, Krishna, Kaveri and in the foothills of Piedmont plains.

(ii) **Composition** Alluvial soil is composed of various nutrients like potash and lime.

(iii) **Characteristics** Alluvial soil is light brown or yellowish-brown in colour and is formed by the deposition of very fine particles of soil called Alluvium.

Q.2 State the difference between alluvial soils found in the lower course and the upper course of the rivers.

Ans. The differences between alluvial soils in the lower and upper courses of the river are

Alluvial Soil in Lower Course	Alluvial Soil in Upper Course
It is finer in the lowest section. It is known as Khadar soil.	It is coarser i.e. particles are bigger in size. It is known as Bhangar soil.
It is moist and more compact.	It is dry and less compact.
It is more fertile than the upper course soil as new layers are deposited year after year during monsoonal floods.	It is less fertile than the soils of lower courses.

Q.3 Answer the following. **(ICSE 2020)**

(i) What are the two types of alluvial soil?

(ii) Name an area where alluvial soil is found.

(iii) Name two crops that grow well in this soil.

Ans. (i) Alluvial soil can be classified into two groups

(a) **Khadar** It is a fertile, newly deposited alluvial soil found in the floodplains of rivers. It is rich in nutrients, making it ideal for agriculture.

(b) **Bhangar** It is the older alluvium. It is less fertile than Khadar soil and is found in higher regions from the riverbanks. It is less suitable for agriculture.

(ii) Alluvial soil is mainly found in the entire Northern plains including parts of Punjab, Uttar Pradesh, Uttarakhand, Arunachal Pradesh, Assam, Bihar, etc.

(iii) Sugarcane and wheat are the two crops that grow well in this soil.

Q.4 Distinguish between alluvial soil and red soil in three points.

Ans. Alluvial soil and red soil can be distinguished as follows

Alluvial Soil	Red Soil
It is formed by river deposition in floodplains and delta regions.	It is formed by the weathering of crystalline rocks in dry regions.
It is highly fertile.	It is usually less fertile. It requires fertilisers.
It is light brown or dark in colour due to the presence of rich organic content.	It is reddish in colour due to iron oxide content.

Q.5 With reference to black soil of India, answer the following questions. **(ICSE 2025)**

(i) How is this soil formed?

(ii) How is this soil able to retain moisture for a long period?

(iii) Mention any two minerals present in this soil.

Ans. (i) Black soil is formed from the weathering of volcanic rocks, primarily from the Deccan Plateau region.

(ii) Black soil has a high clay content, which allows it to absorb and retain moisture for a long time, even during dry seasons.

(iii) Two minerals present in this soil are iron and magnesium.

Q.6 Mention any three characteristics of black soil which make the soil fertile.

Ans. The characteristics of black soil that make it fertile are:

(i) Black soil is rich in lime, iron, potash, magnesium carbonate and calcium carbonate, that is good for cotton crops.

(ii) It is made up of extremely fine clayey material that gives it a fine texture which makes it ideal for cotton crops.

(iii) It has the capacity to hold or retain moisture that is useful for the cotton crop.

Q.7 With reference to the red soil, explain the following.

(i) Distribution (ii) Composition

(iii) Characteristics

Ans. (i) **Distribution** It is found in low rainfall areas of Tamil Nadu, Odisha, Madhya Pradesh, Karnataka, Maharashtra, Andhra Pradesh, the Chota Nagpur plateau areas of Chhattisgarh, Jharkhand and in some parts of North-East India.

(ii) **Composition** It is rich in minerals like iron, magnesium and potassium but it lacks nitrogen, phosphorus and humus.

(iii) **Characteristics** Red soil is rich in iron, well-drained and is slightly acidic in nature.

Q.8 With reference to red soils in India, answer the following questions. **(ICSE 2013)**

(i) Name two states where it is found.

(ii) State two advantages of this type of soil.

(iii) Mention two important crops grown in this soil.

Ans. (i) It is found in Tamil Nadu and Karnataka.

(ii) Advantages of red soil are

(a) It has high iron oxide and potash content.

(b) It becomes productive with fertilisers.

(iii) Two important crops grown in red soil are rice and sugarcane.

Q.9 With reference to laterite soil, explain the following.

(i) Distribution (ii) Composition

(iii) Characteristics

Ans. (i) **Distribution** It is found primarily in the areas of Peninsular plateaus i.e. summits of Eastern and Western Ghats, Odisha, Karnataka, Kerala, Tamil Nadu, Andhra Pradesh, Maharashtra, etc.

(ii) **Composition** It is composed of minerals like iron-oxide, aluminium and potash but lacks phosphate, calcium and nitrogen

(iii) **Characteristics** Laterite soil is hard and coarse in texture. It is yellowish-red in colour and becomes hard when exposed to air.

Q.10 Give a geographic reason for each of the following.

(i) Alluvial soil is extremely fertile. **(ICSE 2015)**

(ii) Need for soil conservation. **(ICSE 2014)**

Or Soil conservation is the need of the hour. **(ICSE 2025)**

(iii) Reafforestation should be practised extensively.

Ans. (i) Alluvial soil is extremely fertile because it is rich in potash and humus, received annually non porous transported soil which brings lots of minerals.

(ii) Soil conservation is needed to prevent soil erosion, loss of fertility, and desertification. It helps maintain soil health, improves agricultural productivity and protects ecosystems.

(iii) Reafforestation should be practiced extensively to restore deforested areas, improve biodiversity, prevent soil erosion and combat climate change. It helps absorb carbon dioxide, provides habitats for wildlife and maintains the balance of natural ecosystems.

Q.11 Give geographical reasons for the following.

(i) Black soil is residual soil. **(ICSE Specimen 2023)**

(ii) Red soil has a poor water retention capacity.

(iii) Alluvial soil differs in texture.

Ans. (i) Black soil is residual soil as it is formed where they are found.

(ii) Red soil has a high sand content and low clay content, which makes it porous and less compact. Due to this, water drains quickly through the soil, reducing its water retention capacity.

(iii) It is due to the fact that alluvial soils are formed due to erosional, transportational and depositional activities of the Himalayan rivers. The upper reaches of the river valleys have coarse soil while the lower reaches of the river have fine textured soil.

Q.12 Give geographical reasons for the following. **(ICSE 2018)**

(i) Red soils require irrigation.

(ii) Afforestation prevents soil from getting eroded.

(iii) Laterite soil is red in colour.

Ans. (i) Red soil is light in texture, friable and porous and does not retain moisture for long time. Thus, require irrigation.

(ii) Afforestation prevents soil erosion by holding soil with tree roots, reducing wind speed, absorbing excess water and improving soil structure through organic matter.

(iii) Laterite soil is red in colour as it is made up of high levels of iron content.

Q.13 Name the soil which **(ICSE 2014)**

(i) is good for the cultivation of cashew nuts.

(ii) covers almost all of West Bengal.

(iii) is a result of leaching.

Ans. (i) **Laterite soil** is good for the cultivation of cashew nuts.

(ii) **Alluvial soil** covers almost all of West Bengal.

(iii) **Laterite soil** is formed as a result of leaching.

Q.14 Briefly answer the following. **(ICSE 2019)**

(i) Mention one way in which man is responsible for soil erosion.

(ii) How can deepening of the river bed help in preventing soil erosion?

(iii) Mention a physical characteristic of laterite soil.

Ans. (i) Faulty practice of farming like faulty ways of ploughing, shifting cultivation, etc done by man is responsible for soil erosion.

(ii) Deepening of the river bed helps in preventing soil erosion as by deepening of river beds, the bed could hold more water during heavy rainy season and water would get more space to flow easily without breaching the embankment and nearby areas.

(iii) The laterite soil is red in colour and coarse in texture.

Q.15 Soil conservation and water retention measures were rolled out across 40 tribal villages in the Tirupattur Forest Division as part of a project aimed at reclaiming and improving tribal lands.

The Times of India, 28th Oct, 2024

(i) Explain how soil conservation is beneficial for agriculture?

(ii) Name two methods of soil conservation.

Ans. (i) Soil conservation is beneficial for agriculture as it helps maintain soil health, enhances crop productivity, prevents desertification, and ensures sustainable land use for future generations.

(ii) Two methods of soil conservation are Afforestation and Contour ploughing.

Q.16 What is soil conservation? State a method of soil conservation in the **(ICSE 2017)**

(i) Arid and semi-arid regions

(ii) River valleys prone to flood

Ans. Soil Conservation is a method to maintain soil fertility, prevent soil erosion and exhaustion and improve the degraded condition of the soil.

(i) **Arid and Semi-arid region** In these regions, overgrazing of forests and grass land by animals should be checked, separate grazing grounds should be provided. Belts of trees and shrubs should be planted to check the velocity of wind and thus, prevent wind erosion.

(ii) **River valleys prone to flood** Soil erosion by floods can be prevented by constructing dams or barrages over such rivers which are responsible for flood.

TYPE - 5 — 10 Marks

Structured Questions

Q.1 (i) Nathu, a farmer in Bihar, does not get good yields as the soil he tills is coarse and has a fair proportion of kankars. Motilal on the other hand has his field closer to the river and gets better yields. **(ICSE Specimen 2025) (2)**

(a) Identify the two soils that are being discussed in the above passage.

(b) Give a possible reason why Motilal benefits from having his field along the river banks.

(ii) With reference to soil erosion in India, answer the following questions. **(2)**

(a) State any two human activities that have led to soil erosion in India.

(b) Mention any two innovative agricultural techniques that can help to prevent soil erosion.

(iii) With reference to red soil, answer the following. **(3)**

(a) How is it formed?

(b) Why is it good for Dry farming?

(c) Name any two areas where it is found.

(iv) Give a reason for the following statements. **(3)**

(a) Black soil has self-ploughing properties.

(b) Laterite soil is not suitable for cultivation.

Or Laterite soils are infertile. **(ICSE 2025)**

(c) Alluvial soil is extensively found in the Northern plains.

Ans. (i) (a) In this passage, the first soil is Bhangar (a type of Alluvial soil) as it contains the proportion of kankars. Second is Khadar as it is helping to get better yields.

(b) Proximity to the river bank helps Motilal to get better yield because along the river banks, Khadar (a type of alluvial soil) is predominantly found. Secondly, closeness to the river bank can provide better irrigation facilities and soil can get replenished every year.

(ii) (a) Overgrazing and Deforestation are the two human activities that led to soil erosion in India.

(b) Strip farming and Contour ploughing are the two innovative agriculture methods that can help to prevent soil erosion.

(iii) (a) It is formed due to weathering of igneous and metamorphic rocks.

(b) Good drainage properties and the presence of high amounts of nutrients make the Red soil good for dry farming.

(c) It is usually found in the low-rainfall areas of Odisha and the Chota Nagpur plateau areas of Chhattisgarh.

(iv) (a) Black soil has self-ploughing properties due to its clayey nature, which helps loosen the soil structure naturally.

(b) Laterite soil is not suitable for cultivation due to its low fertility, poor water retention and its coarse texture.

(c) Alluvial soil is found in the Northern plains because rivers deposit nutrient-rich sediments.

Q.2 (i) Why is black soil found suitable for the production of cotton? (Any two points) **(ICSE 2024) (2)**

(ii) Give one difference between each of the following. **(2)**

(a) Alluvial soil of Uttarakhand and alluvial soil of West Bengal

(b) Transported soil and residual soil

(iii) With reference to laterite soil, answer the questions that follow. **(3)**

(a) How is laterite soil formed?

(b) How can laterite soil be made productive?

(c) Name one region where laterite soil is found.

(iv) (a) Mention two causes of soil erosion in India. **(3)**

(b) Mention a soil conservation method suitable for hilly areas.

Ans. (i) Black soils is found suitable for the production of cotton due to the following reasons

- **High moisture retention capacity** Black soil retains moisture which helps the cotton plants stay hydrated during dry periods.
- **Presence of essential nutrients** Black soil is rich in essential nutrients like calcium, magnesium and iron which are beneficial for the growth of cotton crops.

(ii) (a) Alluvial soil in Uttarakhand is coarser in texture due to the presence of hilly terrains whereas, the alluvial soil in West Bengal is finer and more clayey.

(b) Transported soil is formed when soil particles are moved from their original location by agents like wind or water eg. Alluvial soil. While the residual soil forms where the parent material breaks down without being transported. eg. Black soil.

(iii) (a) Laterite soil forms through intense weathering and leaching in tropical regions with high rainfall.

(b) It can be improved by adding organic matter like manure and crop rotation.

(c) It is found primarily in the summits of Western and Eastern Ghats of Kerala, Tamil Nadu, etc.

(iv) (a) Deforestation and Overgrazing are two major causes of soil erosion in India. Deforestation leads to the loss of protective vegetation, leaving the soil vulnerable to wind and water erosion. Overgrazing by livestock damages the soil's structure, reducing its ability to retain moisture and increasing erosion risks.

(b) Terrace farming is a method of growing crops on stepped, flat areas built into the side of a hill or mountain. It involves creating terraces or platforms by cutting into the slope to prevent soil erosion and make the land easier to farm.

Q.3 **(i) Soil conservation incorporates all such means that help in shielding the dirt from disintegration, form terracing and bunding, developing bunds across ravines, evening out of uneven land, and raising grass and other vegetation ashore are the little estimates which are typically taken by ranchers to safeguard soil from disintegration.**

Geeksforgeeks.org **(2)**

(a) What are some methods used in soil conservation to prevent soil erosion?

(b) How does crop rotation help in maintaining soil fertility?

(ii) (a) Name one cash crop usually found in alluvial soil **(2)**

(b) Name one cash crop usually found in black soil.

(iii) With reference to the given picture below, answer the following questions. **(3)**

(a) What type of farming is shown in the picture given above?

(b) Name another method used which is similar to the one shown above.

(c) Write a benefit of this farming.

(iv) Name the following **(3)**

(a) A soil that occurs in situ and is good for cotton crops.

(b) Soil that is formed due to high temperatures and heavy rainfall.

(c) Define the term 'Residual' soil.

Ans. (i) (a) Some methods used for soil conservation are

- **Shelter Belts** In this method, rows of trees are planted between the fields which slow down the wind and reduces wind erosion.
- **Terrace Farming** In this farming method, step-like terraces are built on slopes. They prevent the soil from being washed away by running water.

(b) Crop rotation helps maintain soil fertility by alternating crops with different nutrient requirements, preventing nutrient depletion.
It improves soil structure and enhances organic matter, ensuring balanced nutrient use and sustainable agricultural productivity.

(ii) (a) Sugarcane is a common cash crop usually grown in Alluvial soil.

(b) Cotton is a well-known cash crop usually grown in Black soil.

(iii) (a) Terrace Farming

(b) Contour Ploughing is another method which is similar to the Terrace Farming

(c) Terrace farming prevents erosion of the top soil from running water or wind rushing downhill and carrying away the soil.

(iv) (a) Black soil

(b) Laterite soil

(c) Residual soil is the soil that forms from rocks breaking down in the same place and stays there without moving for a long time.

NATURAL VEGETATION

- Natural vegetation refers to the plant life that grows naturally in an area without human influence. It includes forests, grasslands, deserts and other ecosystems.
- Natural vegetation of India mainly depends on two important factors: rain and relief.

Importance of Forests

A forest is a large area covered with trees, plants and wildlife. Forests are important because

- They provide food, shelter and breeding grounds for various species.
- They play an important role in the prevention and control of soil erosion, desertification and floods.
- They absorb carbon dioxide from the air which helps to maintain the climate and keeps the Earth's temperature stable.
- They regulate the water cycle. The trees absorb water from the ground and release it into the atmosphere which helps to form clouds and precipitation.

Types of Vegetation

Vegetation can be categorised into

- **Based on Rainfall**
  - (i) Tropical Evergreen Forests
  - (ii) Tropical Deciduous Forests
  - (iii) Desert and Semi Desert Forest (Tropical Desert Forests)
  - (iv) Thorn and Scrub Forests
- **Based on Variation of Relief**
  - (i) Mountain or Mixed Forests
  - (ii) Mangrove or Tidal or Littoral Forests

Tropical Evergreen Forests

Tropical Evergreen Forests

- These forests are very dense with tall trees and also have a number of climbing plants.
- Due to continuous rainfall throughout the year, the trees do not shed their leaves and hence they are called evergreen forests.
- **Correlation with the Environment** These forests are mostly found in tropical areas where the annual rainfall is more than 200 cm with an average annual temperature between 25°C and 27°C. Hence, they are also called tropical rain forests.
- **Distribution** These forests are found in the Western Ghats, Lakshadweep, Andaman and Nicobar Islands and in some parts of North-Eastern India.
- **Important Species**
  - (i) Rosewood

    Economic Importance Used for making expensive furniture.

    Characteristics Hard, fine grained and durable.
  - (ii) Sisam

    Economic Importance Used for making expensive furniture.

    Characteristics Provides hard wood.

(iii) Gurjan

Economic Importance Used for making railway sleepers, furniture and house building.

Characteristics It has excellent strength and durability.

Tropical Deciduous Forests

- These are the most widespread forests in India and are also called the monsoon forests.
- Trees of these forests shed their leaves in hot weather when the scarcity of water is acute.
- They occupy a large area than the evergreen forests.
- Trees of these forests are found in pure strands.
- They are most important economically as they are not dense and provide valuable timber.
- **Correlation with the Environment** These forests are found in rainfall areas of 150 cm to 200 cm and having the mean annual temperature of 24°C to 27°C.
- **Distribution** In India, these forests are found in the belt running along the Western Ghats, on Eastern slopes, Shivalik Range and Chota Nagpur Plateau.
- **Important Species**

  (i) Teak

  Economic Importance Used for making furniture, construction of houses and ship building.

  Characteristics Can resist white ants and does not erode or rust iron nails.

  (ii) Sal

  Economic Importance Used for making railway sleepers and house building.

  Characteristics Hard and resistible to white ant.

  (iii) Sandalwood

  Economic Importance Used for making handicrafts and carving. Sandalwood oil is used in perfumes and cosmetics.

  Characteristics It is hard, heavy and strongly scented.

  (iv) Semul

  Economic Importance Used for making matchboxes, toys and packing cases.

  Characteristics Soft and white.

  (v) Myrobolan

  Economic Importance Used for tanning leather and for dyeing purposes.

  Characteristics It is a tall tree with umbrella shaped crown and wide branches.

Desert and Semi Desert Forests (Tropical Desert Forests)

- These forests are found in dry, arid regions with less vegetation. These are also known as tropical thorn forests.
- Babool, palm, khair, cactus, etc. are some plant species found in these forests.
- The trees in these forests are called xerophytes. Their stems and leaves are often covered by sharp spines.
- The trees have long roots to drain water. They have thick fleshy stems to store water.
- **Correlation with the Environment** These forests are found in areas having a mean annual temperature of 25°C to 27°C and annual rainfall less than 50cm.
- **Distribution** In India, these forests are distributed in Haryana, South-West Punjab, Central and Western parts of Rajasthan and some parts of Madhya Pradesh and Maharashtra.
- **Important Species** Babul and Khair (yield strong and hard wood used for fuel).

Thorn and Scrub Forests

- The vegetation in these forests include low scrub and stunted trees, shrubs with long roots and thorns.
- The vegetation in these forests have long tapering roots, thorny branches and small fleshy leaves.
- **Correlation with the Environment** These forests are found in areas which receive rainfall less than 100 cm and have mean annual temperature of 25°C to 30°C.
- **Important Species**

  (i) **Khair** Useful as timber and provides material for making dyes for tanning.

  (ii) Wild dates

Mountain Forests

- These forests are found in mountainous areas at high altitudes.
- They are found in the transition zone of mixed and coniferous forests.
- **Correlation with the Environment** These forests are found in areas where annual temperature is less than 20°C and rainfall is between 150 cm and 250 cm.
- **Distribution** These forests are found in mountainous areas of Jammu and Kashmir, Himachal Pradesh, Uttarakhand, Sikkim and Arunachal Pradesh. They are also found in Vindhyas, Nilgiris and Western Ghats.
- **Important Species**
  - (i) **Chirpine** Used for extraction of resin and turpentine and provides softwood for making packing cases for tea.
  - (ii) **Silver Fir** Used for making paper pulp, matches, planking and packing cases.
  - (iii) **Deadar** Used for railway sleepers and house construction.

Mountain Forests

Littoral Forests

- These forests are found in wet, marshy areas, river deltas, swampy areas, sea coasts, etc. These are also called Mangrove forests.
- The trees of these forests have stilt roots which remain submerged under water.
- **Correlation with the Environment** These forests are found in areas where the temperature remains between 26°C and 29°C and the rainfall is less than 200cm.
- **Distribution** In India, these forests are found around deltas (Ganga Brahmaputra Delta), estuaries and creeks.
- **Important Species**
  - (i) **Sundari** Provides hard, strong and durable wood.
  - (ii) Gurjan
  - (iii) Hital

Littoral Forests

Forest Conservation

Forest conservation is the practice of protecting and caring for forests to keep them healthy. It involves preventing deforestation and planting new trees.

To conserve forests, many practices have to be undertaken. Some of them are

- Discouraging deforestation and promoting afforestation.
- Growing trees around the urban areas and industrial units.
- Using non-conventional or renewable sources of energy like solar energy, tidal energy, etc.
- Making strict conservation measures and laws to restrict deforestation.
- Participation of people in planning, decision making and implementation of forest programs.

Measures toward Forest Conservation

- **The National Forest Policy** It was implemented in 1988 to protect, conserve and develop forests across the country.
- **Van Mahotsav** It was launched in the year 1950 by Shri Kanhaiyalal M. Munshi for promoting the conservation of forests. This festival is celebrated every year in July and during this festival, lakhs of trees are planted.
- **Social Forestry** It refers to managing and protecting forests and planting trees on barren lands to help in the environmental, social and rural development.
- **Agro-Forestry** It refers to the sustainable system in which trees or shrubs are grown around or among crops or pasture land.
- **Joint Forest Management (JFM) Programs** These programs have been launched by various state governments. Under these programs, village communities are given the responsibility to protect and manage nearby forests.

EXAM ORIENTED QUESTIONS

TYPE - 1 (1 Mark)

Multiple Choice Questions

Q.1 Which of the following statements is correct regarding natural vegetation?

(a) It refers to the plant life that grows naturally in an area

(b) It has not been disturbed by humans

(c) It includes forests, grasslands, deserts and other ecosystems.

(d) All of the above

Ans. (d) All of the above

Q.2 Plants of a particular area or time period, classified as species and considered as a group are known as ....

(a) Flora (b) Forest

(c) Vegetation (d) All of these

Ans. (a) Flora

Q.3 Which of the following is not a function of forests?

(a) Regulating local climate patterns

(b) Enhancing biodiversity and ecosystem stability

(c) Contributing to the urban heat island effect

(d) Stabilising water cycles and groundwater levels

Ans. (c) Contributing to the urban heat island effect

Q.4 If forests are lost, what would likely be the consequence for the environment and why?

(a) Improved agricultural production, as more land becomes available.

(b) Increased biodiversity, due to expansion of other habitats.

(c) Soil degradation and erosion, because of the loss of tree roots and ground cover.

(d) Increased balanced ecosystems, because of the introduction of new species.

Ans. (c) Soil degradation and erosion, because of the loss of tree roots and ground cover.

Q.5 Trees like rosewood, mahogany, cinchona, etc. are found in which type of forests?

(a) Tropical evergreen forests

(b) Tropical deciduous forests

(c) Littoral forests

(d) Mountain forests

Ans. (a) Tropical evergreen forests

Q.6 Tropical evergreen forests are mostly found in tropical areas where the annual rainfall is ....

(a) less than 200 cm (b) more than 200 cm

(c) between 50-100 cm (d) between 100-150cm

Ans. (b) more than 200 cm

Q.7 Name the type of natural vegetation that is found in the windward side of the Western Ghats.

(a) Tropical evergreen (b) Tropical deciduous

(c) Mangrove forest (d) Mountain forest

Ans. (a) Tropical evergreen

Exp. Tropical evergreen forests are found on the windward side of the Western Ghats due to heavy rainfall caused by monsoon winds which are forced to rise, cool and release moisture that is helpful for evergreen forests to grow.

Q.8 In which vegetation belt, multiple layers of trees are found?

(a) Tropical deciduous

(b) Tropical evergreen

(c) Thorn and scrub forest

(d) Tidal forest

Ans. (b) Tropical evergreen

Exp. Multiple layers of trees are found in the tropical rainforests vegetation belt like emergent layer, canopy layer, understory layer, forest floor, etc.

Q.9 Which of these forests are also known as 'monsoon forests'?

(a) Tropical evergreen forests

(b) Tropical deciduous forests

(c) Littoral forests

(d) Mountain forests

Ans. (b) Tropical deciduous forests

Exp. Tropical deciduous forests are called monsoon forests because they flourish in regions with a distinct monsoon season, receiving heavy rainfall during the wet season and shedding leaves during the dry season.

Q.10 Which of these forests are found in areas having a mean annual temperature of 23°C to 27°C?

(a) Tropical thorn forests (b) Mountain forests

(c) Tropical deciduous forests (d) Littoral forests

Ans. (c) Tropical deciduous forests

Q.11 Which are the most widespread forests of India? **(ICSE Specimen 2023)**

(a) Tropical rain forests

(b) Tropical thorn forests

(c) Tropical deciduous forests

(d) Littoral forests

Ans. (c) Tropical deciduous forests

Q.12 Teak and Sheesham are the typical trees of which of the following natural vegetation belt? **(ICSE Specimen 2024)**

(a) Tropical evergreen (b) Tropical deciduous

(c) Tropical desert (d) Littoral

Ans. (b) Tropical monsoon

Q.13 What are the chief characteristics of monsoon forests? **(ICSE Specimen Semester - 1 2022)**

(a) These regions receive moderate rainfall

(b) The trees shed their leaves in the dry season

(c) The trees are found in pure strands.

(d) All of the above

Ans. (d) All of the above

Q.14 Teak: Tropical deciduous forest **(ICSE Specimen 2025)**

(a) Mahogany: Furniture

(b) Stilted roots: Mangrove vegetation

(c) Ebony: Tropical rainforest

(d) Spines: Tropical desert vegetation

Ans. (c) Ebony: Tropical rainforest

Q.15 Which of the following is one of the characteristics of Tropical deciduous forests?

(a) Trees shed their leaves during the spring for 6-8 weeks.

(b) Yield valuable timber.

(c) Trees are found in pure strands.

(d) All of the above

Ans. (d) All of the above

Q.16 Which type of forest is found in the shaded region of the image as given below?

(a) Thorn forests (b) Mountain forests

(c) Tropical deciduous forests (d) Littoral forests

Ans. (a) thorn forests

Q.17 Trees with thick leaves and succulent (juicy) stems are usually found in which type of forests?

(a) Mountain forests

(b) Tropical evergreen forests

(c) Tropical deciduous forests

(d) Thorn forests

Ans. (d) Thorn forests

Exp. The trees of these forests have thick, juicy stems to store water, reduce water loss, and survive in dry areas with little rainfall.

Q.18 Manoj hails from Western Rajasthan. He was asked to name the type of forests found there. He replied ....

(a) Evergreen forests (b) Littoral forests

(c) Mountain forests (d) Thorn forests

Ans. (d) Thorn forests

Q.19 Trees like chestnut, oak, pine, etc. are found in which type of forests?

(a) Mountain forests (b) Tropical desert forests

(c) Littoral forests (d) Tropical deciduous forests

Ans. (a) Mountain forests

Q.20 The type of natural vegetation shown in the picture given below is found in **(ICSE 2025)**

(a) Tropical desert (b) Tropical deciduous

(c) Tropical evergreen (d) Littoral forest

Ans. (d) Littoral forest

Q.21 Which type of forest is found mostly in the coastal areas of India? **(ICSE 2023)**

(a) Tropical evergreen forests

(b) Tropical desert forests

(c) Littoral forests

(d) Tropical deciduous forests

Ans. (c) Littoral forests

Exp. They are found in coastal areas because they flourish in saline water, protect shorelines from soil erosion and adapt to tidal conditions.

Q.22 What is the other name of Littoral forests? **(ICSE Specimen Semester-1 2022)**

(a) Rain forests (b) Monsoon forests

(c) Tidal forests (d) Scrub lands

Ans. (c) Tidal forests

Q.23 The Littoral forests have pneumatophores or breathing roots because

(a) they want oxygen

(b) they can resist the tidal waves

(c) for beauty

(d) to survive in marshes and submerged areas.

Ans. (d) to survive in marshes and submerged areas.

Q.24 Why do we need forest conservation? **(ICSE Semester I 2022)**

(a) Forests provide food for growing population

(b) Forests helps in earning foreign exchange

(c) Forests help in maintaining ecological balance

(d) Forests look beautiful

Ans. (c) Forests help in maintaining ecological balance

Q.25 What are the various forest conservation methods that can be undertaken? **(ICSE Specimen Semester I 2022)**

(a) Afforestation and stopping indiscriminate felling of trees.

(b) Large scale of deforestation and overgrazing.

(c) Allowing animals to graze in farmland.

(d) Maintaining records of forest areas.

Ans. (a) Afforestation and stopping indiscriminate felling of trees.

Q.26 During which month do we celebrate Van Mahotsav every year in India? **(ICSE Semester I 2022)**

(a) In December to February time period

(b) In July to September time period

(c) In March to May time period

(d) In November to January time period

Ans. (b) In July to September time period

Q.27 A sustainable system in which trees or shrubs are grown around or among crops or pasture land is called ....

(a) Reforestry (b) Agro-forestry

(c) Social forestry (d) All of these

Ans. (b) Agro-forestry

Q.28 This type of forestry combines agriculture and forestry.

(a) Social Forestry (b) Farm Forestry

(c) Afforestation (d) Agro-Forestry

Ans. (d) Agro-Forestry

Q.29 Program that promotes commercial tree growing by farmers on their own land.

(a) Agro-Forestry (b) Farm Forestry

(c) Social Forestry (d) Afforesty

Ans. (b) Farm Forestry

Q.30 Trees found on the windward side of the Western Ghats.

(a) Chir (b) Deodar

(c) Hintal (d) Rosewood

Ans. (d) Rosewood

Q.31 Sunderlal Bahuguna is associated with the movement known as

(a) Van Mahotsav (b) Narmada Bachao

(c) Chipko Movement (d) All of these

Ans. (c) Chipko Movement

Q.32 Oil of this tree is used in perfumery and cosmetics.

(a) Neem (b) Tendu

(c) Sandalwood (d) Palas

Ans. (c) Sandalwood

Q.33 Read the table and identify the pair that is correctly matched.

	Types of Forests	Areas
P	Evergreen forests	Uttar Pradesh
Q	Desert forests	Assam
R	Littoral forests	West Bengal
S	Mountain forests	Rajasthan

(a) P (b) Q (c) R (d) S

Ans. (c) R

Q.34 Read the table and identify the pair that is correctly matched. **(ICSE 2024)**

	Natural Vegetation Belt	Tree
P	Tropical evergreen	Babool
Q	Tropical deciduous	Teak
R	Littoral	Ebony
S	Mountain forests	Banyan

(a) P (b) Q

(c) R (d) S

Ans. (b) Q

Q.35 Read the table and identify the pair that is correctly matched.

	Natural Vegetation Belt	Tree
P	Tropical evergreen forest	Babool
Q	Tropical deciduous forest	Sandalwood
R	Mountain forest	Cinchona
S	Tidal forest	Sal

(a) P (b) Q

(c) R (d) S

Ans. (b) Q

TYPE - 2 — 1 Mark

Assertion-Reason Questions

Q.1 Assertion (A) Forests play an important role in regulating the water cycle.

Reason (R) Trees in the forests absorb water from the ground and release it into the atmosphere, which helps to form clouds and precipitation, contributing to the water cycle.

(a) Both A and R are true and R is the correct explanation of A
(b) Both A and R are true, but R does not explain A
(c) A is true, but R is false
(d) A is false, but R is true

Ans. (a) Both A and R are true and R is the correct explanation of A

Q.2 Assertion (A) Chestnut, oak, and pine trees are commonly found in mountain forests.

Reason (R) The leaves of the trees are thick and small which makes them suitable for high-altitude areas.

(a) Both A and R are true and R is the correct explanation of A
(b) Both A and R are true, but R does not explain A
(c) A is true, but R is false
(d) A is false, but R is true

Ans. (c) A is true, but R is false

Q.3 Assertion (A) Mountain forests are found in various regions across India, such as Jammu and Kashmir, Himachal Pradesh and the Western Ghats.

Reason (R) These places have extensive marshy areas which are required for the growth of these forests.

(a) Both A and R are true and R is the correct explanation of A
(b) Both A and R are true, but R does not explain A
(c) A is true, but R is false
(d) A is false, but R is true

Ans. (c) A is true, but R is false

Q.4 Assertion (A) Forest conservation is essential for mitigating climate change.

Reason (R) Forests absorb carbon dioxide, which helps reduce the concentration of greenhouse gases in the atmosphere.

(a) Both A and R are true and R is the correct explanation of A
(b) Both A and R are true, but R does not explain A
(c) A is true, but R is false
(d) A is false, but R is true

Ans. (a) Both A and R are true and R is the correct explanation of A

Q.5 Assertion (A) Van Mahotsav was launched in 1950 by Shri Kanhaiyalal M Munshi to create enthusiasm for the conservation of forests.

Reason (R) It is celebrated every year in the month of July and its main objective is to promote the importance of planting trees.

(a) Both A and R are true and R is the correct explanation of A
(b) Both A and R are true but R does not explain A
(c) A is true, but R is false
(d) A is false, but R is true

Ans. (a) Both A and R are true and R is the correct explanation of A

TYPE - 3 — 2 Marks

Short Answer Type Questions

Q.1 What is meant by natural vegetation? List the types of ecosystems included in natural vegetation.

Ans. Natural vegetation refers to the plant life that grows naturally in an area without human influence. It includes forests, grasslands, deserts and other ecosystems.

Q.2 How do the forests help in maintenance of air quality? **(ICSE 2025)**

Ans. The forests help in maintenance of air quality in the following ways

- **Absorption of Carbon Dioxide** Trees absorb CO_2 during photosynthesis, reducing greenhouse gases and improving air quality.
- **Release of Oxygen** Forests release oxygen (O_2), which is essential for life.

Q.3 State two ways by which forests help in protecting the environment. **(ICSE 2020,2023)**

Ans. Two ways by which forests help in protecting the environment are

(i) After oceans, forests are the world's largest storehouses of carbon. These absorb harmful greenhouse gases.

(ii) They provide habitats to a number of wild animals and birds.

Q.4 'A great diversity of flora is found in India.'
Give three geographical factors that are responsible for this diversification.

Or Give any two reasons for the great diversity of natural vegetation in India. **(ICSE 2025)**

Ans. Three geographical factors responsible for the great variety of flora found in India are

(i) Varied relief features (ii) Varied landforms
(iii) Variation in daily and annual temperature

Q.5 Mention two main characteristics of tropical evergreen rainforests. **(ICSE Specimen 2023)**

Ans. Two main characteristics of tropical rainforests are

(i) Due to continuous rainfall throughout the year, the trees of these forests do not shed their leaves at the same time and hence, such forests are called 'evergreen forests'.

(ii) They are dense and have a variety of trees.

Q.6 With reference to forest, answer the following.

(i) Name the forests which grow on the windward slope of the Western Ghats. **(ICSE 2016)**

(ii) Why do such forests grow in this region?

Ans. (i) Tropical evergreen forests grow on the windward slope of the Western Ghats.

(ii) Tropical evergreen forests grow on the windward slope of the Western Ghats due to favourable climatic conditions such as rainfall of more than 200 cm, average annual temperature between 25° to 27°C and humidity of more than 70%.

Q.7 With reference to tropical monsoon forests, answer the following.

(i) Name an area in India where tropical monsoon forests are found. **(ICSE 2018)**

(ii) How are these forests of great commercial value to India?

Ans. (i) Tropical monsoon forests are found in the Andaman and Nicobar Islands, the Western Ghats, the Coastline of Peninsular India and also in North-East India.

(ii) These forests are of great commercial value to India as they provide valuable timber.

Q.8 With reference to tropical deciduous forests, answer the following questions. **(ICSE 2020)**

(i) Name two states where it is found.

(ii) Name two important trees found in these forests.

Ans. (i) Madhya Pradesh and Uttar Pradesh are the two states where these forests are found.

(ii) Teak and Sal are two important trees found in these forests.

Q.9 State two characteristics of the tropical deciduous forests. **(ICSE 2015)**

Ans. Two characteristics of tropical deciduous forests are

(i) The trees in these forests shed their leaves during spring and early summer.

(ii) These forests provide valuable timber and other forest products.

Q.10 State two reasons why deciduous forests are commercially more valuable than other types of forests. **(ICSE 2014)**

Ans. Deciduous forests are commercially more valuable than other forests because

(i) Trees in these forests are more appropriate for commercial exploitation.

(ii) These forests are not as dense as the tropical evergreen forests. The tree species like sal, sheesham, teak, jamun, etc are very durable woods and are in great demand. These are mainly used for making furniture, railway sleepers, agricultural equipment, construction work, etc.

Q.11 How do trees in the tropical desert forests adapt themselves to the dry climate? **(ICSE 2017)**

Or Mention two ways in which tropical desert vegetation has adapted to its environment. **(ICSE 2023)**

Ans. The trees in tropical desert forests adapt themselves to the dry climate as in the lack of moisture, they have small leaves that minimise evaporation and the stems are succulent (juicy) which helps to conserve water.

Q.12 Mention the climatic condition that leads to the development of tropical desert vegetation. **(ICSE 2024)**

Ans. Tropical desert vegetation typically develops in regions with a hot and dry climate, characterised by very low annual rainfall (less than 250 mm) and high temperatures throughout the year. These areas often have clear skies and high evaporation rates.

The scarcity of water forces plants to adapt to extreme heat, drought, and limited moisture availability, leading to the growth of hardy, drought-resistant vegetation like cacti.

Q.13 Mention the climatic condition suitable for the development of tropical evergreen forest. **(ICSE 2025)**

Ans. The climatic condition suitable for the development of tropical evergreen forest are

- **High Temperature** The temperature remains warm and humid throughout the year, typically ranging between 25°C to 27°C.
- **Heavy Rainfall** These forests require more than 200 cm of annual rainfall, which is evenly distributed throughout the year.

Q.14 What types of trees are found in mountain forests? How do these trees adapt to the challenges of high altitudes?

Ans. Mountain forests usually consist of coniferous trees such as pines, firs, oaks, maples, etc. in lower altitudes.

These trees adapt to high altitudes by having needle like leaves that reduce water loss and thick bark to protect against the cold. Some conifers have a conical shape which prevents branches from breaking under heavy snowfalls.

Q.15 What are 'tidal forests'? Name two typical trees found there.

Ans. Tidal forests are usually found in wet marshy areas, in river deltas, saline or swampy areas along the sea coast. These forests consist of evergreen species with stilt roots that are submerged under the water. Two types of trees found in these forests are sundari and casuarina.

Q.16 With reference to littoral forest, answer the following questions. (ICSE 2018)

(i) Why do the trees in this forest grow aerial roots?

(ii) Name one area in India where this forest is found.

Ans. (i) Littoral forests refer to trees that grow in the shore region. In such regions, soil is accumulated with salt and cannot be aerated as normal soils, so trees grow upwards. Such roots are called aerial roots and they are adventitious in nature.

(ii) Littoral forests or tidal forests are found in delta regions and along the marshy coasts. Sunderbans in West Bengal is one of the areas in India where littoral forests are found.

Q.17 (i) Mention two conditions required for the growth of littoral forest. (ICSE 2019)

(ii) State one characteristic feature of the forest found in the Nilgiri hills.

Ans. (i) Two conditions required for the growth of littoral forests are

(a) Littoral forests grow in areas with a tropical or subtropical climate, characterised by high humidity, moderate to high rainfall and warm temperatures. These conditions support the diverse plant species typical of coastal regions.

(b) Littoral forests are found along coastlines, so the plants must be tolerant to saltwater. The species in these forests, such as mangroves, are adapted to survive in saline soil and water, often having specialised mechanisms to manage salt.

(ii) Forests found in the Nilgiri Hills are also known as monsoon forests. A feature of these forests is that they spread over the region receiving rainfall between 70 and 200 cm.

Q.18 Give two characteristics of littoral forests.

Ans. Two characteristics of littoral or tidal forests are

(i) These forests help in the formation of a delta by blocking the sea.

(ii) These forests also act as a major carbon sink.

Q.19 Name the tree as per its characteristics given below. (ICSE 2017)

(i) The wood is hard and suitable for ship building.

(ii) The stilt roots are underwater during high tide.

Ans. (i) Sundari (ii) Mangrove vegetation

Q.20 Give two reasons to explain as to why we need to conserve our forest resources. (ICSE 2019)

Ans. We need to conserve our forest resources because

(i) **Oxygen and Biodiversity** Forests produce oxygen and provide habitats for diverse plant and animal species, ensuring balanced ecosystems.

(ii) **Climate Regulation and Soil Protection** Forests help regulate the climate, absorb carbon dioxide, and prevent soil erosion, maintaining environmental stability.

Q.21 State two ways in which forests help in protecting the environment. (ICSE 2023, 2020)

Ans. Forests help in protecting the environment in the following ways

(i) Forests contribute to preserving soil and supporting wildlife leading to the protection of the environment.

(ii) Forests play an important role in the global water cycle, moving water across the Earth by releasing water vapour and capturing rainfall.

Q.22 India has lost 2.33 million hectares of tree cover since the year 2000. This is equivalent to a six percent decrease in tree cover during this period. (ICSE 2025)

Source: The Indian Express. Date. 12th April, 2024

(i) Mention any two causes of the decrease in the forest cover of India.

(ii) Name a conservation method that may be used to help in increasing the forest cover.

Ans. (i) Two causes of the decrease in forest cover in India

- **Deforestation for agriculture and urbanisation** Large areas of forests are cleared to make space for farming, industries, and expanding cities.
- **Illegal logging and overexploitation** Excessive cutting of trees for timber, firewood and other commercial purposes leads to forest depletion.

(ii) A conservation method that may be used to help in increasing the forest cover is afforestation, i.e, planting new trees in deforested areas.

TYPE - 4 3 Marks

Long Answer Type Questions

Q.1 With reference to natural vegetation, answer the following

(i) What is meant by vegetation?

(ii) How much natural is the natural vegetation left in India today?

Ans. (i) Vegetation includes all plant life such as trees, bushes, herbs, etc. that grow naturally in an area and have been left undisturbed by humans for a long time.

(ii) Today, natural vegetation has not been left natural anymore because of the following reasons

- Various new species of plants are raised in laboratories and they are planted to have better results.
- Human interference is continuously increasing day by day which is deteriorating the nature and is harmful for humans too.

Q.2 With reference to forests, answer the following.

(i) Why are tropical evergreen forests called 'evergreen'? **(ICSE 2020)**

(ii) Why is afforestation essential in the cities that have iron and steel industries?

(iii) How do forests act as a source of income for the people?

Ans. (i) The regions of tropical evergreen forests receive heavy rainfall throughout the year. As there is no particular dry season, the trees do not shed their leaves at the same time. Thus, the forests always appear green. That's why they are called evergreen forests.

(ii) Afforestation is essential in and around the iron and steel industries because it provides a clean environment as trees take up carbon dioxide and give out oxygen.

(iii) Forests provide important sources of income to many rural people. Forest products such as bushes and fuel wood are gathered and traded at local and regional markets. Forests also provide the raw materials for artisan and processing activities.

Q.3 What are the favourable climatic conditions required for tropical evergreen forests? Also, mention the regions where these are found.

Ans. Tropical Evergreen or Rainforest requires the following climatic conditions

(i) They require abundant rainfall (200-300 cm annually) throughout the year with a short dry season.

(ii) The average temperature required is about 25°C to 27°C which is hot and extremely humid (more than 70% humidity) with almost no seasonal variation.

These forests are found on the Western slopes of the Western Ghats, both groups of islands (Lakshadweep, Andaman and Nicobar Islands), the coast of Tamil Nadu, Odisha, Bhabar and Terai regions, in North-Eastern India (in parts of Assam, Meghalaya, Tripura, Manipur and Nagaland).

Q.4 Distinguish between the tropical evergreen and tropical desert forest.

Ans. The differences between tropical evergreen and tropical desert forests are

Tropical Evergreen Forests	Desert Forests
These are found on the Westward slope of the Western Ghats and the North-Eastern parts of Assam, Meghalaya.	These are found in the Punjab, Haryana and in the Southern peninsula.
These are found where rainfall is over 200 cm.	These are found where rainfall is less than 50 cm.
The main species are Ebony, Rose-wood, Sheesham etc.	The main species are Neem, Babool, Kikar etc.
Very dense and are of less economic importance.	They are known as xerophytes, have long roots and thick fleshy stem.

Q.5 With reference to tropical evergreen forests, answer the following

(i) Give two reasons to explain why the tropical evergreen forests are difficult to exploit for commercial purposes. **(ICSE 2019)**

(ii) Name any two trees found in tropical evergreen forests.

Ans. (i) Two reasons for difficulty in exploiting tropical evergreen forests for commercial purposes are

(a) Tropical evergreen forests do not occur in pure strands i.e. main canopy does not consist of a single species.

(b) These forests are dark and dense, so it is difficult for commercial exploitation.

(ii) Rosewood, Seasame and Gurjan are the trees found in tropical evergreen forests.

Q.6 Name any three trees found in monsoon deciduous forests and state one use of each of these trees.

Ans. Three trees of monsoon deciduous forests and their uses are

(i) **Sal** It is used for furniture making, railway sleepers, etc.

(ii) **Teak** It is used for house construction and furniture making.

(iii) **Sandalwood** It is used in cosmetics and making handicrafts, perfumes, etc.

Q.7 **Explain three main features of tropical moist deciduous forests.**

Ans. The main features of tropical moist deciduous forests are

(i) These forests are found in the areas receiving rainfall of 100 to 200 cm.

(ii) The height and density of the trees in these forests are much lower than in the tropical evergreen forests.

(iii) Due to seasonality of moisture, the trees in these forests shed their leaves for about 6 to 8 weeks in dry summer.

Q.8 **With reference to forests, answer each of the following.** **(ICSE 2019)**

(i) The trees in the desert forests have stunted growth.

(ii) There has been a gradual increase in the forest cover in India in recent times.

(iii) The trees in monsoon deciduous forests shed their leaves for about 6-8 weeks during March and April.

Ans. (i) The trees of tropical desert forests have stunted growth because they receive low or scanty rainfall due to low humidity and high temperature.

(ii) There has been a gradual increase in the forest cover in India in recent times due to the work done by the Central Government in the direction of increasing the forest cover areas in the country by formulating different policies and programs.

(iii) Monsoon deciduous forests shed their leaves for about 6-8 weeks during March and April as water is not enough to retain their leaves.

Q.9 **State any three differences between tropical deciduous and tropical desert Vegetation.** **(ICSE 2025)**

Ans. The three differences between tropical deciduous and tropical desert vegetation are

Tropical Deciduous Vegetation	Tropical Desert Vegetation
Found in monsoon regions with moderate rainfall (100-200 cm).	Found in areas with extremely low rainfall (less than 25 cm), hot and dry climate.
They Shed leaves in dry season to conserve water.	They have small, thorny, or wax-coated leaves to reduce water loss.
Examples sal, teak, and neem	Examples cactus, acacia and date palm

Q.10 **Explain any three features of the tropical desert forests or thorn and scrubs.**

Ans. The features of tropical desert forests or thorn and scrubs are

(i) Trees of these forests are scattered and have long roots penetrating deep into the soil in order to get moisture.

(ii) The stems of the trees in these forests are succulent to conserve water.

(iii) Leaves of the trees in these forests are mostly thick and small to minimise evaporation.

Q.11 **Explain three characteristics of mountain forests.**

Ans. Three characteristics of mountain forests are

(i) Mountain forests exhibit a range of plant species that vary with altitude. At lower elevations, they contain dense deciduous trees, while higher altitudes are home to coniferous trees like pines, firs, etc.

(ii) They are found in the transition zone of mixed and coniferous forests.

Q.12 **Answer the following questions based on image given below.**

(i) Identify the type of forests. Also, name some regions where these forests are found.

(ii) Mention two conditions required for the growth of these forests.

Ans. (i) These are the mangrove/littoral forests.

The deltaic tracts of Ganga, Godavari, Krishna, Kaveri and Mahanadi are ideally suited for Mangrove type of forests.

In India, these forests are mainly found along the coast of Odisha, Andhra Pradesh, West Bengal (Sunderbans), Tamil Nadu and some areas of Kutch, Kathiawar, Gulf of Khambhat and Andaman and Nicobar Islands.

(ii) Two conditions required for the growth of these forests are

(a) These forests are specialised tropical type of vegetation that grows in coastal areas where the saline sea water encroaches at the time of high tides and fresh water of rivers continuously mixes with the saline water. So, these can survive in salty as well as in fresh water.

(b) These forests occur in areas receiving 100 to 150 cm rainfall and have temperatures ranging between 25°C to 27°C.

Q.13 **Name the natural vegetation found in the following regions** **(ICSE 2017)**

(i) The Western slopes of the Western Ghats

(ii) The Nilgiris

(iii) Western Rajasthan

Ans. (i) Tropical evergreen forests

(ii) Tropical evergreen forests

(iii) Desert and semi-desert vegetation and scrub and thorn forests.

Q.14 **Which type of forest do the following trees belong to?**

(i) Hintal and Sundari **(ICSE 2016)**

(ii) Rosewood and Ebony

(iii) Deodar and Chir Pine

Ans. (i) Hintal and sundari belong to littoral or tidal forests.

(ii) Rosewood and ebony belong to tropical evergreen or Rain forests.

(iii) Deodar and chir pine belong to montane forests.

Q.15 **Distinguish between afforestation and deforestation.** **(ICSE 2015)**

Ans. Afforestation and deforestation can be distinguished as follows

Afforestation	Deforestation
It means planting trees in an area where there were no previous forests.	It is the removal or destruction of forests or trees.
It increases biodiversity by providing habitats for wildlife.	It reduces biodiversity and disrupts ecosystems.
It leads to sustainable development and ecological balance.	It leads to environmental degradation and habitat loss.

Q.16 **Name the natural vegetation largely found in the following regions** **(ICSE 2014)**

(i) The delta of the Ganga river

(ii) The windward side of the Western Ghats

(iii) The Deccan plateau

Ans. (i) Tidal forests

(ii) Tropical evergreen forests

(iii) Deciduous monsoon forests and scrub/thorn forests

Q.17 **Mention three forest conservation schemes and methods followed in India.**

Ans. Three forest conservation schemes and methods followed in India are

(i) **Social Forestry** It refers to managing and protecting forests and planting trees on barren lands to help in the development and conservation of forests.

(ii) **Agro-Forestry** It refers to the sustainable system in which trees or shrubs are grown around pasture land. The main aim is to achieve a combined production of forest and agricultural crops through the improvement of land.

(iii) **Joint Forest Management (JFM) Programmes** These programs have been launched by various state governments. Under these programs, village communities are given the responsibility to protect and manage nearby forests.

Q.18 **India informed the United Nations Forum on Forests (UNFF) that it has made significant advancements in forest conservation and management, leading to a consistent increase in forest cover over the past 15 years.** *Press Trust of India New Delhi, 12th May, 2024*

(i) What is the primary goal of forest conservation?

(ii) How does the practice of forest conservation help prevent deforestation and degradation?

(iii) Name two schemes/programs/initiatives of Government of India to conserve forests.

Ans. (i) The primary goal of forest conservation is to ensure the protection, restoration of forest ecosystems and balancing ecological needs with human activities.

(ii) The practice of forest conservation prevents deforestation and degradation by safeguarding forests from harmful activities such as illegal logging, promoting sustainable practices and restoring degraded lands through reforestation.

(iii) Two schemes/programs/initiatives by the Government of India to conserve forests are - Van Mahotsav and Joint Forest Management (JFM) Program.

Q.19 **With reference to the forests, answer the following questions** **(ICSE 2024)**

(i) Mention any two forest conservation methods that may be adopted to protect the forests.

(ii) How has the rising population of India resulted in the loss of forest cover? (Any one point)

Ans. (i) Two forest conservation methods that may be adopted to protect the forests are

(a) Planting new trees or afforestation can help restore ecosystems and increase green cover.

(b) Limiting the number of livestock in forest areas prevents overgrazing which will allow forests to regenerate.

(ii) The rising population in India has led to increased demand for land for agriculture, urbanisation and infrastructure development. As a result, forests are cleared for farming, housing and industries, resulting in the loss of forest cover.

TYPE - 5 — 10 Marks

Structured Questions

Q.1 (i) Mahesh went for an excursion with his friend and came across a marshy area with trees that had stilt like roots. **(ICSE Specimen 2025) (2)**

(a) Which natural vegetation belt did he come across?

(b) Name an area in India where this kind of vegetation is found.

(ii) (a) Why is tropical deciduous forest commercially the most important forest belt of India? **(2)**

(b) Why are long and deep roots a typical characteristic of desert vegetation?

(iii) Give three reasons why forest conservation is the need of the hour. **(3)**

(iv) (a) Name a forest conservation method that involves the local community. **(3)**

(b) Which primitive system of agriculture had led to large scale destruction of forest in the past?

(c) Name the process which involves planting two saplings for each tree that is felled.

Ans. (i) (a) Mahesh came across Littoral/Mangrove vegetation/forests.

(b) West Bengal (Sunderbans)

(ii) (a) Tropical deciduous forests are commercially the most important forest belt of India because they provide a wide range of valuable timber, including species like teak, sal, and sandalwood which are vital for the country's economy.

(b) Long and deep roots are a typical characteristic of desert vegetation because they help plants to access water stored deep underground, which is essential for survival in arid conditions with limited rainfall, ensuring they can thrive despite the harsh and dry environment.

(iii) Three reasons why forest conservation is the need of the hour are

(a) Forests are home to diverse species and conservation helps preserve habitats and prevent extinction.

(b) They play an important role in the prevention and control of soil erosion, desertification and floods.

(c) They absorb carbon dioxide from the air. This helps maintain climate and keeps the Earth's temperature stable.

(iv) (a) Agro-Forestry

(b) The primitive system of agriculture that led to large-scale destruction of forests in the past was slash-and-burn agriculture. This method involved clearing forested areas by cutting and burning vegetation to make way for crops, resulting in deforestation.

(c) Afforestation

Q.2 (i) Answer the following questions based on image given below

(a) Identify the type of vegetation. **(2)**

(b) Give two characteristics of this vegetation.

(ii) Name the forest which is found in the delta of the river Ganga. Name two trees which are found here. **(2)**

(iii) Give geographical reasons for the following **(3)**

(a) Xerophytic plants have long roots.

(b) Forests prevent floods.

(c) Tropical deciduous forests are commercially most exploited.

(iv) Give a reason to explain each of the following. **(3)**

(a) Mountains have varied vegetation.

(b) Stilt like / aerial roots are a typical feature of littoral forests.

(c) The tropical evergreen forests do not look bare at any time of the year.

Ans. (i) (a) The vegetation in the above image is mountain vegetation.

(b) Three characteristics of mountain vegetation are (any two)

- The plants of this vegetation can survive cold temperatures and harsh winds.
- This vegetation varies with altitude, with trees at lower elevations and alpine plants at higher altitudes.
- At higher altitudes, coniferous trees like pines, oaks and firs are predominantly found due to their ability to withstand cold and heavy snow.

(ii) The forests found in the delta of the river Ganga are called the Sundarbans mangrove forest. Two trees commonly found here are Sundari and Agar.

(iii) (a) Xerophytic plants have long roots to access deep water in dry environments.

(b) Forests prevent flooding by absorbing excess rainwater and preventing soil erosion.

(c) Tropical deciduous forests are commercially most exploited because these forests are heavily used for timber, fuelwood and other resources, making them economically important.

(iv) (a) Mountains have varied vegetation that changes with altitude, ranging from forests to alpine plants.

(b) Stilt-like/aerial roots are a typical feature of littoral forests as these roots help plants survive in coastal and waterlogged areas.

(c) Tropical evergreen forests do not look bare at any time of the year as these forests remain lush and green throughout the year due to constant rainfall.

Q.3 **(i) Forests play an important role in the global water cycle, moving water across the Earth by releasing water vapour and capturing rainfall. They also filter out pollution and chemicals, improving the quality of water available for human use. The destruction of forests has a knock-on effect on agriculture and can affect the production of the food we eat.** *Source: wwf.panda.org* **(2)**

(a) How do forests help in preventing erosion and protecting communities from landslides and floods?

(b) What impact does the destruction of forests have on agriculture and food production?

(ii) Name the natural vegetation extensively found at the following altitudes **(2)**

(a) At lower altitudes between 1000-2000 m.

(b) At altitudes between 1500-3000 m.

(iii) (a) In which natural vegetation belt is Sundari tree found?

(b) Why is the tropical deciduous forest commercially the most exploited forest belt of India? (Two points) **(3)**

(iv) (a) Name one region in India where tropical evergreen forest is found. **(3)**

(b) Mention the temperature and rainfall conditions suitable for its growth.

Ans. (i) (a) Forests prevent erosion by holding soil together with their roots, reducing the risk of landslides and floods.

(b) Destroying forests leads to soil degradation which reduces the fertility of the soil to grow crops.

(ii) (a) Wet temperate forests are found at lower altitudes between 1000 and 2000m with broad leaf trees.

(b) Temperate forests are found at altitude between 1500 and 3000 m.

(iii) (a) Sundari tree is found in littoral/mangrove vegetation.

(b) Two reasons why the tropical deciduous forest is commercially the most exploited forest belt are

- These forests have valuable tree species like teak and sal, which are essential for the economy.
- These forest are not very dense.
- These forests provide essential products such as resin, fruits and medicinal plants.

(iv) (a) Tropical evergreen forests are found in Western Ghats, North-East India particularly in the states of Assam, Meghalaya and Arunachal Pradesh, etc.

(b) These forests are mostly found in tropical areas where the annual rainfall is more than 200 cm with an average annual temperature between 25°C and 27°C.

6

WATER RESOURCES

- Water resources refer to the available sources of water, such as rivers, lakes, groundwater, and rainfall which is used for drinking, irrigation, and other purposes.
- 97% of water available on the Earth is saline water and the remaining 3% is fresh water. Over 2.3% of this freshwater is frozen in glaciers and ice caps.

Sources of Water

- **Surface Water** Water present on the surface of the Earth is called surface water. In India, 60% of the total surface water is provided by the rivers.
- **Groundwater** Water present under the surface of the Earth is called Groundwater. Groundwater makes up 98% of the freshwater on the planet.

Need for Conservation of Water

Conservation of water is the practice of using water efficiently and to prevent unnecessary wastage of water.

Conservation of water is necessary due to the following reasons

- The excessive use of groundwater leads to a decline in the water table.
- Loss of vegetation causes a reduction in rainfall.
- Irrigation consumes more than 90% of total fresh water.
- An increase in population results in a shortage of water.

Water Conservation Practices

Water conservation practices are the methods used to reduce wastage of water and ensure efficient use of water resources. These include Rainwater Harvesting, Watershed Management, etc.

Rainwater Harvesting

It is the process of collecting and storing rainwater for future use. In this method, rainwater is collected and stored especially for irrigation, drinking, irrigation, etc. It is mainly of two types

(i) **Surface Runoff Harvesting or Groundwater Recharge** It is the collection, accumulation and storing of rainwater for its eventual reuse. It has various structures that are used to recharge or refill groundwater such as

- **Recharge Pits** These are the man-made structures designed to store rainwater. They are typically dug into the Earth and filled with layers of coarse material like gravel or sand which helps filter and slow down the water.
- **Dug wells or Borewells** These are shallow, deep wells drilled into the ground to access groundwater. These are recharged by drain pipes which carry the water.
- **Percolation Pits (Soakaway)** These are small, dug-out pits or trenches designed to facilitate the infiltration of rainwater or surface runoff into the ground.

(ii) **Rooftop Rainwater Harvesting** It is the practice of collecting rainwater from the roof of the building. It comprises a simple scheme to replenish the groundwater and increase its level.

Rooftop Rainwater Harvesting

REVISION NOTES

Rainwater harvesting is widely practiced in states like Rajasthan, Gujarat, Andhra Pradesh, Assam and Karnataka. In India, there are various regional names for rainwater harvesting systems

- Khatri and Kuhl in the Western Himalayas
- Baolis and Dighis in the Gangetic plains
- Dongs in Assam
- Bhandaras or Kere in the Deccan plateau region
- Zing in Ladakh
- Cheruvu in Andhra Pradesh
- Tankas and Khadin in Gujarat

Importance of Rainwater Harvesting

- It reduces the volume of rainwater flowing into drains, which helps in preventing flooding.
- It allows water to seep back into the ground which helps to restore underground water.
- It is an excellent source of water free from contamination and soil pollution.

Irrigation

Irrigation is the process of supplying water to plants or crops from wells, tanks, canals, etc. to help them grow.

Importance of Irrigation

- In case of uncertain and less rainfall, irrigation is necessary to provide sufficient water to the agricultural fields.
- Irrigation facilities help in the growing of multiple crops in a year which enhances agriculture production and productivity.
- It generates employment by developing allied activities like means of transport, etc.
- Irrigation is important for different crops according to their needs.

Traditional Methods of Irrigation

- **Canal Irrigation** A canal is a man-made waterway used for irrigation, transport, or draining water. This method of irrigation is very popular in Northern plains due to the presence of perennial rivers. It is of two types - inundation canals and perennial canals.
- **Tank Irrigation** Tank refers to a small bunds (embankment) of stones built across a stream to impound water. This method is popular in the Deccan region where rivers dry up when there is no rain.
- **Well Irrigation** A well is a small hole dug in the surface of the Earth to obtain underground water. Around 40% of India's irrigated land is supplied by wells. It is popular in the Northern plains, the Deccan region and in some areas of Karnataka and Tamil Nadu. It is of two types - lined wells and unlined wells.
- **Tube Well Irrigation** In this method, a deep borewell is dug at a depth of about 30 m and water is taken out with the help of an electric or diesel motor. It is also called the lift method. This method is popular in Punjab, Haryana, Uttar Pradesh, Bihar, West Bengal, etc.

Modern Methods of Irrigation

Sprinkler Irrigation

It is a method where water is sprayed over the plants using a system of pipes and sprinklers.

Advantages

- No loss of water by seepage or evaporation.
- Best method to conserve water.
- Best suited in acid & semi-acid regions.

Disadvantages

- High initial cost.
- Water efficiency is affected by direction of wind.
- High maintenance requirement.
- Water must be free from sand, debris, salt.

Sprinkler Irrigation

Drip Irrigation

In this method, plastic pipes are placed between the rows of crops or buried along the roots of plants and water is dripped directly to the crops.

Advantages

- Minimal loss of fertiliser & nutrients.
- High water application efficiency.
- Fields with irregular shapes can be irrigated.
- Less erosion of soil.
- No wastage of water through evaporation.

Drip Irrigation

Disadvantages

- High initial cost.
- Sun can affect the tubes used for drip irrigation.
- Clogging of pipes.

Bamboo Irrigation

A 200 year old system of irrigation in Meghalaya by using bamboo pipes.

Bamboo Irrigation

Advantages

- Does not need any fuel.
- It can be used in the regions where bamboo is available for free of cost.

Disadvantage

- Can not be used in the areas where bamboo are not available.
- Bamboo starts to rot in rain.

EXAM ORIENTED QUESTIONS

TYPE - 1 — 1 Mark

Multiple Choice Questions

Q.1 Which of the following is a groundwater source? **(ICSE 2023)**

(a) Pond (b) Lake
(c) Spring (d) River

Ans. (c) Spring

Q.2 Why is there a need to conserve water in India?
(a) A lot of water is polluted
(b) No water is found below the land in India
(c) Water is in abundance in India
(d) We receive lot of rain in summer

Ans. (a) A lot of water is polluted

Q.3 What are the advantages of rainwater harvesting?
(a) Recharge of groundwater and conservation of water
(b) Provide water through canals to the farms and its conservation
(c) It helps in harvesting of crops and its storage
(d) Provide water for multinational companies to produce packaged drinking water

Ans. (a) Recharge of groundwater and conservation of water

Q.4 What is the main purpose of Rainwater Harvesting?
(a) To store rainwater for future use
(b) To purify water
(c) To reduce pollution
(d) To increase rainfall

Ans. (a) To store rainwater for future use

Q.5 Which of the following may be used for the recharging of underground water? **(ICSE Specimen 2025)**
(a) Planting of shelterbelts
(b) Plugging of gullies and ravines
(c) Percolation pit
(d) Tube-well irrigation

Ans. (c) Percolation pit

Exp. Percolation pits are small, dug-out pits or trenches designed to facilitate the infiltration of rainwater or surface runoff into the ground.

Q.6 Which is not an objective of rain water harvesting?
(a) Avoid flooding roads (b) Polluting water
(c) Reduce surface run off (d) Reduce soil erosion

Ans. (b) Polluting water

Q.7 Read the table and identify the pair that is correctly matched.

	Harvesting System Names	Regions
P.	Zing	Karnataka
Q.	Dighi	Tamil Nadu
R.	Dongs	Assam
S.	Cheruvu	Gujarat

(a) P (b) Q
(c) R (d) S

Ans. (c) R

Q.8 What is the meaning of irrigation? **(ICSE Specimen Semester I 2022)**
(a) The water received by rainfall.
(b) The man-made arrangements of supplying water to the fields.
(c) The storage of rainwater.
(d) Growing of crops.

Ans. (b) The man-made arrangements of supplying water to the fields.

Q.9 Which means of irrigation can be developed with minimum expenditure? **(ICSE 2024)**
(a) Tube well (b) Canal
(c) Well (d) Drip irrigation

Ans. (b) Canal

Q.10 Which of the following is a type of canal found in India? **(ICSE Specimen semester I 2022)**
(a) Perennial canal
(b) River canal
(c) Artificial canal
(d) Ground canal

Ans. (a) Perennial canal

Exp. Perennial canals are those canals that supply water throughout the year.

Q.11 Why do the inundation canals have limited use? **(ICSE Specimen semester I 2022)**

(a) They get water only when the rivers are in flood
(b) They are taken out from a perennial river
(c) They are constructed to store rain water
(d) It occupies a lot of space

Ans. (a) They get water only when the rivers are in flood

Q.12 Why is canal irrigation more popular in the Northern Plains?

(a) The surface of land is almost flat and soft soil is easy to dig
(b) To supply water to a number of cities in Plain area
(c) Rocky surface of the plain helps in their conservation
(d) Rivers are seasonal and canals are needed

Ans. (a) The surface of land is almost flat and soft soil is easy to dig

Q.13 Which of the following is not a suitable condition for the development of tank irrigation?

(a) Presence of natural depressions
(b) Permeable rock structure
(c) Plenty of rain in rainy period
(d) Hard substance rock structure

Ans. (b) Permeable rock structure

Q.14 Read the table and identify the pair that is correctly matched.

	Methods of Irrigation	Regions
P.	Tube well	Karnataka
Q.	Tank	Punjab
R.	Lined well	Uttar Pradesh
S.	Canal	Mizoram

(a) P (b) Q (c) R (d) S

Ans. (c) R

Q.15 If Rahul had to maintain a public park in his colony, which method of irrigation should he prefer?

(a) Drip irrigation (b) Sprinkler irrigation
(c) Furrow irrigation (d) Spray irrigation

Ans. (b) Sprinkler irrigation

Exp. Rahul should prefer a sprinkler irrigation system in the park because it evenly distributes water over a large area and ensures uniform growth of the grass and less wastage of water.

Q.16 Sprinkler irrigation: Rainfall

(a) Drip irrigation: River flow
(b) Spray irrigation: Water pooling
(c) Furrow irrigation: Stream channeling
(d) Tank irrigation: Raindrops

Ans. (c) Furrow irrigation: Stream channeling

Q.17 Why is Sprinkler irrigation efficient but still not a very commonly used method of irrigation by Indian farmers? **(ICSE Specimen 2022)**

(a) There is no loss of water by seepage.
(b) It is an expensive method of irrigation.
(c) There is no loss of water by evaporation.
(d) Farmers are scared of getting wet.

Ans. (b) It is an expensive method of irrigation.

Q.18 Which is the most advanced and efficient method of irrigation? **(ICSE Specimen semester I 2022)**

(a) Canal irrigation (b) Well irrigation
(c) Drip irrigation (d) Tank irrigation

Ans. (c) Drip irrigation

Exp. Drip irrigation is considered advanced and efficient because it delivers water directly to plant roots, minimising water wastage, evaporation, and promoting better growth with less water.

Q.19 What is the importance of drip irrigation?

(a) It is an ultra modern system of irrigation
(b) It is cheaper than other sources
(c) It can irrigate more areas with less usage of water
(d) It is used by almost all farmers in India

Ans. (c) It can irrigate more areas with less usage of water

Q.20 Identify the type of irrigation method depicted in the image below.

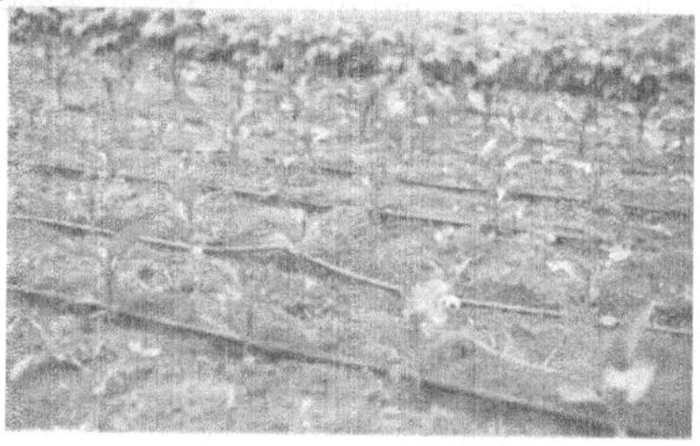

(a) Furrow irrigation
(b) Drip irrigation
(c) Spray irrigation
(d) Sprinkler irrigation

Ans. (b) Drip irrigation

Q.21 Which of the following prevents wastage of water? **(ICSE 2025)**

(a) Canal (b) Well
(c) Sprinkler (d) Tube well

Ans. (c) Sprinkler

Q.22 Most advanced and efficient method of irrigation consisting of pipes

(a) Sprinkler irrigation
(b) Drip irrigation
(c) Spray irrigation
(d) Furrow irrigation

Ans. (b) Drip irrigation

Q.23 A watershed development project by Central Government aiming at conservation water.
(a) Rainwater Harvesting (b) Conservation of water
(c) Johads (d) Haryali

Ans. (d) Haryali

Q.24 Canal irrigation is not very prominent in North-East because
(a) land is hilly (b) no agricultural land
(c) dense forest (d) due to other mode of irrigation

Ans. (a) land is hilly

Q.25 Most popular means of irrigation in India.
(a) Well (b) Drip (c) Canal (d) Tubewell

Ans. (a) Well

Q.26 Most efficient means of irrigation in South India.
(a) Sprinkle (b) Drip (c) Tank (d) Canal

Ans. (c) Tank

Q.27 State that leads in irrigation by wells in India.
(a) Karnataka (b) Maharashtra
(c) Rajasthan (d) U.P.

Ans. (d) U.P.

Q.28 Rajasthan canal is also know as
(a) Narendra Modi (b) Rajnath canal
(c) Indira Gandhi canal (d) Ambedkar canal

Ans. (c) Indira Gandhi canal

Q.29 Inundation canals can be used
(a) throughout the year
(b) only during rainy season
(c) only in the summer season
(d) only in winter

Ans. (b) only during rainy season

Q.30 Persian wheel method uses .... for irrigation.
(a) buckets only (b) draught animal only
(c) cart (d) draught animal & buckets both

Ans. (d) Draught animal & buckets both

TYPE - 2 1 Mark

Assertion-Reason Questions

Q.1 Assertion (A) Conservation of water is important because it helps prevent the decline of the water table, loss of vegetation, and water shortages.

Reason (R) Overuse of groundwater, deforestation, excessive irrigation and population growth are leading to serious water scarcity issues.
(a) Both A and R are true and R is the correct explanation of A
(b) Both A and R are true, but R does not explain A
(c) A is true, but R is false (d) A is false, but R is true

Ans. (a) Both A and R are true and R is the correct explanation of A

Q.2 Assertion (A) Rainwater harvesting can lead to excessive flooding in urban areas.

Reason (R) Properly designed rainwater harvesting systems store water effectively and reduce surface runoff.
(a) Both A and R are true and R is the correct explanation of A
(b) Both A and R are true, but R does not explain A
(c) A is true, but R is false
(d) A is false, but R is true

Ans. (d) A is false, but R is true

Q.3 Assertion (A) Tubewell irrigation is mostly used in regions with high agricultural output.

Reason (R) Tubewell irrigation involves using a deep borewell to extract water using an electric or diesel motor.
(a) Both A and R are true and R is the correct explanation of A.
(b) Both A and R are true, but R does not explain A
(c) A is true, but R is false (d) A is false, but R is true

Ans. (b) Both A and R are true, but R does not explain A

Q.4 Assertion (A) Drip irrigation is suitable for areas with water scarcity.

Reason (R) Drip irrigation uses high volumes of water which leads to excessive water wastage.
(a) Both A and R are true and R is the correct explanation of A
(b) Both A and R are true, but R does not explain A
(c) A is true, but R is false (d) A is false, but R is true

Ans. (c) A is true, but R is false

Q.5 Assertion (A) Spray irrigation involves spraying water in fine droplets over plants using nozzles or sprayers.

Reason (R) It differs from sprinkler irrigation as it uses nozzles to spray water in fine droplets, while sprinkler irrigation uses a network of pipes.
(a) Both A and R are true and R is the correct explanation of A
(b) Both A and R are true, but R does not explain A
(c) A is true, but R is false
(d) A is false, but R is true

Ans. (a) Both A and R are true and R is the correct explanation of A

TYPE - 3 2 Marks

Short Answer Type Questions

Q.1 The combination of climate change and population growth poses a serious threat to India's water scarcity and without adequate measures to address these challenges *Source - Business standard*

Give two main reasons why water scarcity occurs in India. (ICSE 2013)

Ans. The two main reasons due to which water scarcity occurs in India are

(i) Transformation of society into urban and industrial has increased the requirement of water.

(ii) Rainfall is irregular and unpredictable in India.

Q.2 Mention any two methods of recharging groundwater aquifers. (ICSE 2020)

Ans. Two methods of recharging groundwater aquifers are

(i) Constructing recharging wells.

(ii) Constructing recharge pits and shafts.

Q.3 Suggest any two measures to overcome scarcity of water in the metropolitan cities of India. (ICSE 2025)

Ans. Two measures to overcome water scarcity in metropolitan cities of India are

- **Rainwater Harvesting** Collecting and storing rainwater from rooftops and open spaces can help in recharging groundwater and meeting daily water needs.
- **Wastewater Recycling and Reuse** Treating and recycling wastewater for non-drinking purposes like gardening, cleaning and industrial use can reduce water wastage.

Q.4 With reference to rainwater harvesting, answer the following. (ICSE 2016)

(i) Explain Rainwater harvesting.

(ii) Mention two objectives of rainwater harvesting. (ICSE 2025)

Or State the significance of rainwater harvesting. (ICSE 2015)

Ans. (i) It is the process of collecting and storing rainwater for future use. In this method, rainwater is collected and stored especially for drinking, irrigation, etc.

(ii) Two objectives of rainwater harvesting are

(a) Recharging the groundwater and raising its level.

(b) Preventing the rainwater from being wasted as there is water scarcity.

Q.5 Mention two advantages of rainwater harvesting.

Ans. Two advantages of rainwater harvesting are

(i) It helps reduce the dependency on groundwater and other water sources.

(ii) It is an excellent source of water for landscape irrigation, contains fewer chemicals, leading to better soil health and plant growth.

Q.6 "There is plenty of rain in India during the rainy season, yet we need irrigation." Give two reasons to support this statement. (ICSE 2018)

Ans. Yes, there is plenty of rain in India, yet we need irrigation because

(i) Rainfall in India is unevenly distributed. Some areas received heavy rains while others remain dry.

(ii) Rainfall in India is uncertain i.e. there may be good rainfall in one year and there may be a drought in another year.

Q.7 "Without irrigation, development of agriculture is difficult in India." Give two reasons.

Ans. 'Without irrigation, the development of agriculture is difficult in India' because of

(i) the irregular and unpredictable monsoon of India which makes irrigation difficult.

(ii) uneven distribution of rainfall in different parts of the country.

Q.8 With reference to irrigation, answer the following. (ICSE 2020)

(i) Name the most common means of irrigation used in India.

(ii) Give one reason for the popularity of this means of irrigation in our country.

Ans. (i) Canals are the most common source of irrigation used in India. In Punjab, Haryana, Delhi, Uttar Pradesh, Bihar and Northern Rajasthan, canals are used to irrigate the soil.

(ii) Canals are popular as means of irrigation in our country because they give higher productivity per hectare of land as compared to traditional methods.

Q.9 Give a reason for the significance of irrigation in

(i) Punjab (ii) Rajasthan (ICSE 2017)

Ans. (i) Punjab is the major wheat producing state in India. Rainfall in the state is irregular. Thus irrigation is required extensively in Punjab through canals or wells.

(ii) Rajasthan receives scanty rainfall due to high temperature and alingment of Aravallis parallel to the South-West Monsoon winds.

Q.10 With reference to irrigation, answer the following. **(ICSE 2018)**

(i) Name three traditional means of irrigation.

(ii) Why do we need different modes of irrigation?

Ans. (i) The three traditional means of irrigation are

(a) Tank irrigation (b) Canal irrigation

(c) Well irrigation

(ii) We need different modes of irrigation because of topographical features, availability of surface water, groundwater, soil types and climatic conditions.

Q.11 With reference to the methods of irrigation, answer the following questions

(i) What are perennial canals?

(ii) What is a tank?

Ans. (i) Perennial canals maintain their water flow throughout the year either from the river or from reservoirs of the river projects.

(ii) A tank is a man-made/natural structure that is used for storing rainwater.

Q.12 With reference to canals, answer the following.

(i) Mention two types of canals used in canal irrigation.

(ii) How does canal irrigation benefit farmers in the Northern plains of India?

Ans. (i) The two types of canals used in canal irrigation are Inundation canals and Perennial canals.

(ii) Canal irrigation benefits farmers in the Northern plains by providing a reliable and consistent water supply from perennial rivers, which is essential for irrigation during the summer season.

Q.13 Give two reasons why well irrigation is popular in North India? **(ICSE Specimen 2018)**

Ans. Well irrigation is popular method of irrigation in North India due to the following reasons

(i) North India has widespread deposition of alluvial soil which is soft and can be dug very easily.

(ii) North India has abundant groundwater resources which makes well irrigation an effective way to access water.

Q.14 Mention any one advantage and any one disadvantage of well irrigation. **(ICSE 2025)**

Ans. Advantage of Well Irrigation

- **Low Cost and Easy to Construct** Wells can be dug at a low cost and require simple technology, making them accessible for small farmers.

Disadvantage of Well Irrigation

- **Limited Water Supply** Wells depend on groundwater, which can dry up during summers or in areas with low water tables.

Q.15 Mention two factors that are essential for the development of tubewell irrigation. **(ICSE 2016)**

Ans. The factors essential for the development of tube wells irrigation are

(i) Water level should be high with perennial water supply.

(ii) The ground should be soft, preferably alluvial soil, to facilitate deep digging.

Q.16 Name two states in which tube wells are extensively used. Give a reason to explain its importance as a source of irrigation.

Ans. Uttar Pradesh and Punjab are the states where tube wells are extensively used. The importance of tube wells as a source of irrigation is

(i) These are very useful during drought conditions when surface wells dry up.

(ii) These can irrigate a large area as compared to surface wells or tanks.

Q.17 With reference to irrigation, answer the following

(i) Why is the sprinkler irrigation method suitable for arid and semi-arid region?

(ii) Which area of India is famous for bamboo irrigation system?

Ans. (i) The Sprinkler irrigation method is suitable for arid and semi-arid regions because these do not involve any loss of water by seepage.

(ii) The bamboo irrigation system is very popular in North-East part of India. This is 200 years old system used by the tribal farmers of Khasi and Jaintia hills.

Q.18 Mention two modern methods of irrigation. State one important reason for their growing popularity. **(ICSE 2015)**

Or "The modern means of irrigation are gaining popularity". Give two reasons to justify this statement. **(ICSE 2019)**

Ans. Two modern methods of irrigation are as follows

(i) Drip irrigation method

(ii) Sprinkler irrigation method

In the conventional methods of irrigation, a large quantity of water is wasted due to water logging which often results in the gradual salinity of the soil. This has made the modern methods of irrigation more popular.

Q.19 (i) How does drip irrigation deliver water to plants?

(ii) What is one major benefit of drip irrigation?

Ans. (i) Drip irrigation delivers water directly to the roots of plants through a system of pipes and tubes in controlled amounts.

(ii) It reduces water wastage by delivering water directly to the plant roots.

Q.20 Distinguish between Drip irrigation and Furrow irrigation.

Ans. The differences between Drip irrigation and Furrow irrigation are as follows

Drip Irrigation	Furrow Irrigation
Water is delivered directly to the plant roots through a system of pipes and emitters.	Water is applied in furrows or channels between crop rows, allowing it to flow over the soil.
It is highly efficient, reducing water wastage by targeting only the roots of the plants.	It is less efficient as water can evaporate or be absorbed unevenly by the soil, often leading to wastage.

Q.21 Explain the following types of irrigation.
(i) Spray Irrigation (ii) Sprinkler irrigation

Ans. (i) In Spray irrigation, water is sprayed in a fine mist over the crops, usually through a set of nozzles or sprayers. It differs from a sprinkler irrigation system as it uses nozzles to spray water in fine droplets over plants, while in sprinkler irrigation, a network of pipes is used.

(ii) Sprinkler irrigation is a method where water is sprayed over the plants using a system of pipes and sprinklers.

TYPE - 4 (3 Marks)

Long Answer Type Questions

Q.1 Distinguish between surface water and groundwater. **(ICSE 2018)**

Ans. Surface water and groundwater can be distinguished as follows

Surface Water	Groundwater
The water found on the surface of the Earth is known as surface water.	The water that is located below the Earth's surface is referred to as groundwater.
Due to less minerals it is also known as soft water.	Due to more amount of minerals, it is considered as hard water.
It is easier to extract surface water.	It is comparatively difficult to extract groundwater.

Q.2 Why there is a need for the conservation of water? Mention three reasons.

Ans. Conservation of water is necessary due to the following reasons

(i) The excessive use of groundwater leads to a decline in the water table. As the water level in underground aquifers decreases, it becomes more challenging and costly to access water.

(ii) Loss of vegetation causes a reduction in rainfall. Loss of vegetation due to deforestation or land degradation reduces the amount of moisture released into the air, leading to a decrease in rainfall.

(iii) Irrigation consumes more than 90% of total fresh water. This extensive use of water for crops can lead to depletion of available water resources.

Q.3 (i) Why is the world in danger of facing a severe water shortage in the coming future? Give two reasons to support your answer. **(ICSE 2015)**

(ii) State one measure the government should adopt to handle the present water crisis.

Ans. (i) The world is in danger of facing a severe water shortage in the future due to several factors

(a) As the population grows, the need for water increases, putting pressure on available resources.

(b) Changing weather patterns, including droughts and unpredictable rainfall disrupt the natural replenishment of freshwater sources.

(ii) One measure the government should adopt to handle the present water crisis is rainwater harvesting to recycle and reuse water.

Q.4 With reference to water conservation, answer the following

(i) What type of regions are expected to face water shortage?

(ii) In which areas, rainwater harvesting is used?

(iii) Name regions where rainwater harvesting techniques are used.

Ans. (i) Regions with low rainfall, low water table, desert and drought-prone areas are expected to face water shortage.

(ii) Rainwater harvesting is used in the states of Rajasthan, Gujarat, Andhra Pradesh, Assam and Karnataka.

(iii) (a) Dong's technique is used in Assam by Bodo tribes.

(b) Cheruva technique is used in Andhra Pradesh.

Q.5 Mention any three water harvesting systems practiced in India.

Ans. The three water harvesting systems practiced in India are

(i) **Rooftop Rainwater Harvesting** It is a system of harvesting rainwater where it falls. In this technique, the roof becomes the catchment and the rainwater is collected from the roof of the building.

(ii) **Kuls** In hills and mountainous regions, people built diversion channels like the 'guls' or 'kuls'. It is common in the Western Himalayas and largely used for irrigation.

(iii) **Johads and Khadins** In arid and semi-arid regions, agricultural fields were converted into rain-fed storage structures that allowed the water to retain and moisten the soil. This is known as Khadins in Jaisalmer and Johads in other parts of Rajasthan.

Q.6 With reference to rainwater harvesting, answer the following. **(ICSE 2018)**

(i) Name two methods of water harvesting in India.

(ii) Mention any two objectives of rainwater harvesting.

Ans. (i) The two methods of water harvesting in India are

(a) Rooftop rainwater harvesting

(b) Recharge of groundwater

(ii) The two objectives of rainwater harvesting are

(a) It prevents soil erosion or flooding of the surrounding area.

(b) It meets the demands of water requirements in the dry season.

Q.7 Explain any three components of the rooftop rainwater harvesting system.

Ans. The components of rooftop rainwater harvesting are

(i) **Catchment** The surface that receives rainfall directly is the catchment, e.g. sloping roof or flat roof.

(ii) **Water Pipes** Rainwater from the rooftop is carried down through water pipes or drains to the storage/ harvesting system.

(iii) **First Flush** It is a device used to flush off the water received in the first shower. First rain contains contaminants of the atmosphere and catchment roof thus, first rain separator should be made at the outlet of each drain pipe.

Q.8 With reference to the following image, answer the following questions. **(ICSE 2017)**

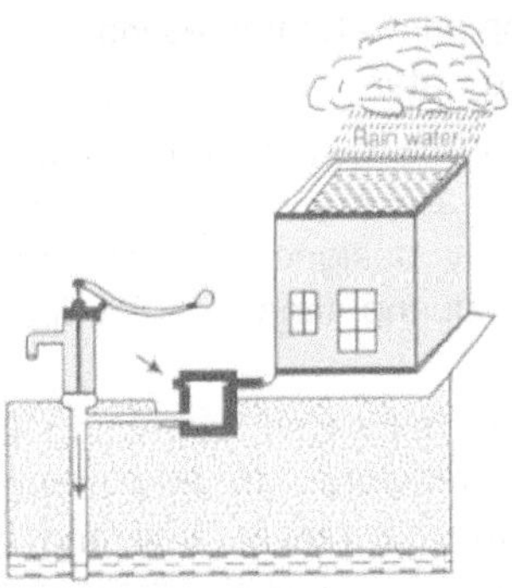

(i) Name the activity shown in the diagram.

(ii) Give two objectives of the activity.

Ans. (i) The activity shown in the diagram is of rooftop rainwater harvesting method.

(ii) Two objectives of the rainwater harvesting method are

(a) It is a simple scheme to replenish the groundwater and increase its level.

(b) The purpose of rainwater harvesting is to utilise the rainwater to its maximum and not to let it run off or go waste.

Q.9 Ravi, a farmer in a drought-prone village is struggling with water shortages during the dry seasons. To combat this, he decided to set up a rainwater harvesting system on his property. He installed a collection system on his rooftop, directing the rainwater into large storage tanks. This allowed him to have enough water for his crops and household needs even when the rainfall was scarce.

(i) How did Ravi's decision to install a rainwater harvesting system reflect his proactive approach to water management?

(ii) In what ways does rainwater harvesting potentially offer a sustainable solution for farmers in drought-prone areas like Ravi's village?

(iii) How did Ravi's experience with rainwater harvesting inspire other farmers to adopt similar practices, and what could be the economic and environmental benefits for the village?

Ans. (i) Ravi's decision showed foresight in addressing water scarcity, ensuring a reliable water source for his crops.

(ii) Rainwater harvesting ensures that farmers have water during dry spells, reducing reliance on external sources. It can boost community water security by preserving groundwater and reducing strain on local water systems.

(iii) Ravi's success could encourage neighbouring farmers to adopt rainwater harvesting, leading to better water availability and more stable agricultural output, benefitting the village's economy and improving the local environment by reducing over-extraction of groundwater.

Q.10 Give a geographical reason for each of the following. **(ICSE 2014)**

(i) Irrigation is necessary despite the monsoon.

(ii) Canal irrigation leads to the unproductivity of grounds around it.

Ans. (i) Irrigation is necessary even with the monsoon because rainfall can be uneven, insufficient, or unpredictable. It helps ensure a steady water supply for crops especially during dry season or when monsoon rains are delayed.

(ii) Canal irrigation can lead to unproductivity around it due to waterlogging and salinization. Excess water from canals can raise the water table which causes soil to become waterlogged or salt-rich.

Q.11 Give a reason for each of the following. **(ICSE 2019)**

(i) **Most of the South Indian states are not suitable for development of canal irrigation.**

(ii) **There is an urgent need for water conservation in India.**

(iii) **Development of irrigation is essential for the growth of the agriculture sector of India.**

Ans. (i) Most of the South Indian states are located over a rocky surface. The digging of canals in rocky and uneven areas is difficult and uneconomic. Thus, these states are not suitable for canal irrigation.

(ii) Conservation of water resources is essential in India due to following reasons

- To safeguard ourselves from health hazards as the quality of water is badly affected by discharge of urban wastes, industrial effluents, pesticides and fertilisers.
- The underground water has been exploited and the water table has been lowered.
- Uneven rainfall patterns and changing climate is making it essential to conserve water.

(iii) Development of irrigation is essential for the growth of the agriculture sector of India because Indian agriculture mostly depends on monsoon rainfall which is inadequate and fluctuates every year.Thus, to minimise this dependence, different methods of irrigation should be developed in the country.

Q.12 Give a reason for each of the following. **(ICSE Specimen 2018)**

(i) **Inundation canals are being converted into perennial canals.**

(ii) **Groundwater reserves are depleting at a fast rate.**

(iii) **Drip irrigation reduces loss of water through evaporation.**

Ans. (i) Inundation canals are being converted into perennial canals to ensure a steady and reliable water supply throughout the year. Unlike inundation canals, which are seasonal and dependent on rainfall, perennial canals provide waer continuously, regardless of seasonal variations.

(ii) Groundwater reserves are depleting at a fast rate due to following reasons

- Overexploitation of groundwater to satisfy the needs of a growing population.
- Agricultural needs require a large amount of groundwater.

(iii) Drip method has highest water application efficiency and directly reaches the roots of the plant, thus, conserving water.

Q.13 (i) **Where in India is tank irrigation most widely used?** **(ICSE Specimen 2023)**

(ii) **Give one factor that has led to its popularity in the region mentioned by you.**

(iii) **Mention one advantage of using a tank as a means of irrigation.**

Ans. (i) The tank irrigation systems are widely found in the states of Tamil Nadu, Andhra Pradesh, Maharashtra, etc.

(ii) Tank irrigation is popular in these regions because of the presence of hard rocks in Peninsular India that makes it difficult to dig canals.

(iii) One advantage of using a tank for irrigation is that it stores rainwater, providing a reliable water source during dry periods or when rainfall is insufficient.

Q.14 Give one reason for each of the following. **(ICSE 2016)**

(i) **The Northern Plain of India is found suitable for canal irrigation.**

(ii) **Tank irrigation is an important method of irrigation in Karnataka.**

(iii) **Although expensive, sprinkler irrigation is gaining popularity in recent times.**

Ans. (i) The Northern Plain of India is suitable for canal irrigation because it has low-level relief, deep fertile soils and a perennial source of water.

(ii) Tank irrigation is important in Karnataka due to the state's irregular rainfall and the presence of many traditional water tanks. These tanks store rainwater during the monsoon and provide a reliable water source during dry periods.

(iii) Although considered an expensive source, sprinkler irrigation has gained popularity in recent times because in this type of irrigation, there is no loss of water by seepage and evaporation.

Q.15 With reference to water resources, explain the following terms. **(ICSE 2019)**

(i) **Inundation canal**

(ii) **Rooftop rainwater harvesting**

(iii) **Surface water**

Ans. (i) These are a type of canals used for irrigation, primarily in areas with seasonal river flow. These are especially designed to carry water from rivers or streams during times of flooding or high water levels.

(ii) Rooftop rainwater harvesting is a system of collecting rainwater. In this technique, the roof becomes the catchment area and the rainwater is collected at the roof of the building. This method is less expensive and very effective and if implemented properly, it helps in augmenting the groundwater level of the area.

(iii) Surface water is the water present in the water bodies which are found on the surface of the ground, e.g. rivers, lakes, ponds, lagoons, backwater, etc.

Q.16 **Give one reason to explain each of the following.** **(ICSE 2025)**

(i) Tank irrigation is not common in Northern India.

(ii) Canal irrigation is important in Punjab.

(iii) All farmers do not use tube well irrigation even if the geographical condition is favourable.

Ans. (i) Tank irrigation is not common in Northern India because of flat terrain. Northern India, especially the Indo-Gangetic Plain, has a flat landscape, making it difficult to construct tanks, which require natural depressions to store water.

(ii) Canal irrigation is important in Punjab because the region has a network of perennial rivers like the Satluj, Beas and Ravi, which provide a continuous water supply for irrigation through canals.

(iii) All farmers do not use tube well irrigation even if the geographical conditions are favourable because the installation and maintenance of tube wells are expensive. Small and marginal farmers may not afford the high initial cost of setting up tube wells and the electricity or diesel expenses required to operate them.

Q.17 **Give two advantages and one disadvantage that tube wells have over surface wells.**

Ans. The advantages of tube wells are

(i) Tubewells do not result in evaporation of water like surface wells.

(ii) It irrigates a large area (400 hectares) as compared to surface wells.

A disadvantage of tube well is that it is only possible in areas where the groundwater level is not too low and power is needed to drain water. On the other hand, water can be stored in a surface well even if there is no groundwater.

TYPE - 5 — 10 Marks

Structured Questions

Q.1 **(i) State two reasons why there is a need for irrigation in India.** **(ICSE Specimen 202, 2024) (2)**

(ii) Distinguish between Inundation Canals and Perennial Canals. **(2)**

(iii) (a) Name a state in India where tube wells are commonly used. **(3)**

(b) Give two geographical conditions that favour tube well irrigation in this state.

(iv) (a) What is meant by rainwater harvesting? **(3)**

(b) Mention any two water harvesting practices followed in India.

Ans. (i) Two reasons why there is a need for irrigation in India are

(a) **Uneven Distribution of Rainfall** India experiences seasonal rainfall with heavy rains in some regions and droughts in others. Northern and Western parts have irregular or insufficient rainfall, making irrigation essential for maintaining agricultural productivity throughout the year.

(b) **Dependence on Monsoon** Indian agriculture depends on the monsoon season for water. However, crop yields can suffer if the monsoon is delayed or insufficient. Irrigation provides a stable water supply, ensuring that crops can grow even in the absence of timely monsoon rains.

(ii) The differences beween inundation canals and perennial canal are as follows

Inundation Canal	Perennial Canal
Derived from seasonal rivers and floods, only active during the rainy season.	Derived from permanent water sources such as reservoirs or perennial rivers, providing water year-round.
Water supply is available only during the monsoon or flood season.	Water is available throughout the year, ensuring continuous irrigation.

(iii) (a) Punjab/Haryana/Uttar Pradesh

(b) Two geographical conditions that favour tube well irrigation in Northern India are

- **Availability of Groundwater** Northern India, especially the Indo-Gangetic Plain area, has plenty of groundwater, making tube well irrigation possible.
- **Flat Terrain** The region generally has a flat or gently sloping terrain, which makes it easier and cost-effective to install tube wells and distribute water across agricultural fields.

(iv) (a) It is the process of collecting and storing rainwater for future use. In this method, rainwater is collected and stored especially for drinking, irrigation, etc.

(b) Two water harvesting practices followed in India are

- **Rainwater Harvesting** Collecting and storing rainwater from rooftops or open surfaces for later use.

- **Watershed Management** It refers to the efficient management and conservation of both the surface and groundwater resources.

Q.2 (i) Mention one advantage and one disadvantage of using tank irrigation. **(ICSE 2024) (2)**

(ii) Define **(2)**

(a) What is the advantage of using drip irrigation?

(b) Why is Drip irrigation not practiced on a large scale in India?

(iii) Give a reason to explain each of the following. **(3)**

(a) Sprinkler irrigation is gaining popularity in recent times.

(b) Tube well irrigation is used in Punjab.

(c) North India has more area under canal irrigation.

(iv)

(3)

(a) Name the water conservation practice shown in the above picture.

(b) How does this system help to reduce floods?

(c) Why is water conservation necessary? (Any two reasons)

Ans. (i) One advantage and one disadvantage of using tank irrigation are as follows

- **Advantage** Tank irrigation stores rainwater, ensuring a consistent water supply during dry periods or droughts.
- **Disadvantage** Tanks can be expensive to build and maintain, and they may not hold enough water during prolonged dry spells.

(ii) (a) The advantage of using drip irrigation is that it delivers water directly to the plant roots, minimising wastage of water.

(b) Drip irrigation is not practiced on a large scale in India due to its high cost and complex installation process. Additionally, many farmers find it difficult to access the required technology and maintenance support, especially in rural areas.

(iii) (a) Sprinkler irrigation is gaining popularity in recent times because it efficiently distributes water over crops, and is suitable for areas with uneven terrain and can be used for a variety of crops.

(b) Tube well irrigation is used in Punjab because the region relies heavily on groundwater for irrigation due to its high agricultural demands. The availability of deep groundwater helps ensure a consistent water supply.

(c) North India has more area under canal irrigation due to the availability of major river systems like the Ganges, the Indus, and the Yamuna. These rivers provide a reliable source of water and canal systems are developed to distribute water efficiently across large agricultural areas.

(iv) (a) Rooftop water harvesting is shown in the above picture.

(b) Rooftop water harvesting helps reduce floods by capturing and storing rainwater, which prevents excess water from overflowing drainage systems and causing runoff. By collecting rainwater in reservoirs, ponds or underground systems, it reduces surface water flow and allows the ground to absorb more water, lowering the risk of floods.

(c) Water conservation is necessary because water is a limited resource and overuse of water can lead to shortages. It also helps protect the environment, ensuring that plants, animals, and ecosystems have enough water to flourish.

Q.3 (i) Mention two conditions necessary for the construction of wells. **(ICSE Specimen 2023) (2)**

(ii) Define

(a) Surface water (b) Groundwater **(2)**

(iii) Mention one advantage of canals and two disadvantages of tanks. **(3)**

(iv) Mention three ways by which you as an individual can reuse and conserve water. **(3)**

Ans. (i) Two conditions necessary for the construction of wells are

(a) **Presence of Groundwater** There must be enough groundwater available beneath the surface for the well to draw from.

(b) **Permeable Soil or Rock** The soil or rock in the area should allow water to flow easily into the well.

(ii) (a) **Surface water** Water present on the surface of the Earth is called surface water. In India, 60% of the total surface water is provided by the rivers.

(b) **Groundwater** Water present under the surface of the Earth is called Groundwater. Groundwater makes up 98% of the freshwater on the planet.

(iii) **Advantage of canals**

- **Efficient Irrigation** Canals provide a continuous and controlled supply of water for crops, improving irrigation efficiency.

Disadvantages of tanks

- **Loss due to evaporation** Water in tanks can evaporate quickly, especially in hot climates, leading to water loss.
- **Silting** Over time, tanks may fill up with silt, reducing their storage capacity and effectiveness.

(iv) Three ways to reuse and conserve water are

- **Rainwater Harvesting** Collecting rainwater from rooftops to use for watering plants or cleaning helps conserve groundwater.
- **Use Water-Efficient Appliances** Using water-saving devices like low-flow showerheads and toilets reduces water usage.
- **Use a Bucket for Car/Bike Washing** Instead of using a hose, we can wash our car/bike with a bucket of water to save a large amount of water.

Q.4 (i) Groundwater irrigation covers more than half of the total irrigated area in India — and its rapid depletion is a major concern in the country. But this isn't just an India-specific problem. Irrigated agriculture remains the largest user of water globally, a trend encouraged by the fact that farmers in most countries do not pay for the full cost of the water they use. *www.Indiatoday.in* **(3)**

(a) How does the overuse of groundwater in irrigation impact the sustainability of agriculture in India?

(b) Why is irrigated agriculture the largest user of water globally, and how does this affect water management practices?

(ii)

(2)

(a) Identify the type of irrigation as shown in the figure above.

(b) Give one advantage of using this irrigation.

(iii) Aadarsh visits a village in Western Uttar Pradesh and listens to the conversation of two people who were discussing about the water scarcity problem in the area during the dry season. Aadarsh notices that this area receives sufficient amount of rainfall but still faces water scarcity due to underutilisation of the rain water. **(2)**

(a) What methods for conserving water can be used in the area which Aadarsh visits?

(b) How did rainwater harvesting improve water scarcity?

(iv) With reference to utilisation of water resources, answer the following

(a) What geographical conditions make irrigation necessary in the country? **(3)**

(b) How has irrigation changed the cropping pattern in India?

(c) Why is there a scarcity of surface water in our country?

Ans. (i) (a) Overuse of groundwater for irrigation in India causes water resources to deplete quickly. This lowers the water table, making it harder and more expensive for farmers to access water, which reduces crop production and threatens the future of farming.

(b) Irrigated agriculture uses the most water globally because crops need a lot of water. Since farmers often don't pay the full cost, they use water inefficiently, leading to over-extraction and water scarcity. This highlights the need for better water conservation.

(ii) (a) Spray irrigation is shown in the picture.

(b) It ensures the even distribution of water, thereby reducing the wastage of water.

(iii) (a) Traditional methods like talabs and kunds and modern methods such as rooftop rainwater harvesting can be used to conserve water in the area which Aadarsh visits.

(b) Rainwater harvesting improve water scarcity by capturing and storing rainwater. This stored water could then be used during dry periods, providing a reliable water source for irrigation, drinking and other needs.

(iv) (a) Uneven rainfall distribution in India leads to some areas receiving very little rainfall, making irrigation essential for agriculture. Additionally, India relies heavily on seasonal monsoons. Furthermore, in certain regions, the soil has poor moisture retention, requiring additional water for farming to support crop growth.

(b) Irrigation has helped farmers grow crops year-round and shift to multiple cropping cycles. Irrigation has enabled the cultivation of water-intensive crops like rice, sugarcane and cotton in areas where they couldn't be grown before.

(c) There is a scarcity of surface water in India due to uneven rainfall, with some areas receiving very little rain. Overuse of rivers and reservoirs for irrigation also depletes water supplies.

7

MINERAL AND ENERGY RESOURCES

Minerals

Minerals are natural, solid, inorganic substances found in the Earth, with a specific chemical composition and structure. These are found in three forms i.e. metallic, non-metallic and energy minerals.

Mineral resources are valuable, can be extracted and used for various purposes, such as building and manufacturing.

Major Minerals

Minerals	Distribution	Uses
Iron Ore It is a type of rock from which iron is extracted. It is the backbone of industries. It contains iron minerals in the form of iron oxides, like haematite and magnetite. There are four types of iron ore found in India - Magnetite (Black Ore), Haematite, Limonite and Siderite.	Around 20% of the world's total reserves of iron ore are found in India, particularly in the states of Odisha, Jharkhand, Chhattisgarh, Karnataka, etc. Odisha is the leading producer of iron ore in India.	• It is primarily used for making steel. • Black iron oxide is used as pigments in polishing compounds, medicine and magnetic inks. • Low-grade iron ore is used in manufacturing sponge iron.
Manganese It is an iron-like metal that occurs as a natural oxide. It is a hard and black metal that is used in industries like steel, battery and dye manufacturing industries. India ranks third in the world in Maganese production.	In India, it is mainly found in Odisha, Karnataka, Maharashtra and Madhya Pradesh. Odisha is the largest producer of Manganese in India.	• It is commonly used in the steel industry to improve the strength and hardness of steel. • It is used in industries for manufacturing dry-cell batteries, coloured glass, etc. • It is used in industries for manufacturing bleaching powder and insecticides.
Copper It is a reddish-brown metal that is highly conductive of electricity and heat. It occurs in three main combinations sulphides, oxides and carbonates.	In India, Madhya Pradesh, Rajasthan, Jharkhand are the leading producers of copper.	• It is used in the electrical industry due to its property of good electrical conductivity. • It is a good conductor of heat, so it is extremely useful in refrigeration, utensils and wires. • It is alloyed with aluminium to make duralumin.
Bauxite It is the ore of aluminium. It is mainly found in tertiary deposits.	In India, Odisha, Chhattisgarh, Jharkhand and Gujarat are the major producers of Bauxite. Odisha is the largest producer of bauxite in India.	• It is a good conductor of electricity hence, it is used in the electrical industry. • It is used for making aircraft, ships and utensils, as it is light in weight and resists rust. • It is also used in making mirrors, headlight reflectors and in telescopes.

Energy Resources

Resources which are used for generating power or energy are called Energy resources. These resources are categorised into Conventional and Non-Conventional energy sources.

Conventional Sources

- These are traditional sources that have been used for a long time.
- These resources cannot be renewed or replenished. They are exhaustible in nature. Examples - Coal, Petroleum, Natural gas, etc.

Resources	Distribution	Advantages	Disadvantages
Coal It is a type of fossil fuel found in sedimentary rocks. It is composed of carbon, hydrogen, oxygen, nitrogen and a small amount of sulphur and phosphorus. It is mainly of four types; Anthracite, Bituminous, Lignite and Peat.	In India, coal is found in two rock sequences i.e. Gondwana deposits and Tertiary coal deposits. • **Gondwana deposits** These coal fields are mostly located in Damodar Valley, particularly in the states of West Bengal, Jharkhand, Chhattisgarh, Odisha, etc. Jharia and Raniganj coal fields in West Bengal are the largest coal fields in India. • **Tertiary Coal Deposits** These are found in Assam, Arunachal Pradesh, Meghalaya, Nagaland and Kashmir. The important coal mining areas of these deposits are Darangiri and Cherrapunji in Meghalaya, Makum in Assam, Namchik in Arunachal and Kalakot in Jammu and Kashmir.	• It is also used for making iron and steel. • It produces high energy upon its combustion. • It is used in thermal power plants as raw material.	• Carbon emissions due to the burning of coal harm the environment. • The production and transportation costs of coal is very high. • Due to its mining, deforestation and land degradation take place and habitats of wildlife also get affected.
Petroleum Petroleum is a natural liquid found beneath the surface of the Earth and is made up of hydrocarbons. It is known as Liquid gold due to its scarcity and multiple uses.	Mumbai High, Oilfields of Eastern and Western Region are the main petroleum deposits in India. Mathura, Jamnagar, Haldia, Barauni, Panipat, Refineries, etc. are the major refineries in India. Digboi in Assam is the oldest and the biggest oilfield in India.	• It has a large amount of energy per unit, making it an efficient fuel. • It can be transported easily through pipelines, ships and tankers. • It is used widely in many industries, mainly the petrochemical, fertilisers and chemical industries.	• It is inflammable and can readily catch fire. • On burning, it emits large amounts of Carbon dioxide (CO_2) and other harmful gases. • It is toxic to humans, animals and other forms of wildlife like plants and animals.
Natural Gas It is a naturally occurring hydro-carbon gas consisting primarily of methane and a small amount of propane and ethane. It is a fossil fuel used as a source of energy for heating, cooking and electricity generation.	Natural gas reserves in India are found in Andhra Pradesh (Krishna-Godavari basin), Gujarat (Khambhat Basin), Rajasthan (Jaisalmer), Tamil Nadu, Assam and Tripura. The Mumbai region accounts for about 70% of the country's total gas reserves.	• It is affordable and eco-friendly. • It is an efficient energy source having high calorific value. • It has multiple uses, e.g. generating electric power, powering vehicles, fertilisers, etc.	• It is a non-renewable source of energy. • It has limited reserves. • Leakage of natural gas cannot be detected and can cause fire or explosions.

Hydel Power

- Hydropower or hydel power is derived from the energy of falling water or fast-running water.
- It is a source used for generating electricity. It is a cheap, clean, environmentally friendly and renewable source of energy.

Importance of Hydel Power

- Hydel power is a renewable source of energy, harnessing water flow to generate electricity without depleting natural resources or emitting harmful pollutants.
- It provides a consistent and reliable source of electricity, especially in regions with abundant water resources, and can meet peak energy demands.
- Compared to fossil fuels, hydel power has a lower environmental impact, as it reduces greenhouse gas emissions and air pollution, making it a sustainable energy source.

Bhakra Nangal Dam

Major Dams Generating Hydel Power

The major dams used to generate hydel power are

Bhakra Nangal Dam

- It is located on the Satluj river in Himachal Pradesh. It is the second-highest dam in India and is part of a multipurpose river valley project.
- The power generated from Bhakra dam is supplied to Punjab, Haryana, Rajasthan, Himachal Pradesh, Chandigarh and Delhi.

Hirakud Dam

- The Hirakud dam is located on the Mahanadi river in Odisha. It is one of the longest earthen dams in the world.
- It is also a multipurpose dam and serves purposes such as irrigation, hydropower generation and water supply.
- The Hirakud dam benefits the areas in the state of Odisha, particularly the districts of Sambalpur, Bolangir, Bargarh and Jharsuguda.
- It provides irrigation to a large area, helps in flood control, and generates hydroelectric power.

Non-Conventional Sources

- Non-conventional or renewable sources of energy are automatically replenished by nature, i.e. solar energy, water, tides, wind, air, etc.
- These sources include solar energy, wind energy, tidal energy, geothermal energy, nuclear energy and biogas.

Resources	Generation	Advantages	Disadvantages
Solar Energy Energy produced through the Sunlight is called solar energy.	Solar energy can be generated through the following • **Solar Cookers** These are devices that use sunlight to cook food. They capture and concentrate sunlight using mirrors or reflective surfaces to heat up a cooking container. • **Photovoltaic Cells** These are made up of semiconductor materials and convert solar energy into electricity. Hence, they are also called solar cells. • **Solar Heater** It is a device that captures Sunlight to heat water.	• It can be used in heating, drying and cooking. • Large amounts of free and clean energy can be produced due to the high availability of Sunlight. • It saves fossil fuels and is used to produce large amounts of electricity.	• Cannot be created during night. • The power generation is reduced during times of cloud cover. • Installation is quite expensive.

Resources	Generation	Advantages	Disadvantages
Wind Energy Energy produced through wind is called wind energy.	It is generated by using windmills. The blades of windmills rotate because of the wind and generate electricity.In India, large wind farms are found in Tamil Nadu, Andhra Pradesh, Gujarat, etc.	• It is cost-effective and a clean energy source. • It has a low operational cost. • It doesn't emit harmful emissions or pollutants, helping to reduce greenhouse gases.	• Depends upon local winds. • Wind turbines can pose a threat to birds and bats.
Tidal Energy It is a form of renewable energy generated from the movement of ocean tides.	Tidal energy is generated by the movement of oceanic tides, which can be used to generate electricity by using turbines or other technologies.	• It is a cleaner and safer form of energy. • The maintenance of tidal plants is quite low. • It is more efficient compared to solar or wind energy.	• May disupt the natural movement of marine animals. • Intermittent energy source. • May be far away from the exact location where it is needed.
Geothermal Energy The heat generated from the Earth's internal sources, such as hot water or steam from beneath the surface is called geothermal energy.	It is generated when water seeps into the Earth's crust through cracks and gets heated due to the high temperature inside. The heated water becomes steam.	• It is highly efficient and requires low maintenance. • It involves simple and less complex procedures. • It has low emissions of sulphur, carbon dioxide and greenhouse gases.	• Leads to release of hydrogen sulphides. • Possibility of depletion. • High investment and installation cost.
Nuclear Power The main raw material used for generation of atomic energy is Uranium, Plutonium, Beryllium and Thorium.	The first nuclear power station was developed in Tarapur. Other plants are in Kalpakkam (T.N.) Rana Pratap Sagar (Kota), Narora (U.P.) Kakrapara (Gujarat)	• Less amount of fuel is required. • Alternative to fossil fuel. • Less use of fossil fuel lowers the greenhouse gas emission.	• Once used, disposal is a problem. • High cost. • Nuclear accidents. • Radioactive waste.
Biogas It refers to a mixture of different gases produced by the decomposition of organic matter in the absence of oxygen. It is composed of carbon dioxide, methane, hydrogen and hydrogen sulphide.	Biogas is generated in a digester tank which is filled with bacteria. The bacteria absorb the organic waste and give flammable gas.	• It is a clean and non-polluting source of energy. • It helps reduce soil and water pollution. • It is cost-effective and can be used for heating, electricity and many other operations.	• High cost of production. • Requires large area for installation.

EXAM ORIENTED QUESTIONS

TYPE - 1

1 Mark

Multiple Choice Questions

Q.1 Minerals are deposited and accumulated in the stratified form of .... rocks.

(a) sedimentary (b) igneous
(c) metamorphic (d) sandstone

Ans. (a) sedimentary

Q.2 Minerals need to be conserved because they are ....

(a) expensive
(b) hard to find
(c) exhaustible
(d) None of the above

Ans. (c) exhaustible

Q.3 Siderite and Limonite are the types of which mineral?

(a) Iron ore (b) Copper
(c) Bauxite (d) Manganese

Ans. (a) Iron ore

Q.4 Which of the following states is one of the leading producers of iron ore in India?

(a) Assam (b) Odisha
(c) Rajasthan (d) Tamil Nadu

Ans. (b) Odisha

Q.5 Which of the following is the best quality iron ore and contains around 70% of iron content?

(a) Limonite (b) Siderite
(c) Haematite (d) Magnetite

Ans. (d) Magnetite

Q.6 Rourkela Steel plant was built with the cooperation of .... **(ICSE Specimen 2023)**

(a) USSR (b) Germany
(c) Japan (d) France

Ans. (b) Germany

Q.7 Which of the following is not a centre for the iron and steel industry? **(ICSE 2024)**

(a) Bhilai
(b) Bengaluru
(c) Rourkela
(d) Vishakhapatnam

Ans. (b) Bengaluru

Q.8 What is the primary use of manganese in industry?

(a) Construction of power plants
(b) Manufacturing of steel
(c) Production of plastics
(d) Extraction of aluminium

Ans. (b) Manufacturing of steel

Q.9 Which of the following states is the leading producer of manganese in India?

(a) Uttar Pradesh (b) Punjab
(c) Andhra Pradesh (d) Madhya Pradesh

Ans. (d) Madhya Pradesh

Q.10 Kendujhar and Sundergarh mines in Odisha are related to which of the following minerals?

(a) Copper (b) Manganese
(c) Bauxite (d) Iron ore

Ans. (b) Manganese

Q.11 Which of the following is not a use of manganese?

(a) Cement manufacturing
(b) Alloy manufacturing
(c) Making insecticides
(d) Manufacturing of coloured glasses

Ans. (a) Cement manufacturing

Q.12 Khetri mines in Rajasthan are related to which of the following minerals?

(a) Iron ore (b) Manganese
(c) Copper (d) Bauxite

Ans. (c) Copper

Q.13 If Ravi wants to produce brass in his manufacturing firm, which of the following metals he should mix with copper?

(a) Zinc (b) Tin (c) Aluminium (d) Iron

Ans. (a) Zinc

Exp. Brass is an alloy which is produced by mixing copper and zinc.

Q.14 To make duralumin, copper is alloyed with which metal?

(a) Zinc (b) Aluminium
(c) Iron (d) Bauxite

Ans. (b) Aluminium

Exp. To make duralumin, copper is alloyed with aluminium. Duralumin is widely used in the aerospace, automotive and construction industries due to its high strength and corrosion resistance.

Q.15 Which of the following states is the leading producer of copper in India?

(a) Madhya Pradesh (b) Assam
(c) Karnataka (d) Kerala

Ans. (a) Madhya Pradesh

Q.16 Bauxite is the ore of **(ICSE 2024)**

(a) Aluminium (b) Copper (c) Manganese (d) Iron

Ans. (a) Aluminium

Q.17 Which of the following states is the leading producer of Bauxite in India?

(a) Odisha (b) Karnataka
(c) Tamil Nadu (d) Maharashtra

Ans. (a) Odisha

Q.18 Bolangir and Koraput mines are related to which of the following minerals?

(a) Iron ore (b) Bauxite
(c) Copper (d) Manganese

Ans. (b) Bauxite

Q.19 Which of the following is not a use of bauxite?

(a) Used in making surgical equipment.
(b) Used in producing aluminium.
(c) Used in shipbuilding.
(d) Used in electrical industry.

Ans. (a) Used in making surgical equipment.

Q.20 Read the table and identify the pair that is correctly matched.

	Mines	State
P.	Singhbhum	Jharkhand
Q.	Malanjkhand	Odisha
R.	Ratnagiri	Andhra Pradesh
S.	Badampahar	Madhya Pradesh

(a) P (b) Q (c) R (d) S

Ans. (a) P

Q.21 Which of the following is an example of a conventional source of energy?

(a) Geothermal (b) Dams (c) Biomass (d) Wind

Ans. (b) Dams

Q.22 Which type of coal is referred to as industrial coal? **(ICSE Specimen 2024, 2025)**

(a) Peat (b) Lignite
(c) Bituminous (d) Anthracite

Ans. (c) Bituminous

Exp. Bituminous coal is called industrial coal due to its high carbon content and heating value which makes it ideal for power generation, steel production, industrial uses, etc.

Q.23 .... is the largest coalfield in India. **(ICSE Specimen 2023)**

(a) Raniganj (b) Jharia
(c) Bokaro (d) Karanpura

Ans. (a) Raniganj

Q.24 .... is considered the highest grade coal.

(a) Peat
(b) Lignite
(c) Bituminous
(d) Anthracite

Ans. (d) Anthracite

Q.25 .... is considered the lowest grade coal.

(a) Peat (b) Bituminous
(c) Lignite (d) Anthracite

Ans. (c) Lignite

Q.26 Petroleum is called 'Liquid Gold'

(a) because it is as rare as gold and has multiple uses.
(b) because it is found in the same locations as gold and is used in jewellery.
(c) because it has the same colour as gold when refined.
(d) because it is a renewable resource with an unlimited supply.

Ans. (a) because it is as rare as gold and has multiple uses.

Q.27 Balaghat : Manganese : : Mumbai High : .... **(ICSE 2025)**

(a) Copper (b) Coal
(c) Iron Ore (d) Petroleum

Ans. (d) Petroleum

Q.28 Which is the largest oil refinery in India?

(a) Mathura (b) Barauni
(c) Haldia (d) Jamnagar

Ans. (d) Jamnagar

Q.29 Which of the following is the oldest oilfield in India?

(a) Ankaleshwar (b) Digboi
(c) Naharkatiya (d) Aliabet

Ans. (b) Digboi

Q.30 Identify the source of energy that leads to pollution. **(ICSE 2024)**

(a) Tidal energy (b) Wind energy
(c) Natural gas (d) Geothermal energy

Ans. (c) Natural gas

Q.31 Which of the following is the main constituent of the natural gas?

(a) Propane (b) Butane
(c) Ethane (d) Methane

Ans. (d) Methane

Exp. Methane makes up about 70-90% of the composition of natural gas.

Q.32 In India, where are the largest natural gas reserves located?

(a) Assam (b) Rajasthan (c) Mumbai (d) Karnataka

Ans. (c) Mumbai

Q.33 Photovoltaic cells are made up of ....

(a) Aluminium (b) Silicon
(c) Boron (d) Polonium

Ans. (b) Silicon

Exp. Photovoltaic cells are made of silicon because it is abundant, efficient in converting sunlight into electricity and has excellent semiconductor properties, making it ideal for solar energy generation.

Q.34 Identify the state which is the leading producer of the energy type shown in the figure.

(a) Andhra Pradesh (b) Kerala
(c) Tamil Nadu (d) Gujarat

Ans. (d) Gujarat

Exp. Gujarat is the leading producer of wind energy shown in the figure. Gujarat's long coastline provides strong and consistent wind currents that are ideal for wind energy generation.

Q.35 What could be the possible environmental concern that can be associated with tidal energy?

(a) Noise pollution from turbines
(b) Overfishing
(c) Disruption of marine ecosystems
(d) Large-scale use of freshwater

Ans. (c) Disruption of marine ecosystems

Q.36 Geothermal energy can be used for which of the following applications?

(a) Residential heating (b) Generating electricity
(c) Industrial processes (d) All of these

Ans. (d) All of these

Q.37 Which of the following is not a typical raw material for biogas production?

(a) Animal manure (b) Food waste
(c) Coal (d) Crop residues

Ans. (c) Coal

Exp. Coal is unsuitable for biogas production as it is non-biodegradable, lacks organic compounds for methane production and cannot undergo microbial anaerobic digestion.

Q.38 Identify the correct statements regarding the primary purpose of constructing a dam.

(a) Dams are made to create artificial lakes for recreational activities.
(b) Dams are made to control the flow of rivers and prevent floods.
(c) Dams are made to store water for future.
(d) Dams are made to conserve aquatic life.

Ans. (b) Dams are made to control the flow of rivers and prevent floods.

Q.39 On which river is the Hirakud dam situated?

(a) Godavari (b) Krishna
(c) Cauvery (d) Mahanadi

Ans. (d) Mahanadi

TYPE - 2 — 1 Mark

Assertion-Reason Questions

Q.1 **Assertion** (A) Iron ore mining in India is primarily concentrated in the states of Odisha, Chhattisgarh, and Jharkhand.

Reason (R) These states have large reserves of high-quality iron ore, especially haematite and magnetite.

(a) Both A and R are true and R is the correct explanation of A
(b) Both A and R are true, but R is not the correct explanation of A
(c) A is true, but R is false
(d) A is false, but R is true

Ans. (a) Both A and R are true, and R is the correct explanation of A

Q.2 **Assertion** (A) Copper is widely used in electrical wiring.

Reason (R) Copper has high electrical conductivity, which makes it an ideal material for electrical cables and wires.

(a) Both A and R are true and R is the correct explanation of A
(b) Both A and R are true, but R is not the correct explanation of A
(c) A is true, but R is false
(d) A is false, but R is true

Ans. (a) Both A and R are true, and R is the correct explanation of A

Q.3 Assertion (A) Coal releases Carbon dioxide which affects the environment leading to greenhouse Gas emissions and the global warming effect.

Reason (R) Most of the coal found in India is of poor quality.

(a) Both A and R are true and R is the correct explanation of A

(b) Both A and R are true, but R is not the correct explanation of A

(c) A is true, but R is false

(d) A is false, but R is true

Ans. (b) Both A and R are true, but R is not the correct explanation of A

Q.4 Assertion (A) Coal is used extensively in power plants to generate electricity.

Reason (R) Coal is used in power plants because it is a renewable source of energy.

(a) Both A and R are true and R is the correct explanation of A

(b) Both A and R are true, but R is not the correct explanation of A

(c) A is true, but R is false

(d) A is false, but R is true

Ans. (c) A is true, but R is false

Q.5 Assertion (A) Solar energy is generated using photovoltaic cells.

Reason (R) Photovoltaic cells convert solar radiation into electricity.

(a) Both A and R are true and R is the correct explanation of A

(b) Both A and R are true, but R is not the correct explanation of A

(c) A is true, but R is false

(d) A is false, but R is true

Ans. (a) Both A and R are true, and R is the correct explanation of A

Q.6 Assertion (A) Hydroelectric dams use steam generated from boiling water to turn turbines and generate electricity.

Reason (R) Hydroelectric plants convert the potential energy of water into kinetic energy to generate electricity through turbines.

(a) Both A and R are true and R is the correct explanation of A

(b) Both A and R are true, but R is not the correct explanation of A

(c) A is true, but R is false

(d) A is false, but R is true

Ans. (d) A is false, but R is true

TYPE - 3 — 2 Marks

Short Answer Type Questions

Q.1 With reference to minerals, answer the following.

(i) Define minerals.

(ii) Name two ferrous minerals.

Ans. (i) Minerals are the combination of two or more than two elements through definite chemical composition which are formed by inorganic processes.

(ii) Nickel and Manganese

Q.2 With reference to ore, answer the following.

(i) Define Ore.

(ii) Name any two iron ores.

Ans. (i) A naturally occurring solid material from which a valuable metallic mineral can be extracted profitably is called 'Ore'.

(ii) Two iron ores are Haematite and Magnetite.

Q.3 Give the names of four important types of iron ore found in India. **(ICSE 2017)**

Ans. Four important iron ore found in India are

(i) Magnetite (ii) Haematite

(iii) Limonite (iv) Siderite

Q.4 With reference to the iron ore, answer the following. **(ICSE 2020)**

(i) Why is iron ore called the backbone of our modern industry?

(ii) Two uses of iron ore.

Ans. (i) Iron ore is called the backbone of modern industry because

(a) It is the main source material for producing iron and steel, which are crucial for the growth and operation of numerous industries.

(b) This sector has helped in the generation of several small-scale industries supporting the power, transport and communication industries in India.

(ii) Two uses of iron ore are

(a) It is used to make steel which is essential for construction, manufacturing, transportation, and various other industries.

(b) It is used to create tools, machinery and equipment needed for industrial operations, agriculture and infrastructure development.

Q.5 What grade of iron-ore is mostly mined in India? Name two leading iron-ore producing states. **(ICSE Semester II 2022)**

Ans. Iron-ore like haematite and magnetite is mostly mined in India. Odisha and Jharkhand are the leading iron-ore producing states.

Q.6 Ravi is a metallurgist working in a steel manufacturing company. He is responsible for ensuring that the steel produced is of high quality and meets industry standards. One of Ravi's key tasks involves overseeing the use of manganese in the steel production process.

(i) How does Ravi utilise manganese in the steel production process?

(ii) Besides steel production, what are two other industries in which manganese is used?

Ans. (i) Ravi uses manganese as a deoxidising agent in the steel production process. It prevents the formation of iron oxide during the production of steel, which helps to enhance the strength and hardness of the steel.

(ii) Besides steel production, manganese is used in making lithium-ion and alkaline batteries, and in producing chemicals, such as fertilisers. It is also used in making aluminium and other non-ferrous metals.

Q.7 With reference to minerals, answer the following.

(i) Name two manganese-producing states in India.

(ii) Give any one use of the manganese.

Ans. (i) Odisha and Karnataka are two manganese producing states in India.

(ii) Manganese is used to improve the quality of many alloys, e.g. iron and steel.

Q.8 Give reasons for the following.

(i) Copper is used to make electrical wires.

(ii) Manganese is used to make duralumin.

Ans. (i) Copper is used to make electrical wires because it is an excellent conductor of electricity. Additionally, it is relatively malleable and ductile, allowing it to be easily drawn into thin wires.

(ii) Manganese is used to make duralumin because it enhances the strength, toughness, and resistance to corrosion of the alloy.

Q.9 Name two states where copper is found in India. Mention one use of it. **(ICSE Specimen 2023)**

Ans. Two states where copper is found in India are Rajasthan and Jharkhand.

One use of copper is in electrical wiring due to its excellent conductivity.

Q.10 Give reasons for the following.

(i) Why is copper considered a good conductor of electricity?

(ii) Why copper is used in the utensils industry?

Ans. (i) Copper is considered a good conductor of electricity due to the following reasons

- It has high electrical conductivity, hence it allows electric current to flow through it easily.
- It is malleable and ductile so it can be drawn into wires easily.

(ii) Copper is used in the utensils industry due to the following reasons

- Copper has excellent thermal conductivity, allowing it to heat up rapidly and evenly. This property makes copper utensils perfect for cooking.
- Copper is a strong and durable metal that can withstand high temperatures and heavy use.

Q.11 Give one important use of each of the following.

(i) Bauxite (ii) Iron ore **(ICSE 2015)**

Ans. (i) **Bauxite** It is the main source of aluminium which is lightweight, strong and rust-resistant. Aluminium is mainly used for making automobiles, aircrafts, wagons, coaches and in the shipping industry, etc.

(ii) **Iron ore** It is mainly used to make steel. Raw iron is alloyed with other elements to make good quality steel which is used for construction, automobiles and other forms of transportation, etc.

Q.12 With reference to bauxite, answer the following questions.

(i) Where are the largest bauxite deposits found in India?

(ii) Why is bauxite important for the aluminium industry?

Ans. (i) The largest bauxite deposits in India are found in the states of Odisha and Jharkhand.

(ii) It is the primary source of aluminium, making it essential for aluminium production, which is used in various industries such as construction, transportation and packaging.

Q.13 With reference to coal, answer the following questions. **(ICSE 2016)**

(i) Name any three types of coal found in India.

(ii) Which type of coal is mostly used in iron and steel industries?

Ans. (i) There are four varieties of coal found in India i.e. lignite, peat, bituminous and anthracite.

(ii) Anthracite is mostly used in iron and steel industries.

Q.14 Mention one advantage and one disadvantage of coal found in India. **(ICSE Specimen 2023)**

Ans. One advantage of coal is that coal is easy to burn and produces high energy upon combustion.

One disadvantage of coal found in India is that coal generates carbon emission which is responsible for air pollution.

Q.15 Which are the two different varieties of coal used for domestic purposes and why? **(ICSE 2014)**

Ans. Anthracite and Bituminous are two varieties of coal used for domestic purposes because they have high carbon content and hence best suited as fuel and emits less smoke.

Q.16 Distinguish between anthracite and peat coal.

Ans. The differences between the anthracite and peat coal are as follows

Anthracite Coal	Peat Coal
It has a very high carbon content (around 70%)	It has a very low carbon content (around 40-50%)
It burns with a clean, hot flame, with minimal smoke.	Burns with a lot of smoke and lower heat.
Due to high carbon content it is used in the production of high quality steel.	It is used as a fuel source for heating in rural households.

Q.17 With reference to petroleum, answer the following. **(ICSE 2017)**

(i) An off-shore oil field in the Gulf of Cambay.

(ii) An oil refinery in Bihar.

Ans. (i) Aliabet Island close to Bhavangarh is an off-shore oil field in the Gulf of Cambay.

(ii) Barauni refinery

Q.18 Give two advantages and disadvantages of petroleum.

Ans. Two advantages and disadvantages of petroleum are

Advantages of Petroleum

(i) It has a large amount of energy per unit, making it efficient for fuel.

(ii) It can be transported easily through pipelines, ships and tankers.

Disadvantages of Petroleum

(i) It is a non-renewable source of energy and is inflammable.

(ii) On burning, it emits large amounts of Carbon dioxide (CO_2) and other harmful gases.

Q.19 Give two advantages of using natural gas over coal. **(ICSE Specimen Semester-II 2022)**

Ans. Two advantages of using natural gas over coal are

(i) Natural gas is more eco-friendly than coal.

(ii) It is more efficient than coal plants in generating electricity.

Q.20 Give two advantages and disadvantages of natural gas.

Ans. Two advantages and disadvantages of natural gas are

Advantages of Natural Gas

(i) It is affordable and eco-friendly.

(ii) It is an efficient energy source having high calorific value.

Disadvantages of Natural Gas

(i) It is a non-renewable source of energy with limited reserves.

(ii) Leakage of natural gas cannot be detected and can cause fire or explosions.

Q.21 With reference to solar energy, answer the following questions.

(i) How does solar energy help in reducing environmental pollution?

(ii) Explain the generation of solar energy by photovoltaic cells.

Ans. (i) Solar energy is a type of clean energy. It helps reduce environmental pollution by producing electricity without emitting harmful pollutants such as carbon dioxide, sulphur dioxide, etc.

(ii) Photovoltaic cells generate solar energy by absorbing sunlight, exciting electrons in semiconductor materials, and creating an electric current. This current is converted from DC to AC for use in electrical devices.

Q.22 Distinguish between solar and wind energy.

Ans. The differences between solar and wind energy are as follows

Solar Energy	Wind Energy
It is derived from sunlight using solar panels or photovoltaic cells.	It is generated from the movement of air (wind) through wind turbines.
Available only during daylight hours.	Not dependent on daylight. Only dependent on wind speed and direction.

Q.23 **Distinguish between tidal and geothermal energy.**

Ans. The differences between tidal and geothermal energy are as follows

Tidal Energy	Geothermal Energy
It is generated from the gravitational pull of the Moon and Sun, causing ocean tides.	It is generated from the heat stored beneath the Earth's surface.
Mostly found in coastal areas with significant tidal movements.	Found in regions with volcanic activity or geothermal hot spots.

Q.24 **With the rising price of fossil fuel every passing day, it is very important to develop non-conventional energy resources.**
Bulletin - Department of non-conventional sources of energy **(ICSE 2025)**

(i) Name a non-conventional energy source that can be harnessed by taking advantage of India's vast coastline.

(ii) State one advantage of using geothermal energy.

Ans. (i) A non-conventional energy source that can be harnessed using India's vast coastline is Tidal Energy.

(ii) Geothermal energy is a clean and sustainable source of power, producing minimal pollution and reducing dependence on fossil fuels.

Q.25 **Distinguish between nuclear energy and geothermal energy.**

Ans. The differences between nuclear energy and geothermal energy are as follows

Nuclear Energy	Geothermal Energy
Generates energy through controlled nuclear fission reactions in reactors.	Generates energy by harnessing the Earth's natural heat through geothermal plants.
Produces radioactive waste and requires careful disposal and management.	Produces minimal waste and is considered environmentally friendly.

Q.26 **With reference to nuclear energy, answer the following.**

(i) Explain nuclear energy.

(ii) Give one advantage of using this energy.

Ans. (i) Nuclear energy is the energy released during nuclear fission, a process where the nucleus of an atom is split into smaller parts, releasing a large amount of energy in the form of heat. This heat is used to produce steam, which drives turbines connected to electricity generators.

(ii) One advantage is that a small amount of nuclear fuel can generate large amounts of energy.

Q.27 **With reference to biogas, answer the following.**

(i) What is biogas?

(ii) Give one advantage of using biogas.

Or **(i) How is biogas formed?**

(ii) Mention any one advantage of biogas over other non-conventional energy resources. **(ICSE 2025)**

Ans. (i) Biogas is a renewable gas produced from the breakdown of organic waste like food scraps, animal manure, and plant material. It mainly consists of methane.

(ii) It is a clean and non-polluting source of energy and is also cost-effective.

Q.28 **Give two advantages of using biogas as a source of power.** **(ICSE 2019)**

Ans. Two advantages of using biogas as a source of power are

(i) Biogas produces fewer greenhouse gas emissions compared to fossil fuels, helping to reduce air pollution and mitigate climate change.

(ii) It helps in managing organic waste by converting it into useful energy, reducing landfill waste and minimising environmental pollution.

Q.29 **Name the following.**

(i) A metallic mineral for which the Balaghat district of Madhya Pradesh is famous.

(ii) The multi-purpose project based on the River Sutlej.

Ans. (i) Copper (ii) Bhakra Nangal

Q.30 **"Dams play a crucial role in providing water for irrigation, power generation, and flood control." Explain.**

Ans. Dams store water for irrigation, ensuring consistent crop growth, generating hydroelectric power through water flow, and helping control floods by regulating water levels. These functions contribute to agricultural productivity, energy supply, and protection against natural disasters.

Q.31 **Mention two advantages of using non-conventional sources of power.** **(ICSE Specimen 2018)**

Ans. Two advantages of using non-conventional sources of power are

(i) They are renewable and inexhaustible sources of energy.

(ii) They are available at low cost.

Q.32 **Name the following.** **(ICSE 2023)**

(i) The non-conventional energy source that has the most widespread potential usage in India.

(ii) A mineral used to generate nuclear energy.

Ans. (i) Solar energy (ii) Uranium

TYPE - 4 — 3 Marks

Long Answer Type Questions

Q.1 With reference to minerals, answer the following.

(i) Mention two reasons why minerals are important.

(ii) Name one area in Odisha and one in Chhattisgarh, where iron-ore is mined.

Ans. (i) Minerals are important due to the following reasons

(a) They are used to make things like buildings, machines, etc. which help economies grow.

(b) Minerals like coal, oil and natural gas are crucial for generating electricity and fuel.

(ii) Odisha Keonjhar; Chhattisgarh Bailadila

Q.2 Mention some important iron ore-producing regions found in India. Explain all of them.

Ans. The important iron ore-producing regions are

- **Odisha** Iron ore found in Odisha contains 55 to 68% iron content and belongs to the haematite variety. Important mines are located at Gorumahisani, Sulaipet and Badampahar in Mayurbhanj district, Kiruburuaburu in Kendujhar district and Bonai in Sundergarh district.
- **Karnataka** It has large reserves of haematite and magnetite. Important mines are located at Donai Malai in the Bellary-Hospet region, Baba Budan Hills in the Chikmagalur district and Kudremukh in the Chitradurg district.
- **Chhattisgarh** Important mines are located at Dalli Rajhara in Durg district and Bailadilla in Bastar district.

Q.3 With reference to manganese, answer the following.

(i) Mention any two uses of manganese.

(ii) Give the names of some regions where manganese is found in India.

Ans. (i) Uses of manganese are as follows

- It is used to prepare alloys or mixtures of different metals to acquire special properties for the minerals.
- It is used in industries for manufacturing bleaching powder and insecticides.

(ii) In India, most of the manganese is found in Bonai, Kendujhar of Odisha, Balaghat-Chhindwara-Nimar-Mandla and Jhabua districts of Madhya Pradesh, Dharwar, Ballari, Bolgaum (Belagavi) of Karnataka, etc.

Q.4 Explain the distribution of copper in India. (Any 3)

Ans. The distribution of copper in India is as follows

- In Jharkhand, Singhbhum and Hazaribagh districts have good reserves of copper.
- Malanjkhand copper belt and the Balaghat district have rich reserves of copper in Madhya Pradesh.
- Khetri copper belt, Jhunjhunu and Dariba in Alwar district have important reserves of copper in Rajasthan.
- Bhandara, Chandrapur, Gadchiroli and Nagpur districts are copper-producing regions in Maharashtra.
- Guntur, Prakasam and Kurnool are the copper-producing regions of Andhra Pradesh.

Q.5 Answer the following. **(ICSE Semester II 2022)**

(i) State one industrial use of copper.

(ii) Name the metal that toughens steel and makes it rust-proof.

(iii) Name the state that is the leading producer of Manganese.

Ans. (i) Copper is used in the electrical industry in the form of copper wires and numerous kinds of electrical equipment.

(ii) Manganese is used in steel industries to make steel tough and rust-proof.

(iii) Madhya Pradesh

Q.6 With reference to the minerals and energy resources, answer the following. **(ICSE 2018)**

(i) Name the metal obtained from bauxite. Give one use of the metal mentioned by you.

(ii) Which multipurpose project provides power to both Punjab and Himachal Pradesh?

Ans. (i) Aluminium metal is obtained from bauxite. Aluminium is used in a huge variety of products including cans, foils, kitchen utensils, airplane parts, etc.

(ii) The Bhakra Nangal multipurpose dam provides power to both Punjab and Himachal Pradesh. It is built on the River Sutlej.

Q.7 Mention three disadvantages of conventional sources of energy.

Ans. The three disadvantages of conventional sources of energy are

(i) These are non-renewable sources of energy.

(ii) These are not environment-friendly and release harmful gases.

(iii) These are exhaustible sources of energy.

Q.8 Mention three advantages that non-conventional energy resources have over conventional energy resources.

Ans. The three advantages of non-conventional energy resources over conventional energy resources are as follows

(i) Non-conventional energy resources, like solar and wind, produce little to no pollution, whereas conventional energy sources like coal and petroleum contribute to air pollution and climate change.

(ii) Non-conventional energy sources are renewable and sustainable, as they rely on natural processes, unlike conventional energy resources which are finite and depleting over time.

(iii) After initial installation, non-conventional energy systems, such as solar panels and wind turbines, have lower operating and maintenance costs compared to conventional systems, which require ongoing fuel supply and maintenance.

Q.9 Distinguish between conventional and non-conventional energy sources.

Ans. The differences between conventional and non-conventional energy sources are as follows

Conventional	Non-conventional
These are the traditional energy sources that have been in use for a long time.	These are the new and emerging energy sources that are more sustainable and eco-friendly.
These are limited and depleting over time.	These are abundant and widely available in most regions.
Examples are coal, petroleum, natural gas, nuclear power.	Examples are solar energy, wind energy, geothermal energy, tidal energy and biomass.

Q.10 Explain any three types of coal found in India. **(ICSE 2016)**

Ans. There are mainly three types of coal found in India - Anthracite, Bituminous, Lignite.

Anthracite Coal

- It is a hard and compressed variety of coal with the highest carbon content of 70-80% and has a high calorific value.
- In India, it is found only in Jammu and Kashmir.

Bituminous Coal

- It is a black, hard, brittle and compact coal with 50% to 60% of carbon content in it.
- In India, it is found in Odisha, Jharkhand, Chhattisgarh, West Bengal and Madhya Pradesh.

Lignite Coal

- It is a soft brown combustible coal with 40-50% carbon content.
- In India, it is found in Tamil Nadu, Rajasthan, Kerala, West Bengal, etc.

Q.11 Give three disadvantages of using coal. **(ICSE Semester II 2022)**

Ans. Three advantages of using coal are

(i) Coal emits deadly pollutants into the air including mercury, arsenic and sulphur dioxide.

(ii) The sulphur dioxide emitted by coal also causes acid rain.

(iii) Coal creates large amounts of greenhouse gases that contribute to global warming.

Q.12 State an important use of **(ICSE 2017)**

(i) Manganese (ii) Coal
(iii) Aluminium

Ans. (i) **Manganese** It is the most important mineral for making steel.

(ii) **Coal** It is the main source of power generation in India.

(iii) **Aluminium** It is used for packing in various forms such as cans, foils, tubes and bottle tops.

Q.13 Name the following. **(ICSE 2015)**

(i) Largest oil refinery in the public sector.
(ii) State the largest producer of coal.
(iii) Best variety of iron ore.

Ans. (i) Kochi refinery is the largest oil refinery in the public sector in India.

(ii) Jharkhand is the largest producer of coal in India.

(iii) The best variety of iron ore is magnetite which constitutes the best quality of iron ore.

Q.14 Give three advantages and three disadvantages of Petroleum.

Ans. The three advantages and three disadvantages of petroleum are as follows

Advantages

(i) Petroleum has a high calorific value, making it efficient for use in transportation and industry.

(ii) It has multiple uses and various other products can be formed like gasoline, diesel, kerosene and in petrochemical industries for producing plastics and chemicals.

(iii) It can be transported easily through pipelines, ships and tankers.

Disadvantages

(i) The combustion of petroleum releases greenhouse gases, leading to air pollution and global warming.

(ii) Accidental oil spills can cause severe environmental damage to marine and coastal ecosystems.

(iii) It is a non-renewable source of energy and is inflammable.

Q.15 Give a reason for each of the following. **(ICSE 2025)**

(i) Iron ore is called a versatile mineral.

(ii) Windmills set up on agricultural lands are beneficial to farmers.

(iii) Coal is the most preferred source of energy in Indian industries.

Ans. (i) Iron ore is called a versatile mineral because it is the primary raw material for making steel, which is used in various industries like construction, transportation, machinery and infrastructure development.

(ii) Windmills set up on agricultural lands are beneficial to farmers because they generate additional income for farmers through land lease payments while allowing them to continue farming activities beneath the wind turbines.

(iii) Coal is the most preferred source of energy in Indian industries because it is abundantly available, affordable and provides a reliable energy source for industries like steel, cement and power generation.

Q.16 Give a geographic reason for each of the following. **(ICSE 2015)**

(i) Port cities have their refineries.

(ii) Petroleum is called a fossil fuel.

(iii) Coal is called a versatile material.

Ans. (i) Port cities have refineries because they provide easy access to import crude oil via ships, facilitating efficient transportation. Also, the closeness to shipping routes helps in the quick export of refined products.

(ii) Petroleum is called a fossil fuel because it is formed from the remains of ancient plants and animals that lived millions of years ago. These remains of plants and animals, over millions of years, changed into petroleum due to heat and pressure deep under the Earth's surface.

(iii) Coal is called a versatile material because it can be used in various ways, such as for energy production, industrial processes and making steel. It can also be converted into liquid fuels and chemicals.

Q.17 Tanu performed a web search about the petroleum reserves in India. She found that there are few reserves of petroleum in India which are mostly located along the coast in Mumbai High and Gujarat or in the North-East in Assam.

(i) Mention two reasons behind the location of petroleum reserves in the above areas.

(ii) Name some regions in India which are known for petroleum reserves.

Ans. (i) Two reasons behind the location of petroleum reserves in the above areas are

(a) Most of the petroleum occurrences in India are associated with anticlines and fault traps in the rock formations of the tertiary age.

(b) In regions of folding, anticlines or domes, it occurs where oil is trapped in the crest of the upfold.

(ii) In India, some common petroleum reserves found are Mumbai high, Gujarat, Assam, etc.

Q.18 (i) Mention two advantages of nuclear power.

(ii) What is the advantage of using solar energy in place of the conventional sources of energy? **(ICSE Semester II 2022)**

Ans. (i) The advantages of nuclear power are

(a) It is one of the most low-carbon energy sources.

(b) It is reliable and cost-effective.

(ii) The main advantage of using solar energy is its sustainability and eco-friendliness. Unlike conventional sources like coal, oil and gas, solar energy is renewable, non-polluting and helps reduce greenhouse gas emissions, combating climate change. It also lowers energy costs over time, reduces dependence on fossil fuels and requires minimal maintenance after installation.

Q.19 Mention two advantages of using natural gas over petroleum. Name an area where natural gas is found.

Ans. Two advantages of using natural gas over petroleum are as follows

(i) Natural gas is a cleaner fuel. It is less harmful to the environment than petroleum as it has less carbon dioxide emissions.

(ii) It can easily stored and transferred through pipelines.

An area where natural gas is found is Mumbai.

Q.20 Give answer of the following questions. **(ICSE 2020)**

(i) Mention one disadvantage of using natural gas as a source of power.

(ii) How is the residue from a biogas plant put to use?

(iii) Why is the use of alternative sources of energy becoming essential in modern time?

Ans. (i) Natural gas is explosive and can cause a fire hazard if the pipeline bursts.

(ii) The residue left out in the biogas plant is slurry which is essentially used in the manure.

(iii) As the consumption of energy grows, the population depends more and more on fossil fuels such as coal, oil and gas day by day. Thus, there is a need to use alternative sources of energy.

Q.21

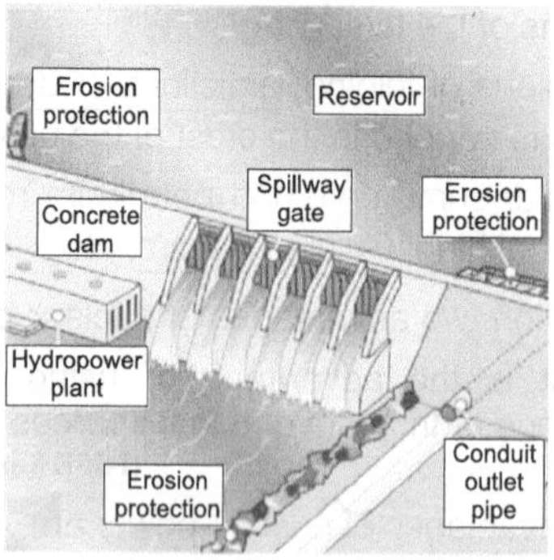

(i) Identify the type of energy being generated in the picture given above. **(ICSE 2025)**

(ii) State why this type of energy is cheaper in the long run.

(iii) Name a power project associated with the generation of this energy in the northern part of India.

Ans. (i) The type of energy being generated in the picture is Hydroelectric Energy.

(ii) This type of energy is cheaper in the long run because

- It uses renewable water resources, which do not require fuel costs.
- Hydroelectric power plants have low operational and maintenance costs after initial construction. (any one point)

(iii) A power project associated with the generation of this energy in Northern India is the Bhakra Nangal Hydroelectric Project on the Sutlej river.

Q.22 Mention three advantages of Hydroelectric power over petroleum and coal.

Ans. Three advantages of Hydro-electric power over petroleum and coal are

(i) Hydroelectric power generates electricity without emitting pollutants or greenhouse gases, unlike petroleum and coal, which contribute to air pollution and climate change.

(ii) It is a renewable energy source, while petroleum and coal are non-renewable resources that will eventually be depleted.

(iii) Its operational costs are relatively low compared to petroleum and coal plants, which require ongoing fuel and maintenance.

Q.23 With reference to Bhakra Nangal project, answer the following.

(i) State any two features of this project.

(ii) Which man-made lake is associated with this project?

Ans. (i) Two features of the Bhakra Nangal project are as follows

(a) The Bhakra Nangal project is designed for irrigation, hydroelectric power generation and flood control.

(b) It is located on the Sutlej river in Himachal Pradesh and is one of the largest dams in the country.

(ii) Gobind Sagar lake is associated with this project.

Q.24 Give a reason for each of the following. **(ICSE 2019)**

(i) Odisha has benefitted greatly from the Hirakud project.

(ii) Copper is used to make electric wires.

(iii) India's location is advantageous for the generation of solar power.

Ans. (i) Odisha is benefitted from the Hirakud project as water from the Hirakud dam is used in various industries, e.g. in minerals processing and thermal power plants.

(ii) Copper is a good conductor of heat and electricity, so it is extremely useful in refrigeration, utensils and in wires.

(iii) India's location is advantageous for the generation of solar power as the country receives adequate solar radiation for 300 clear and sunny days. India is located North of the Equator which helps to increase the amount of sunlight.

Q.25 Unlike conventional energy sources, non-conventional energy is environmentally friendly, producing little to no pollution and having a minimal impact on natural resources. As concerns over climate change and depleting fossil fuels grow, non-conventional energy sources are becoming increasingly important in meeting global energy needs while promoting a cleaner, more sustainable future. ***Source - www.business-standard.com***

(i) What is a major advantage of using solar energy as a non-conventional source of energy?

(ii) How does wind energy contribute to reducing environmental pollution?

Ans. (i) A major advantage of solar energy is that it is renewable, abundant and environmentally friendly, producing no pollution or greenhouse gases while generating electricity.

(ii) Wind energy generates electricity without producing harmful emissions of pollutants, making it a clean, renewable energy source that helps reduce reliance on fossil fuels and lower carbon emissions.

TYPE - 5   10 Marks

Structured Questions

Q.1 (i) (a) Name any three varieties of coal produced in India. **(ICSE 2024) (2)**

(b) Name the variety of coal widely used in the iron and steel industries of India.

(ii) (a) Name the state that is the largest producer of iron ore in India. **(2)**

(b) Name any one mining area of iron ore from the state mentioned by you.

(iii) (a) Mention two ways in which the Hirakud dam has helped the people of Odisha. **(3)**

(b) Across which river is the Hirakud dam built?

(iv) Give reasons for each of the following. **(3)**

(a) Geothermal energy is not popular in India.

(b) Solar energy is gaining popularity.

(c) Petroleum is considered a harmful source of energy.

Ans. (i) (a) Anthracite, Bituminous and Lignite are the three varieties of coal produced in India.

(b) The variety of coal widely used in the iron and steel industries of India is coking coal. It is essential for producing coke, which is used in blast furnaces to make steel.

(ii) (a) Odisha is the largest producer of iron ore in India.

(b) Barbil-Joda (Odisha)/ Bailadila (Chhattisgarh)/ Bellary-Hospet (Karnataka) (Only 1)

(iii) (a) Two ways in which the Hirakud dam has helped the people of Odisha are

- The Hirakud dam provides irrigation to vast agricultural lands, boosting crop production in Odisha.
- It helps in controlling floods by regulating the flow of the Mahanadi river and protecting nearby areas.

(b) Hirakud dam is built on Mahanadi river.

(iv) (a) Geothermal energy is not popular in India due to limited geothermal resources, high initial setup costs and technical challenges in harnessing and maintaining geothermal power plants, making it less feasible than other energy sources.

(b) Solar energy is gaining popularity due to its renewable nature, low environmental impact, decreasing installation costs and ability to provide clean, sustainable power, making it an attractive alternative to conventional energy sources.

(c) Petroleum is considered harmful due to its environmental impact, including air pollution and greenhouse gas emissions. Its extraction also leads to habitat destruction and oil spills.

Q.2 (i) Today, non-conventional energy sources are no longer a novelty. They are a vital part of the global energy mix, contributing significantly to electricity generation. Research and development continue to improve the efficiency and affordability of these renewable resources. **(2)**

(a) Give one advantage of using non-conventional energy resources.

(b) Mention any two examples of conventional energy sources.

(ii) Answer the following questions, based on the image given below. **(2)**

(a) Considering the image, which category of energy does the power plant belong to? **(2)**

(b) Mention two advantages of this type of energy.

(iii) (a) Name the mineral used to make brass and bronze. **(3)**

(b) Name two Indian states where bauxite is found.

(c) Name the two oldest nuclear power plants in India.

(iv) (a) Name some minerals used in the petrochemical industry. **(3)**

(b) Give one difference between tidal and nuclear energy.

(c) What are the environmental impacts of using fossil fuels for energy?

Ans. (i) (a) One advantage of using non-conventional energy resources is that they are environmentally friendly. Unlike fossil fuels, they produce little to no pollution or greenhouse gas emissions, helping to reduce the impact of climate change.

(b) Two examples of conventional energy sources are **coal** and **petroleum**.

(ii) (a) Nuclear energy

(b) Two advantages of nuclear energy are

- It generates a large amount of power from a small amount of fuel.
- It produces minimal greenhouse gas emissions during electricity generation.

(iii) (a) Copper is used to make both brass and bronze.

(b) Odisha and Jharkhand

(c) The two oldest nuclear power plants in India are Tarapur (Maharashtra) and Rawatbhata (Rajasthan)

(iv) (a) Sulphur, Limestone, Clay, etc.

(b) Tidal energy relies on the movement of ocean tides to generate power, while nuclear energy uses nuclear reactions to produce heat and generate electricity.

(c) Fossil fuel use leads to air pollution, climate change, habitat destruction, and water pollution, harming the environment and contributing to global warming.

Q.3 (i) There is ample potential for setting up biogas plants in India. The National Bioenergy Programme has been recommended by the concerned ministry, for implementation in two phases. The spread of biogas technology is a boon for Indian farmers with its direct and guaranteed benefits. *https://biogas.mnre.gov.in*

(Specimen 2025) (2)

(a) Why do you think generation of biogas can be achieved in every household in rural India?

(b) Mention two ways in which the generation of this form of energy proves to be a boon for Indian farmers.

(ii) With reference to the Hirakud project answer the following. **(2)**

(a) On which river is it based?

(b) Name an Indian state that benefitted from the project.

(iii) (a) Give any one use of iron ore. **(3)**

(b) Name the mineral used to strengthen steel.

(c) Name two Indian states where copper is found.

(iv) With reference to the given image, answer the following. **(3)**

(a) Identify the type of energy being harnessed in the above picture.

(b) Mention why this form of energy is preferred over fossil fuels.

(c) Why does India stand at an advantage in the production of this type of energy?

Ans. (i) (a) Biogas generation can be achieved in rural households in India because it utilises readily available organic waste, like agricultural residues and livestock manure, and provides a sustainable, cost-effective energy source for cooking and lighting.

(b) The two ways in which the generation of this form of energy proves to be a boon for Indian farmers are

- **Utilisation of Organic Waste** Farmers can use agricultural waste and livestock manure to generate biogas, reducing waste and improving farm hygiene.
- **Affordable Energy** Biogas provides a cost-effective, reliable energy source for cooking and lighting, reducing dependence on expensive and polluting fuels.

(ii) (a) Hirakud is based on Mahanadi river.

(b) Odisha

(iii) (a) One use of iron ore is in the production of steel.

(b) Manganese improves the hardness, toughness and durability of steel.

(c) In India, copper is found in Rajasthan and Odisha.

(iv) (a) Solar Energy

(b) Solar energy is preferred over fossil fuels because it is renewable, environmentally friendly and sustainable, whereas fossil fuels contribute to pollution and climate change, and are finite resources.

(c) India stands at an advantage in the production of solar energy due to its abundant sunlight throughout the year, especially in the Western and Northern regions, making solar energy a highly viable and renewable resource for the country.

8

AGRICULTURE

The term 'Agriculture' is derived from two latin words 'ager' meaning 'land' and 'culture' meaning 'cultivation'. Thus, agriculture can be defined as the cultivation of soil to grow crops and raising livestock.

Indian Agriculture

- Agriculture is a primary source of livelihood in India. Indian agriculture is very important for food security, rural growth and the economy. It also supplies raw materials for many industries.
- National Agriculture Policy is announced by Indian Government to remove major problems of agriculture and improve the complications of agriculture.

Importance of Agriculture

- It employs a large section of the population in India.
- It provides food and food products to the human population and fodder for livestock.
- It is the source of raw material for many agro-based as well as non-agro-based industries.
- It brings foreign exchange through the export of many crops like tea, jute, cotton, etc.

Problems of Indian Agriculture

- **Unreliable Rainfall** The agricultural sector in India is heavily dependent on monsoon rainfall which is very unreliable and irregular.
- **Soil Erosion** It decreases the fertility of the soil. The indiscriminate clearing of forests, overgrazing by cattle and faulty agricultural practices have led to the degradation of soil quality in India.
- **Lack of Irrigation facilities** India is a vast country with large irrigated areas but still a large portion of the area lacks good irrigation facilities.
- **Frequent Floods and Drought** This is one of the most detrimental elements that leads to damage to crops as well as a decrease in the fertility of the soil.
- **Demand for Food Crops** There are two main food crops that are grown extensively with repetition in the country, i.e. rice and wheat. Due to repetition, these crops deplete the soil fertility.
- **Financial Constraints and Indebtedness** Crop failures and low returns from agriculture force small and marginal farmers to fall into the trap of indebtedness.

Reforms in Agriculture

- **Green Revolution** In the 1960s, the Indian Government introduced Green Revolution where modern technology like HYV seeds, modern machinery and fertilisers were introduced in the production of rice and wheat.
- **Minimum Support Price (MSP)** It was introduced by the Government to ensure that farmers are able to sell their products at proper rates.
- **Kisan Credit Cards** These were issued to farmers so that they could get cheap and early loans. The government also provides a Personal Accident Insurance Scheme to the card holders.
- **Indian Council of Agricultural Research (ICAR)** It was set up under the Ministry of Agriculture to promote agricultural research and development.
- **National Agricultural Policy** It was launched by the Government of India in 2000 to strengthen rural infrastructure and promote agriculture.

Types of Farming in India

- **Subsistence Farming** It is a type of agriculture where farmers grow crops and raise livestock primarily to meet the needs of their own families, with little surplus for sale or trade. It is mainly practiced in Madhya Pradesh, Orissa, Andhra Pradesh and North-East India.
- **Commercial Farming** In this type of farming, crops are cultivated mainly for commercial purposes i.e. for selling in the market, e.g. sugarcane, tobacco, oilseeds, etc. It is commonly practiced in Punjab, Haryana, UP, Gujarat, etc.
- **Shifting Farming** In this type, a patch of forest is cleared by cutting trees and burning the remaining vegetation. The ash after burning is used as manure. It is also known as **Slash-and-Burn** agriculture. It is practiced in Bihar, Orissa, Madhya Pradesh, Madhya Pradesh and North-East India.
- **Intensive Farming** It is an agricultural system that aims to maximise crop and livestock production by using high levels of labour, capital, and inputs. This method focusses on achieving high yields and productivity in a small area. This farming is practiced in Punjab, Rajasthan, Uttar Pradesh and Madhya Pradesh.
- **Extensive Farming** It is an agricultural system that involves large-scale farming with lower inputs of labour, capital, and resources. It typically takes place on large areas of land. It is practiced in Uttar Pradesh, Punjab, Haryana and Madhya Pradesh.
- **Plantation Farming** This type of farming is practiced on a large (continuous) piece of land where the cultivation of a single crop (mainly cash crops) like tea, coffee, rubber, spices, etc is done on a large scale. It is widely practiced in Karnataka, Kerala, Assam, Gujarat, Maharashtra and Madhya Pradesh.
- **Mixed Farming** The practice of cultivation of crops as well as raising of animals/livestock simultaneously is popularly known as Mixed Farming. Crop rotation is an important feature of this farming. It is practiced mainly in Punjab, Haryana, Gujarat and Western Uttar Pradesh.

Agricultural Seasons

- **Rabi Crops** These crops are grown in October and November during the winter season and harvested in March and April. Examples - wheat, barley, peas, gram, mustard, etc.
- **Kharif Crops** These crops are grown during the months of June and July and harvested in September and October during the autumn months. Examples - rice, bajra, ragi, maize, sugarcane, jute, etc.
- **Zaid Crops** These crops are grown for a short time period between kharif and rabi crops, mainly from March to June. Examples - cucumber, muskmelon, vegetables, fodder crops, etc.

Major Crops in India

Rice (Tropical and Sub-Tropical Crop)

It is a Kharif crop and accounts for one-third production of food grains in India.

Climatic Conditions

- **Temperature** It requires an average temperature of about 24°C.
- **Rainfall** It requires a sufficient amount of water and the average rainfall required is about 150 cm to 300 cm.
- **Soil** It is cultivated in the alluvial soils around the river banks. The soil should be capable of retaining water in the field. It should be deep fertile clayey or friable loam soil.

Methods of Cultivation

- **Broadcasting or Scattering** In this method, seeds are sprinkled all over the field by hand.

  Advantage Cheap and saves time.

  Disadvantage
  - Seeds are distributed unevenly.
  - Does not ensure that all the seeds are sown at correct depth.
- **Dribbling** In this method, seeds are dropped at regular intervals in the furrows with the help of plough or dibber.

  Advantage Less seeds are required and there is no wastage of seeds.

  Disadvantage Time consuming, cost is high and more labour is required.

- **Drilling** In this method, seeds are dropped through bamboo shaft.

  Advantage There is no wastage of seed, less seeds are required, and there is rapid germination if seeds are prior soaked.

  Disadvantage Very time consuming, cost is high and more labour is required.

- **Transplantation** In this method, seeds are first sown in nurseries and after 4-6 weeks, they are planted to other fields. It is the best method.

  Advantage
  - Lot of manual labour is required (provides work to farmers and solves the problem of unemployment).
  - Weeds are removed.
  - Less wastage of seeds.
  - Precise spacing allows the crop to mature uniformly.

  Disadvantage
  - Labour cost is high.
  - Seeds are not exposed.
  - Plants grow slowly because of recovery time after transplantation.
  - More time consuming as nursery preparation and pulling of seedlings is required.

- **Japanese Method** In this method, seedlings are transplanted in rows to make weeding and fertilising easy.

  Advantage
  - Use of good quality seeds
  - Higher yield

  Disadvantage Much use of manure for higher yield.

Processing

- **Threshing** Rice is threshed and crushed by bullocks to separate the kernel from the seed.
- **Winnowing** The process of removing the unwanted husk from the grain is called winnowing.
- **Milling** It is the process of removing the yellowish outer cover of the grain. The rice is then polished which makes it attractive.

Distribution

India is the second largest producer of rice in the world.

Some major rice-producing states in India are West Bengal, Uttar Pradesh, Andhra Pradesh, Telangana, Punjab, Bihar, Assam, Odisha, Gujarat, etc.

Wheat (Temperate Crop)

It is the second most important staple food in India after rice. It is grown in winter and harvested in March or April.

Climatic Conditions	Methods of Cultivation	Processing	Distribution
• **Temperature** It requires an average temperature of about 10°C to 15°C at the time of sowing. But higher temperature (20°C to 25°C) at the time of ripening. • **Rainfall** It requires rainfall of about 50 - 100 cm during growing period. Fog and slight rainfall are good for this crop in North India. • **Soil** It requires well-drained, fertile, loamy and alluvial soils of clayey type. In India, it is mainly grown in the flat alluvial plains of North India.	• Sowing, harvesting and processing.	Wheat is processed into various grades of flour by cleaning, tempering, grinding, sifting (refining) and purifying. Then the flour is sold in the markets.	India is the second-largest wheat producer in the world, after China. Wheat is the staple food of India. It is mainly grown in Uttar Pradesh, Punjab, Haryana, Madhya Pradesh, etc. Punjab is called the Granary of India.

Millets

Millets are a kharif crop grown in comparatively less fertile areas where rice and wheat cannot be cultivated. These are important fodder for cattle and are a good source of iron, calcium, zinc and magnesium. It contains mainly jowar, bajra and ragi.

Millets	Climatic Conditions	Methods of Cultivation	Processing	Distribution
(i) Jowar	• **Temperature** It requires an average temperature of 26°C to 33°C. • **Rainfall** It requires rainfall less than 30-100 cm. • **Soil** Medium, regur clayey black soil.	It does not require the preparation of fields. However, soil management plays an important role.	In the processing of jowar, threshing may be done with mechanical threshers or stone roller threshing or cattle threshing may be done and the grain should be stored in airtight containers.	Maharashtra is the largest producer of jowar. It is also grown in Karnataka, Madhya Pradesh, Andhra Pradesh, Telangana, Tamil Nadu, Rajasthan, Gujarat and Uttar Pradesh.
(ii) Bajra	• **Temperature** It requires an average temperature of 25°C to 35°C. • **Rainfall** It requires rainfall less than 100 cm. • **Soil** It can be grown on a wide range of soils but grows best in black, sandy soil with good drainage.	Bajra is sown in the middle or last week of July through the drilling or dibbling method and harvested when grains become hard enough and contain moisture.	Bajra grains are separated either by beating the earheads with sticks or by trampling the earheads under bullock feet.	In India, it is grown mainly in Rajasthan, Maharashtra, Gujarat, Uttar Pradesh, Tamil Nadu and Haryana. India is the largest producer of Bajra.
(iii) Ragi	• **Temperature** It requires an average temperature of 20°C to 30°C. • **Rainfall** It is suited for cultivation in areas with an annual rainfall of 50-100 cm. • **Soil** Red, light black and sandy soil.	• **Sowing** Ragi is mainly a kharif crop which is sown between May and August. The broadcasting method is mainly used for this crop, but its seeds are also sown with the help of drills and even transplanted. • **Harvesting** It is harvested between September and January.	The processing of ragi includes milling and malting. Ragi can be milled by wet conditioning.	Karnataka and Tamil Nadu are the leading producers of ragi in India. Other important producers are Uttarakhand, Maharashtra, Andhra Pradesh, Odisha, Jharkhand and Gujarat.

Pulses

Pulses are the main source of protein in a vegetarian diet. They occupy about 11 percent of the total cropped area in India. Pulses are rabi crops that provide essential vegetable proteins.

Climatic Conditions	Methods of Cultivation	Processing	Distribution
• **Temperature** Pulses are best grown in mild, cool and comparatively dry climates with temperatures ranging from 20°C to 25°C. • **Rainfall** These need rainfall between 50-100 cm. Severe cold and excessive rain are harmful for pulses. • **Soil** Loamy soil.	• **Sowing** Being a rabi crop, pulses are sown between September and November. It gets matured in 150 days. • **Harvesting** Pulses are harvested in February and April. After leaves turn to reddish brown from green, it is pulled up and dry under Sun. It is threshed or trampled by bullocks.	Pulses are processed in the following manner- cleaning and grading, pitting, pre-treatments with oil, conditioning, de-husking and polishing.	The cultivation of pulses in the country is largely concentrated in the dry lands of deccan and central plateaus and North-Western parts of the country. Pulses are mainly grown in Madhya Pradesh, Maharashtra, Uttar Pradesh, Himachal Pradesh, Rajasthan, Haryana, Andhra Pradesh, West Bengal, Karnataka, etc.

Sugarcane

It is one of the important cash/commercial crops of India. It is a tropical crop that belongs to the bamboo family and it is indigenous to India.

Climatic Conditions	Methods of Cultivation	Processing	Distribution
• **Temperature** Sugarcane requires a hot and humid climate with temperatures ranging from 20°C to 30°C. • **Rainfall** It requires a rainfall of about 75-120 cm. It cannot resist water stagnation. • **Soil** It grows best in alluvial clayey loams of the Indo-Gangetic plains and the black soil of Southern India.	• **Sowing** Sugarcane is generally sown from January to April, in most parts of the country. It can be planted through the ratooning, sett method and by harrowing also. • **Harvesting** Harvesting is done with the use of a long curved knife before the cane begins to flower. Its harvesting and crushing period is from October-November to April.	It must be processed within 48 hours of cutting to preserve its sugar content. In the mills, the sugarcane is trampled/ crushed between rollers. It is boiled soon after the juice is extracted. Lime is added to it to remove the impurities.	Sugarcane is cultivated in the Sutlej-Ganga plains of Uttar Pradesh, Punjab and Bihar in North India. The soil in these regions is fertile alluvium. It is also cultivated in the black soil region of Maharashtra and Tamil Nadu.

Oilseeds

Oilseeds are primarily grown for the extraction of oil. The oil extracted from these seeds is rich in fats and essential fatty acids which makes them a vital component of the human diet. In India, several oilseeds are grown, such as groundnut, mustard and soybean.

Oilseeds	Climatic Conditions	Methods of Cultivation	Processing	Distribution
(i) Groundnut It is the most important edible oilseed in India. It is both a kharif and rabi crop but is mostly grown as a kharif crop. It was introduced in India from Brazil during the 16th century.	• **Temperature** It requires a temperature ranging from 20°C to 25°C. It is a tropical crop. Warm and dry weather is suitable for the ripening of the crop. • **Rainfall** It requires about 50-100 cm of rainfall. • **Soil** Groundnut grows well in sandy loams, red and black soils which allow enough aeration. Red, yellow and black cotton soils are good for this crop.	• **Sowing** The seeds of the plant are sown in the month of June or July generally by the process of broadcasting or drilling. Oilseeds has the property of fixing atmospheric nitrogen and increases the fertility of soil, hence it is used as rotation crop for millets as well as other crops. • **Harvesting** The whole crop takes a time of about 4-5 months to be ready for harvesting. It is harvested between October-December. It needs cheap and abundant labour.	The whole plant is removed from the soil, including its roots. After that, they are collected and dried in the Sun. They are shelled and seeds are collected and then sent to mills after packaging (in sacks).	India is the second largest producer of groundnut. The major producers of groundnut are Andhra Pradesh, Telangana, Tamil Nadu and Gujarat.

Oilseeds	Climatic Conditions	Methods of Cultivation	Processing	Distribution
(ii) Mustard It is a tropical crop that is grown in the rabi season. The seeds are pressed to obtain mustard oil which is an edible oil.	• **Temperature** It is a tropical crop which needs a moderate, cool climate with a temperature range of 10°C to 20°C. • **Rainfall** It requires a rainfall of about 25-40 cm. • **Soil** It grows best in the alluvial soils of the Northern plains of Ganga and Sutlej. These plains are rich in alluvial deposits.	• **Sowing** Mustard is sown by broadcasting and drilling methods. Mustard and rapseed take around 4 to 5 months to mature. • **Harvesting** Mustard takes 3 months to mature and becomes ready as soon as the crop turns yellow.	Processing of mustard involves pre-cleaning of seeds, grading of seeds, conditioning for de-husking, separation and proper conditioning of de-husked granules.	It is grown extensively in Uttar Pradesh, Rajasthan and Haryana.
(iii) Soybean It is a rainfed kharif crop in India. It is a rich source of protein and vitamins. It is in great demand due to its varied uses like soyabean oil, soya milk, soya sauce, cheese, etc.	• **Temperature** Soybean requires a temperature between 13°C and 24°C. During the time of flowering, the temperature should be between 20°C and 25°C. • **Rainfall** The plant grows well in dry areas so it requires rainfall from 40-60cm. • **Soil** The soil needed for the cultivation of soybeans is the one that can retain moisture i.e. well-drained fertile loamy acidic soil.	• **Sowing** Soybeans is sown in the summer month (June). It is sown by drill method in rows, 40 to 50 cm apart from each other. • **Harvesting** It is harvested in October before the arrival of winter. Thus, the crop gets ready within 3-4 months.	The first step in processing is to properly prepare the soybean for dehulling which involves using magnets to remove metal and screening to remove impurities. After this, extraction process is used in which the soybean oil is washed from the prepared soybean flakes by using hexane or other solvents. After this, desolventising process is used in which solvent is removed from both the flakes and soybean oil. The desolventised flakes are now a product and ready for sale.	In India, soybean is generally grown in Madhya Pradesh and Uttar Pradesh.

Agro-Fibers

Cotton (Rabi and Kharif Crop)

It is a very important fiber crop that supplies raw materials to the textile industry. It is a tropical crop and it is grown in India as a kharif crop.

Climatic Conditions	Methods of Cultivation	Processing	Distribution
• **Temperature** Cotton needs mild, cool and comparatively dry climate having a temperature of 21°C to 27°C and abundant sunshine during its growth period. • **Rainfall** Cotton plants need a moderate rainfall of 50-80 cm which should be well distributed throughout the year. Stagnant water and excessive rainfall are harmful. • **Soil** Cotton is grown on a variety of soils, but it is grown mainly in the black (regur) soil of the deccan plateau and malwa plateau, as this soil has the ability to retain moisture.	• **Sowing** In Punjab and Haryana, cotton is sown as Rabi crop and in Peninsular India, it is grown as Kharif crop. It is mostly used as a rotation crop with maize, jowar, seasame and groundnut. Regular manure and fertilisers are essential as it quickly absorb the nutrients. • **Harvesting** Cotton takes 6-8 months to mature. Frost is the worst enemy of cotton. Cotton gets ready by October. Less humidity and warm temperature help in ripening and bursting of cotton bolls.	Picking and ginning are the main activities in the processing of cotton which is mostly done by hand. Ginning is the process of separation of seeds and fiber from the raw material known as lint.	India is the second largest producer of cotton in the world. It is mainly grown in Punjab, Maharashtra, Gujarat, and Haryana.

Jute

It is also an important fiber crop. It is known as the golden fiber of India because of the versatile nature of its colour and India earns valuable foreign exchange by exporting good quality of jute.

Climatic Conditions	Methods of Cultivation	Processing	Distribution
• **Temperature** It requires a temperature ranging from 24°C to 35°C. The hot and humid climate is very useful for jute production. • **Rainfall** It requires a high relative humidity of about 80% to 90%. It requires huge rainfall of 170 cm to 200 cm. • **Soil** Jute grows best in the alluvial loamy soil.	• **Sowing** It is generally sown in February on lowlands and in March-June on upland. Sowing is mostly done by drilling or broad-casting methods. • **Harvesting** It is harvested from July to September.	Retting is used for processing jute. After harvesting the plant, it is tied into bundles. It is dried and stripped of unwanted leaves and is kept submerged in water for 2 to 3 weeks. This process is known as retting. Retting is a micro-biological process. It softens the outer bark and facilitates the easy removability of the fibers from the stalk.	India is the largest producer of jute in the world. In India, it is mainly found in the states of West Bengal, Bihar Assam, Odisha, etc. West Bengal is the largest producer of jute in india.

Tea

It is an important beverage crop in India. Commercial planting of tea was started in India in 1840s in the Brahmaputra valley of Assam.

Climatic Conditions	Methods of Cultivation	Processing	Distribution
• **Temperature** Tea plant requires a temperature ranging from 20°C to 30°C, but the ideal temperature would be 25°C. • **Rainfall** It requires heavy rainfall of about 150-250 cm and is distributed well throughout the year. Alternate cool and warm breezes are very helpful for tea plants. • **Soil** It requires well-drained, deep, friable (easily crumbled) light loamy soils. The soil should be rich in humus and iron content.	• **Sowing** The sowing of tea plants includes the following methods - transplantation and clonal planting method. • **Harvesting** Tea planters start the pruning (trim) of the bush after two years. It is done to maintain the height and diameter of the tea plant limited to one meter.	Processing of tea includes withering, rolling, fermentation, drying, sorting, blending and packing.	In India, tea is mainly produced in North-East India and South India. Assam accounts for about 53.2 percent of the total cropped area under tea plants and contributes more than half of the total production of tea in the country.

Coffee

It is the second most important beverage in India after tea. The first plantation of coffee in India was set up by the Britishers near Chikmagalur in Karnataka in 1840. In India, there are mainly three types of coffee grown - Arabica, Robusta and Liberica.

Climatic Conditions	Methods of Cultivation	Processing	Distribution
• **Temperature** Coffee is a tropical plant that requires high temperatures, ranging from 13°C to 35°C throughout the year. Bright sunlight and warm weather are necessary for harvesting and growth of the berries. • **Rainfall** It requires a rainfall of about 125 to 200 cm which should be well distributed throughout the year. • **Soil** It grows well in deep, porous soil having high humus content and minerals like iron and calcium.	• **Sowing** The coffee seeds are grown in the nursery for 9 to 12 months, till they grow into a proper seedlings. • **Harvesting** Generally, harvesting of coffee is done in the 4th or 5th year after planting. Coffee picking is done by hand by removing the ripe berries from the stalk.	• **Dry Method** Under this method, cherries are put under the Sun to dry. After drying, the covering is removed and the seeds are obtained. • **Wet Method** Under this method, crushing, fermenting, washing and drying is done. Machines are also used in this method.	Coffee in India is majorly produced in three states i.e. Karnataka, Kerala and Tamil Nadu. The states are referred to as traditional coffee-producing areas.

EXAM ORIENTED QUESTIONS

TYPE - 1 1 Mark

Multiple Choice Questions

Q.1 Why is agriculture important for economic development?
(a) It provides employment opportunities in the industrial sector.
(b) It generates income through the export of crops and livestock.
(c) It reduces the need for natural resources.
(d) It decreases the population in rural areas.

Ans. (b) It generates income through the export of crops and livestock.

Q.2 Agriculture is an important economic sector for a country like India because
(a) India has a large population size.
(b) Agriculture provides its maximum share to GDP.
(c) Many industries get their raw material from agriculture.
(d) All of the above

Ans. (d) All of the above

Q.3 How does agriculture contribute to food security?
(a) By reducing food production costs.
(b) By ensuring a steady supply of food to the population.
(c) By increasing the demand for industrial goods.
(d) By encouraging people to migrate to urban areas.

Ans. (b) By ensuring a steady supply of food to the population.

Q.4 What is a common issue in the agricultural sector regarding soil quality?
(a) Excessive organic content
(b) Soil erosion and degradation
(c) Overuse of natural fertilisers
(d) Surplus soil moisture

Ans. (b) Soil erosion and degradation

Q.5 Which of the following is not a problem of Indian agriculture? **(ICSE 2023)**
(a) Dependence on monsoon
(b) Small land holdings
(c) Two main cropping seasons
(d) Use of traditional methods of farming

Ans. (c) Two main cropping seasons

Q.6 What is the full form of HYV?
(a) High Yielding Vegetables
(b) High Yielding Variety
(c) High Yielding Volume
(d) High Yielding Variations

Ans. (b) High Yielding Variety

Q.7 With reference to agriculture, what does ICAR stand for?
(a) Indian Council of Agricultural Research
(b) International Council of Agricultural Research
(c) Indian Centre for Agricultural Research
(d) International Centre for Agricultural Research

Ans. (a) Indian Council of Agricultural Research

Q.8 What is a major characteristic of subsistence farming?
(a) High crop diversity and surplus production
(b) Low levels of technology and limited mechanisation
(c) Extensive use of synthetic fertilisers and pesticides
(d) Large-scale commercial production for urban markets

Ans. (b) Low levels of technology and limited mechanisation

Q.9 What is the main objective of commercial farming?
(a) To produce food for personal consumption.
(b) To generate surplus crops for sale and profit.
(c) To sustain local agricultural traditions.
(d) To focus on organic farming practices.

Ans. (b) To generate surplus crops for sale and profit.

Q.10 A major environmental concern of shifting farming is
(a) Overuse of chemical fertilisers.
(b) Deforestation and loss of biodiversity.
(c) High water consumption.
(d) Monoculture farming leads to soil degradation.

Ans. (b) Deforestation and loss of biodiversity

Q.11 Which of the following farming methods is also known as slash-and-burn agriculture?
(a) Subsistence (b) Commercial
(c) Intensive (d) Shifting

Ans. (d) Shifting

Exp. Shifting agriculture is also known as slash-and burn agriculture. In this method, land is cleared by cutting down and burning vegetation to create fields for growing crops.

Q.12 Which of the following is a characteristic of intensive farming?

(a) Large land areas with low input costs.
(b) High use of labor, capital, and technology on small land areas.
(c) Limited use of fertilisers and pesticides.
(d) Low yield and minimal crop production.

Ans. (b) High use of labour, capital, and technology on small land areas.

Q.13 Which of the following farming methods is used to grow tea on a large scale? **(ICSE 2024)**

(a) Subsistence farming (b) Plantation farming
(c) Mixed farming (d) Shifting agriculture

Ans. (b) Plantation farming

Exp. Plantation farming is a type of large-scale agriculture where a single crop, often commercial like tea, coffee, or rubber is grown on vast areas of land for profit.

Q.14 Mixed farming involves

(a) Growing a single crop on large land areas.
(b) Combining both crop cultivation and livestock farming.
(c) Farming with minimal use of technology and inputs.
(d) Focusing on animal husbandry with minimal crop production.

Ans. (b) Combining both crop cultivation and livestock farming.

Q.15 Cultivation of crops and raising of animals is a feature of .... **(ICSE Specimen 2023)**

(a) Intensive farming (b) Plantation farming
(c) Mixed farming (d) Commercial farming

Ans. (c) Mixed farming

Exp. Mixed farming is an agricultural practice where both crops and livestock are raised on the same farm. This approach helps diversify income, improves soil fertility and reduces risks.

Q.16 Identify the agricultural season associated with the crop shown in the image below.

(a) Rabi (b) Kharif (c) Zaid (d) None of these

Ans. (a) Rabi

Q.17 The crops grown between the months of March and June are called ....

(a) rabi crops (b) kharif crops
(c) zaid crops (d) commercial crops

Ans. (c) zaid crops

Q.18 Which of the following is a staple food grain of Indians? **(ICSE 2023)**

(a) Wheat (b) Rice (c) Gram (d) Arhar

Ans. (b) Rice

Q.19 Which method is not used for the sowing of rice?

(a) Drilling (b) Dibbling
(c) Retting (d) Broadcasting

Ans. (c) Retting

Exp. Retting is the process of soaking plant fibers, like jute or flax in water to soften and separate the fibers from the stalks, making them easier to extract and use.

Q.20 Which of the following is a key requirement for the successful cultivation of wheat?

(a) High rainfall throughout the year.
(b) Warm temperatures and irrigation.
(c) Cool temperatures with moderate rainfall.
(d) Coastal regions with high humidity.

Ans. (c) Cool temperatures with moderate rainfall.

Q.21 Millets are typically grown in which type of climate?

(a) Cool and humid (b) Warm and dry
(c) Cold and wet (d) Tropical and rainy

Ans. (b) Warm and dry

Q.22 If Ravi, a farmer, alternates wheat and legumes during each season to maintain soil fertility, which of the following farming methods he is using?

(a) Crop rotation (b) Intensive farming
(c) Mixed farming (d) Shifting cultivation

Ans. (a) Crop rotation

Q.23 Which crop is associated with Ratooning? **(ICSE Specimen 2025)**

(a) Sugarcane (b) Jute
(c) Rice (d) Cotton

Ans. (a) Sugarcane

Exp. Ratooning is an agricultural practice where new crops are grown from the stubble or roots of the previous crop, without replanting seeds. It's commonly used for crops like sugarcane, rice, and bananas, allowing farmers to harvest additional yields from the same plant.

Q.24 In which of the following climates is sugarcane ideally cultivated?

(a) Dry and arid (b) Cool and temperate
(c) Tropical and subtropical (d) Polar regions

Ans. (c) Tropical and subtropical

Q.25 Mustard: Rabi Crop

(a) Rice: Rabi Crop
(b) Cucumber: Kharif Crop
(c) Maize: Zaid Crop
(d) Peas: Rabi Crop

Ans. (d) Peas: Rabi Crop

Q.26 Which of the following soils is most suitable for the cultivation of cotton and sugarcane? **(ICSE Specimen Semester I 2022)**

(a) Laterite soil (b) Black soil
(c) Alluvial soil (d) Red soil

Ans. (b) Black soil

Q.27 A microbiological process that loosens the bark of a crop and facilitates removal of fibre from the stalk. **(ICSE 2025)**

(a) Rolling
(b) Ratooning
(c) Retting
(d) Fermentation

Ans. (c) Retting

Q.28 Read the table and identify the pair that is correctly matched.

	Type of Crop	Area
P.	Tea	Assam
Q.	Jute	Punjab
R.	Coffee	Rajasthan
S.	Cotton	Haryana

(a) P (b) Q
(c) R (d) S

Ans. (a) P

Q.29 .... crops are associated with laterite soil. **(ICSE Specimen 2023)**

(a) Wheat and rice (b) Sugarcane and rice
(c) Maize and bajra (d) Tea and coffee

Ans. (d) Tea and coffee

Q30 Arabica and Robusta are a type of which of the following crops?

(a) Tea (b) Coffee
(c) Sugarcane (d) Oilseeds

Ans. (b) Coffee

Q.31 Identify the states that are major producers of coffee in India.

(a) Maharashtra and Gujarat
(b) Andhra Pradesh and Odisha
(c) Karnataka and Kerala
(d) Uttar Pradesh and Bihar

Ans. (c) Karnataka and Kerala

Q.32 Maharashtra is the leading producer of which of the following cash crops?

(a) Jute (b) Cotton
(c) Coffee (d) Tea

Ans. (b) Cotton

Q.33 Winnowing is associated with

(a) tea (b) wheat
(c) cotton (d) jute

Ans. (b) wheat

Q.34 State that grows long stapled cotton

(a) Rajasthan (b) Kerala
(c) Punjab (d) Assam

Ans. (c) Punjab

Q.35 Pruning is associated with

(a) coffee (b) sugarcane
(c) tea (d) cotton

Ans. (c) tea

Q.36 The yield per hectare of sugarcane is higher in

(a) Southern states
(b) Northern states
(c) Eastern states
(d) Western states

Ans. (a) Southern states

Q.37 Pulses are important food crops as

(a) they are warm weather grasses.
(b) being leguminous, they fix atmospheric nitrogen in the soil
(c) it is the staple food of Indians
(d) India is the largest consumer of pulses

Ans. (b) being leguminous, they fix atmospheric nitrogen in the soil

Q.38 Disease that can harm the cultivation of sugarcane

(a) Boll worms (b) Rust
(c) Smut (d) Stem-rot

Ans. (c) Smut

Q.39 A fungal disease called .... that affects the crop of wheat

(a) wilts (b) smut
(c) red rot (d) rust

Ans. (d) rust

Q.40 A method where cuttings are taken from good high yielding mother plant of tea rather than its seeds

(a) Transplantation
(b) Clone planting
(c) Fine plucking
(d) Retting

Ans. (b) Clone planting

TYPE - 2 1 Mark

Assertion-Reason Questions

Q.1 **Assertion** (A) Subsistence farming is a type of agriculture where the farmer grows enough crops to sustain themselves and their family.

Reason (R) The farmers have small land and do not use fertilisers and thus the yield is low.

(a) Both A and R are true and R is the correct explanation of A
(b) Both A and R are true but R does not explain A
(c) A is true but R is false
(d) A is false but R is true

Ans. (b) Both A and R are true but R does not explain A

Q.2 **Assertion** (A) Rabi crops are sown in winter and harvested in the spring season.

Reason (R) Rabi crops require a cool climate with moderate rainfall for optimal growth.

(a) Both A and R are true and R is the correct explanation of A
(b) Both A and R are true but R does not explain A
(c) A is true but R is false
(d) A is false but R is true

Ans. (a) Both A and R are true and R is the correct explanation of A

Q.3 **Assertion** (A) In kharif season, the crops are grown in the months of June and July and harvested in September and October.

Reason (R) Rice, jowar, sugarcane, bajra and jute are some examples of Kharif crop.

(a) Both A and R are true and R is the correct explanation of A
(b) Both A and R are true but R does not explain A
(c) A is true but R is false
(d) A is false but R is true

Ans. (b) Both A and R are true but R does not explain A

Q.4 **Assertion** (A) Millets are coarse and dry grains such as jowar, bajra, and ragi, which are used as food grains.

Reason (R) Millets can grow in poor soil and withstand extreme weather conditions. They require less rainfall, so they are also known as 'Dry Crops.'

(a) Both A and R are true and R is the correct explanation of A
(b) Both A and R are true but R does not explain A
(c) A is true but R is false
(d) A is false but R is true

Ans. (a) Both A and R are true and R is the correct explanation of A

Q.5 **Assertion** (A) Sugarcane is primarily grown in tropical and subtropical regions of the world.

Reason (R) Sugarcane requires a cold climate for optimal growth and sugar production.

(a) Both A and R are true and R is the correct explanation of A
(b) Both A and R are true but R does not explain A
(c) A is true but R is false
(d) A is false but R is true

Ans. (c) A is true but R is false

TYPE - 3 2 Marks

Short Answer Type Questions

Q.1 Mention any two points explaining the importance of agriculture in India. **(ICSE Specimen 2022)**

Ans. The importance of agriculture can be defined by the following points

(i) It provides food and food products to the human population and fodder for livestock.

(ii) It is the source of raw material for many agro-based as well as non-agro-based industries.

Q.2 Mention any two problems of agriculture in India.

Ans. The two problems of agriculture in India are

(i) The agricultural sector in India is heavily dependent on monsoon rainfall which is very unreliable and irregular.

(ii) Flood and drought are the most detrimental elements that leads to damage to crops as well as a decrease in the fertility of the soil.

Q.3 "Poverty and fragmentation of land are one of the biggest problems of agriculture in India". Explain. **(ICSE 2014)**

Ans. Poverty and fragmentation of land are one of the biggest problems of agriculture in India. This can be explained by the following points

- Due to poverty, farmers are not able to afford modern farming techniques, quality seeds and fertilisers which leads to low productivity.
- Land fragmentation due to inheritance results in smaller piece of lands, making it difficult for farmers to practice efficient farming methods which impacts the agricultural output.

Q.4 **Mention any two steps taken by the Government of India to boost agricultural production.** **(ICSE 2019)**

Ans. Following are the two steps taken by the Government of India to boost agricultural production

(i) Minimum Support Price (MSP) was introduced by the Government to ensure that farmers are able to sell their products at proper rates.

(ii) In the 1960s, the Indian Government introduced Green Revolution where modern technology like HYV seeds, modern machinery and fertilisers were introduced in the production of rice and wheat.

Q.5 **Describe any two main features of subsistence agriculture.** **(ICSE 2005)**

Ans. Two main features of subsistence agriculture are

(i) Farmers produce for their own needs only.

(ii) Farms are mainly small and only the farmer's family works on it to cultivate food crops such as rice, wheat, pulses, etc.

Q.6 **Distinguish between subsistence and commercial farming.** **(ICSE Specimen 2017)**

Ans. The differences between subsistence and commercial farming are as follows

Subsistence Farming	Commercial Farming
The main aim of this farming is to produce food for the farmer's family.	This farming is primarily done to produce crops for sale and profit.
Low investment in inputs and infrastructure is required.	High investment in seeds, machinery and irrigation are required.

Q.7 **What is mixed farming? Mention any one benefit of mixed farming.** **(ICSE 2017)**

Ans. Mixed farming is a cultivation of arable crops and the rearing of livestock on the same farm.

Its benefit is that it reduces dependence on external inputs like fertilizers because the crop and animal components in the farm support each other.

Q.8 **With reference to the commercial farming, answer the following questions.**

(i) Define commercial farming.

(ii) Name any two crops of commercial farming

Ans. (i) In commercial farming, crops are cultivated mainly for commercial purposes i.e. to sale it in the market. It involves large-scale production using modern techniques, machinery and high capital investment.

(ii) Sugarcane and coffee are the two crops of commercial farming.

Q.9 **Explain shifting cultivation. Mention one disadvantage of this.**

Ans. Shifting cultivation is a traditional farming technique that involves clearing a piece of land by cutting and burning trees. It is also called slash-and-burn agriculture. This method is commonly used by tribal communities in the states of Mizoram, Arunachal Pradesh, Assam, Tripura, etc.

One major disadvantage of shifting cultivation is deforestation. As farmers repeatedly clear new patches of forest for cultivation, it leads to the destruction of valuable forests.

Q.10 **Distinguish between intensive and extensive farming.** **(ICSE Specimen 2018, ICSE 2013)**

Ans. The differences between intensive and extensive farming are as follows

Intensive Farming	Extensive Farming
In intensive farming, small land area is used.	In extensive farming, large land area is used.
Yield per unit of land is high due to the use of advanced techniques and inputs.	As crops are grown on larger areas with fewer inputs, yield per unit is low.

Q.11 **With reference to the rice cultivation, answer the following.** **(ICSE 2018)**

(i) Why does the cultivation of rice require a lot of manual labour?

(ii) Mention any two geographical conditions which suit the cultivation of rice.

Ans. (i) Rice cultivation requires a lot of manual labour because it involves tasks like planting, transplanting, weeding and harvesting which are often done by hand.

(ii) Two geographical conditions suited for rice cultivation are (any two)

(a) Temp-16°C-32°C (b) Rainfall-150 cm-200 cm

(c) Soil-deep fertile clays.

Q.12 **With reference to plantation farming, answer the following questions**

(i) How does plantation farming contribute to the economy of tropical regions?

(ii) What are the main crops commonly grown in plantation farming systems?

Ans. (i) Farming contributes significantly to the economy of tropical regions by generating employment, providing raw materials for industries (such as rubber, tea, coffee, and cocoa) and contributing to exports that drive national income.

(ii) The main crops grown in plantation farming systems include tea, coffee, sugarcane, rubber, cocoa, bananas, etc.

Q.13 Mention any two features of plantation farming with two examples. **(ICSE 2014)**

Ans. Two features of plantation farming are

(i) Plantation farming focuses on the large-scale cultivation of a single cash crop, such as tea, coffee, rubber, sugarcane, etc.

(ii) It requires a significant amount of labor for planting, maintenance and harvesting of crops.

Q.14 Give a geographical reason for each of the following **(ICSE 2019)**

(i) Practicing mixed farming gives security to farmers.

(ii) Cultivation of wheat is confined to the Northern part of India.

Ans. (i) Mixed farming provides security by diversifying income sources, reducing risks, improving sustainability, increasing productivity and offering market flexibility, ensuring farmers can better withstand environmental, economic and market uncertainities.

(ii) The cultivation of wheat is primarily confined to the Northern part of India due to the following reasons

- Wheat grows best in cool, dry winters and moderate temperatures which are prevalent in the Northern part of India.
- The fertile alluvial soil found in the Northern plains, especially in the Indo-Gangetic region is ideal for wheat cultivation.

Q.15 With reference to kharif crops, answer the following questions

(i) When are kharif crops sown and harvested?

(ii) Name the cash crop which is also a kharif crop.

Ans. (i) Kharif crops are sown in June and July with the arrival of the monsoon rains. They are harvested in October and November.

(ii) Cotton is a cash crop and also a kharif crop in peninsular India.

Q.16 State an important difference between the climatic requirements for growing cotton and jute. **(ICSE 2015)**

Ans. Important differences between the climatic requirements for growing cotton and jute are given below

- **Cotton** It requires 21°C to 27°C temperature range with 50 cm to 80 cm rainfall.
- **Jute** It requires 25°C to 35°C temperature and an amount of 170cm to 200cm of rainfall.

Q.17 With reference to agriculture, answer the following questions **(ICSE Specimen Semester-II 2022)**

(i) Name two agriculture seasons of India.

(ii) Name one crop that grows in each season.

Ans. (i) Two agriculture seasons of India are rabi and kharif.

(ii) Wheat is a rabi crop and rice is a kharif crop.

Q.18 A farmer in Punjab has traditionally grown rice during the kharif season but is considering switching to wheat for the rabi season due to water scarcity and increasing input costs. The farmer has limited access to irrigation and is concerned about the timing of sowing and harvest.

(i) Based on the situation of the farmer, explain the advantages and challenges of cultivating wheat as a rabi crop in comparison to rice.

(ii) What factors should the farmer consider before making this switch and how can they ensure optimal growth of the wheat crop?

Ans. (i) Switching to wheat offers water efficiency and lower input costs compared to rice, making it suitable for areas with limited irrigation. However, the farmer must ensure proper sowing timing (October to December) and soil preparation.

(ii) Factors like climate, soil health and market prices should be considered before making the switch. Efficient irrigation, pest control and proper fertilisation will help ensure optimal wheat growth.

Q.19 Name two non-edible oilseeds grown in India. State one use of each. **(ICSE Specimen 2017)**

Ans. Two non-edible oilseeds grown in India are

(i) **Linseed** It is used for manufacturing paints and varnishing.

(ii) **Castor Seed** It is used as a lubricant in various machines.

Q.20 Explain the climatic conditions and soil requirements that are required for wheat to grow.

Ans. Following are the climatic conditions and soil requirements that are required for wheat

- **Temperature** It requires an average temperature of about 10°C to 15°C at the time of sowing. But higher temperature (20°C to 25°C) at the time of ripening.
- **Rainfall** It requires rainfall of about 50 - 100 cm during the growing period. Fog and slight rainfall are good for this crop in North India.
- **Soil** It requires well-drained, fertile, loamy and alluvial soils of clayey type. In India, it is mainly grown in the flat alluvial plains of North India.

Q.21 Distinguish between Jowar and Bajra in terms of climatic conditions.

Ans. Jowar and bajra differ in terms of climatic conditions as follows

Jowar	Bajra
It grows well in hot, dry climates with high temperatures i.e. 28°C to 32°C.	It grows in arid and semi-arid regions, requiring high temperatures and low rainfall.
It requires moderate rainfall.	It requires low rainfall.

Q.22 Give any two reasons why Maharashtra has emerged as an important sugarcane producing state. **(ICSE 2025)**

Ans. Maharashtra has emerged as an important sugarcane producing state due to the following reasons

- **Favourable Climate** The state has a tropical climate with hot and humid conditions, which are ideal for sugarcane cultivation. Additionally, moderate rainfall and well-distributed irrigation facilities support high yields.
- **Well-Developed Irrigation Facilities** Despite having relatively low rainfall in some regions, Maharashtra has well-developed canal and well irrigation systems, ensuring a continuous water supply for sugarcane crops.

Q.23 Give any two geographical requirements for the cultivation of the sugarcane crop. **(ICSE 2017)**

Ans. The geographical requirements for the cultivation of sugarcane are

(i) **Temperature and rainfall** Sugarcane requires a hot and humid climate with temperatures ranging from 20°C to 30°C and annual rainfall of about 75-120 cm.

(ii) **Soil** It grows best in alluvial clayey loams of the Indo-Gangetic plains and the black soil of Southern India.

Q.24 Mention any two geographical conditions necessary for the cultivation of groundnuts.

Or Mention two climatic conditions that favour the cultivation of groundnut. **(ICSE 2025)**

Ans. The geographical conditions necessary for the cultivation of groundnuts are

(i) **Temperature and rainfall** It requires a temperature ranging from 20°C to 25°C and rainfall of about 50-100 cm.

(ii) **Soil** Groundnut grows well in sandy loams, red and black soils which allow enough aeration.

Q.25 Explain the following terms **(ICSE 2017)**

(i) Ginning (ii) Retting

Ans. (i) **Ginning** It is the process of separating cotton fibers from seeds. The process involves removing the seeds from the cotton bolls to produce clean cotton fibers, which can then be spun into yarn or thread for textile production.

(b) **Retting** It is the process of breaking down the pectins that bind fibers to the stalks of plants like flax, hemp, or jute, to separate the fibers from the rest of the plant material.

Q.26 With reference to the coffee plantation, answer the following questions. **(ICSE 2013)**

(i) What geographical conditions are favourable for the cultivation of coffee?

(ii) Name any two states in India where coffee plantations are found.

Ans. (i) Geographical conditions that are favourable for the cultivation of coffee are

- **Temperature** Coffee is a tropical plant that requires high temperatures, ranging from 15°C to 28°C throughout the year with an annual rainfall of about 150-200cm.
- **Soil** It grows well in deep, porous soil having high humus content and minerals like iron and calcium.

(ii) Two states in India where coffee plantations are found are Karnataka and Kerala.

Q.27 State any two methods for the processing of coffee berries.

Ans. The two methods of processing the coffee berries are dry method and wet method.

(i) **Dry method** Under this method, cherries are put under the Sun to dry. After drying, the covering is removed and the seeds are obtained.

(ii) **Wet method** Under this method, crushing, fermenting, washing and drying is done. Machines are also used in this method.

TYPE - 4

3 Marks

Long Answer Type Questions

Q.1 Distinguish between rabi, kharif and zaid crops. Also, give one example of each.

Ans. The differences between the rabi, kharif and zaid crops are as follows

Rabi Crops	Kharif Crops	Zaid Crops
These are sown in the winter season during the months of October-November.	These are sown in the monsoon season during the months of June-September.	These are sown in the summer season during the months of March-June.
These requires cool temperatures and moderate rainfall.	These requires warm temperatures and high rainfall.	These requires hot and dry conditions with less water.
Examples - wheat, barley	Examples - rice, cotton	Examples - cucumber, melons

Q.2 With reference to rice crop, explain the process of

(i) Threshing (ii) Winnowing

(iii) Milling

Ans. (i) **Threshing** Rice is threshed and crushed by bullocks to separate the kernel from the seed.

(ii) **Winnowing** The process of removing the unwanted husk from the grain is called winnowing.

(iii) **Milling** It is the process of removing the yellowish outer cover of the grain. The rice is then polished which makes it attractive.

Q.3 Study the given picture below and answer the following questions

(i) Name the crop which is being planted. Give one benefit of this method of planting this crop.

(ii) Mention the climatic conditions which favour the cultivation of the crop being planted.

Ans. (i) Rice is being planted using the transplantation method. One benefit is that weeds (wild/unwanted plants) are removed at the time of transplantation.

(ii) Rice requires 16°C to 32°C temperature and rainfall ranging from 150 to 300 cm.

Q.4 Give a geographical reason for each of the following. **(ICSE 2019)**

(i) Cultivation of wheat is confined to the Northern part of India.

(ii) Practicing mixed farming gives security to farmers.

(iii) Ratoon cropping is gaining popularity among sugarcane cultivators.

Ans. (i) The cultivation of wheat is confined to the Northern part of India because wheat grows best in temperatures between 10°C to 15°C and requires a winter season for proper growth, which is found in the Northern states. Additionally, these areas have fertile alluvial soil and adequate irrigation, making them ideal for wheat farming.

(ii) Mixed farming, which involves growing crops and raising livestock together, provides security to farmers by diversifying their sources of income. If one crop or livestock fails due to weather or disease, the other can help sustain the farmer's livelihood

(iii) Ratoon cropping is gaining popularity among sugarcane cultivators because it allows for multiple harvests from the same plant. After the initial harvest, new shoots (ratoons) sprout from the roots which reduces the need for replanting. This method saves time, labour, and costs.

Q.5 With reference to rice cultivation, answer the following. **(ICSE Semester II 2022)**

(i) Name the soil found suitable for its growth.

(ii) Name the state that is the largest producer of this crop in India.

(iii) In which cropping season is it generally grown in India?

Ans. (i) The soil which is found suitable for the growth of rice is deep fertile clay or friable loam soil.

(ii) The state that is the largest producer of rice crop in India is West Bengal.

(iii) Rice is generally grown in India in the Kharif cropping season.

Q.6 Give a geographical reason for each of the following.

(i) The growth of pulses is important in India. **(ICSE 2018)**

(ii) Pulses are grown as rotational Crops. **(ICSE Specimen 2018)**

(iii) Cultivation of pulses is mostly confined to Central and Northern India.

Ans. (i) The growth of pulses is important in India due to its suitability for the Indian climate and soil. Pulses play a crucial role in soil fertility, as they are leguminous plants that fix nitrogen in the soil, enriching it for subsequent crops. Additionally, these provide a significant source of protein.

(ii) Pulses are grown as rotational crops due to their ability to improve soil fertility. Geographically, pulses are well-suited for crop rotation because they are leguminous plants. By rotating pulses with other crops like cereals, farmers can maintain soil fertility without the need for excessive chemical fertilisers. This practice helps reduce soil depletion.

(iii) Central and Northern India experience semi-arid and dry conditions with moderate rainfall, which is ideal for pulses like chickpeas, pigeon peas, and lentils. The alluvial and loamy soils found in the Indo-Gangetic plains and the deccan plateau are rich in nutrients, making them suitable for pulse cultivation.

Q.7 Give a geographical reason for each of the following

(i) Oil cake is a useful residue.

(ii) The yield per hectare of sugarcane is higher in the Southern states.

Ans. (i) Oil cake is a useful residue because it is rich in nutrients, particularly nitrogen and phosphorus, which can be used as an organic fertiliser to improve soil fertility. It is commonly produced after oil extraction from seeds like groundnut or mustard.

(ii) The climate in the Southern states, with abundant rainfall and a longer growing season, supports optimal growth of sugarcane, leading to higher yields. Additionally, better irrigation facilities and soil conditions in states like Tamil Nadu and Karnataka also contribute to higher productivity.

Q.8 With reference to sugarcane, answer the following questions.

(i) Mention two different ways in which it is propagated.

(ii) Why is a lot of labour required for its cultivation?

(iii) Why must the sugar mills be near the sugar fields?

Ans. (i) Two different ways in which sugarcane is propagated are

(a) **By planting setts** Small sections of sugarcane stalks (called setts) are planted in the soil, from which new shoots grow.

(b) **Ratooning** In this method after the first-crop the sugarcane is cut leaving the root intact in soil.

(ii) It requires a lot of labour because it involves manual tasks such as planting setts, weeding, irrigating, applying fertilisers, and harvesting.

(iii) Sugar mills are located near the sugar fields because sugarcane is heavy and perishable raw material. Therefore it has to be crushed within 24 hrs, else the sucrose content is reduced. Transportation cost is reduced if mills are located near the sugarcane field.

Q.9 With reference to sugarcane, answer the following questions.

(i) The yield of sugarcane is higher in the Deccan. Give two reasons for this.

(ii) Give one advantage and disadvantage of ratoon cropping.

Ans. (i) The yield of sugarcane is higher in the Deccan for the following two reasons

(a) The climatic conditions are ideal with the absence of too high temperature and frost free winters.

(b) The black lava soil with high fertility and rententivity are found.

(c) Better methods, manures and fertilisers are used for cultivation in South.

(ii) One advantage and disadvantage of ratoon cropping is as follows

- **Advantage** Ratoon cropping is cost-effective because the sugarcane plant regrows from the root system after the first harvest, eliminating the need to plant new setts and reducing labour and input costs.
- **Disadvantage** The yield from ratoon crops decreases with each successive harvest as the soil becomes depleted.

Q.10 (i) Mention two reasons why sugarcane cultivation is gaining importance in Peninsular India.

(ICSE Specimen 2023)

(ii) State one problem of sugarcane growers of Uttar Pradesh

Ans. (i) Two reasons why sugarcane cultivation is gaining importance in peninsular India are

(a) The tropical climate and black soil of Peninsular India results in higher yield per unit hectare of land.

(b) There is a long crushing season for sugarcane crops in Peninsular India.

(ii) One problem of sugarcane growers of Uttar Pradesh is that they are dependent on canal irrigation for water requirements. The canals are often non-perennial and so the supply of water is uncertain. The dry winds loo also affect the growth of sugarcane.

Q.11 Give the geographic term for each of the following. **(ICSE 2015)**

(i) Cultivation of sugarcane from the rootstock of the cane which has been cut.

(ii) The residue left behind after the crushing of oil seeds.

(iii) The process by which latex is converted into a thick, spongy mass by adding acetic acid or formic acid.

Ans. Geographic term for each of the following are

(i) Ratooning (ii) Oil cake (iii) Coagulation

Q.12 Mention any three uses of groundnuts.

Ans. Three uses of groundnuts are as follows

(i) Groundnuts are processed to produce peanut oil, commonly used for cooking and frying.

(ii) Oil cake made from these can be used as cattle fodder.

(ii) Groundnuts are eaten as snacks and are also used in peanut butter, sweets and confectionery.

Q.13 Jute is one of the most important fiber crops grown in India. It is mainly grown during the kharif season. India is the largest producer and exporter of jute, which is used for making sacks, ropes, and other products.

(i) Why is jute considered a kharif crop?

(ii) What are the main uses of jute in various industries?

(iii) State any one geographic condition for jute cultivation.

Ans. (i) Jute is grown mainly in the kharif season, with planting done in late spring and harvesting during the monsoon. It grows well because of the rain and warm weather during this period.

(ii) The main uses of jute in various industries include making sacks, ropes, bags, mats and carpets. It is also used in the production of eco-friendly packaging materials due to its biodegradable nature.

(iii) One geographic condition for jute cultivation is the availability of fertile alluvial soil along riverbanks which provides the necessary nutrients and proper drainage for the growth of jute.

Q.14 Give one reason to explain each of the following **(ICSE 2025)**

(i) Trees are planted in between the rows of coffee plants.

(ii) Cotton cultivation requires plenty of cheap labour.

(iii) Hill slopes are best suited for tea cultivation.

Ans. (i) Trees are planted in between the rows of coffee plants to provide shade and protect the coffee plants from direct sunlight and strong winds, which can affect their growth and quality.

(ii) Cotton cultivation requires plenty of cheap labour because most of the processes, like sowing, picking, and ginning, are done manually, requiring a large workforce.

(iii) Hill slopes are best suited for tea cultivation because they ensure proper drainage, preventing waterlogging, which is harmful to tea plants. Additionally, the cool and humid climate of hills favours tea growth.

Q.15 Give a geographical reason for each of the following. **(ICSE 2015)**

(i) Clonal planting is the best method for tea propagation.

(ii) Cotton grows widely in Maharashtra.

(iii) Oilseeds are an important commercial crop grown in India.

Ans. (i) Clonal planting helps to produce superior quality, better yield and special flavour of the mother plants.

(ii) Black soil is widely found in Maharashtra and is best suited for cotton.

(iii) Oilseeds provide raw material to various industries which extract the oil for use such as paints, varnishes, soaps, cosmetic items, medical items etc. The residue of oil seed forms an important part of cattle-feed and manure.

TYPE - 5 — 10 Marks

Structured Questions

Q.1 (i) Mention two agricultural reforms done by the government for the betterment of the agricultural sector. **(ICSE Specimen 2025) (2)**

(ii) (a) State one point of difference between rabi and kharif cropping seasons. **(2)**

(b) Name the state that is the leading producer of groundnut in India.

(iii) With reference to the cultivation of pulses answer the following. **(3)**

(a) Name a soil found suitable for the growth of pulses.

(b) Name any two varieties of pulses grown in India.

(c) Give a reason why pulses are a popular food crop in India.

(iv) Rohan, a farmer, hired some labourers to help him with 'ginning'. **(3)**

(a) Name the crop grown by Rohan.

(b) Mention any two climatic conditions suitable for this crop.

Ans. (i) Two agricultural reforms done by the government for the betterment of the agricultural sector are

(a) **Green Revolution** The government introduced high-yielding variety seeds, chemical fertilisers, and modern irrigation techniques to boost agricultural production, especially for staple crops like wheat and rice.

(b) **The Kisan Credit Card (KCC)** It offers farmers easy access to short-term credit for activities like buying seeds, fertilisers, pesticides, and for irrigation purposes. The KCC provides low-interest loans, helping farmers manage their cash flow during the planting and harvesting seasons. It also allows farmers to withdraw money from any bank branch or ATM.

(ii) (a) Rabi crops are sown in October-November and harvested in March-April while kharif crops are sown in June-July and harvested in September-October.

(b) Gujarat is the leading producer of groundnut in India.

(iii) (a) Alluvial or black soil is found suitable for the growth of pulses. However, these can also be grown on laterite or red soils.

(b) Urad and chana are the two varieties of pulses grown in India.

(c) Pulses are a popular food crop in India because they are an excellent source of protein and are a vital part of the vegetarian diet. They also grow well in diverse climatic conditions and are relatively drought-resistant, making them suitable for cultivation across various regions of India.

(iv) (a) Cotton crop is grown by Rohan.

(b) Two climatic conditions suitable for cotton cultivation are

- **Warm temperature** Cotton grows best in temperatures between 25°C to 35°C.
- **Dry weather** Cotton requires a dry climate with low humidity, especially during the flowering and harvesting stages.

Q.2 (i) Why is agriculture considered an important sector of the Indian economy? (Any two points) **(2)**

(ii) (a) What is mixed farming? **(2)**

(b) Mention any one advantage of mixed farming.

(iii) Give one reason to explain each of the following.

(a) West Bengal is a leading producer of jute. **(3)**

(b) Millets are fast becoming a popular food crop.

(c) More than two ratoon crops are not advisable for sugarcane farmers.

(iv) Explain the following. **(ICSE 2025)**

(a) Mixed farming

(b) Zayad

(c) Transplantation

Ans. (i) Agriculture is considered a crucial sector of the Indian economy for several reasons

- **Source of Livelihood** A large portion of India's population depends on agriculture for their livelihood. This makes it a primary source of income and employment.
- **Contribution to GDP** Agriculture plays a significant role in India's Gross Domestic Product (GDP). Though its share has declined over time with industrialisation and services growth, it still contributes a substantial portion to the overall economy and supports many industries related to food processing, textiles and more.

(ii) (a) The practice of cultivation of crops as well as raising of animals/livestock simultaneously is popularly known as mixed farming.

(b) Under mixed farming, if crop production fails, farmers can still earn from their livestock, ensuring a more stable income. This is an advantage of mixed farming.

(iii) (a) West Bengal is a leading producer of jute because of the ideal climate and fertile alluvial soil along the riverbanks which are perfect for jute cultivation. The region also benefits from adequate rainfall and a humid climate which are essential for growing high-quality jute.

(b) Millets are becoming a popular food crop because they are nutritious, rich in fiber, vitamins, and minerals and are considered a healthier alternative to rice and wheat. Additionally, they are drought-resistant and require less water, making them suitable for cultivation in regions with limited water resources.

(c) More than two ratoon crops are not advisable for sugarcane farmers because the soil fertility declines with each successive harvest, leading to lower yields.

(iv) (a) Mixed farming is a type of agriculture where both crops and livestock are raised on the same farm.

(b) Zayad is the short cropping season between the Rabi and Kharif seasons in India, from March to June.

(c) Transplantation is the process of growing seedlings in a nursery and then shifting them to the main field for better growth.

Q.3 (i) Give two advantages of the transplantation method of sowing rice. **(2)**

(ii) (a) Why is pruning essential for tea crops? **(2)**

(b) Name the largest producer of tea in India.

(iii) A broad range of valuable bioactive compounds has been obtained from oilseeds either in pure form or in a homogenous mixture. Oilseed cake or meal had been undervalued by-products or waste, which conventionally had been utilised for feed in many countries. *Source: pmc.ncbi.nlm.nih.gov* **(3)**

(a) Name some oilseeds grown for edible oil production in India?

(b) How does the climate affect the cultivation of oilseeds like sunflower and soybean?

(c) What is the significance of oilseed crops in the global economy?

(iv) Study the picture and answer the following questions. **(3)**

(a) Mention the climatic conditions that are suitable for the cultivation of this crop.

(b) Name the state that produces the largest amount of this crop.

(c) In which cropping season is this crop grown in India?

Ans. (i) Two advantages of the transplantation method of sowing rice are

(a) **Higher yields** Transplanting ensures healthier, well-established seedlings, leading to better growth and higher crop yields.

(b) **Weed control** Transplanted rice is better able to compete with weeds, reducing the need for manual weeding or herbicides.

(ii) (a) Pruning is essential for tea leaves because it determines the productivity of tea bushes. Delay in pruning decreases the size and weight of growing tea shoots.

(b) **Assam** is the largest producer of tea in India.

(iii) (a) The main oilseeds grown for edible oil production include soybean, sunflower, groundnut (peanut), mustard, and canola.

(b) Oilseeds like sunflower and soybean require warm temperatures and adequate rainfall. Sunflowers thrive in sunny, dry conditions, while soybeans grow best in moderate, humid climates.

(c) Oilseed crops are significant in the global economy as they are key sources of edible oils, protein meals for animal feed, and raw materials for various industries, contributing to food security and agricultural trade.

(iv) (a) Cotton needs a mild, cool and comparatively dry climate having a temperature of 21°C to 30°C and abundant sunshine during its growth period and annual rainfall between 50-80cm.

(b) Gujarat produces the largest amount of cotton.

(c) Cotton is grown primarily during the Kharif season in India.

9

MANUFACTURING INDUSTRIES

- Manufacturing industries are the sectors that engage in the production of goods through the transformation of raw materials into finished products.
- These include industries like textiles, automobiles, electronics, chemicals, etc. where goods are produced on a large scale for consumption or further use.

Importance of Industries in India

- Industries are the backbone of the Indian economy. They provide finished goods for consumption and intermediate goods for other sectors.
- Industries help to strengthen our agricultural system by providing tools and implements to be used in agriculture.
- Industries help to produce goods and equipment for the defence sector of our country.
- Industries help to reduce dependency on foreign countries and make India self-reliant.

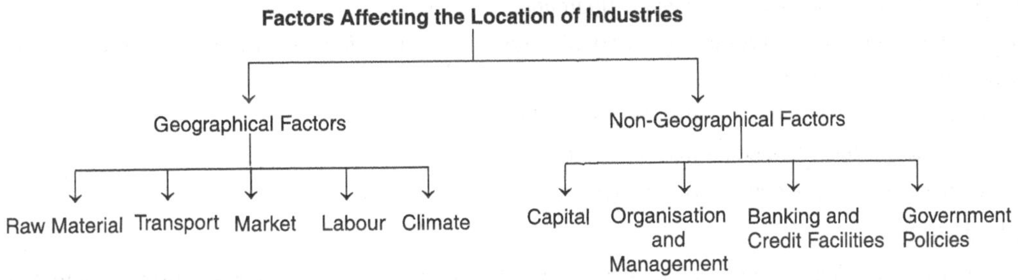

Classification of Industries

Based on the type of raw material, its size, location and type of product manufactured, industries can be classified into the following groups

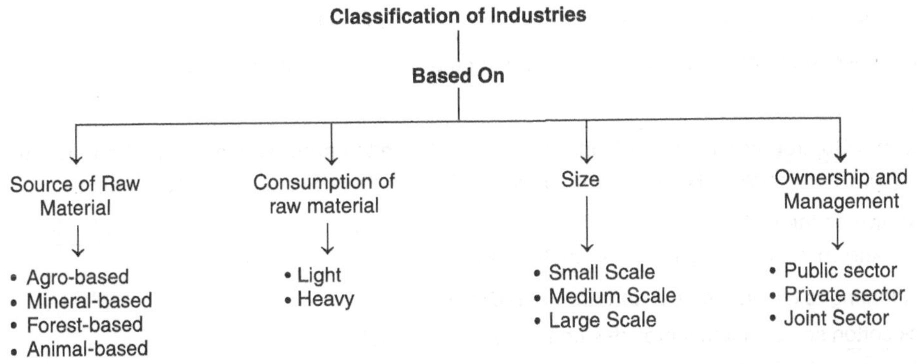

Agro-Based Industry

- An Agro-based industry is an industry that uses agricultural products like crops, fruits and livestock as raw materials for the production of goods.
- **Examples** Sugar, textiles and dairy industries.

Sugar Industry

- It is the second-largest organised industry in India and contributes around 8% of the total sugar production in the world.
- Factors affecting the location of sugar industry
  (i) Heavy and perishable raw material therefore it has to be crushed within 24 hours else sucrose content isreduced.
  (ii) Cannot be easily transported over long distance.
- Molasses, pressmud and bagasse are some important byproducts of sugarcane.
- Gur, Jaggery, Khandsari, White sugar are some of its products.

Distribution

- The sugar industry in India is primarily concentrated in states like Uttar Pradesh, Bihar, Haryana and Punjab in North and Maharashtra, Karnataka, Tamil Nadu, Andhra Pradesh in South.
- These states have favourable conditions such as climate, soil type, and availability of raw materials like sugarcane which support large-scale sugar production.

Problems

- The quality of sugarcane produced in India is poor having low yield and sucrose content is also very low.
- The sugarcane is grown by small farmers who sell their crops to sugar factories at fixed prices by the government. When farmers do not get attractive prices they switch the other profit-making crops.
- The by-products produced by the sugar industry are not utilised properly. Hence, they can't be converted into other useful products.

Reasons for shifting of Sugar Mills from North India to South India

(i) Tropical climate which is ideal for growing sugarcane.
(ii) The black soil, higher temperature, good amount of rainfall, irrigation facilities & frost free growing season.
(iii) The sucrose content is higher in South.
(iv) The crushing season is longer in South as compared to North.
(v) Better managed cooperative sugar mills in South.
(vi) In South, mills are equipped with modern machinery.

Textile Industry

- The textile industry involves the production of fibers, yarns and fabrics that are used to make clothing, home furnishings and other textile products.
- The major textile industries in India include the cotton and silk industries.

Cotton Textile Industry

- Cotton textile manufacturing is the largest organised modern industry in the country.
- It employs a huge number of people thereby supporting the economy of the country.

Distribution

- Maharashtra and Gujarat produce more than 60% of the total cotton produced in India. The remaining is produced by West Bengal, Uttar Pradesh, Rajasthan, Madhya Pradesh, Andhra Pradesh and Karnataka.
- Mumbai is known as the Cottonopolis of India, Ahmedabad in Gujarat is known as the Manchester of India and Coimbatore is known as the Manchester of South India.
- Factors contributing textile industry in and around Mumbai
  (i) The black cotton soil in Mumbai provides cotton as raw material.
  (ii) Humid Climate which is ideal for this industry is available there.
  (iii) Cheap hydroelectric power is available from Tata Hydroelectric grid.
  (iv) Mumbai's location as an international port.
  (v) Cheap skilled and unskilled labour.
  (vi) Banking facility is easily available.

Problems

- Many mills in India are very old and are very inefficient. They have old types of machinery as compared to some other developed countries.
- As compared to other developed countries, the labour productivity of India is low.
- Indian cotton textiles have to face stiff competition from synthetic fibers which are cheaper and need less maintenance.
- Inadequate power supply with increasing population is becoming acute.

Silk Industry

- Silk Industry is considered as a small-scale industry in India.
- The art of rearing silkworms for silk production is called sericulture.
- In India, mulberry silk accounts for about 90% of total natural silk produced.
- Golden yellow muga silk is produced in Assam.

Distribution

- In India, the major silk-producing states are Karnataka, West Bengal, Srinagar, Assam, Andhra Pradesh, Jharkhand, Bihar and Odisha. Around 70% of the total silk is produced in Karnataka alone.

Factors Responsible for Sericulture in Karnataka

(i) Favourable climate for rearing silkworm.
(ii) Availability of mulberry plant.
(iii) Silkworm known as Bombyxmori, is reared throughout the year.

Problems

- As compared to advanced countries like Japan and China, India does not have latest and modern technology for producing silk.
- It is facing tough competition from artificial silk which is cheaper and needs less maintenance.

Mineral Based Industry

The industries that require minerals as their raw materials are called mineral based industries.

Iron and Steel Industry

- Iron and steel industries are the main mineral based industries in India.
- An integrated steel plant is one where all the three processes from melting of iron ore in the blast furnance to steel making, shaping of metal is carried out under one complex.
- Mini steel plant which manufactures steel using scrap iron are decentralised secondary units.
- It involves the production of iron and steel through processes like smelting iron ore and refining it into various steel products.

Tata Iron and Steel Company (TISCO)

- Often know as basic or key industry.
- The first unit to produce pig iron was started in 1874 at Kulti, which was named as Bengal Iron Works Company.

Tata Iron and Steel Company (TISCO)

- It is a private-sector iron and steel plant established in 1907 by Jamshedji Tata at Jamshedpur in Jharkhand. The production of this plant started in 1911.
- TISCO mainly produces high-grade carbon steel, acid steel and special alloy steel.

Favourable Factors

(i) High grade haematite iron ore from Noamundi mines of Singhbhum & Mayurbhanj, Odisha.
(ii) Coal from Jharia coal fields.
(iii) Manganese from Keonjhar.
(iv) River Subarnarekha provides water for cooling purpose.
(vi) Ideal transport facilities.

REVISION NOTES

Bhilai Iron and Steel Plant

- This was the first plant under the public sector. It was set up in collaboration with the erstwhile USSR in the Durg district of Chhattisgarh.
- It started production in 1959. This plant produces rails, railway sleepers, beams, billets, angles, etc.

Favourable Factors

(i) Iron-ore from Dalli-Rajhara, Bhilai.
(ii) Limestone from Nandani Quarries.
(iii) Manganese from Balaghat (M.P.).
(iv) Water supply from Tendula canal.
(v) Thermal power from Korba thermal power station.

Rourkela Steel Plant

- This plant was set up in the Sundergarh district of Odisha with the technical help of German firm, Krupps and Demag in 1959.
- Known for latest technology in steel making, related to Indian Space Satellite Programme.
- Produces sheets, steel plates and strips for railway wagons, coaches and shipbuilding.

Favourable Factors

(i) Iron ore is obtained from Sundargarh & Keonjhar
(ii) Coal from Jharia, Talcher & Korba
(iii) Power from Hirakud Project
(iv) Manganese from Barajmda
(v) Water supply from Brahmani river.

Visakhapatnam Steel Plant

Visakhapatnam Steel Plant

- It is the first seashore-based steel plant which started its production in 1992. It is managed by Rashtriya Ispat Nigam Limited.
- This plant contributes heavily to the shipbuilding industry and uses the advantage of being a large seaport of India.
- It produces liquid steel and saleable steel which is exported to China and South-East Asia.
- It is the second largest producer of iron and steel in the country.

Favourable Factors

(i) Iron ore is obtained from Bailadila mines in Chhattisgarh.
(ii) Coking coal from Pookkii and Bhalore coal mines in Jharkhand.
(iii) Limestone from Jaggayyapeta in Andhra Pradesh.
(iv) Dolomite from Birmitrapur in Odisha.

Problems of Iron and Steel Industry

- **Huge Investment** This industry requires huge capital for its setup which is difficult for a developing country like India.
- **Outdated and Low Technical Development** Outdated machinery has increased the cost of production of iron and steel. This has also reduced the profit margin of the iron and steel plants.
- **Inefficiency in Production** The production units do not utilise the full potential of employees. Labour productivity is low as compared to other countries which increases the cost of production.
- **Rise in Import** India has to import iron and steel from foreign countries as it is not able to fulfil its demand for steel. The rise in imports leads to greater spending on foreign exchange.

Petrochemical Industry

- It is an important organic chemical industry that derives its chemicals from petroleum resources and products like LPG and coal.
- Petrochemicals are used for manufacturing various goods like synthetic rubber, plastics, dyestuffs, drugs, etc.
- Some examples of petrochemical industries are Union Carbide India Ltd., The Udex Plant, Indian Petrochemical Corporation Ltd., National Organic Chemical Industries Ltd., Reliance Industries, etc.
- They are gaining importance as they are cost effective, economically stable, cheaper and raw material is easily available.

Electronics Industry

- The electronics industry involves the design, manufacturing and sale of electronic devices and components, such as smartphones, computers, semiconductors and medical equipment.
- Some important electronic industries are Bharat Electronics Ltd., India Telephone Industries (ITI), Electronics Corporation of India Ltd. (ECIL), etc.

Bharat Electronics Limited

Electronics play a crucial role in the communication, software and entertainment industries. Some of the applications of electronics are as follows

- **Space Technology** India has successfully launched indigenously built satellites such as the Aryabhatta and INSAT series with the help of electronics industry.
- **Software Industry** The software industry has emerged as one of the fastest-growing sectors in electronics in India. Bengaluru and Hyderabad are the leading sectors of the software industry.
- Bengaluru is called the 'Silicon Valley of India' due to large number of information technology companies located there.

Favourable Factors for the Growth of Software Industry in Bengaluru are

(i) Progressive government policies.
(ii) World class information technology infrastructure.
(iii) Pleasant and comfortable climate.
(iv) Centre for international conferences & workshops.

Television and Audio

The television and audio industries came into existence in the 1990s due to the progress of the electronics industry. Mumbai, Kolkata, Chennai and Pune are important centers of production.

EXAM ORIENTED QUESTIONS

TYPE - 1

1 Mark

Multiple Choice Questions

Q.1 Why are industries considered the backbone of the economy?
(a) They provide consumer goods.
(b) They create job opportunities for a large population.
(c) They provide finished goods for consumption and intermediate goods for other sectors.
(d) They focus only on the production of raw materials.

Ans. (c) They provide finished goods for consumption and intermediate goods for other sectors.

Q.2 Cotton, jute, textile and sugar industries come under which category?
(a) Mineral Based Industries
(b) Agro Based Industries
(c) Animal Based Industries
(d) Forest Based Industries

Ans. (b) Agro Based Industries

Q.3 Which of the following is a basic/key industry? **(2023)**
(a) Iron and steel industry
(b) Furniture production industry
(c) Electronic Industry
(d) Cotton textile manufacturing industry

Ans. (a) Iron and steel industry

Exp. Basic industries (or key industries) are those industries that produce raw materials or primary goods to all other industries.

Q.4 Banking, railways, post and telegraph industries are examples of which type of sector?
(a) Primary (b) Secondary
(c) Tertiary (d) Basic

Ans. (c) Tertiary

Q.5 .... industries are also known as household industries.
(a) Basic (b) Cooperative
(c) Cottage (d) None of these

Ans. (c) Cottage

Exp. Cottage industries are small-scale, home-based businesses where goods are produced by individuals or families using simple tools and low capital. Hence, they are called household industries.

Q.6 Molasses, pressmund and bagasse are the byproducts of ....
(a) silk industry (b) textile industry
(c) sugar industry (d) iron industry

Ans. (c) sugar industry

Q.7 Which of the following is a major problem faced by the sugar industry in India?
(a) Excessive government subsidies for sugar exports.
(b) Over-reliance on mechanisation in sugar mills.
(c) Fluctuating sugar prices and high production costs.
(d) Lack of demand for sugar in both domestic and international markets.

Ans. (c) Fluctuating sugar prices and high production costs.

Q.8 Name the by-product of the sugar industry used for making wax, carbon paper and shoe polish.
(a) Press mud (b) Khandsari
(c) Molasses (d) Bagasse

Ans. (a) Press mud

Exp. Press mud is a by-product produced during the sugar extraction process from sugarcane or sugar beet. It is a residue left after the juice is extracted from the crushed cane or beet in sugar mills.

Q.9 Which city is known as the 'Manchester of India'?
(a) Mumbai (b) Surat
(c) Ahmedabad (d) Kanpur

Ans. (c) Ahmedabad

Exp. It is because of the historical prominence of Ahmedabad in the textile industry, similar to Manchester in the United Kingdom.

Q.10 Which of the following states is the leading producer of silk?
(a) Rajasthan (b) Assam
(c) Uttar Pradesh (d) Karnataka

Ans. (d) Karnataka

Q.11 Varanasi in Uttar Pradesh is famous for ..... .
(a) cotton (b) silk (c) electronics (d) sugar

Ans. (b) Silk

Q.12 The rearing of silkworms for the production of silk is known as ....
(a) sericulture (b) horticulture
(c) pisciculture (d) apiculture

Ans. (a) sericulture

Q.13 In which year was the Tata Iron and Steel Company (TISCO) established?
(a) 1905 (b) 1907 (c) 1912 (d) 1915

Ans. (b) 1907

Q.14 The steel plant given in the image is situated in which state?

(a) Jharkhand (b) Karnataka
(c) Uttar Pradesh (d) Haryana

Ans. (a) Jharkhand

Q.15 Which among the following is the oldest steel plant in India?
(a) TISCO (b) IISCO
(c) Durgapur Steel Plant (d) Bhilai Steel Plant

Ans. (a) TISCO

Q.16 The Bhilai Steel Plant was established with the help of which nation?
(a) USSR (b) Germany (c) UK (d) USA

Ans. (a) USSR

Q.17 Bhilai steel plant is located in Durg district of ....
(a) West Bengal (b) Chhattisgarh
(c) Madhya Pradesh (d) Odisha

Ans. (b) Chhattisgarh

Q.18 Which steel plant amongst the following was set up in collaboration with Germany? **(ICSE Specimen 2024, 2025)**
(a) Bhilai (b) Tata Steel
(c) Visakhapatnam (d) Rourkela

Ans. (d) Rourkela

Q.19 Sachin and his friend are talking about the largest steel making company of India. To which of the following companies they are talking about?
(a) Steel Manufacturing Unit of India
(b) JSW Steel
(c) Steel Authority of India
(d) Rashtriya Ispat Nigam Limited

Ans. (c) Steel Authority of India

Q.20 Which of the following is not a centre for the iron and steel industry? **(ICSE 2024)**
(a) Bhilai (b) Bengaluru
(c) Rourkela (d) Visakhapatnam

Ans. (b) Bengaluru

Exp. Bengaluru in Karnataka is a centre for Electronics and IT industry.

Q.21 Read the table and identify the pair that is correctly matched.

Name of Plant	State
P. Rourkela	Assam
Q. Bhilai	Chhattisgarh
R. TISCO	Maharashtra
S. Visakhapatnam	Tamil Nadu

(a) P (b) Q (c) R (d) S

Ans. (b) Q

Q.22 Visakhapatnam steel plant obtains iron ore from .... in Chhattisgarh.
(a) Korba (b) Talcher
(c) Bailadila (d) Durg

Ans. (c) Bailadila

Q.23 Which of the following is a significant problem faced by the iron and steel industry in India?
(a) Low demand for iron and steel in the global market.
(b) Lack of water resources.
(c) High cost of production due to outdated technology and inadequate infrastructure.
(d) Consistent and stable prices of iron and steel in domestic markets.

Ans. (c) High cost of production due to outdated technology and inadequate infrastructure.

Q.24 What is one major advantage of using petrochemicals?
(a) They are biodegradable and environmentally friendly.
(b) They are renewable and easily replenishable.
(c) They are versatile and used in a wide range of products.
(d) They require no energy to produce.

Ans. (c) They are versatile and used in a wide range of products.

Q.25 Which industry amongst the following has revolutionised the lifestyle of the Indian masses in recent years? **(ICSE 2025)**
(a) Cotton Textile (b) Electronic
(c) Iron and Steel (d) Sugar

Ans. (b) Electronic

Q.26 Industries which are owned and controlled by state or Central Government:
(a) Agro-based
(b) Joint sector
(c) Public sector
(d) Mini industries

Ans. (c) Public sector

Q.27 Which of the following household products 1s associated with the petrochemical industry? **(ICSE 2025)**

(a) Glass bottle
(b) Wooden chopping board
(c) Kitchen knife
(d) Plastic mug

Ans. (d) Plastic mug

Q.28 Non - mulberry silk such as muga, tassar and eri are produced in

(a) Assam (b) Gujarat (c) Nagaland (d) Kerala

Ans. (a) Assam

Q.29 Bombyx mori is associated with

(a) cotton textile (b) jute industry
(c) silk industry (d) sugar industry

Ans. (c) silk industry

Q.30 Industry has a tendency to migrate towards South

(a) Cotton textile (b) Iron-steel (c) Sugar (d) Silk

Ans. (c) Sugar

TYPE - 2 1 Mark

Assertion-Reason Questions

Q.1 Assertion (A) The cotton industry in India provides employment to millions of people.

Reason (R) Cotton cultivation and processing are labour-intensive activities that require a large workforce in both rural and urban areas.

(a) Both A and R are true, and R is the correct explanation of A
(b) Both A and R are true but R does not explain A
(c) A is true, but R is false
(d) A is false, but R is true

Ans. (a) Both A and R are true, and R is the correct explanation of A

Q.2. Assertion (A) The silk industry in India faces challenges due to high production costs and limited raw material availability.

Reason (R) India is highly dependent on imports for silk raw materials such as cocoons.

(a) Both A and R are true and R is the correct explanation of A
(b) Both A and R are true, but R does not explain A
(c) A is true, but R is false (d) A is false, but R is true

Ans. (c) A is true but R is false

Q.3 Assertion (A) The iron and steel industry in India faces challenges such as high production costs.

Reason (R) Most of the steel plants in India use modern technology methods.

(a) Both A and R are true and R is the correct explanation of A
(b) Both A and R are true, but R does not explain A
(c) A is true,but R is false
(d) A is false,but R is true

Ans. (c) A is true, but R is false

Q.4 Assertion (A) TISCO was established in 1907 and is one of the largest steel manufacturing companies in India.

Reason (R) The plant is strategically located near the mineral-rich region of Jamshedpur to ensure easy access to raw materials for steel production.

(a) Both A and R are true and R is the correct explanation of A
(b) Both A and R are true, but R does not explain A
(c) A is true,but R is false
(d) A is false,but R is true

Ans. (a) Both A and R are true and R is the correct explanation of A

Q.5 Assertion (A) The software industry in India contributes significantly to the economy of the country.

Reason (R) India's software exports have become a major source of foreign exchange earnings and employment generation.

(a) Both A and R are true and R is the correct explanation of A
(b) Both A and R are true, but R does not explain A
(c) A is true, but R is false
(d) A is false, but R is true

Ans. (a) Both A and R are true and R is the correct explanation of A

TYPE - 3 2 Marks

Short Answer Type Questions

Q.1 With reference to industrialisation, answer the following questions.

(i) How has industrialisation helped India?
(ii) What is the need for rapid industrialisation in India?

Ans. (i) Industrialisation has helped India by boosting economic growth, creating jobs, improving infrastructure, fostering technological advancements, increasing exports, promoting rural development and raising the standard of living for many people.

(ii) Rapid industrialisation strengthens the economy by providing employment to a large number of the population.

Q.2 **Mention two reasons, why industrial development is important for India?**

Or How are the industries important for India. (ICSE 2023)

Ans. Two reasons why industrial development is important for India are

- It provides employment to a large number of people.
- It supports agriculture by providing farm machinery, fertilisers, etc.

Q.3 **With reference to the basic industries, answer the following. (ICSE 2020)**

(i) What are basic industries?

(ii) Give one example of a basic industry in India.

Ans. (i) Basic industries are the industries that produce raw materials or essential goods used by other industries to manufacture finished products. Examples - Mining, steel production, oil extraction, etc.

(ii) Iron and steel industry.

Q.4 **With reference to the classification of industries, answer the following questions.**

(i) How would you classify industries?

(ii) Mention the classification of industries on the basis of ownership in India.

Ans. (i) The industries are classified on the basis of raw materials, size, location, type of product manufactured, etc.

(ii) The industries are classified on the basis of ownership in India as public sector, private sector, joint sector and co-operative sector.

Q.5 **The heavy industry sector has been a key player in ensuring job security and enabling India to become one of the fastest-growing economies in the world. The sector has contributed significantly to the country's socio-economic development and urbanisation, due to which energy demand has been on the rise.** *www.theclimategroup.org*

(i) What is the most important requirement for the heavy engineering industry in India?

(ii) Name one important centre for ship building and aircraft construction.

Ans. (i) The most important requirement for the heavy engineering industry in India is the availability of raw materials like iron ore, coal and steel along with skilled labour and good infrastructure.

(ii) One important center for shipbuilding in India is Kochi and aircraft construction In Bengaluru.

Q.6 **Distinguish between agro-based and mineral-based industries with one example of each. (ICSE 2017)**

Ans. Agro-based and mineral-based industries can be differentiated as follows

Agro-Based Industries	Mineral-Based Industries
These industries derive their raw material from agricultural products.	These industries are derive their raw material from minerals or ores.
These produces products related to food, clothing or raw materials for other industries.	These produces goods used in construction, manufacturing and heavy industries.
Examples - textile industry, sugar industry	Examples - steel industry, cement industry

Q.7 **Mention two advantages of setting up a small scale industry. (ICSE Specimen 2018)**

Ans. Two advantages of setting up a small scale industry are

(i) Small-scale industries require less capital investment, making it easier for entrepreneurs to start and manage the business.

(ii) These industries create job opportunities, particularly in rural and semi-urban areas, helping reduce unemployment.

Q.8 **Distinguish between a public sector industry and private sector industry? Give an example of industry in each of the two sectors. (ICSE Specimen Semester-I, 2022)**

Ans. Public and private sector industries can be distinguished as follows

Public Sector Industry	Private Sector Industry
These are owned and managed by the government.	These are owned and managed by private individuals or companies.
Primarily aims at public welfare and service.	Aimed at profit generation and wealth creation.
Examples - BHEL, BEL	Examples - TISCO, Reliance Industries

Q.9 **Explain the terms (ICSE Specimen 2023)**

(i) Ancillary industry (ii) Public sector industry

Ans. (i) An ancillary industry is a small-scale industry that supports and supplies goods or services to a larger industry. These industries provide essential components, raw materials, or services that help the industries, like automobile or manufacturing.

(ii) Public sector industry is an industry that is owned and operated by the government. The aim of this industry is to provide essential services, promote economic development by serving the public interest.

Q.10 **State four geographical factors which should be kept in mind while setting up an agro-based industry.**

Ans. Four geographical factors to consider when setting up an agro-based industry are

(i) **Climate** The region should have a suitable climate for growing the raw materials required for the industry.

(ii) **Soil Type** The quality and fertility of the soil should support the cultivation of the specific agricultural products used in the industry.

(iii) **Water Availability** Access to adequate water sources is crucial for both agriculture and the processing of raw materials.

(iv) **Proximity to Raw Materials** The location should be near areas where raw agricultural products are grown to reduce transportation costs and ensure fresh supply.

Q.11 **Give reason for each of the following.**

(i) Sugar industry has developed in Maharashtra.

(ii) Silk plays an important role for the Indian economy.

Ans. (i) (a) Maharashtra has hot and humid climate conditions which are ideal for growing sugarcane.

(b) Also, the state has a well-developed irrigation system which provides a regular supply for the irrigation of sugarcane.

(ii) India is a major producer of silk, providing jobs to millions. The silk industry boosts exports and supports the textile sector.

Q.12 **'Though Uttar Pradesh has the largest number of sugar mills yet Maharashtra is the largest producer of sugar'. Give any two reasons to justify the statement.** **(ICSE 2017)**

Ans. Two reasons why Maharashtra is the largest producer of sugar are

(i) Maharashtra has a more suitable climate and better irrigation facilities which support higher sugarcane yields compared to Uttar Pradesh.

(ii) Farmers in Maharashtra use more advanced farming techniques and better crop management practices.

Q.13 **State any two factors that are responsible for the growth of the cotton textile industry in Kolkata.** **(ICSE 2025)**

Ans. The growth of the cotton textile industry in Kolkata is due to the following factors

- **Availability of Cheap Labour** Kolkata has a large workforce, including migrant labourers from neighbouring states like Bihar and Odisha, which helps in keeping production costs low.
- **Well-Connected Transportation System** The city has a good network of roads, railways and a major port, making it easy to transport raw materials (cotton) and finished goods both within India and internationally.

Q.14 **Give two reasons why the cotton textile industry has developed in Mumbai.** **(ICSE Specimen 2018)**

Ans. Two reasons why the cotton textile industry has developed in Mumbai are

(i) Mumbai has a well-developed port system, which facilitates the easy import of raw cotton and the export of finished textile products.

(ii) Mumbai's humid climate is ideal for cotton spinning and weaving, as it helps maintain the moisture content needed for cotton processing.

Q.15 **Mention two problems of the cotton textile industry in India.** **(ICSE 2016, 2018)**

Ans. Two problems of the cotton textile industry in India are

- Many mills in India are very old and are very inefficient. They have old types of machinery as compared to some other developed countries.
- Indian cotton textiles have to face stiff competition from synthetic fibers which are cheaper and need less maintenance.

Q.16 **Give two reasons why Ahmedabad in Gujarat is famous for cotton textile Industry.** **(ICSE Specimen 2017)**

Ans. Two reasons why Ahmedabad in Gujarat is famous for the cotton textile industry are

- Ahmedabad is located near major cotton-producing regions which ensures a regular supply of raw cotton for textile mills.
- The city has well-developed transportation and a large number of spinning and weaving mills, making it a hub for the cotton textile industry.

Q.17 **'Karnataka has developed an important state for the growth of the silk industry'. Give two reasons to justify the statement.**

Or **Karnataka is the leading state for silk production in India. Give any two reasons to justify the above statement.** **(ICSE 2025)**

Ans. Two reasons why Karnataka has developed as an important state for the growth of the silk industry are

- Karnataka has a warm, humid climate ideal for sericulture (silk farming) which supports the growth of mulberry trees, the primary food for silkworms.

- The state has well-developed infrastructure, including a network of silk-producing regions and government support, which has helped promote silk farming and processing in the state.

Q.18 **With reference to the silk industry in India, answer the following questions**
(i) **Why is the silk industry considered as a small scale industry?**
(ii) **Name two types of silk produced in India.**

Ans. (i) The silk industry is considered a small-scale industry due to its low capital investment and labour-intensive nature. Setting up a silk farm or a small silk processing unit requires relatively less investment compared to large-scale industries.

(ii) Tasar and muga are the two types of silk produced in India.

Q.19 **Give two reasons for the importance of the silk industry in India.**

Ans. Two reasons for the importance of the silk industry in India are
- Silk industry provides employment to lakhs of people.
- The silk industry contributes significantly to India's economy by generating foreign exchange through exports of silk products like sarees, garments and textiles.

Q.20 **With reference to the silk industry in India, answer the following questions.**
(i) **Define sericulture** **(ICSE Specimen 2017)**
(ii) **Name the state that is the leading producer of silk in India.** **(ICSE 2015)**

Ans. (i) Sericulture is the practice of farming silkworms to produce silk. It involves rearing silkworms, feeding them mulberry leaves, and collecting the silk threads from their cocoons after they are spun.

(ii) Karnataka is the leading producer of silk in India.

Q.21 **The silk handloom industry is favourable in Mysore. Give two reasons.** **(ICSE 2014)**

Ans. The silk handloom industry is favourable in Mysore for the following two reasons

(i) Mysore is known for its abundant supply of mulberry silk which is essential for producing fine silk fabrics.

(ii) Mysore has a long tradition of silk weaving with a skilled workforce proficient in the craft.

Q.22 **With reference to industries, answer the following questions**
(i) **From where Tata Steel gets its supply of coal, iron ore and water supply from?** **(ICSE Specimen 2023)**
(ii) **What is the significance of the electronics industry for education, entertainment and research?**

Ans. (i) Tata Steel sources its raw materials as follows
- **Coal** From Jharia coal field
- **Iron Ore** The company sources iron ore from Noamundi Mines (Jharkhand) and Mayurbhanj (Odisha)
- **Water** water supply from nearby rivers, such as the Subarnarekha and Kharkai rivers, for its steel production processes.

(ii) The electronics industry is crucial for education by providing tools like computers and e-learning platforms. In entertainment, it powers devices such as TVs and gaming consoles, enabling digital media consumption. For research, electronics supplies instruments that help in data collection and experimentation.

Q.23 **Give two reasons why iron and steel industries are concentrated in the Chhota Nagpur region.**

Ans. Two reasons why iron and steel industries are concentrated in the Chhota Nagpur region are
- The Chhota Nagpur region is rich in essential raw materials like iron ore, coal and limestone, which are crucial for iron and steel production.
- The Chhota Nagpur belt has well-developed transport networks, including railways and roads, which facilitate the easy movement of raw materials to factories and finished goods to markets.

Q.24 **The iron and steel industry in India has faced several challenges, such as high production costs, outdated technology, and environmental concerns. However, the industry continues to grow.**
(i) **Explain why the iron and steel industry in India continues to grow despite the challenges of high production costs and outdated technology.**
(ii) **How have government policies contributed to the growth of the iron and steel industry in India?**

Ans. (i) The continued growth of the iron and steel industry in India can be attributed to the abundant availability of raw materials such as iron ore, coal and limestone. These essential materials are crucial for steel production and are found in large quantities within India.

(ii) Government policies have supported the growth of India's iron and steel industry through subsidies, tax incentives and investment in infrastructure. Policies ensuring a steady supply of raw materials and promoting exports have also played a key role in boosting the industry.

Q.25 **With reference to the iron and steel industry, answer the following questions.**

(i) **Why is iron and steel industry called a basic industry?**

(ii) **From where does the Bhilai iron and steel plant get the supply of limestone?**

Ans. (i) The iron and steel industry is called a basic industry because it provides essential raw materials like steel and iron which are used in the production of a wide range of other goods and industries, such as construction, automobiles and machinery.

(ii) The Bhilai Iron and Steel Plant receives its supply of limestone from the Kodarma region in Jharkhand which is rich in limestone deposits.

Q.26 **'The Iron and steel industry constitutes the backbone of modern industrial economy'. Give two reasons to justify the statement.** **(ICSE 2017)**

Ans. Two reasons why the iron and steel industry constitutes the backbone of a modern industrial economy are

(i) Iron and steel are essential raw materials used in the production of machinery, infrastructure, transportation and various other industrial products which makes it a key driver for economic growth and industrialisation.

(ii) The iron and steel industry generates significant employment opportunities and contributes to the development of infrastructure which supports other sectors of the economy, thus boosting overall economic growth.

Q.27 Give reasons for the following questions

(i) **Iron and steel industries are not found in the Western part of India.**

(ii) **Most of the iron and steel plants in India are public sector undertakings.**

Ans. (i) The Western part of India lacks sufficient natural resources like coal and iron ore which are essential for iron and steel production.

(ii) The iron and steel industry requires heavy investment in infrastructure, technology and raw materials which often makes it difficult for private companies to establish and sustain such industries. To promote industrial growth and ensure national control over key resources, the Indian government has invested heavily in establishing public sector undertakings (PSUs) in this sector.

Q.28 With reference to the integrated steel plants, answer the following questions

(i) What are integrated steel plants?

(ii) Name any one integrated steel plant of the public sector in India.

Ans. (i) Integrated steel plants are large factories where all stages of steel production take place from processing raw materials like iron ore and coal toproducing finished steel. These plants have facilities for smelting iron, converting it into steel, and shaping it into products like sheets, rods and bars.

(ii) Bhilai Steel Plant

Q.29 **With reference to the petrochemicals, answer the following questions**

(i) **Define petrochemicals.**

(ii) **Name any two petrochemical industries in India.**

Ans. (i) Petrochemicals are chemical products derived from petroleum or natural gas. They are used to create a wide range of products, including plastics, fertilisers, synthetic rubber, detergents and various industrial chemicals. These chemicals are produced through refining and processing raw oil and gas materials.

(ii) Reliance Industries Limited (RIL) and Hindustan Petroleum Corporation Limited (HPCL) are the two petrochemical industries.

Q.30 **Mention two reasons why petrochemical products are replacing traditional raw materials.**

Ans. Two reasons why petrochemical products are replacing traditional raw materials are

(i) Petrochemical products are often cheaper to produce and more readily available compared to traditional raw materials, making them an attractive alternative for industries.

(ii) Petrochemical products, such as plastics and synthetic materials are highly versatile, durable and can be tailored to suit various industrial applications, making them more efficient and long-lasting than traditional materials.

Q.31 **Give two reasons why most of the petrochemical units are in Maharashtra and Gujarat.**

Ans. Two reasons why most of the petrochemical units are in Maharashtra and Gujarat are

(i) Both Maharashtra and Gujarat have well-developed ports like Mumbai and Vadodara which facilitate easy import of raw materials like crude oil and export of petrochemical products.

(ii) These states have advanced industrial infrastructure, including transport networks, skilled labour and access to power which supports the growth of petrochemical industries.

Q.32 Mention two reasons for the development of the petro-chemical industry in India. **(ICSE Semester II 2022)**

Ans. Two reasons for the development of the petro-chemical industry in India are

(i) **Availability of Raw Materials** India has abundant reserves of petroleum and natural gas which provide the essential raw materials for the production of petrochemicals.

(ii) **Growing Domestic Demand** The increasing demand for petrochemical products in industries like textiles, packaging, pharmaceuticals and automotive has increased the growth of the petrochemical sector in India.

Q.33 Mention two reasons for the importance of the electronic industry in India's development.

Ans. Two reasons for the importance of the electronic industry in India's development are

(i) The electronic industry drives innovation and technological progress, contributing to sectors like communication, IT, healthcare and defense which are crucial for India's overall development.

(ii) The industry creates millions of job opportunities in manufacturing, research and development and services, helping reduce unemployment and improve the economy.

Q.34 Give two geographical reasons for the growth of IT industries in Bengaluru.

Ans. Two geographical reasons for the growth of IT industries in Bengaluru are

(i) Bengaluru is well-connected by road, rail and air, giving easy access to national and international markets, making it a favourable location for IT businesses.

(ii) The city has well-developed infrastructure, including office spaces, power supply and communication networks which support the operations of IT companies and encourage industry growth.

TYPE - 4 — 3 Marks

Long Answer Type Questions

Q.1 With reference to the sugar industry, answer the following questions **(ICSE 2019)**

(i) Why should these industries be located near sugarcane growing areas?

(ii) Name any two byproducts of the sugar industry.

(iii) Mention one leading sugar-producing state in North India and one in South India.

Ans. (i) (a) Sugar industries are located near sugarcane growing areas to reduce transportation costs.

(b) Sugarcane is perishable raw material, it has to be crushed within 24 hrs else the sucrose content is reduced.

(ii) Molasses, Bagasse

(iii) **North India** Uttar Pradesh

South India Maharashtra

Q.2 Lakshmi, a farmer from Tamil Nadu, plays a vital role in the sugar industry of the Peninsular region of India. The sugar industry in this region, particularly in states like Maharashtra, Karnataka and Tamil Nadu, not only supports thousands of farmers like Lakshmi but also contributes significantly to the economy through employment, rural development and the production of various by-products such as ethanol and jaggery.

Mention three factors that have helped the sugar industry flourish in the peninsular region rather than in the Northern regions of India. **(ICSE 2014)**

Ans. Three factors that have helped the sugar industry flourish in the peninsular region are

(i) The warm, tropical climate in Southern India is ideal for sugarcane cultivation.

(ii) The region experiences a longer sugarcane growing season which gives better yields.

(iii) Proximity to ports facilitates easy export of sugar.

Q.3 Raghav has been given a project by his teacher in which he has to write about the by-products of an industry that is used for preparing shoe polish, carbon paper and cardboard. **(ICSE 2025)**

(i) Which industry will he be writing about?

(ii) Name any two by-products of the industry mentioned by you.

Ans. (i) Raghav will be writing about the Sugar Industry because its by-products are used in making shoe polish, carbon paper, and cardboard.

(ii) Two by-products of the sugar industry are bagasse and molasses.

Q.4 With reference to the cotton textile industry, answer the following questions. **(ICSE Specimen Semester-II 2022)**

(i) Mention two reasons for the importance of the cotton textile industry.

(ii) Mention two reasons responsible for its poor performance.

Ans. (i) The two reasons for importance of the cotton textile industry are

(a) It provides employment to a large section of the population.

(b) It brings a lot of foreign exchange.

(ii) Two reasons responsible for the poor performance of cotton textile industry are

(a) **Lack of Raw Material** After the partition, India had to bear a huge loss of long-staple cotton as most of the centres went to Pakistan. Thus, in order to fulfil its requirement, India imports cotton from Pakistan, Kenya, Uganda, Sudan, Egypt, USA and Peru.

(b) **Old and Obsolete Machinery** Many mills in India are very old and are very inefficient. They have obsolete machinery as compared to some other developed countries. This proves to be an obstruction in higher production.

Q.5 Give a geographical reason for each of the following. **(ICSE 2018)**

(i) Silk industry is doing particularly well in Karnataka.

(ii) Petrochemical products are gaining popularity in modern times.

(iii) The electronics industry is proving to be an asset for our country in the field of education.

Ans. (i) The silk industry in Karnataka is doing well due to favourable climatic conditions for mulberry cultivation, skilled workforce, government support and a rich tradition of silk weaving.

(ii) Petrochemical products are gaining popularity because they are versatile, cost-effective and used in a wide range of industries, like plastics, textiles, pharmaceuticals and packaging, making them essential in modern life.

(iii) The electronics industry is an asset to education by providing essential tools like computers, tablets, projectors and interactive whiteboards. These technologies enhance learning, enable online education and improve access to information, making education more interactive and accessible.

Q.6 With reference to the silk industry, answer the following questions. **(ICSE 2014)**

(i) Why is Karnataka the largest producer of mulberry silk?

(ii) Mention two varieties of silk other than mulberry that are produced in India.

(iii) Name one silk weaving centre each in Uttar Pradesh and Maharashtra.

Ans. (i) Karnataka is the largest producer of mulberry silk due to its favourable climate, abundant mulberry cultivation and well-developed sericulture infrastructure along with government support and skilled labour for silk production.

(ii) Tasar and Muga

(iii) Varanasi (Uttar Pradesh) and Pune (Maharashtra)

Q.7 Give a geographic term for each of the following. **(ICSE 2017)**

(i) Non-mulberry silk produced in Madhya Pradesh.

(ii) Rejected cane after crushing.

(iii) The rearing of silk worms to obtain silk.

Ans. (i) Tasar Silk (ii) Bagasse

(iii) Sericulture

Q.8 State any three advantages of mini steel plants.

Ans. Three advantages of mini steel plants are

(i) Mini steel plants do not require huge capital investment like integrated steel plants.

(ii) Mini steel plants use scrap or sponge iron as raw materials, that is easily available and also helps in the recycling of iron.

(iii) These plants are set up in local areas so they suit local needs and cater to local demands.

Q.9 Study the picture given below and answer the following questions.

(i) Name the industry shown in the picture.

(ii) Give a brief description of this industry.

(iii) Name two public sector organisations related to this industry.

Ans. (i) This industry shown in the picture is the iron and steel industry.

(ii) The iron and steel industry produces iron and steel from raw materials like iron ore, coal and limestone. Iron is extracted through smelting and steel is made by refining iron further. This industry is crucial for manufacturing products such as construction materials, vehicles, and machinery, but it is also energy-intensive and has environmental impacts.

(iii) Indian Iron and Steel Company (IISCO) and Steel Authority of India Limited (SAIL).

Q.10 (i) Name the Iron and Steel industry located at Chhattisgarh. **(ICSE 2025)**

(ii) From where does the industry named by you above get its supply of the following?

(a) Iron ore (b) Coal

Ans. (i)The Iron and Steel industry located in Chhattisgarh is the Bhilai Steel Plant.

(ii) Sources of raw materials for Bhilai Steel Plant

(a) **Iron Ore** Sourced from the Dalli-Rajhara mines in Chhattisgarh.

(b) **Coal** Supplied from the Korba and Jharia coalfields.

Q.11 With reference to the Rourkela steel plant answer the following **(ICSE Specimen Semester-II 2022)**

(i) Name the state in which it is located.

(ii) Which country helped India to establish this steel plant?

(iii) From where it gets

(a) Iron ore (b) Limestone

Ans. (i) Rourkela steel plant is situated in Odisha.

(ii) Germany helped India to establish the Rourkela steel plant in the country in 1959 during the Second Five-Year Plan.

(iii) (a) Iron ore comes from the Bonaigarh, Mayurbanj and Keonjhar districts.

(b) It gets limestone from Birmitrapur.

Q.12 With reference to industries in India, answer the following. **(ICSE 2020)**

(i) From where does the Rourkela steel plant obtain its supply of coal?

(ii) Tata Iron and Steel plant obtains its supply of iron ore from which areas?

(iii) Name two cities that are important for the production of electronics.

Ans. (i) Rourkela steel plant obtains its supply of coal from the Jharia, Talcher and Korba coal fields.

(ii) Tata Iron and Steel plants obtain their supply of iron ore from Noamundi of Singhbhum region and Mayurbhanj.

(iii) Bengaluru and Hyderabad are important for the production of electronics.

Q.13 Give names of the following.

(i) First seashore-based city on the East coast of India which has an iron and steel industry.

(ii) The iron and steel plant set-up with German collaboration.

(iii) A city which has a plant manufacturing Maruti cars.

Ans. (i) Visakhapatnam is the first seashore-based steel plant which was started in 1992.

(ii) The Rourkela plant was set up in the Sundergarh district of Odisha with the technical help of German firm Krupps and Demag in 1959 during the Second Five-Year Plan.

(iii) Gurugram in Haryana has a plant manufacturing Maruti cars.

Q.14 Name a manufacturing centre for each of the following industries. **(ICSE 2014)**

(i) Engines for MIG aircraft (ii) Diesel locomotives

(iii) Software

Ans. (i) Koraput has the engine division of Hindustan Aeronautics Limited (HAL), which is a defence enterprise of the Government of India. This factory manufactures aircraft engines for MIG and Sukhoi fighter aircraft.

(ii) The diesel locomotives are manufactured by the diesel locomotive works in Varanasi.

(iii) The manufacturing centers of software industries are Bengaluru and Pune.

Q.15 With reference to the electronics industry, answer the following questions. **(ICSE Specimen 2023)**

(i) What is the significance of the electronics industry in recent times?

(ii) Name two cities that have leading software companies.

Ans. (i) The significance of the electronics industry is that it has revolutionised the lifestyle of people today. It covers a wide range of products including transistor sets, televisions, telephone exchanges, telecommunication, computers and various equipment for posts and telegraph, defence, railway and meteorological departments.

(ii) Bengaluru and Pune

Q.16 Give a reason for each of the following.

(i) The largest mineral-based industry in India.

(ii) Mini-steel plants cause less pollution than integrated steel plants.

(iii) The electronic industry has made an impact on both entertainment and education.

Ans. (i) The iron and steel industry is the largest mineral-based industry in India as iron and steel are the important elements in the heavy industrial structure and form the backbone of industrial development. It gives the raw material for other industries such as automobiles, locomotives, railways, shipbuilding, machine and tools, dams, manufacture of defence equipment etc.

(ii) Mini-steel plants cause less pollution because they use electric and induction furnaces for processing.

(iii) The electronic industry gives us various products like televisions, computers, laptops, tabs, radio, DTH, etc. All these electronic products have become a major source of entertainment as well as education. For example, electronic gadgets with the help of the internet provide us with the information we require for educating ourselves and our children.

Q.17 (i) Name the two most important centres of the electronic industry in India. **(ICSE Specimen 2017)**

(ii) Name the largest and the oldest integrated iron and steel plant in the private sector in India.

(iii) What is meant by a mini steel plant? State its advantages.

Ans. (i) The two most important centres of the electronic industry in India are Bengaluru and Hyderabad.

(ii) The largest and the oldest integrated iron and steel plant in the private sector is Tata Iron and Steel Company Limited at Jamshedpur.

(iii) A mini steel plant uses electric arc and induction furnaces for processing scrap iron and sponge iron to produce alloy steel, mild steel and stainless steel.

Its major advantage is that it uses mostly steel scrap as raw material, which is relatively cheap.

Q.18 Today, due to the explosion of the Silicon Age paradigm and the digital era lifestyle globally, electronics system design and manufacturing (ESDM) has emerged as one of the fastest-growing industries globally.

(i) Explain the significance of the electronics industry in India.

(ii) How does the electronics industry contribute in the growth of the aerospace sector of India?

(iii) What factors are driving the growth of the electronics industry in India?

Ans. (i) The electronics industry in India is crucial for economic growth, contributing significantly to GDP, employment and technological advancements. It drives innovation, supports sectors like telecommunications, consumer goods, manufacturing, etc. and enhances India's competitiveness in the global market.

(ii) The electronics industry supports India's aerospace sector by providing advanced electronic systems for avionics, navigation, communication and control systems. These components are essential for aircraft development, satellite systems and defense technologies, enhancing the sector's capabilities and innovation.

(iii) Key factors include increased domestic demand for consumer electronics, government initiatives like 'Make in India' and PLI schemes, foreign investments, a growing middle class, digitalisation, and advancements in technology like IOT, AI and 5G which create new market opportunities.

TYPE - 5

10 Marks

Structured Questions

Q.1 (i) Mention two points of difference between small scale and large scale industry. **(2)** **(ICSE Specimen 2025)**

(ii) Explain two ways in which the cotton textile industry is important for India's economy. **(2)**

(iii) With reference to the petrochemical industry, answer the following **(3)**

(a) State a reason for the growing popularity of this industry in recent times.

(b) Why is it located close to oil refineries?

(c) Name any two petrochemical products.

(iv) Give one reason to explain each of the following **(3)**

(a) Sugar production is gradually gaining importance in peninsular India.

(b) Indian silk products are becoming less popular in the international market.

(c) The importance of the iron and steel industry will never decline.

Ans. (i) The differences between small scale and large scale industry are

Small Scale Industry	Large Scale Industry
Smaller production units with limited capacity.	Large-scale operations with extensive infrastructure.
Requires lower capital investment.	Requires significant capital investment and advanced technology.

(ii) The cotton textile industry is important for India's economy due to the following reasons

- It is a major source of employment in India, providing jobs to millions of people, particularly in rural areas. It supports workers in various stages of production from cotton cultivation to manufacturing and distribution.
- The cotton textile industry contributes significantly to India's export revenue. India is one of the largest exporters of cotton textiles, including garments, fabric and yarn which strengthens the country's trade balance and supports foreign exchange earnings and cost effective.

(iii) (a) The petrochemical industry is growing due to the increasing demand for plastic, synthetic fibers and other chemical products used in various sectors like packaging, automotive and healthcare.

(b) Petrochemical industries are located near oil refineries to ensure easy access to raw materials like petroleum and natural gas, which are essential for producing petrochemical products.

(c) Polyethylene and polyester are the two petrochemical products.

(iv) (a) Peninsular India has a favourable climate for growing sugarcane along with fertile land and irrigation facilities which boost sugar production in the region.

(b) The increasing competition from cheaper synthetic fibers and low-cost silk production in other countries has led to a decline in the global demand for Indian silk products.

(c) The importance of the iron and steel industry will never decline as they are essential materials for construction, infrastructure development and manufacturing, making the industry fundamental to economic growth and technological advancements.

Q.2 (i) State the difference between agro-based industry and forest-based industry. Give one example for each type of industry. **(2)**

(ii) India, however, far outranks China in terms of its consumption of silk. Data suggests India is the world's highest silk consumer, much of which has traditionally been consumed in the handloom space. *www.globaltextilesource.com* **(2)**

(a) Why is the silk industry of India losing the market in recent times?

(b) Which type of silk is most produced in India?

(iii) (a) Mention two problems faced by the sugar industry of India. **(3)**

(b) During which five-year plan was the Bhilai steel plant established?

(c) Name two Indian cities that are famous for silk production.

(iv) Study the picture given below and answer the following questions. **(3)**

(a) Which type of industry is shown in the image above?

(b) How do petrochemicals contribute to the manufacturing of plastics?

(c) Name two common products made from petrochemicals.

Ans. (i) The difference between agro and forest-based industry is as follows

- **Agro-based** These industries rely on agricultural products as raw materials for production. They primarily focus on processing crops and other farm products. Example - cotton textile.
- **Forest-based** These industries depend on forest resources such as timber, wood, and other forest products for manufacturing goods. Example - paper and pulp industry.

(ii) (a) The silk industry in India is losing market share due to competition from cheaper synthetic fibers like polyester and nylon which are more affordable and easier to maintain. Also, the high production costs and labour-intensive nature of silk production make it less competitive globally.

(b) The most produced type of silk in India is mulberry silk.

(iii) (a) Two problems faced by the sugar industry in India are

- The sugar industry faces irregularities in the supply of sugarcane due to dependency on monsoons which leads to fluctuations in production levels.
- The industry struggles with low sugarcane yield and outdated farming practices which results in lower efficiency and higher production costs.

(b) It was established during the second five-year plan.

(c) Bangalore and Mysore

(iv) (a) Petrochemical Industry

(b) Petrochemicals contribute to the manufacturing of plastics by providing key raw materials such as ethylene, propylene and butadiene. These compounds are derived from crude oil and natural gas and are polymerised to create various types of plastics.

(c) Plastic and synthetic fibers

Q.3 (i) (a) Based on the ownership, what type of industry is Visakhapatnam steel plant? **(ICSE 2024) (2)**

(b) What is meant by cooperative sector industry?

(ii) Explain the following terms **(2)**

(a) Sericulture

(b) Integrated steel plant

(iii) Give one reason to explain each of the following **(3)**

(a) Mini-steel plants help in conservation of coal.

(b) Location of the sugar industry is shifting to the Southern part of India.

(c) The electronic industry is growing at a fast rate.

(iv) (a) State two conditions that favour the location of cotton textile industry in Ahmedabad. **(3)**

(b) State any one advantage of locating iron and steel industry at Rourkela.

Ans. (i) (a) The Visakhapatnam steel plant is a public sector industry. It is owned and operated by Rashtriya Ispat Nigam Limited (RINL), which is a government-owned company under the Ministry of Steel, Government of India.

(b) A cooperative sector industry refers to an industry that is owned and operated by a group of individuals who work together for their mutual benefit.

(ii) (a) Sericulture is the process of growing silkworms to produce silk threads which are used to make fabrics.

(b) An Integrated steel plant is a facility that produces steel by processing raw materials like iron ore, coal and limestone through various stages, including smelting, refining and casting. It integrates all stages of steel production, from raw material processing to finished products at one location.

(iii) (a) Mini-steel plants help in the conservation of coal by utilising scrap steel as their primary raw material instead of relying heavily on iron ore and coal. They primarily use electric arc furnaces or induction furnaces which consume much less coal compared to traditional blast furnaces.

(b) The sugar industry is shifting to Southern India due to the region's favourable climate for sugarcane cultivation, higher crop yields, better irrigation, government incentives and proximity to ports.

(c) The electronic industry in India is growing rapidly due to rising consumer demand, technological advancements, government support like "Make in India", increased local manufacturing and the expansion of digital infrastructure and e-commerce.

(iv) (a) Two conditions that favour the location of the cotton textile industry in Ahmedabad are

- Ahmedabad is near major cotton-producing regions, which helps in a steady supply of raw material for the textile industry.
- Moist climate as located near the sea.
- Ahmedabad has well-developed road, rail and port connectivity which facilitates easy transportation of raw materials and finished goods.

(b) One advantage of locating the iron and steel industry at Rourkela is its proximity to essential raw materials (coal from Jharia, iron from Sundargarh) that are required for iron and steel industry, which are readily available in the surrounding areas, ensuring a steady supply for steel production.

10

TRANSPORT

Transport refers to the movement of goods and services from one place to another using various means such as roads, railways, airways and waterways.

Importance of Transport

- It helps in transportation of raw material to industries.
- It helps in connecting distant or remote regions with urban centers.
- It plays a major role in the tourism industry by making travel accessible.

Roadways

It is a very important means of transportation for the development of a country as it is capable of connecting every area of a region with another and provides door to door service. India has the second largest road network in the world after the USA.

Road networks are classified as National Highways, Expressways, Golden Quadrilateral.

National Highways

- These roads are constructed and maintained by the Central Government and are meant for inter-state transport.
- The longest highway in India is NH-7 which is from Varanasi to Kanyakumari.
- The National Highway Authority of India (NHAI) is responsible for the development, maintenance and management of National Highways in India.

Expressways

- Expressways are high-speed, multi-lane roads designed for long-distance traffic with limited access points.
- Some of the major expressways of India are - Agra-Lucknow Expressway, Yamuna Expressway, Delhi-Gurgaon Expressway, etc.
- Expressways are constructed to ensure smooth travel. Mostly they are toll roads.

Golden Quadrilateral

It is a network of highways connecting four major cities in India - Delhi, Mumbai, Chennai and Kolkata. These highways form a quadrilateral across the country.

Objectives/Benefits of Golden Quadrilateral

(i) The purpose is to reduce the time and distance.

(ii) Helps in industrial growth of smaller towns through which it passes.

(iii) Provides job opportunities.

North-South and East-West Corridors

- These corridors are a part of the Golden Quadrilateral project. It consists of 4/6 lane expressways.
- North-South corridor connects Srinagar with Kanyakumari.
- The East-West corridor connects Silchar in Assam with Porbandar in Gujarat.

Advantages of Roadways

- Cheapest means of transportation.
- Roadways help to connect the remotest villages and hilly areas to towns, cities and plain areas.
- Roads provide the facility of door-to-door service. They minimise the cost of loading and unloading of products and goods.
- Roads can be constructed even in irregular land and hilly regions where other transport systems are difficult to develop.

Disadvantages of Roadways

- It is not considered a safe mode of transport as road accidents frequently take place.
- Village roads are unmetalled and badly maintained.
- Increased road traffic contributes to air pollution, noise pollution and higher fuel consumption which affects the environment.
- Roads require frequent maintenance and repairs.
- Traffic Jams.

Railways

- Railways constitute a principal means of transportation for freight and passengers. India has the fourth-largest railway network in the world, covering over 67,000 kilometers.
- There are three gauges - Broad Gauge (1.676 mt), Meter Gauge (1m) Narrow Gauge (0.762 m).
- The railways in India started in 1853 from Mumbai to Thane which covered a distance of about 34 km.
- There are a total of 16 railway zones in which the railway network has been divided.

Advantages of Railways

- It is an affordable means of transportation, especially for long-distance travel and freight.
- It is considered a safer travel option. Railways generally have a lower accident rate compared to road transport.
- It can carry a large number of passengers and significant amounts of goods, making it efficient for mass transport.
- Unites people from one corner to the other.

Disadvantages of Railways

- Building and maintaining rail infrastructure, including tracks, stations and bridges is expensive.
- Rail services can be delayed or disrupted due to issues like natural disasters, accidents or track maintenance.
- Trains cannot cross seas and oceans. It cannot be laid on the landscape which has a loose soil base.
- Face tough connection with road transport as road provide door to door service.
- Obsolete machinery, track and equipment.

Airways

- Airways refers to the system of air transportation that includes the movement of passengers and goods through aircrafts.
- Air transport in India was started in 1911 when airmail operations commenced between Allahabad and Naini.
- The Airports Authority of India (AAI) is the nodal agency that provides safe and efficient air traffic services in the country.
- Airport can be classified into - International Airport, National Airport, Pawan Hans Helicopters Ltd.
- Jet Airways (India) Ltd, Spicejet Ltd., Vistara, Go Airlines (India) Pvt. Ltd. are some of the private airlines in India.

Advantages of Airways

- It is a comfortable and the fastest means of transportation.
- It connects countries and continents, promoting international trade, tourism and businesses.
- It provides access to places that are difficult to reach by road or rail.

Disadvantages of Airways

- It is often more expensive than other modes of transport.
- Flight schedules can be disrupted by adverse weather conditions.
- Airports are generally located in or near cities which makes air transport less accessible to rural areas.

Waterways

- Waterways are bodies of water like rivers, lakes and seas that are used for transporting goods and people.
- Water transport can be broadly categorised into two groups which are
  (i) **Inland Waterways** These are navigable rivers, lakes-canals, etc. used for transporting goods and passengers within a country. Inland Waterways Authority of India (IWAI) is the statutory authority that looks after the development and regulation of inland waterways in India.
    - National Waterway 1- On Ganga starts from Allahabad to Haldia.
    - National Waterway 2- On Brahmaputra river from Sadia to Dhubri.
    - National Waterway 3- Coast of Kerala, runs from Kollan to Kottapuram.

  (ii) **Oceanic Waterways** These are the major sea routes used for the transportation of goods and passengers across oceans and seas.

Ports

- A port is a maritime facility comprising one or more loading areas, where ships load and discharge cargo and passengers.
- In India, ports are administered by the Central Shipping Ministry.
- Some important ports in India are Kandla Port (Gujarat), Jawaharlal Nehru Port (Maharashtra), Marmagao Port (Goa), New Mangalore Port (Karnataka), Kochi Port (Kerala), Tuticorin Port and Ennore Port (Tamil Nadu), Paradip Port (Odisha), Haldia and Kolkata Port (West Bengal).

Advantages of Waterways

- It is the cheapest mode of transporting bulk goods over long distances.
- The traffic in waterways is much less as compared to other modes of transport like roadways and railways.
- It consumes less fuel and is very safe in terms of conservation of environment.

Disadvantages of Waterways

- Water transport is slower compared to road, rail or air transport which makes it unsuitable for time-sensitive deliveries.
- Adverse weather conditions, like storms or high tides can disrupt travel.
- Many ports are not well linked with their hinterland which obstructs the smooth movement of goods.

EXAM ORIENTED QUESTIONS

TYPE - 1   1 Mark

Multiple Choice Questions

Q.1 Which of the following is a key advantage of road transport?
(a) It is the fastest mode of transport for long distances.
(b) It has low accessibility to remote and rural areas.
(c) It offers flexibility in routes and schedules.
(d) It requires less infrastructure investment.

Ans. (c) It offers flexibility in routes and schedules.

Q.2 India has the .... largest road network in the world.
(a) second (b) fourth
(c) fifth (d) sixth

Ans. (a) second

Q.3 Which is the longest highway in India?
(a) NH-1 (b) NH-77 (c) NH-44 (d) NH-2

Ans. (c) NH-44

Q.4 Yamuna Expressway: Uttar Pradesh
(a) Panipat Expressway: Rajasthan
(b) Western Peripheral Expressway: Maharashtra
(c) Puravanchal Expressway: Bihar
(d) Bundelkhand Expressway: Uttar Pradesh

Ans. (d) Bundelkhand Expressway: Uttar Pradesh

Exp. The Bundelkhand Expressway connects Chitrakoot to Etawah districts of Uttar Pradesh and is approximately 296 kilometers long.

Q.5 Raman, dairy farmer in Ludhiana, supplies milk within the city on a daily basis. Which mode of transport is he most likely to use? **(ICSE 2025)**
(a) Railway
(b) Roadway
(c) Airway
(d) Waterway

Ans. (b) Roadway

Q.6 District roads are maintained by the
(a) State Public Works Department
(b) Zila Parishad
(c) Block Development Office
(d) Panchayat

Ans. (b) Zila Parishad

Q.7 Roads that link a state capital with its district headquarters are called
(a) National Highways (b) State Highways
(c) District roads (d) Rural roads

Ans. (b) State Highways

Q.8 Which of the following is the Northern terminal of the North-South corridor?
(a) Srinagar (b) Nangal
(c) Kashmir (d) Gulmarg

Ans. (a) Srinagar

Q.9 The East-West corridor connects which two cities?
(a) Kolkata and Mumbai
(b) Silchar and Porbandar
(c) Guwahati and Ahmedabad
(d) Itanagar and Jodhpur

Ans. (b) Silchar and Porbandar

Q.10 How many zones are the Indian Railways divided into?
(a) 14 (b) 16 (c) 20 (d) 22

Ans. (b) 16

Q.11 The railway track system is based on which of the following?
(a) Length of the track (b) Breadth of the track
(c) Height of the track (d) Load of the track

Ans. (b) Breadth of the track

Q.12 The distance between rails in a metre-gauge is ....
(a) 1.67m (b) 1.00m (c) 1.12m (d) 1.35m

Ans. (b) 1.00m

Exp. There are three main types of gauges used in railways
(i) **Broad gauge** 1.676 m
(ii) **Meter gauge** 1.000 m
(iii) **Narrow gauge** 0.762m or 0.610 m

Q.13 If you have to transport perishable goods over a long distance, which mode of transport will you use and why? **(ICSE Specimen 2025)**
(a) Air transport because it is the fastest.
(b) Road transport as it is economical.
(c) Rail transport as it is eco-friendly.
(d) Water transport as it can handle large amounts of goods.

Ans. (a) Air transport because it is the fastest.

Q.14 Which of the following means of transport has the best use during floods/earthquakes? **(ICSE 2024)**
(a) Airways (b) Railways (c) Roadways (d) Waterways

Ans. (a) Airways

Q.15 Which of the following is a primary advantage of airways over other modes of transportation?
(a) Lower operating costs compared to road and rail transport.
(b) Ability to transport bulk goods less effectively than sea transport.
(c) Speed and efficiency for long-distance travel with fewer geographic limitations.
(d) Greater environmental sustainability due to less fuel consumption.

Ans. (c) Speed and efficiency for long-distance travel with fewer geographic limitations.

Q.16 .... transport supplements the other modes of transport. **(ICSE Specimen 2023)**
(a) Airways (b) Roadways (c) Waterways (d) Railways

Ans. (b) Roadways

Q.17 Read the table and identify the pair that is correctly matched.

Port	State
P. Kandla	West Bengal
Q. Tuticorin	Kerala
R. Ennore	Tamil Nadu
S. Haldia	Andhra Pradesh

(a) P (b) Q (c) R (d) S

Ans. (c) R

Q.18 Which of the following ports is located in the shaded region as given in the image.

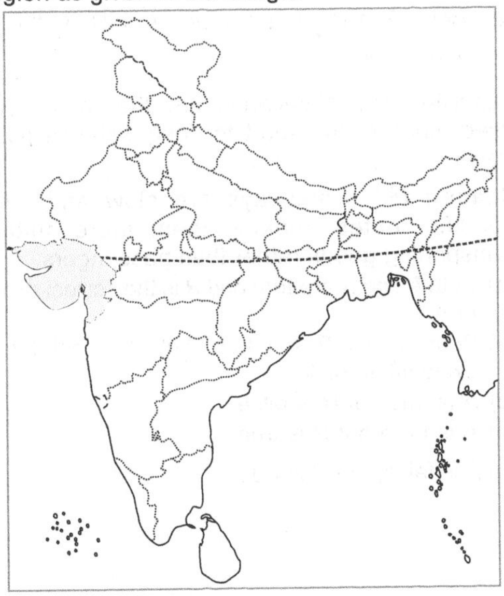

(a) Jawaharlal Nehru Port (b) Paradip Port
(c) Marmagao Port (d) Kandla Port

Ans. (d) Kandla Port

Q.19 Which is the busiest artificial port of India? **(ICSE Specimen 2024)**
(a) Goa (b) Mumbai
(c) Chennai (d) Vishakhapatnam

Ans. (b) Mumbai

Q.20 .... is the longest waterway in India.
(a) NW-1 (b) NW-3
(c) NW-6 (d) NW-2

Ans. (a) NW-1

Exp. NW-1 is the longest waterway in India which connects Allahabad (Uttar Pradesh) to Haldia (West Bengal) and is 1620 kilometers long.

Q.21 A port on the East coast which is often hit by cyclones
(a) Kandla
(b) Mumbai
(c) Haldia
(d) Vishakhapatnam

Ans. (d) Vishakhapatnam

Q.22 Wide and smooth roads where six to eight vehicles can run along parallel lanes.
(a) Freeways (b) Expressways
(c) National ways (d) Highways

Ans. (b) Expressways

Q.23 National Highways are maintained by
(a) National Highway Authority of India (NHAI)
(b) Public Works Department (PWD)
(c) National Govt. of India. (NGI)
(d) Central Public Work Department (CPWD)

Ans. (d) Central Public Work Department (CPWD)

Q.24 To boost up the trade and economic development of the country, the government has undertaken the project known as
(a) Expressways
(b) National Highways
(c) National Highway Development Projects (NHDP)
(d) Central Public Works Department.

Ans. (c) National Highway Development Projects (NHDP)

Q.25 The majority of village roads are constructed by
(a) Pradhan Mantri Highway Development
(b) Highway Authority of India
(c) Pradhan Mantri Grameen Sadak Yojna
(d) Sarkari Sadak Yojna

Ans. (c) Pradhan Mantri Grameen Sadak Yojna

Q.26 The Air service that gives support to the petroleum sector as ONGC and Oil India Ltd.

(a) Raj Hans Helicopter
(b) Pawan Hans Helicopter
(c) Ganga Helicopter
(d) Bharat Raksha Helicopter

Ans. (b) Pawan Hans Helicopter

Q.27 National waterway that connect Sadiya to Dhubri

(a) National Waterway 1 (b) National Waterway 2
(c) National Waterway 3 (d) National Waterway 4

Ans. (b) National Waterway 2

Q.28 National Waterway 1 is on river

(a) Brahmaputra (b) Ganga
(c) Yamuna (d) Godavari

Ans. (b) Ganga

Q.29 A seaport located in West cost

(a) Vishakhapatnam (b) Ennore
(c) Goa (d) Kolkata

Ans. (c) Goa

Q.30 Meter Gauge railway lines are generally found in

(a) plains (b) hills
(c) Western parts (d) Southern parts

Ans. (b) hills

TYPE - 2

1 Mark

Assertion-Reason Questions

Q.1 Assertion (A) Road transport is considered the most flexible mode of transport because it can reach areas that are not accessible by other modes of transport.

Reason (R) Roadways can be constructed in remote areas, providing direct access to villages, towns and cities which other transport modes cannot.

(a) Both A and R are true and R is the correct explanation of A
(b) Both A and R are true, but R is not the correct explanation of A
(c) A is true, but R is false
(d) A is false, but R is true

Ans. (a) Both A and R are true and R is the correct explanation of A

Q.2 Assertion (A) Railways is the fastest mode of transport in India, providing the quickest travel times between major cities.

Reason (R) It is generally slower than air transport and is often subject to delays due to infrastructure limitations.

(a) Both A and R are true and R is the correct explanation of A
(b) Both A and R are true, but R is not the correct explanation of A
(c) A is true, but R is false
(d) A is false, but R is true

Ans. (d) A is false, but R is true

Q.3 Assertion (A) Rail gauge is the distance between the inner sides of the two parallel rails that make up a single railway line.

Reason (R) On the basis of the width of the railway track, the Indian Railways are divided into three categories.

(a) Both A and R are true and R is the correct explanation of A
(b) Both A and R are true, but R is not the correct explanation of A
(c) A is true, but R is false
(d) A is false, but R is true

Ans. (b) Both A and R are true, but R is not the correct explanation of A

Q.4 Assertion (A) Airways are the fastest mode of transport for long-distance travel.

Reason (R) Air transport offers direct routes between cities, reducing travel time compared to other modes like road or rail.

(a) Both A and R are true and R is the correct explanation of A
(b) Both A and R are true, but R is not the correct explanation of A
(c) A is true, but R is false
(d) A is false, but R is true

Ans. (a) Both A and R are true, and R is the correct explanation of A

Q.5 Assertion (A) Waterways are the most commonly used mode of transport for long-distance passenger travel.

Reason (R) Waterways are slow and limited to specific routes, making them more suitable for transporting goods rather than passengers.

(a) Both A and R are true and R is the correct explanation of A
(b) Both A and R are true, but R is not the correct explanation of A
(c) A is true but R is false
(d) A is false but R is true

Ans. (d) A is false, but R is true

TYPE - 3

2 Marks

Short Answer Type Questions

Q.1 Why is a well-developed transport network important for India? **(ICSE 2025)**

Ans. A well-developed transport network is important for India because

- **Boosts Trade and Economy** Efficient transport helps in the movement of goods across the country and supports industries, agriculture and exports.
- **Enhances Connectivity** It connects remote and rural areas with cities, improving access to markets, healthcare and education.

Q.2 With reference to the road transport, explain the following terms.

(i) National highways (ii) Expressways

Ans. (i) National highways are the roads that are constructed and maintained by the Central Government and are meant for inter-state transport.

(ii) Expressways are high-speed, multi-lane roads designed for long-distance traffic with limited access points meaning there are fewer intersections and entry/exit points.

Q.3 Mention any two advantages of using roadways. **(ICSE Semester II 2022)**

Or Mention any two advantages of road transport. **(ICSE 2025)**

Ans. Two advantages of using roadways are

(i) Roadways provide door-to-door service, allowing transport to reach the remotest parts of the country.

(ii) Road transport is generally cheaper for short distances and smaller loads compared to rail or air transport.

Q.4 Even though all means of transport are well-developed in India, yet, road transport remains the most popular means of transport. Justify this statement. **(ICSE 2020)**

Ans. Roadways are considered as popular means of transport because of the following reasons

- It is more suitable for short distance travel and connects small villages and remote areas.
- For short distances and smaller loads, road transport is generally cheaper compared to other means of transportation.

Q.5 Give reasons for the following.

(i) Road transport is preferred in the Northern plains.

(ii) Roadways are considered more important than any other means of transport.

Ans. (i) Road transport is preferred in the Northern plains due to its flat terrain, which makes road construction easier. The region has a dense population and extensive agricultural activities which creates a high demand for road transport.

(ii) Roadways are considered more important than other means of transport because they provide flexible and accessible transportation for people and goods. Additionally, roads provide the facility of door-to-door service which is very favourable and minimises the cost of loading and unloading products and goods.

Q.6 Why is road transport considered more useful than rail transport? State two reasons in support of your answer.

Ans. Road transport is considered more useful than rail transport due to the following reasons

(i) Road transport can reach remote and rural areas while rail transport is limited to specific tracks.

(ii) Road transport is faster for delivering small quantities of goods as it doesn't depend on scheduled routes like trains.

Q.7 Distinguish between national highways and state highways.

Ans. National highways and state highways can be distinguished as follows

National Highways	State Highways
These are maintained and funded by the Central Government.	These are maintained and funded by the State Government.
These connect major cities and states across the country.	These connect state capitals, districts and important towns within the state.

Q.8 Mention two reasons why more people use railways rather than airways. **(ICSE 2017)**

Ans. Two reasons why more people use railways rather than airways are

(i) Train tickets are cheaper than flight tickets which makes rail transport a budget-friendly option.

(ii) Trains have more stoppages and routes which make rural and remote areas accessible for the people.

Q.9 Distinguish between broad gauge and metre gauge rail track systems.

Ans. Broad gauge and metre gauge can be distinguished as follows

Broad Gauge	Metre Gauge
In broad gauge, the width between the railway track lines is 1.676 m.	In metre gauge, the distance between the railway track lines is 1 m.
This track system allows higher speeds for trains.	This track system allows limited speeds for trains.

Q.10 Give two reasons why airways are used extensively despite being an expensive mode of transport.

Ans. Two reasons why airways are used extensively despite being an expensive mode of transport are

(i) It offers the fastest travel option which saves time.

(ii) It provides a high level of comfort with amenities like meals, entertainment and spacious seating.

Q.11 With reference to the air transport in India, answer the following questions.

(i) What is AAI and when was it formed?

(ii) What is 'Pawan Hans'? Why was it set up?

Ans. (i) The Airports Authority of India (AAI) is the nodal agency that provides safe and efficient air traffic services in the country. It was set up on 1st April 1995.

(ii) Pawan Hans is a helicopter services company in India. It was set up in 1985 by the government of India to provide air transport services to petroleum sector (ONGC and Oil India Ltd.) and services to North-Eastern states.

Q.12 Mention two advantages of waterways over the other means of transport.

Ans. Two advantages of waterways over the other means of transport are

(i) It is economical for transporting large quantities of goods over long distance.

(ii) It produces less pollution compared to rail, road and air transport which makes it a more eco-friendly option.

Q.13 Give two geographical reasons why water transport is not as popular as land transport in India. **(ICSE 2019)**

Ans. Two geographical reasons why water transport is not as popular as land transport in India are

(i) Major ports in India are concentrated in specific regions which makes it difficult for water transport to reach inland regions efficiently.

(ii) Many rivers in India are seasonal and not navigable for large vessels due to shallow depths and seasonal variations which limits the water transport.

Q.14 Why is the inland waterway declining its importance? Give two reasons to justify your answer. **(ICSE 2017)**

Ans. Inland waterway declining its importance due to the following reasons

(i) The inland waterway network in India is underdeveloped with few navigable rivers and insufficient connectivity between major ports and inland areas.

(ii) Many rivers are seasonal and canals are shallow and their water levels fluctuate with the seasons which makes it difficult for large vessels and cargo transport.

TYPE - 4 — 3 Marks

Long Answer Type Questions

Q.1 In a growing urban city, the transportation system plays a critical role in connecting people, goods, and services. The availability of well-developed public transport, such as buses and trains, reduces traffic congestion and the environmental impact caused by private vehicles.

(i) What are the main challenges faced by India's public transportation system?

(ii) How does traffic congestion in Indian cities contribute to pollution and public health issues?

Ans. (i) The main challenges include inadequate infrastructure, overcrowding, lack of connectivity between different modes of transport, inefficient management and poor maintenance.

(ii) Traffic congestion leads to increased fuel consumption, higher emissions of harmful gases like carbon monoxide and nitrogen oxides and greater air pollution. This not only contributes to environmental degradation but also causes respiratory diseases, cardiovascular problems and other health issues.

Q.2 With reference to rail transport in India, answer the following questions.

(i) State any three problems faced by the railways. **(ICSE Specimen 2018)**

(ii) Mention one disadvantage of rail transport.

Ans. (i) Three problems faced by the railways are

- Overcrowding in trains and stations.
- Poor quality of tracks and outdated infrastructure.
- Frequent accidents and maintenance issues.

(ii) Trains cannot cross seas and oceans. It cannot be laid on the landscape which has a loose soil base.

Q.3 Give reason for each of the following.

(i) Railways are under the public sector. **(ICSE 2020)**

(ii) Roadways are not well developed in North-East India.

(iii) A good network of transport is of great help for the development of the economy.

Ans. (i) Railways are under the public sector in India because they are vital for national connectivity, serve millions of passengers, require heavy investment and need government regulation to ensure safety, fair pricing and uniform services across the country.

(ii) Roadways in North-East India are underdeveloped due to the challenging mountainous terrain, frequent flooding during monsoons, limited connectivity to remote areas and security concerns along the border. These factors make road construction and maintenance difficult and costly.

(iii) A good network of transport is crucial for economic development as it facilitates the efficient movement of goods and people, promotes trade, supports industries, boosts tourism, creates jobs and improves connectivity between regions, leading to overall economic growth.

Q.4 Name the following. **(ICSE 2025)**

(i) The mode of transport that ensures comfortable journey, especially for elders and children.

(ii) The highway connecting Silchar in Assam to Porbandar in Gujarat.

(iii) The cheapest means of transport for bulky goods.

Ans. (i) Rail transport ensures a comfortable journey, especially for elders and children, as trains provide seating, sleeping arrangements and other facilities.

(ii) The highway connecting Silchar in Assam to Porbandar in Gujarat is part of the East-West Corridor.

(iii) The cheapest means of transport for bulky goods is water transport, as it is cost-effective and fuel-efficient, especially for long-distance trade.

Q.5 With reference to the image given below, answer the following questions.

(i) Give two advantages of the type of transport which is shown in the above figure.

(ii) Give one disadvantage of this type of transport.

Ans. (i) The means of transport shown in the above figure is air transport. Two advantages of air transport are as follows

(a) It is the fastest mode of transport to travel long distances.

(b) It can access places that are difficult to reach by road or rail.

(ii) One disadvantage of air transport is that it is more costly than other modes of transport.

Q.6 Give a reason for each of the following **(ICSE 2019)**

(i) Nearly seventy per cent of Indians do not use air transport.

(ii) A well-developed transport is important for industrial growth.

(iii) Water transport is not as popular as land transport in India.

Ans. (i) Nearly seventy percent of Indians do not use air transport due to factors like high prices of tickets and limited access to airports.

(ii) A well-developed transport system is important for industrial growth because it helps move raw materials to factories and finished products to markets faster and more efficiently. This reduces costs and saves time, making it easier for industries to grow.

(iii) Water transport is not as popular as land transport in India because it is limited to certain areas like rivers and coastal regions. Many parts of the country do not have navigable waterways, so it is not easily accessible. It is also slower compared to road and rail transport, making it less suitable for quick delivery of goods.

Q.7 Mention three reasons why inland waterways are better developed in North India than in South India. **(ICSE Specimen 2018)**

Ans. Three reasons why inland waterways are better developed in North India than in South India are

(i) North India has larger and more navigable rivers like the Ganges and Brahmaputra that are suitable for inland water transport.

(ii) The land in North India is relatively flat which makes it easier to develop waterways compared to the hilly terrain in parts of South India.

(iii) Rivers in North India generally have a more consistent and stronger flow which provides better navigation to the ships.

Q.8 Give three reasons why peninsular rivers are not ideal for navigation. **(ICSE 2023)**

Ans. Three reasons why peninsular rivers are not ideal for navigation are as follows

(i) Peninsular rivers are shallow which makes it difficult for large ships or boats to navigate.

(ii) Peninsular rivers pass through rocky and hilly terrains which create obstacles and make navigation challenging.

(iii) Peninsular rivers are short in length and have an uneven flow which makes navigation difficult.

TYPE - 5 — 10 Marks

Structured Questions

Q.1 (i) Mention two disadvantages of using waterways. **(Specimen 2025) (2)**

(ii) The Golden Quadrilateral has contributed towards improvement of the Indian economy. Explain. **(2)**

(iii) (a) Which rail gauge is mostly limited to hilly areas only? **(3)**

(b) Name the organisation responsible for the maintenance of the National Highways of India.

(c) Which inland waterway connects Prayagraj to Haldia?

(iv) Give a reason for each of the following. **(ICSE 2025)**

(a) Airways are the most efficient mode of transport to connect North-East India with the rest of the country.

(b) Railways are easily developed in the Northern Plains of India.

(c) Rivers of peninsular India are not ideal for inland water transport.

Ans. (i) Two disadvantages of using waterways are

(a) Transportation via waterways is slower compared to other modes like road or air which makes it unsuitable for perishable goods or time-sensitive deliveries.

(b) Waterways are dependent on the availability of rivers, canals and ports, restricting their use in landlocked regions or areas without proper water routes or infrastructure.

(ii) The Golden Quadrilateral has enhanced connectivity between major cities, boosting trade and reducing transportation costs. It contributed to industrial growth, improved access to markets for farmers and promoted tourism.

By linking rural areas to urban centers, it has facilitated regional development, created jobs and contributed significantly to India's economic growth.

(iii) (a) The narrow gauge is mostly limited to hilly areas in India. This gauge is used in regions where the terrain is difficult. These tracks are mostly found in hilly and mountainous areas.

(b) The National Highways Authority of India (NHAI) is responsible for the maintenance of the National Highways in India.

(c) The National Waterway 1 (NW-1) connects Prayagraj to Haldia. This waterway follows the course of the Ganges River.

(iv) (a) Airways are the most efficient mode of transport to connect North-East India with the rest of the country because the region has rugged terrain, dense forests and frequent floods, making road and rail transport difficult.

(b) Railways are easily developed in the Northern plains of India because the region has flat and fertile land, which makes track construction and maintenance easier compared to hilly or plateau regions.

(c) Rivers of peninsular India are not ideal for inland water transport because they are seasonal, with water levels fluctuating throughout the year. Additionally, these rivers have many waterfalls, rapids, and rocky beds, making navigation difficult.

Q.2. (i) With reference to the image given below, answer the following questions **(2)**

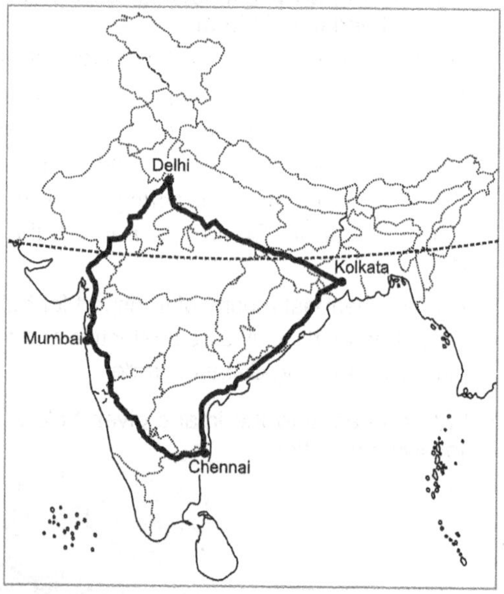

(a) Identify the project given in the above image?

(b) What is the primary purpose of this project?

(ii) India's aviation industry has experienced significant growth in the past 10 years. The number of operational airports in the country has doubled from 74 in 2014 to 157 in 2024 and the aim is to increase this number to 350-400 by 2047.

The domestic air passengers have more than doubled in the past decade, with Indian airlines significantly expanding their fleets. *pib.gov.in* **(2)**

(a) The air transport has contributed towards the improvement of the Indian economy. Explain.

(b) Name any two domestic airlines in India.

(iii) Mention three disadvantages of road transport. **(3)**

(iv) (a) How is a good transport network important for India? **(3)**

(b) Give one difference between oceanic waterways and inland waterways.

Ans. (i) (a) Project Golden Quadrilateral has been given in the image.

(b) The primary purpose of this project is to enhance road connectivity and promote economic growth by connecting key industrial, agricultural and cultural hubs.

(ii) (a) Air transport boosts India's economy by enhancing connectivity, promoting tourism, facilitating trade, supporting e-commerce and generating jobs. It attracts foreign investment, drives regional development and integrates India's economy with global markets efficiently and effectively.

(b) Indigo and Air India are the two domestic airlines in India.

(iii) Three disadvantages of road ransport are

- Roads and vehicles require regular maintenance, which can be expensive.
- It contributes to air pollution and greenhouse gas emissions.
- It is less suitable for bulky or heavy goods compared to rail or water transport.

(iv) (a) A good transport network is important for India because it helps in faster movement of goods and people, boosts the economy, creates employment, connects rural and urban areas, supports trade and tourism and helps in quick disaster response.

(b) Oceanic waterways are used for international trade and connect different countries across seas and oceans while inland waterways operate within a country, using rivers, canals, etc. for domestic transportation.

Q.3 (i) Why is road transport an important means of transport in India? (Any two reasons)

(ICSE 2024) (2)

(ii) Give a reason for each of the following. **(2)**

(a) Northern plain is best suited for the development of Railways.

(b) Railways are managed completely by the Central Government.

(iii) Mention two advantages and one disadvantage of Inland water transport. **(3)**

(iv) Why have airways become more popular than other means of transport? (Any three reasons) **(3)**

Ans. (i) Road transport is an important means of transport in India because

- It connects remote and rural areas.
- It offers flexibility in routes and schedules.

(ii) (a) The Northern Plain is best suited for the development of railways because it has a flat and level terrain which makes it easier to lay railway tracks.

(b) Railways are managed by the Central Government in India because it is a national network that connects all states and regions and acts as the lifeline of the national economy. Such a large system needs government regulations to ensure safety, fair pricing and uniform services across the country.

(iii) Two advantages and one disadvantage of inland water transport in India are as follows

Advantages

- It is cheaper for transporting heavy and bulky goods over long distances.
- It produces less pollution compared to road and rail transport.

Disadvantage

- It is limited to navigable rivers and waterways, so it can only reach certain areas.

(iv) Airways have become more popular than other means of transport for several reasons

(a) It is the fastest mode of transport, which allows people and goods to cover long distances quickly.

(b) It offers comfort with amenities like meals, entertainment and faster check-ins.

(c) It connects different parts of the world giving businesses access to global markets, people to travel internationally and goods to be shipped quickly.

11

WASTE MANAGEMENT

Waste management is the process of collecting, transporting, disposing, recycling or treating waste materials to minimise their impact on the environment.

Impacts of Waste Accumulation

Waste accumulation refers to the gathering of waste materials over time due to improper disposal or inadequate waste management systems. Some of the impacts of waste accumulation are

Spoilage of Landscape

It refers to the dumping of garbage in an open area that destroys the natural beauty of a place and serves as a potential breeding ground.

Pollution

The substances that cause pollution are called pollutants. The sources of pollution are

- **Air Pollution** It is the presence of harmful substances, such as gases, chemicals or particles in the air that can negatively affect human health, the environment and the climate.
- **Water Pollution** It is the contamination of water bodies, such as rivers, lakes and oceans by harmful substances like chemicals, waste and toxins which makes water unsafe for drinking, wildlife and ecosystems.
- **Soil Pollution** It is the degradation and deterioration of soil quality due to the addition of certain solid and semi-solid wastes from agricultural practices, industrial processes, households, etc.
- **Oil Spills** Oil being viscous in nature does not mix in water. The thin layer of oil on the surface of water is called on oil slick.

Health Hazards

Health hazards are the physical, chemical, biological or environmental factors that can cause harm to human health. Following are the factors responsible for health hazards

- Indiscriminate dumping of toxic and non-toxic matter.
- Lead present in petrol, diesel, lead batteries, paints, hair dye products, etc. can cause nervous system damage and cancer.
- The dumping grounds are open pits and thus, become the breeding ground for mosquitoes, flies and insects that cause malaria and dengue.

Effects on Terrestrial Life

- Many toxic chemicals, pesticides, other agricultural wastes released into the environment are taken up by the plants from air, water and soil. These toxins cause different types of leaf injuries, premature leaf fall, decrease in transpiration, reduction in the rate of photosynthesis, reduction in biological nitrogen fixation.
- Several domestic animals like cows, buffalo, goats, etc. often eat polythene and plastic bags along with food material which causes many disorders in them.
- Exposure to high concentrations of pollutants may cause acute injuries like chlorosis and discoloration. Sulphur dioxide is the most toxic pollutant that damages crops.

Effects on Aquatic Life

Freshwater Life

- Sewage from municipalities that is discharged into the rivers, canals and lakes, etc. carries many species of bacteria and other microbes that cause diseases in aquatic organisms.
- Oxygen concentration is reduced considerably due to the heavy accumulation of toxic wastes and sewage drained from cities into water bodies like canals, lakes and rivers. This process is known as Eutrophication.

Marine Water Life

- Herbicides and pesticides that reach the oceans through wind and rivers can contaminate water and cause harm to marine life.
- Massive oil spills can also cause widespread damage to marine life.

Need for Waste Management

- It helps prevent pollution of air, water and soil, protecting ecosystems and wildlife from harmful substances.
- Managing waste effectively helps reduce the amount of waste sent to landfills, preventing them from overflowing and causing environmental issues.
- Proper waste management, including recycling and composting, helps reduce greenhouse gas emissions.

Methods of Safe Disposal

Segregation

It is a method of dividing garbage into different categories as wet or biodegradable and dry or non-biodegradable.

Some methods of segregation are

- In colonies, various types of dustbins are used to segregate garbage as wet and dry waste.
- Techniques like screening, sieving or manual sorting are used to separate materials based on size, shape, or physical properties.
- Magnets are used to extract ferrous metals like iron and steel from mixed waste, commonly used in recycling industries.

Waste Segregation

Dumping/Landfills

It refers to uncovered areas that are used to dump solid waste of all kinds.

Some methods of dumping are

- **Open dumping** In this method, waste materials are dumped in open lowlands far away from the city.
- **Sanitary landfill** In this method, the waste is packed and dumped daily at the site and is covered with soil.
- **Incineration** It is the process of burning waste materials at high temperatures to convert them into ash, gases and heat. It reduces the volume of waste.
- Leachate is formed when rain water leaks into the landfill. Chemical processes turn it acidic and it dissolves toxic chemicals, making soil infertile and also contaminate the ground water.

Composting

It is a natural biological process of decomposing wastes in which organic wastes are broken down into nutrient-rich humus-like material called compost.

Composting

Some methods of composting are

- **Aerobic Composting** In this method, organic materials decompose in the presence of oxygen.
- **Anaerobic Composting** In this method, waste and organic materials breaks down without oxygen with the help of micro-organisms.
- **Vermicomposting** In this method, earthworms are used to decompose organic wastes, such as food scraps, garden waste, etc. and break them into nutrient-rich compost that improves soil fertility.

Need and Methods for Reducing, Reusing and Recycling Waste

The waste material could be managed by using the three R's which are

Reducing

It refers to the practice of minimising the amount of waste and resources consumed.

Three R's

There is a need for reducing waste for the following reasons

- Reducing waste helps conserve natural resources, reduce pollution and minimise the strain on ecosystems.
- By reducing consumption, we can preserve raw materials.

Some methods of reducing waste are

- In Industries, waste generation can be minimised by changing the production process by using materials more efficiently.
- Scientific methods like precipitation and evaporation can help decrease the volume of liquid waste.

Reusing

It refers to the practice of using items or materials multiple times before throwing them.

There is need for reusing waste for the following reasons

- Reusing items helps to decrease the amount of waste that ends up in landfills.
- By reusing products, fewer raw materials are required to make new items.

Some methods of reusing waste are

- Reusing bottles, cans, jars, etc. and refilling them with new products can avoid wastage.
- Replacing disposable plastic bags with reusable cloth or jute bags helps in reducing plastic waste.

Recycling

It is a method in which used waste materials are changed into new and useful products.

There is need for recycling waste for the following reasons

- Recycling helps conserve natural resources by reprocessing materials like paper, metals, plastics, etc.
- Recycling saves energy for producing new products from raw materials.

Some methods of recycling waste are

- Materials like metals and plastics are melted down and reformed into new products
- Paper, cardboard and certain plastics are shredded or ground into smaller pieces, making it easier to process and transform them into new products like insulation or packaging materials.

EXAM ORIENTED QUESTIONS

TYPE - 1

1 Mark

Multiple Choice Questions

Q.1 What is the primary consequence of water pollution?
(a) Increased biodiversity
(b) Contaminated drinking water
(c) Improved aquatic life
(d) Better irrigation

Ans. (b) Contaminated drinking water

Q.2 Which of the following is not a leading cause of soil pollution?
(a) Industrial waste disposal
(b) Excessive use of pesticides and fertilisers
(c) Deforestation
(d) Improper waste disposal

Ans. (c) Deforestation

Q.3 The depletion of oxygen in a water body resulting from pollution is called ....
(a) Decay of water
(b) Eutrophication
(c) Biomagnification
(d) Greenhouse effect

Ans. (b) Eutrophication

Q.4 Read the table and identify the pair that is correctly matched.

Waste Type	Category
P. Dust	Electronic waste
Q. Radioactive elements	Domestic waste
R. Bricks	Construction waste
S. Discarded refrigerators	Nuclear waste

(a) P (b) Q
(c) R (d) S

Ans. (c) R

Q.5 Which of the following is a biodegradable waste? **(ICSE 2024)**
(a) Broken glass
(b) Wastepaper
(c) Polythene
(d) Plastic bags

Ans. (b) Wastepaper

Exp. Biodegradable wastes are materials that can be broken down naturally by micro-organisms like bacteria and fungi into simpler and non-toxic substances. These wastes decompose over time and do not harm the environment. Some examples of Biodegradable wastes are food scraps, leaves, paper and wood.

Q.6 Vegetable peels: Domestic waste
(a) Gases: Chemical waste
(b) Syringes: Domestic waste
(c) Crop residue: Industrial waste
(d) Polythenes: Nuclear waste

Ans. (a) Gases: Chemical waste

Q.7 Ravi has wet waste with him, which colour dustbin should he use to dump his waste?
(a) Blue (b) Red
(c) Green (d) Black

Ans. (c) Green

Exp. Wet wastes are biodegradable wastes, like food scraps, vegetable peels and other organic materials. Green dustbins are used for these types of wastes.

Q.8 Which of the following methods of waste disposal is harmful? **(ICSE 2023)**
(a) Composting (b) Segregation
(c) Dumping (d) Vermicomposting

Ans. (c) Dumping

Q.9 .... is an aerobic method of managing solid wastes.
(a) Incineration (b) Composting
(c) Recycling (d) Dumping

Ans. (b) Composting

Q.10 Composting rejuvenates poor soils by adding ....
(a) nutrients (b) manure
(c) humus (d) oxygen

Ans. (c) humus

Q.11 .... is the cheapest method of waste disposal.
(a) Open dumping (b) Sanitary landfill
(c) Incineration (d) Recycling

Ans. (a) Open dumping

Q.12 To create compost, household organic waste goes through ....
(a) reduction (b) burning
(c) decomposition (d) churning

Ans. (c) decomposition

Exp. Decomposition is the natural process by which organic materials, like food scraps, leaves, or plant matter break down into simpler substances when bacteria, fungi and other micro-organisms feed on the waste. It is then converted into compost which is beneficial for crops.

Q.13 Which of the following practices is part of the 3 R's for waste management?
(a) Releasing waste into water bodies
(b) Reducing resource consumption
(c) Increasing landfill use
(d) Burning waste materials

Ans. (b) Reducing resource consumption

Q.14 Identify the primary goal of reducing the 3 R's of waste management among the following options.
(a) Reducing the amount of energy used in recycling processes.
(b) Reducing the production of waste by consuming fewer resources.
(c) Reducing the number of products that can be recycled.
(d) Reducing the cost of waste disposal through landfill use.

Ans. (b) Reducing the production of waste by consuming fewer resources.

Q.15 Which of the following methods of disposal is best applicable for the waste depicted in the picture below? **(ICSE Specimen 2025)**

(a) Burning waste in open areas
(b) Recycling waste
(c) Dumping
(d) Composting

Ans. (b) Recycling waste

Exp. The best method of disposal for broken glass is to dispose of it in a separate bin designated for non-biodegradable or recyclable waste.

Q.16 Large areas on the outskirts of cities where the waste is deposited above or below the ground covered with Earth
(a) Landfills (b) Dumping
(c) Composting (d) Toxic

Ans. (a) Landfills

Q.17 A method of burning waste to reduce its weight & volume
(a) Eutrophication (b) Incineration
(c) Dumping (d) Composting

Ans. (b) Incineration

Q.18 Set of micro organism involved in the process of composting.
(a) Helminths, Archaea
(b) Bacteria, Fungi
(c) Algae, Protozoa
(d) Viruses, Algae

Ans. (b) Bacteria, Fungi

Q.19 E-waste refers to
(a) electric waste
(b) excreta waste
(c) electronic wastes
(d) environment waste

Ans. (c) electronic wastes

Q.20 The collection of discarded materials and converting them into useful products is **(ICSE 2025)**
(a) Recycling
(b) Processing
(c) Reducing
(d) Composting

Ans. (a) Recycling

TYPE - 2 — 1 Mark

Assertion-Reason Questions

Q.1 **Assertion** (A) Exposure to air pollution increases the risk of respiratory diseases.
Reason (R) Air pollution contains harmful particles and gases that irritate the respiratory system and contribute to long-term lung damage.
(a) Both A and R are true and R is the correct explanation of A
(b) Both A and R are true, but R is not the correct explanation of A
(c) A is true, but R is false
(d) A is false, but R is true

Ans. (a) Both A and R are true and R is the correct explanation of A

Q.2 Assertion (A) Exposure to harmful chemicals in household cleaning products can lead to respiratory problems and skin irritation.

Reason (R) Many cleaning products contain toxic substances like ammonia and bleach that can cause allergic reactions and damage to the respiratory system when inhaled or come into contact with the skin.

(a) Both A and R are true and R is the correct explanation of A

(b) Both A and R are true, but R is not the correct explanation of A

(c) A is true, but R is false

(d) A is false, but R is true

Ans. (a) Both A and R are true and R is the correct explanation of A

Q.3 Assertion (A) Incineration is an environmentally friendly method of waste disposal.

Reason (R) Incineration reduces waste volume and generates energy, making it an efficient method for waste management.

(a) Both A and R are true and R is the correct explanation of A

(b) Both A and R are true, but R is not the correct explanation of A

(c) A is true, but R is false

(d) A is false, but R is true

Ans. (d) A is false, but R is true

Q.4 Assertion (A) Reusing items is less important than recycling in waste management.

Reason (R) Recycling transforms waste into new products, making it a more efficient way to reduce waste compared to reusing.

(a) Both A and R are true and R is the correct explanation of A

(b) Both A and R are true, but R is not the correct explanation of A

(c) A is true, but R is false

(d) A is false, but R is true

Ans. (c) A is true, but R is false

Q.5 Assertion (A) Effective waste management can contribute to resource conservation.

Reason (R) Recyclable materials can be processed and reused to create new products, reducing the need for raw materials.

(a) Both A and R are true and R is the correct explanation of A

(b) Both A and R are true, but R is not the correct explanation of A

(c) A is true, but R is false

(d) A is false, but R is true

Ans. (a) Both A and R are true and R is the correct explanation of A

TYPE - 3

2 Marks

Short Answer Type Questions

Q.1 Delhi and several Northern Indian cities get enveloped in a thick blanket of smog every winter due to smoke, dust, low wind speed, vehicular emissions and crop stubble burning. *www.bbc.com*

(i) What are the main causes of air pollution in urban areas?

(ii) How can industries reduce their environmental impact through sustainable practices?

Ans. (i) Emissions from vehicles, industrial activities, construction dust, burning of fossil fuels, waste incineration, etc. are some of the causes of air pollution in urban areas.

(ii) Industries can reduce their environmental impact by adopting cleaner technologies, recycling waste, conserving water, using eco-friendly materials and improving waste management practices. These actions help minimise pollution, conserve resources and promote sustainable operations for long-term environmental benefits.

Q.2 'Soil pollution can harm human health through contaminated food.' Explain.

Ans. Soil pollution can lead to the contamination of crops and agricultural products. Consuming such contaminated food can lead to health issues like poisoning, developmental disorders and increased risk of various diseases.

Q.3 With reference to the wastes, answer the following. **(ICSE 2015)**

(i) What is understood by biodegradable waste?

(ii) State one source of gaseous waste.

Ans. (i) Biodegradable wastes are those which can be degraded by micro-organisms and by natural processes.

(ii) One source of gaseous waste is the release of carbon monoxide by automobiles.

Q.4 Mention any two sources of industrial waste.

Ans. The two sources of industrial waste are

(i) Waste generated from factories and production units such as metal scrap, chemical by-products, plastics and other materials used in the production process.

(ii) Waste products from mining activities like slag and other materials that are extracted during mineral processing.

Q.5 Why should waste management be practiced in every school? **(ICSE 2023)**

Ans. Waste management should be practiced in every school, as it encourages and makes students learn about the practice of proper waste disposal and management at individual level that can contribute to environment protection and reduction of pollution.

Q.6 Give two reasons why we need to manage our waste? **(ICSE Specimen 2023)**

Ans. Two reasons for why we need to manage our waste are

(i) Hazardous waste can cause depletion of natural resources as they are corrosive and toxic in nature.

(ii) They can cause serious illness to human and animal health.

Q.7 Segregation is considered a safe method of waste disposal. Explain. **(ICSE Specimen Semester II 2022)**

Ans. Segregation is considered a safe method of waste disposal because in this method waste is segregated into different categories like dry and wet or biodegradable and non-biodegradable wastes and can be disposed of accordingly.

Q.8 (i) Give a reason for a substantial rise of E-waste in India. **(ICSE 2025)**

(ii) What is dumping?

Ans. (i) The increase in the use of electronic devices such as mobile phones, computers, televisions, and home appliances, along with rapid technological advancements, has led to a substantial rise in E-waste in India.

(ii) Dumping is the practice of disposing of waste materials, including industrial, household, and hazardous waste, in an uncontrolled manner, often in landfills, open spaces, or water bodies.

Q.9 Mention one advantage and one disadvantage of dumping of waste. **(ICSE 2023)**

Ans. **Advantage** The main benefits of effective waste disposal include environmental protection from pollution or contamination.

Disadvantage Poor waste management contributes to climate change and air pollution and directly affects many ecosystems and species.

Q.10 'You cannot protect environment unless you empower people, you inform them and help them to understand that these resources are their own, that they must protect them. '

-Wangari Maathai (recipient of Nobel Prize 2004 for Sustainable Development)

As a responsible student, how would you contribute to reduce and manage the waste generated in your surroundings. Explain by giving suitable Examples. **(ICSE 2025)**

Ans. As a responsible student, I can contribute to reducing and managing waste in my surroundings through the following steps

- **Reduce Waste Generation** Use reusable items like steel water bottles, cloth bags, and lunch boxes instead of plastic ones.
- **Spread Awareness** Organise cleanliness drives in school and the local community.

Q.11 With reference to the methods of safe disposal of wastes, explain the following. **(ICSE Specimen 2018)**

(i) Open Dumping (ii) Composting

Ans. (i) **Open Dumping** It refers to uncovered areas that are used to dump solid waste of all kinds.

(ii) **Composting** It is a natural biological process of decomposing wastes in which organic wastes are broken down into nutrient-rich humus-like material called compost.

TYPE - 4

3 Marks

Long Answer Type Questions

Q.1 Distinguish between air, water and soil pollution.

Ans. Air, water and soil pollution can be distinguished as follows

Air Pollution	Water Pollution	Soil Pollution
It emits from vehicles, industries, burning of fossil fuels, wildfires, etc.	It is produced by industrial waste, sewage, agricultural runoff, oil spills, etc.	It is generated from pesticides, industrial waste, mining activities and improper waste disposal.
Some of the constituents are - particulate matter, carbon monoxide, sulphur dioxide, nitrogen oxides and volatile organic compounds.	The main pollutants are - chemicals, heavy metals, plastic waste, bacteria and nutrients (nitrogen and phosphorus).	Major pollutants of this type of pollution are pesticides, heavy metals, plastics, chemicals and hazardous waste.
It can harm air quality, contribute to climate change.	It can disrupt aquatic ecosystems, harm aquatic life and affect biodiversity.	It reduces soil fertility, harms plant growth and causes loss of biodiversity.

Q.2 With reference to the image given below, answer the following.

(i) Identify the type of pollution shown in the above image.

(ii) State some harmful effects of this type of pollution.

Ans. (i) Air pollution is shown in the above image.

(ii) Some harmful effects of air pollution are as follows

- It can cause respiratory issues like asthma and bronchitis.
- It can harm ecosystems, damage forests and acidify soil and water bodies.

Q.3 Mention any one way in which waste accumulation affects the following. **(ICSE 2018)**

(i) Terrestrial life (ii) Aquatic life

(iii) Landscape

Ans. (i) **Terrestrial life** Soil contamination from waste accumulation, such as plastics and chemicals can degrade soil quality, harming plant growth and affecting the terrestrial animals that depend on these plants for food.

(ii) **Aquatic life** Water pollution from waste such as plastics and chemicals can lead to the poisoning of aquatic organisms, disrupt ecosystems and cause the death of marine life due to toxins in the water.

(iii) **Landscape** Visual pollution from waste accumulation like litter and discarded items can degrade the natural beauty of landscapes and affect tourism.

Q.4 Give three reasons as to why there is a need for safe waste disposal. **(ICSE 2018)**

Ans. Three reasons as to why there is a need for safe waste disposal are

- Improper waste disposal can lead to the spread of diseases, contamination of water sources and exposure to harmful chemicals which can increase health risks to humans.
- Safe disposal prevents the contamination of soil, air and water, reducing the adverse effects of pollution on ecosystems, wildlife and biodiversity.
- Proper waste management, including recycling and composting, helps conserve valuable natural resources, reducing the need for raw material extraction and minimising environmental degradation.

Q.5 With reference to waste management, answer the following questions.

(i) "Waste segregation is important." Give a reason to support your answer. **(ICSE 2015)**

(ii) Explain briefly how as a student, you can help in the reduction of waste generation.

Ans. (i) Waste segregation is important because it allows for the proper recycling and disposal of different types of waste, reducing contamination and ensuring that recyclable materials are processed efficiently. This helps conserve resources, reduces landfill waste and minimises environmental pollution.

(ii) As a student, we can help in the reduction of waste generation by adopting the 3 R's

- **Reduce** By minimising the use of single-use plastics and opting for digital notes instead of printing.
- **Reuse** By using reusable water bottles, bags and containers and repurposing materials like old notebooks.
- **Recycle** By properly segregating recyclable materials and encouraging your peers to do the same.

Q.6 Briefly answer the following. **(ICSE 2023)**

(i) How is segregation of the waste helpful?

(ii) Mention one way in which we can reuse waste.

(iii) Mention one benefit of composting.

Ans. (i) Segregating waste is helpful because it makes recycling easier and more effective. By separating recyclables like plastic, paper and glass from non-recyclables, we can ensure that materials are properly processed.

(ii) We can reuse the waste by donating the items that are still in a good, usable condition to charities.

(iii) Composting enhances the soil nutrients such as nitrogen and phosphorus. It also enhances the water retention capacity of the soil and the fertility of soil by adding humus.

Q.7 Give a reason for each of the following.

(i) Segregation of waste must be done before disposal. **(ICSE 2019)**

(ii) Trees must be planted in the industrial areas.

(iii) Chemical fertilisers must be replaced by organic manure.

Ans. (i) Segregation of waste before disposal is important because it helps in the effective recycling and management of waste. This improves the efficiency of waste treatment and helps conserve natural resources.

(ii) Trees must be planted in industrial areas to improve air quality by absorbing carbon dioxide and releasing oxygen. They also help in reducing air pollution by filtering harmful gases and particulate matter.

(iii) Chemical fertilisers must be replaced by organic manure because chemical fertilisers can degrade soil health over time, reduce biodiversity and contaminate water sources. Organic manure, on the other hand, improves soil fertility naturally and enhances the long-term sustainability of the soil.

Q.8 Mention three ways to reduce waste generation at home. **(ICSE Semester II 2022)**

Or How will you as an individual reduce and reuse waste at home?

Ans. Three ways to reduce waste generation at home are as follows

- Shop eco-friendly with reusable bags like jute bags instead of plastic bags.
- Develop a habit of composting at home. Fruits and vegetable scraps, egg shells, coffee grounds, grass clippings and leaves can all be composted.
- Buy second hand items and donate used goods. Purchase new items only when it is much needed.

Q.9 With reference to the 3Rs, give a term that best describes each of the following **(ICSE 2025)**

(i) An empty soft drink can is used as a pen stand.

(ii) Old scrap papers are used to manufacture handmade paper.

(iii) No food is wasted in the household.

Ans. (i) **Reuse** Using an item again for a different purpose instead of throwing it away.

(ii) **Recycle** Processing waste materials into new products to prevent waste.

(iii) **Reduce** Using resources wisely to minimise waste generation.

Q.10 With reference to the waste management, answer the following. **(ICSE 2023)**

(i) How is recycling of waste helpful? Give an example of recycling of waste.

(ii) Mention any one initiative taken by the government to manage waste.

Ans. (i) Recycling helps in the protection of the environment, in reducing air, land, water and soil pollution and saving energy. For example, use reusable bags instead of plastic bags.

(ii) Swachh Bharat Mission is the initiative taken by the government to manage waste.

TYPE - 5 10 Marks

Structured Questions

Q.1 (i) With reference to the image, answer the following questions. **(2)**

(a) Identify the type of pollution seen in the image given above.

(b) Mention two methods that can be implemented to reduce this type of pollution.

(ii) Mention one advantage of sanitary landfills and one disadvantage of composting. **(2)**

(iii) Give a reason for the following statements. **(ICSE 2025)**

(a) Organic manure should replace chemical fertilisers.

(b) There should be a ban on the use of polythene and plastic products.

(c) Manual handling of waste must be avoided.

(iv) Your school recently started an initiative to promote environmental awareness among students. As part of the program, the school introduced the concept of the 3R's — Reduce, Reuse, and Recycle. Students were encouraged to bring reusable water bottles, avoid single-use plastics and segregate waste into separate bins for recycling. The school also held workshops on making DIY crafts from waste materials. **(3)**

(a) How does practicing the 3R's help in waste management and environmental conservation?

(b) Why is segregation of waste important for effective recycling?

(c) Suggest two ways in which students can implement the concept of 'Reduce' in their daily lives.

Ans. (i) (a) Water pollution is seen in the image.

(b) Two methods that can be implemented to reduce water pollution are

- **Wastewater Treatment** Treating industrial and domestic wastewater before releasing it into water bodies removes harmful pollutants, preventing contamination of surface and groundwater.
- **Use of Biodegradable Products** Encouraging the use of eco-friendly and biodegradable products reduces the seepage of toxic chemicals and plastics into water sources.

(ii) **Advantage of Sanitary Landfill**

- Prevents contamination of groundwater by isolating waste through protective liners and leachate management.

Disadvantage of Composting

- Requires significant time and space, making it less suitable for managing large volumes of waste quickly.

(iii) (a) Organic manure should replace chemical fertilisers because it improves soil fertility naturally without harming beneficial microbes. Unlike chemical fertilisers, which can degrade soil quality over time, organic manure enhances soil structure and retains moisture, leading to sustainable farming.

(b) There should be a ban on the use of polythene and plastic products because they are non-biodegradable and cause severe environmental pollution. Plastic waste clogs drains, harms marine and wildlife, and releases toxic chemicals when burned, contributing to climate change.

(c) Manual handling of waste must be avoided because it poses serious health risks to workers due to exposure to harmful bacteria, toxic chemicals, and sharp objects. Instead, proper waste management systems, including protective gear and mechanised waste disposal, should be implemented for safety and hygiene.

(iv) (a) Practicing the 3R's minimises waste generation, conserves natural resources, reduces pollution and promotes sustainable use of materials. It aims to generate minimum amount of waste to extract maximum benefit.

(b) Segregation ensures that recyclable materials are not contaminated by non-recyclable waste, making the recycling process efficient and cost-effective.

(c) Two ways in which students can implement the concept of 'Reduce' in their daily lives are

- Use reusable bags instead of single-use plastic bags.
- Minimise paper usage by switching to digital notes.

Q.2 (i) What is the impact of waste generation on the following? **(ICSE Specimen 2025) (2)**

(a) Surface water (b) Landscape

(ii) Why is dumping considered a harmful method of waste disposal? **(2)**

(iii) Fire broke out at the Kochi city waste treatment plant. Thick clouds of toxic smoke engulfed the city. The waste at the plant also contained plastic and biomedical wastes, both of which on combustion are extremely harmful for the general health of people. *Economic Times, 10th March, 2023* **(3)**

(a) Which method of waste management would have helped in reducing health hazards in the above case?

(b) Mention one measure you can adopt in school to reduce waste.

(c) State one way in which domestic waste can be made useful.

(iv) (a) What are landfills? **(3)**

(b) Enumerate two advantages of composting as a method of waste disposal.

Ans. (i) (a) **Impact on Surface Water** Waste generation leads to water pollution as contaminants and toxic substances from improperly managed waste leach into rivers, lakes and ponds which harms aquatic life and affects water quality.

(b) **Impact on Landscape** Waste generation leads to soil contamination as hazardous chemicals and toxins from decomposing waste seep into the ground. This reduces soil fertility and spoils the scenic beauty of the place.

(ii) Dumping is considered a harmful method of waste disposal because it leads to environmental contamination. It can pollute soil, water and air by releasing harmful chemicals and toxins into the environment.

This practice also attracts pests, poses health risks to humans and animals and contributes to the spread of diseases.

(iii) (a) Recycling is the most effective method for reducing plastic waste. It involves collecting, processing, and reusing plastic materials to create new products, reducing the need for new plastic production and minimising environmental impact.

(b) One measure to reduce waste in school is to implement a paper recycling program, encouraging students and staff to reuse and recycle paper products.

(c) One way to make domestic waste useful is by composting organic waste which can be turned into nutrient-rich compost for gardening.

(iv) (a) Landfills are large areas where the waste is deposited above or below the ground and covered it with Earth.

(b) Two advantages of composting as a method of waste disposal are

- Composting converts organic waste into a useful matter.
- The compost enriches soil by adding nutrients, enhancing plant growth.

Q.3 (i) With reference to the picture below, answer the questions that follow. **(ICSE 2024) (2)**

(a) Which waste management method is depicted here?

(b) State one way in which this method may be implemented at our home.

(ii) Explain how waste accumulation can be harmful. (Any two points). **(2)**

(iii) Explain how waste generated in the following sectors may be made useful. (Give one example for each) **(3)**

(a) Household (b) Industry

(c) Agriculture

(iv) (a) Give two uses for composting. **(3)**

(b) Why are landfills set up far away from the city? (Any two reasons).

Ans. (i) (a) Segregation of wastes is depicted here. Here, various types of dustbins are used to segregate garbage.

(b) At our homes, we can segregate hazardous items like batteries, electronics and cleaning chemicals, biodegradable and non-biodegradable wastes to avoid contamination.

(ii) Waste accumulation can be harmful due to the following reasons

- Accumulated waste, especially plastic and non-biodegradable materials can lead to pollution in the air, water and soil. This affects ecosystems, harms wildlife and contributes to climate change.
- Accumulated waste creates an unpleasant environment, reducing the beauty and livability of areas.

(iii) (a) **Household** Household waste especially organic waste like food scraps can be turned into nutrient-rich compost.

(b) **Industry** In industries, scrap metal generated during manufacturing processes can be collected, cleaned and melted down to create new metal products.

(c) **Agriculture** Agricultural waste such as crop residues can be used as feed for livestock.

(iv) (a) Two uses of composting are

- Composting transforms organic waste into nutrient-rich compost that can be added to soil to enhance its fertility.
- Composting helps divert organic waste from landfills, reducing the amount of waste.

(b) Landfills set up far away from the city due to the following reasons

- Landfills produce harmful gases like methane which can contaminate water sources. Placing them far from cities minimises the risk of exposure.
- Landfills require large areas of land for waste disposal. Placing them far from cities helps reduce the unpleasant odours and visual impact on urban areas.

ICSE Solved Paper 2025

ICSE SOLVED PAPER 2025
(FULLY SOLVED)
GEOGRAPHY X

General Instructions

Maximum Marks : 80

Time allowed : Two hours

Answers to this paper must be written on the answer sheet provided separately.

You will **not** be allowed to write during the first **15** minutes.

This time is to be spent in reading the question paper.

The time given at the head of this paper is the time allowed for writing the answers.

Part I is compulsory. All questions from Part I are to be attempted.

A total of **five** questions are to be attempted from **Part II**.

The intended marks for questions or parts of questions are given brackets ().

Part - I

(30 Marks)

Attempt all questions from this Part.

Question 1

Study the extract of the Survey of India Map Sheet No. G43S10 (Map given at the end) and answer the following questions **(2)**

(i) (a) Give the six-figure grid reference for spot height. 437 in the southeastern part of the map extract.

(b) Aman, a local craftsman, wants to sell his product to a large gathering to earn money instantly.

1. Which settlement should he go to?

2. Name the month in which he should visit the settlement named by you above.

(ii) (a) On which bank of the Sukli nadi is the settlement of Pamera situated? **(2)**

(b) Identify the settlement pattern seen in the grid square 6732.

(iii) Roshan, while travelling from Sirori to Tokra, observed that the surface water sources are dry except for the reservoir near Tokra. **(2)**

(a) What according to you may be the reason for the presence of water in the reservoir in 6832 near Tokra settlement?

(b) State whether this reservoir is artificial or natural source of water.

(iv) (a) What is the direct distance between Gulabganj to Pithapura? Give your answer in kilometre. **(2)**

(b) Mention the compass direction of Pithapura from Gulabganj.

(v) (a) Name two man-made features seen in the grid square 6534. **(2)**

(b) Define contour interval.

Question 2

On the outline map of India provided **(10)**

(i) Mark and label the Nathu-La pass.

(ii) Shade and name the coastal plain that occupies a large part of Kerala.

(iii) Mark and label Digboi.

(iv) Mark and label Chilka lake.

(v) Mark with arrows and name the wind that brings rainfall to Tamil Nadu coast during winter.

(vi) Mark and label the River Sutlej.

(vii) Mark and label the Standard Meridian of India.

(viii) Mark and label Satpura range.

(ix) Shade and label the Chota Nagpur plateau.

(x) Mark and label Visakhapatnam.

Question 3

Choose the correct answers to the questions from the given options. (10)
(Do not copy the questions, write the correct answers only.)

(i) **Assertion** (A) Mumbai receives more rainfall than Pune.

Reason (R) Mumbai gets rain from Arabian Sea branch of South-West monsoon.

(a) Both (A) and (R) are true and (R) is the correct explanation for (A).
(b) Both (A) and (R) are true and (R) is not the correct explanation for (A).
(c) (A) is true and (R) is false
(d) (A) is false and (R) is true

(ii) Which of the following pairs of soils displays similar characteristics in terms of their colour and texture?

(a) Alluvial soil and laterite soil
(b) Black soil and red soil
(c) Red soil and laterite soil
(d) Alluvial soil and black soil

(iii) The type of natural vegetation shown in the picture given below is found on

(a) Tropical desert
(b) Tropical deciduous
(c) Tropical evergreen
(d) Littoral forest

(iv) Which of the following prevents wastage of water?

(a) Canal (b) Well

(c) Sprinkler (d) Tube well

(v) Balaghat : Manganese :: Mumbai High :

(a) Copper (b) Coal

(c) Iron Ore (d) Petroleum

(vi) A microbiological process that loosens the bark of a crop and facilitates removal of fibre from the stalk

(a) Rolling (b) Ratooning

(c) Retting (d) Fermentation

(vii) Which industry amongst the following has revolutionised the lifestyle of the Indian masses in recent years?

(a) Cotton Textile (b) Electronic

(c) Iron and Steel (d) Sugar

(vii) Which of the following household products is associated with the petrochemical industry?

(a) Glass bottle (b) Wooden chopping board

(c) Kitchen knife (d) Plastic mug

(ix) Raman, a dairy farmer in Ludhiana, supplies milk within the city on a daily basis. Which mode of transport is he most likely to use

(a) Railway (b) Roadway

(c) Airway (d) Waterway

(x) The collection of discarded materials and converting them into useful products ist

(a) Recycling (b) Processing

(c) Reducing (d) Composting

Part - II

(50 Marks)

Attempt any five questions from this Part.

Question 4

(i) 'Severe cyclonic storms are often formed over the Bay of Bengal during the retreating monsoon season.' **(2)**

(a) Name two states that are affected by tropical cyclones on the eastern coast of India.

(b) The temperate cyclones cause less damage than the tropical cyclones. Give any two points to support this statement.

(ii) (a) Name the local wind that causes rainfall in the states of Assam and West Bengal in the month of April. **(2)**

(b) How is this rainfall beneficial for the states mentioned above?

(iii) With reference to Figure A and Figure B given below, answer the questions that follow. **(3)**

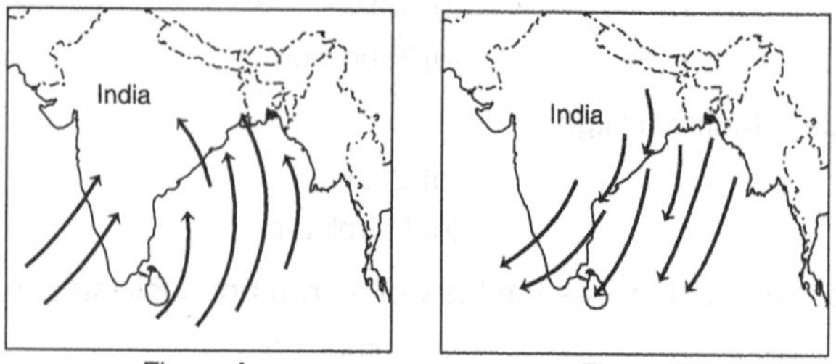

Figure A Figure B

(a) Name the winds shown by arrows in Figure A and Figure B.

(b) How is the wind shown in Figure A different from the one shown in Figure B?

(iv) Study the climate data of station X and answer the following questions **(3)**

Month	Jan	Feb	Mar	Apr	May	Jun	July	Aug	Sep	Oct	Nov	Dec
Temp (°C)	24.0	25.4	26.7	28.3	30.0	28.9	27.6	27.4	27.3	27.1	27.0	25.0
Rainfall (cm)	0.25	0.25	-	-	1.75	50.2	61.0	37.0	27.0	4.75	1.50	-

(a) What is the annual range of temperature for station X?

(b) Which is the wettest month?

(c) Name the wind which brings rainfall for station X during the rainy season.

Question 5

(i) The Ganga Plain is known for its fertile soil, it is often referred to as the Food bowl of India. This region supports a variety of crops such as rice, wheat, pulses, jute and sugarcane. **(2)**

(a) Name the soil that is found in large parts of Ganga plain.

(b) Give two properties of this soil which helps it to produce a variety of crops.

(ii) (a) What is meant by soil erosion? **(2)**

(b) Name any two agents of soil erosion.

(iii) Give a geographical reason to explain each of the following. **(3)**

(a) Soil conservation is the need of the hour.

(b) Red soil has a poor water retention capacity.

(c) Laterite soils are infertile.

(iv) With reference to black soil of India, answer the following questions. **(3)**

(a) How is this soil formed?

(b) How is this soil able to retain moisture for a long period?

(c) Mention any two minerals present in this soil.

Question 6

(i) India has lost 2.33 million hectares of tree cover since the year 2000. This is equivalent to a six percent decrease in tree cover during this period, *Source: The Indian Express, Date 12th April, 2024* **(2)**

(a) Mention any two causes of the decrease in the forest cover of India.

(b) Name a conservation method that may be used to help in increasing the forest cover.

(ii) Mention the climatic condition suitable for the development of tropical evergreen forest. **(2)**

(iii) State any three differences between tropical deciduous and tropical desert vegetation. **(3)**

(iv) (a) Give any two reasons for the great diversity of natural vegetation in India. **(3)**

(b) How do the forests help in maintenance of air quality?

Question 7

(i) Mention any one advantage and any one disadvantage of well irrigation. **(2)**

(ii) Suggest any two measures to overcome scarcity of water in the metropolitan cities of India. **(2)**

(iii) Give one reason to explain each of the following **(3)**

(a) Tank irrigation is not common in Northern India.

(b) Canal irrigation is important in Punjab.

(c) All farmers do not use tube well irrigation even if the geographical condition is favourable.

(iv) State any three objectives of rainwater harvesting. **(3)**

Question 8

(i) With the rising price of fossil fuel every passing day, it is very important to develop non-conventional energy resource. **(3)**

Bulletin-Department of non-conventional sources of energy

(a) Name a non-conventional energy source that can be harnessed by taking advantage of India's vast coastline.

(b) State one advantage of using geothermal energy.

(ii) (a) How is Biogas formed? **(2)**

(b) Mention any one advantage of Biogas over other non-conventional energy resources.

(iii) Give a reason for each of the following. **(3)**

(a) Iron ore is called a versatile mineral.

(b) Windmills set up on agricultural lands are beneficial to farmers.

(c) Coal is the most preferred source of energy in Indian industries.

(iv) **(3)**

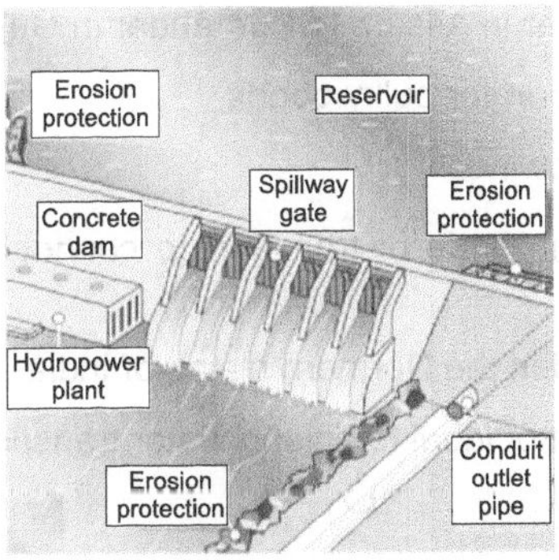

(a) Identify the type of energy being generated in the picture given above.

(b) State why this type of energy is cheaper in the long run.

(c) Name a power project associated with the generation of this energy in the Northern part of India.

Question 9

(i) Mention two climatic conditions that favour the cultivation of groundnut. **(2)**

(ii) Give any two reasons why Maharashtra has emerged as an important sugarcane producing state. **(2)**

(iii) Give one reason to explain each of the following. **(3)**

(a) Trees are planted in between the rows of coffee plants.

(b) Cotton cultivation requires plenty of cheap labour.

(c) Hill slopes are best suited for tea cultivation.

(iv) Explain the following **(3)**

(a) Mixed farming (b) Zayad (c) Transplantation

Question 10

(i) State any two factors that are responsible for the growth of the cotton textile industry in Kolkata. **(2)**

(ii) 'Karnataka is the leading state for silk production in India'. **(2)**

Give any two reasons to justify the above statement.

(iii) (a) Name the Iron and Steel industry located at Chhattisgarh. **(3)**

(b) From where does the industry named by you above get its supply of the following?

1. Iron ore 2. Coal

(iv) Raghav has been given a project by his teacher in which he has to write about the by-products of an industry that is used for preparing shoe polish, carbon paper and cardboard. **(3)**

(a) Which industry will he be writing about?

(b) Name any two by-products of the industry mentioned by you.

Question 11

(i) Why is a well-developed transport network important for India? **(2)**

(ii) Mention any two advantages of road transport. **(2)**

(iii) Name the following **(3)**

(a) The mode of transport that ensures comfortable journey, especially for elders and children.

(b) The highway connecting Silchar in Assam to Porbandar in Gujarat.

(c) The cheapest means of transport for bulky goods.

(iv) Give a reason for each of the following. **(3)**

(a) Airways are the most efficient mode of transport to connect North-East India with the rest of the country.

(b) Railways are easily developed in the Northern plains of India.

(c) Rivers of peninsular India are not ideal for inland water transport.

Question 12

(i) (a) Give a reason for a substantial rise of E-waste in India **(2)**

(b) What is dumping?

(ii) 'You cannot protect environment unless you empower people, you inform them and help them to understand that these resources are their own, that they must protect them'. **(2)**

Wangari Maathar (recipient of Nobel Prize 2004 for Sustainable Developments)

As a responsible student how would you contribute to reduce and manage the waste generated in your surroundings. Explain by giving suitable examples.

(iii) With reference to the 3Rs, give a term that best describes each of the following. **(3)**

(a) An empty soft drink can is used as a pen stand.

(b) Old scrap papers are used to manufacture handmade paper.

(c) No food is wasted in the household.

(iv) Give a reason for the following statements. **(3)**

(a) Organic manure should replace chemical fertilisers.

(b) There should be a ban on the use of polythene and plastic products.

(c) Manual handling of waste must be avoided.

Answers

1. (i) (a) 673295

(b) 1. Malgoan or Pamera both are correct. 2. March

(ii) (a) Right bank (b) Scattered

(iii) (a) Sipu Nadi (b) Artificial

(iv) (a) 2.25 km (b) North-East

(v) (a) Settlement, Roads, Well, Temple, Post-office.

(b) **Contour Interval** A contour interval refers to the vertical distance or elevation difference between adjacent contour lines.

2.

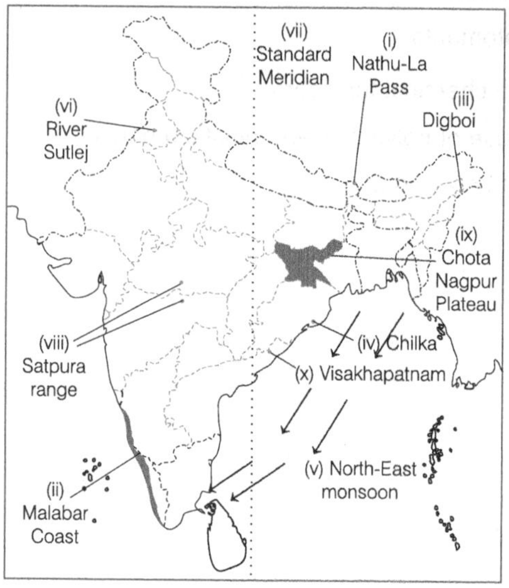

3. (i) (a) Both (A) and (R) are true and (R) is the correct explanation for (A).

(ii) (c) Red soil and laterite soil

(iii) (d) Littoral forest (iv) (c) Sprinkler

(v) (d) Petroleum (vi) (c) Retting

(vii) (b) Electronic (viii) (d) Plastic mug

(ix) (b) Roadway (x) (a) Recycling

4. (i) (a) Two states that are affected by tropical cyclones on the eastern coast of India are West Bengal and Odisha.

(b) The temperate cyclones cause less damage than the tropical cyclones due to the following reasons

- **Lower Wind Speeds** Temperate cyclones have weaker winds than tropical cyclones, causing less damage.
- **Wider Area of Influence** Temperate cyclones affect a larger area with less intensity, while tropical cyclones are more concentrated and destructive.

(ii) (a) The local wind that causes rainfall in the states of Assam and West Bengal in the month of April is the 'Norwesters' or 'Kalbaisakhi'.

(b) This rainfall benefits Assam and West Bengal by aiding crop growth and cooling down temperatures, providing relief from the heat.

(iii) (a) The winds shown by arrows in Figure A represent the South-West monsoon winds. The winds shown by arrows in Figure B represent the North-East monsoon winds.

(b) The wind shown in Figure A is different from the one shown in Figure B in the following ways

- **South-West Monsoon Winds (Figure A)** These winds blow from the Indian Ocean towards the Indian subcontinent during the summer season (June to September), bringing heavy rainfall to most parts of India.
- **North-East Monsoon Winds (Figure B)** These winds blow from the land (India) towards the Indian Ocean during the winter season (October to December), bringing rainfall mainly to the southeastern coast of India (Tamil Nadu, Andhra Pradesh, etc.).

(iv) (a) Annual range of temperature = Highest temperature - Lowest temperature

= 30.0°C (May) - 24.0°C (January)

= 6.0°C

(b) July is the wettest month.

(c) The wind that brings rainfall to station X during the rainy season is the South-West monsoon winds.

5. (i) (a) The soil found in large parts of the Ganga Plain is Alluvial soil.

(b) Two properties of alluvial soil that help in producing a variety of crops

- **High Fertility** It is rich in nutrients like potash, phosphoric acid and lime, which support the growth of crops like rice, wheat and sugarcane.
- **Good Moisture Retention** This soil has the ability to retain water, making it suitable for both rain-fed and irrigated agriculture.

(ii) (a) Soil erosion is the removal of the top fertile layer of soil by natural forces such as wind and water, leading to the loss of nutrients and reduced soil fertility.

(b) Two agents of soil erosion are wind and water.

(iii) (a) Soil conservation is the need of the hour as soil is essential for agriculture and vegetation, but erosion, deforestation, and overuse reduce its fertility. Soil conservation is necessary to prevent land degradation, maintain food security, and protect the environment.

(b) Red soil is rich in iron but has a sandy texture and lacks humus, making it less capable of retaining water. This results in quick drainage and lower moisture availability for crops.

(c) Laterite soil undergoes intense leaching due to heavy rainfall, washing away essential nutrients. As a result, it becomes acidic and lacks fertility, making it unsuitable for most crops without proper treatment.

(iv) (a) Black soil is formed from the weathering of volcanic rocks, primarily from the Deccan Plateau region.

(b) Black soil has a high clay content, which allows it to absorb and retain moisture for a long time, even during dry seasons.

(c) Two minerals present in this soil are iron and magnesium.

6. (i) (a) Two causes of the decrease in forest cover in India

- ***Deforestation for agriculture and urbanisation*** *Large areas of forests are cleared to make space for farming, industries, and expanding cities.*
- ***Illegal logging and overexploitation*** *Excessive cutting of trees for timber, firewood and other commercial purposes leads to forest depletion.*

(b) A conservation method that may be used to help in increasing the forest cover is afforestation, i.e, planting new trees in deforested areas.

(ii) (a) The climatic condition suitable for the development of tropical evergreen forest are

- ***High Temperature*** *The temperature remains warm and humid throughout the year, typically ranging between 25°C to 27°C.*
- ***Heavy Rainfall*** *These forests require more than 200 cm of annual rainfall, which is evenly distributed throughout the year.*

(iii) Three differences between tropical deciduous and tropical desert vegetation are

Tropical Deciduous Vegetation	Tropical Desert Vegetation
Found in monsoon regions with moderate rainfall (100-200 cm).	Found in areas with extremely low rainfall (less than 25 cm), hot and dry climate.
They shed leaves in dry season to conserve water.	They have small, thorny, or wax-coated leaves to reduce water loss.
Examples-Sal, teak, and neem	Examples-cactus, acacia, and date palm

(iv) (a) Two reasons for the great diversity of natural vegetation in India are

- ***Varied Climate*** *India has diverse climatic conditions, ranging from tropical in the South to temperate and alpine in the North. Different temperatures, rainfall patterns and humidity levels support a wide range of vegetation types.*
- ***Diverse Landforms*** *India has mountains, plateaus, plains and coastal regions, each providing unique soil types and environmental conditions that influence the growth of different plant species.*

(b) The forests help in maintenance of air quality in the following ways

- ***Absorption of Carbon Dioxide*** *Trees absorb CO_2 during photosynthesis, reducing greenhouse gases and improving air quality.*
- ***Release of Oxygen*** *Forests release oxygen (O_2), which is essential for life.*

7. (i) **Advantage of Well Irrigation**

- **Low Cost and Easy to Construct** Wells can be dug at a low cost and require simple technology, making them accessible for small farmers.

Disadvantage of Well Irrigation

- **Limited Water Supply** Wells depend on groundwater, which can dry up during summers or in areas with low water tables.

(ii) Two measures to overcome water scarcity in metropolitan cities of India are

- **Rainwater Harvesting** Collecting and storing rainwater from rooftops and open spaces can help in recharging groundwater and meeting daily water needs.
- **Wastewater Recycling and Reuse** Treating and recycling wastewater for non-drinking purposes like gardening, cleaning and industrial use can reduce water wastage.

(iii) (a) Tank irrigation is not common in Northern India because of flat terrain. Northern India, especially the Indo-Gangetic Plain, has a flat landscape, making it difficult to construct tanks, which require natural depressions to store water.

(b) Canal irrigation is important in Punjab because the region has a network of perennial rivers like the Satluj, Beas, and Ravi, which provide a continuous water supply for irrigation through canals.

(c) All farmers do not use tube well irrigation even if the geographical conditions are favourable because the installation and maintenance of tube wells are expensive. Small and marginal farmers may not afford the high initial cost of setting up tube wells and the electricity or diesel expenses required to operate them.

(iv) The three objectives of rainwater harvesting are

- **Conservation of Water** To collect and store rainwater for future use, reducing dependence on groundwater and other water sources.
- **Groundwater Recharge** To replenish underground water levels by allowing rainwater to seep into the soil, preventing depletion.
- **Flood and Soil Erosion Control** To reduce surface runoff, preventing floods and soil erosion, especially in urban and hilly areas.

8. (i) (a) A non-conventional energy source that can be harnessed using India's vast coastline is Tidal Energy.

(b) Geothermal energy is a clean and sustainable source of power, producing minimal pollution and reducing dependence on fossil fuels.

(ii) (a) Biogas is formed through the anaerobic decomposition of organic waste like animal dung, plant material and kitchen waste by bacteria. This process called anaerobic digestion produces methane-rich gas, which can be used as fuel.

(b) Biogas is a continuous and reliable source of energy, unlike solar and wind energy, which depend on weather conditions.

(iii) (a) Iron ore is called a versatile mineral because it is the primary raw material for making steel, which is used in various industries like construction, transportation, machinery and infrastructure development.

(b) Windmills set up on agricultural lands are beneficial to farmers because they generate **additional income** for farmers through land lease payments while allowing them to continue farming activities beneath the wind turbines.

(c) Coal is the most preferred source of energy in Indian industries because it is abundantly available, affordable and provides a reliable energy source for industries like steel, cement and power generation.

(iv) (a) The type of energy being generated in the picture is Hydroelectric Energy.

(b) This type of energy is cheaper in the long run because

- It uses renewable water resources, which do not require fuel costs.
- Hydroelectric power plants have low operational and maintenance costs after initial construction. (any one point)

(c) A power project associated with the generation of this energy in Northern India is the Bhakra Nangal Hydroelectric Project on the Sutlej river.

9. (i) The two climatic conditions that favour the cultivation of groundnut are

- **Warm Temperature** Groundnut requires a warm climate with temperatures between 20°C to 30°C for proper growth.
- **Moderate Rainfall** It grows best in areas with 50-100 cm of rainfall, as excessive moisture can damage the crop.

(ii) Maharashtra has emerged as an important sugarcane-producing state due to the following reasons

- **Favourable Climate** The state has a tropical climate with hot and humid conditions, which are ideal for sugarcane cultivation. Additionally, moderate rainfall and well-distributed irrigation facilities support high yields.
- **Well-Developed Irrigation Facilities** Despite having relatively low rainfall in some regions, Maharashtra has well-developed canal and well irrigation systems, ensuring a continuous water supply for sugarcane crops.

(iii) (a) Trees are planted in between the rows of coffee plants to provide shade and protect the coffee plants from direct sunlight and strong winds, which can affect their growth and quality.

(b) Cotton cultivation requires plenty of cheap labour because most of the processes, like sowing, picking and ginning are done manually, requiring a large workforce.

(c) Hill slopes are best suited for tea cultivation because they ensure proper drainage, preventing waterlogging, which is harmful to tea plants. Additionally, the cool and humid climate of hills favours tea growth.

(iv) (a) Mixed farming is a type of agriculture where both crops and livestock are raised on the same farm.

(b) Zayad is the short cropping season between the Rabi and Kharif seasons in India, from March to June.

(c) Transplantation is the process of growing seedlings in a nursery and then shifting them to the main field for better growth.

10. (i) The growth of the cotton textile industry in Kolkata is due to the following factors

- **Availability of Cheap Labour** Kolkata has a large workforce, including migrant labourers from neighbouring states like Bihar and Odisha, which helps in keeping production costs low.
- **Well-Connected Transportation System** The city has a good network of roads, railways and a major port, making it easy to transport raw materials (cotton) and finished goods both within India and internationally.

(ii) Karnataka is the leading state for silk production in India due to the following reasons

- **Favourable Climate** Karnataka has a moderate climate with suitable temperature and humidity, which is ideal for silkworm rearing and mulberry cultivation.
- **Availability of Mulberry Leaves** The state has extensive mulberry plantations, providing a steady food supply for silkworms, essential for high-quality silk production.

(iii) (a) The Iron and Steel industry located in Chhattisgarh is the Bhilai Steel Plant.

(b) Sources of raw materials for Bhilai Steel Plant

1. **Iron Ore** Sourced from the Dalli-Rajhara mines in Chhattisgarh.
2. **Coal** Supplied from the Korba and Jharia coalfields.

(iv) (a) Raghav will be writing about the Sugar Industry because its by-products are used in making shoe polish, carbon paper and cardboard.

(b) Two by-products of the sugar industry are bagasse and molasses.

11. (i) A well-developed transport network is important for India because

- **Boosts Trade and Economy** Efficient transport helps in the movement of goods across the country and supports industries, agriculture and exports.
- **Enhances Connectivity** It connects remote and rural areas with cities, improving access to markets, healthcare and education.

(ii) Two advantages of road transport are

- **Door-to-Door Service** Road transport provides direct delivery of goods and passengers to their destination, reducing the need for additional handling.
- **Flexibility and Accessibility** Roads can be built in remote areas, making transport possible even in hilly and rural regions where other modes may not be available.

(iii) (a) Rail transport ensures a comfortable journey, especially for elders and children, as trains provide seating, sleeping arrangements and other facilities.

(b) The highway connecting Silchar in Assam to Porbandar in Gujarat is part of the East-West Corridor.

(c) The cheapest means of transport for bulky goods is water transport, as it is cost-effective and fuel-efficient, especially for long-distance trade.

(iv) (a) Airways are the most efficient mode of transport to connect North-East India with the rest of the country because the region has rugged terrain, dense forests and frequent floods, making road and rail transport difficult.

(b) Railways are easily developed in the Northern plains of India because the region has flat and fertile land, which makes track construction and maintenance easier compared to hilly or plateau regions.

(c) Rivers of peninsular India are not ideal for inland water transport because they are seasonal, with water levels fluctuating throughout the year. Additionally, these rivers have many waterfalls, rapids and rocky beds, making navigation difficult.

12. (i) (a) The increase in the use of electronic devices such as mobile phones, computers, televisions and home appliances, along with rapid technological advancements, has led to a substantial rise in E-waste in India.

(b) Dumping is the practice of disposing of waste materials, including industrial, household and hazardous waste, in an uncontrolled manner, often in landfills, open spaces or water bodies.

(ii) As a responsible student, I can contribute to reducing and managing waste in my surroundings through the following steps

1. Reduce Waste Generation

- Use reusable items like steel water bottles, cloth bags and lunch boxes instead of plastic ones.

2. Spread Awareness

- Organise cleanliness drives in school and the local community.

(iii) (a) **Reuse** Using an item again for a different purpose instead of throwing it away.

(b) **Recycle** Processing waste materials into new products to prevent waste.

(c) **Reduce** Using resources wisely to minimise waste generation.

(iv) (a) Organic manure should replace chemical fertilisers because it improves soil fertility naturally without harming beneficial microbes. Unlike chemical fertilisers, which can degrade soil quality over time, organic manure enhances soil structure and retains moisture, leading to sustainable farming.

(b) There should be a ban on the use of polythene and plastic products because they are non-biodegradable and cause severe environmental pollution. Plastic waste clogs drains, harms marine and wildlife, and releases toxic chemicals when burned, contributing to climate change.

(c) Manual handling of waste must be avoided because it poses serious health risks to workers due to exposure to harmful bacteria, toxic chemicals and sharp objects. Instead, proper waste management systems, including protective gear and mechanised waste disposal, should be implemented for safety and hygiene.

ICSE Latest Specimen Paper

Sample Question Paper

ICSE LATEST SPECIMEN PAPER
(FULLY SOLVED)
GEOGRAPHY X

General Instructions

Maximum Marks : 80

Time allowed : Two hours

Answers to this paper must be written on the answer sheet provided separately.

You will **not** be allowed to write during the first **15** minutes.

This time is to be spent in reading the question paper.

The time given at the head of this paper is the time allowed for writing the answers.

Part I is compulsory. All questions from Part I are to be attempted.

A total of **five** questions are to be attempted from **Part II**.

The intended marks for questions or parts of questions are given brackets ().

Part - I

(30 Marks)

Attempt all questions from this Part.

Question 1

Study the extract of the Survey of India Map sheet No. G43S7 and answer the following questions.

(i) (a) Give the six-figure grid reference for .201 in the Eastern part of the map extract. **(2)**

(b) What are the brown patches in the North-East quarter of the map extract? **[Apply & Understanding]**

(ii) Mohan goes on a bicycle from 02 northing to 12 northing in a straight line. If he moves at a speed of 10 kilometers per hour, how much time will he take to reach his destination? **[Apply] (2)**

(iii) (a) What is the compass direction of Rampura (2709) from Kotda (3005)? **(2)**

(b) If you are moving along the left bank of Sipu river, which settlement will you come across? **[Analyse]**

(iv) (a) Ramesh returned to his native place Mahudi Moti (2404) after a gap of ten years and was happy to see the development around his village. What according to you show that the area around his village has developed? **(2)**

(b) What is the black vertical line made between the easting 25 and 26? **[Apply & Remember]**

(v) Mention two man-made and two natural features in the grid square 2508. **[Understanding] (2)**

Question 2

On the outline map of India provided **[Recall]**

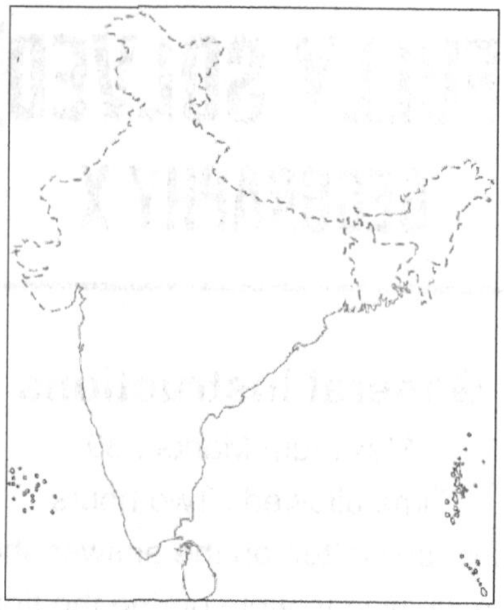

(i) Shade and label an area of alluvial soil in the North-East. **(1)**

(ii) Mark using a dot and name the commercial capital of India. **(1)**

(iii) Mark and name the highest peak of Himalayas in India. **(1)**

(iv) Shade and label Gulf of Kutch. **(1)**

(v) Mark with arrows and name the wind bringing rainfall to Punjab in winter. **(1)**

(vi) Shade and label a sparsely populated area. **(1)**

(vii) Mark and label Eastern Ghats. **(1)**

(viii) Mark and name a tributary of an important peninsular river. **(1)**

(ix) Mark and label the most important latitude passing through the country. **(1)**

(x) Mark and label Coromandel coast. **(1)**

Question 3

Choose the correct answers to the questions from the given options. (Do not copy the question, write the correct answers only). **(10)**

(i) Himalayas have a significant impact on the climate of India as they **[Apply]**

(a) block the North-East monsoon winds
(b) causes rainfall in the Gangetic plains
(c) create a rain shadow area in the Deccan plateau
(d) cause cyclonic disturbance in the Bay of Bengal

(ii) Feel and consistency of soil is called .... of the soil. **[Remember]**

(a) profile (b) parent rock
(c) texture (d) density

(iii) Teak: Tropical Deciduous Forest **[Remember]**

(a) Mahogany: Furniture (b) Stilted roots: Mangrove Vegetation
(c) Ebony: Tropical Rainforest (d) Spines: Tropical Desert Vegetation

(iv) **Which of the following may be used for the recharging of underground water?** **[Understanding]**

(a) Planting of shelter belt
(b) Plugging of gullies and ravines
(c) Percolation pit
(d) Tube-well irrigation

(v) **Which type of coal is referred to as industrial coal?** **[Remember]**

(a) Peat
(b) Lignite
(c) Bituminous
(d) Anthracite

(vi) **Assertion** (A) During the late 1960s, there was a many-fold increase in the production of wheat in Punjab.

Reason (R) The Green Revolution brought about increased use of inputs like HYV seeds, fertilisers and pesticides. **[Analyse]**

Codes

(a) Both A and R are true and R is the correct explanation of A
(b) Both A and R are true, but R is not the correct explanation of A
(c) A is true but, R is false
(d) A is false, but R is true

(vii) **Which crop is associated with Ratooning?** **[Remember]**

(a) Sugarcane
(b) Jute
(c) Rice
(d) Cotton

(viii) **Which steel plant amongst the following was set up with the collaboration with Germany?** **[Remember]**

(a) Bhilai
(b) Tata Steel
(c) Visakhapatnam
(d) Rourkela

(ix) **If you have to transport perishable goods over a long distance, which mode of transport will you use and why?** **[Apply]**

(a) Air transport because it is the fastest.
(b) Road transport as it is economical.
(c) Rail transport as it is ecofriendly.
(d) Water transport as it can handle large amount of goods.

(x) **Which of the following methods of disposal is best applicable for the waste depicted in the picture below?** **[Apply]**

(a) Burning waste in open area
(b) Recycling waste
(c) Dumping
(d) Composting

Part - II

(50 Marks)

Attempt any five questions from this Part.

Question 4

(i) India Meteorological Department (IMD) brings a ray of hope for India's agricultural sector and weather patterns in the upcoming year. After grappling with 'below normal' rains and dry conditions in 2023, the forecast suggested above-normal rainfall in certain regions, including the Southernmost parts of peninsular India, North-West India and several parts of East-Central, East and North-East India. **(2)**

– *Investing.com (01.11.2023)*

(a) As a student of Geography, what according to you may be the possible reason for the 'below normal' rains in 2023?

(b) During which months of the year does most of India receive major amount of its rainfall?

[Analyse & Apply]

(ii) What is the source of winter rainfall in each of the following areas? **(2)**

(a) Punjab (b) Tamil Nadu **[Remember]**

(iii) Give a reason for each of the following. **(3)**

(a) Kerala gets rainfall from the summer monsoons much before Uttar Pradesh.

(b) Visakhapatnam records a low annual range of temperature.

(c) Winds are mostly offshore during the cold season. **[Analyse]**

(iv) Study the climatic data of station X and answer the following questions. **(3)**

Month	Temp (0°C)	Rainfall (cm)
Jan	23.1	7.3
Feb	24.8	1.1
Mar	26.5	0.3
Apr	29.3	0.1
May	32	1.3
Jun	32.8	4.5
July	33.1	6.1
Aug	32.1	8.2
Sep	30.5	8.5
Oct	29.3	20.1
Nov	28.7	20.8
Dec	26.1	9.0

(a) What is the annual range of temperature of station X? **[Apply]**

(b) Which is the driest month? **[Understand]**

(c) Name the wind that brings maximum rainfall to this station. **[Analyse]**

Question 5

(i) Nathu, a farmer in Bihar, does not get good yields as the soil he tills is coarse and has fair proportion of kankars. Motilal on the other hand, has his field closer to the river and gets better yields. **(2)**

(a) Identify the two soils that are being discussed in the above passage.

(b) Give a possible reason why Motilal benefits from having his field along the river banks. **[Remember and Apply]**

(ii) With reference to soil erosion in India answer the following questions. **(2)**

(a) State any two human activities that have led to soil erosion in India.

(b) Mention any two innovative agricultural techniques that can help to prevent soil erosion. **[Apply]**

(iii) With reference to red soil, answer the following. **(3)**

(a) How is it formed? **[Understanding]**

(b) Why is it good for dry farming? **[Apply]**

(c) Name any two areas where it is found. **[Recall]**

(iv) Give a reason for the following statements: **(3)**

(a) Black soil has self-ploughing property.

(b) Laterite soil is not suitable for cultivation.

(c) Alluvial soil is extensively found in the Northern Plains. **[Analyse]**

Question 6

(i) Mahesh went for an excursion with his friend and came across a marshy area with trees that had stilt like roots. **(2)**

(a) Which natural vegetation belt did he come across? **[Apply]**

(b) Name an area in India where this kind of vegetation is found. **[Recall]**

(ii) (a) Why is Tropical Deciduous Forest commercially the most important forest belt of India? **[Evaluate] (2)**

(b) Why are long and deep roots a typical characteristic of desert vegetation? **[Evaluate]**

(iii) Give three reasons why forest conservation is the need of the hour. **[Analyse] (3)**

(iv) (a) Name a forest conservation method that involves the local community. **(3)** **[Remember]**

(b) Which primitive system of agriculture had led to large scale destruction of forest in the past? **[Remember]**

(c) Name the process which involves planting two saplings for each tree that is felled. **[Remember]**

Question 7

(i) State two reasons why there is a need for irrigation in India. **[Understand] (2)**

(ii) Distinguish between Inundation Canals and Perennial Canals. **[Analyse] (2)**

(iii) (a) Name a state in India where tube wells are commonly used. **(3)**

(b) Give two geographical conditions that favour tube well irrigation in this state. **[Analyse]**

(iv) (a) What is meant by rainwater harvesting? **(3)**

(b) Mention any two water harvesting practices followed in India. **[Understand & Remember]**

Question 8

(i) There is ample potential of setting up biogas plants in India. The National Bioenergy Programme has been recommended by the concerned Ministry, for implementation in two phases. The spread of biogas technology is a boon for Indian farmers with its direct and guaranteed benefits. *(https:/lbiogas.mnre.gov.in)* **(2)**

(a) Why do you think generation of biogas can be achieved in every household of rural India?

(b) Mention two ways in which generation of this form of energy proves to be a boon for Indian farmers. **[Analyse & Evaluate]**

(ii) With reference to Hirakud project answer the following: **(2)**

(a) On which river is it based? **[Remember & Apply]**

(b) Name an Indian state benefitted by the project.

(iii) (a) Give anyone use of iron ore. **(3)**

(b) Name the mineral used to strengthen steel.

(c) Name two Indian states where copper is found. **[Apply & Remember]**

(iv) **(3)**

(a) Identify the type of energy being harnessed in the above picture.

(b) Mention why this form of energy is preferred over fossil fuels.

(c) Why does India stand at an advantage in the production of tis type of energy? **[Understand, Evaluate & Apply]**

Question 9

(i) Mention two agricultural reforms done by the government for the betterment of the agricultural sector. **[Understand] (2)**

(ii) (a) State one point of difference between Rabi and Kharif cropping seasons. **(2) [Analyse & Remember]**

(b) Name the state that is the leading producer of groundnut in India.

(iii) With reference to cultivation of pulses, answer the following. **(3)**

(a) Name a soil found suitable for the growth of pulses. **[Understand]**

(b) Name any two varieties of pulses grown in India. **[Remember]**

(c) Give a reason, why is it a popular food crop of India? **[Evaluate]**

(iv) Rohan, a farmer, hired some labourers to help him with 'GINNING'. **(3)**

(a) Name the crop grown by Rohan. **[Apply]**

(b) Mention any two climatic conditions suitable for this crop. **[Recall]**

Question 10

(i) Mention two points of difference between small scale and large scale industry. **[Analyse] (2)**

(ii) Explain two ways in which cotton textile industry is important for India's economy. **(2) [Understand]**

(iii) With reference to petrochemical industry, answer the following. **(3)**

(a) State a reason for the growing popularity of this industry in recent times. **[Apply]**

(b) Why is it located close to oil refineries? **[Evaluate]**

(c) Name any two petrochemical products. **[Remember]**

(iv) Give one reason to explain each of the following. **(3)**

(a) Sugar production is gradually gaining importance in peninsular India.

(b) Indian silk products are becoming less popular in the international market.

(c) The importance of the iron and steel industry will never decline. **[Analyse]**

Question 11

(i) Mention two disadvantages of using waterways. **[Understand] (2)**

(ii) The Golden Quadrilateral has contributed towards improvement of the Indian economy- Explain. **[Understand] (2)**

(iii) (a) Which rail gauge is mostly limited to hilly areas only? **(3)**

(b) Name the organisation responsible for the maintenance of the National Highways of India.

(c) Which is the Inland Waterway that connects Prayagraj to Haldia? **[Understand & Remember]**

(iv) Give a reason for each of the following. **(3)**

(a) At present times, airports are being established even in smaller towns of India.

(b) Railways are well developed in the Northern states of India.

(c) Helicopter services are crucial during emergencies. **[Analyse]**

Question 12

(i) What is the impact of waste generation on the following? **(2)**

(a) Surface water (b) Landscape **[Understand]**

(ii) Why is dumping considered a harmful method of waste disposal? **[Analyse] (2)**

(iii) Fire broke out at the Kochi city waste treatment plant. Thick clouds of toxic smoke engulfed the city. The waste at the plant also contained plastic and biomedical wastes, both of which on combustion are extremely harmful for the general health of people. *– Economic Times, 10.03.2023* **(3)**

(a) Which method of waste management would have helped in reducing health hazard in the above case? **[Analyse]**

(b) Mention one measure you can adopt in school to reduce waste. **[Apply]**

(c) State one way in which domestic waste can be made useful. **[Understand]**

(iv) (a) What are landfills? **(3)**

(b) Enumerate two advantages of composting as a method of waste disposal. **[Remember & Apply]**

Answers

1. (i) (a) 301074 (b) Sand dunes

(ii) One hour

(iii) (a) North West (b) Jhat

(iv) (a) Powerline showing that the village now has electricity

(b) Longitude/Meridian

(v) Natural features : Sand dune, Broken Ground

Man made features : Cart track/Pack track/Permanent hut/temple

2.

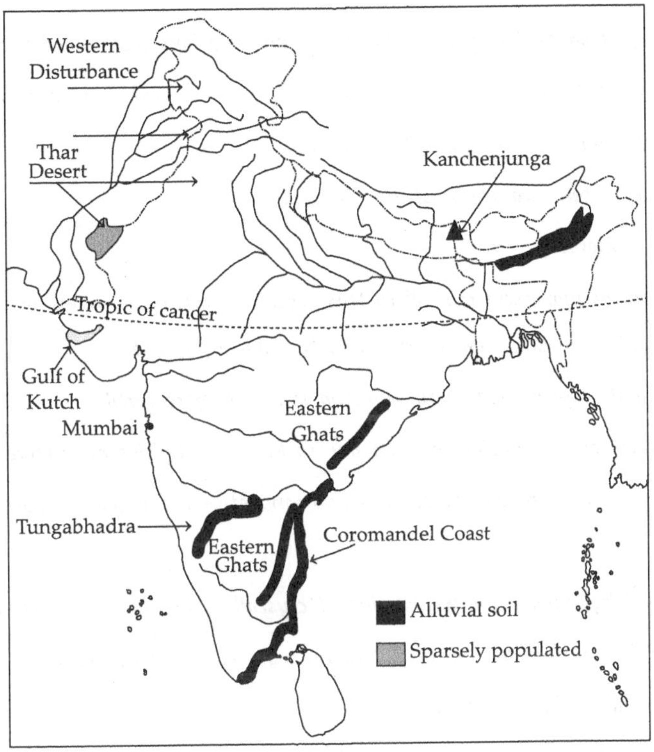

3. (i) (b) Causes rainfall in the Gangetic plains

(ii) (c) texture

(iii) (c) Ebony: Tropical Rainforest

(iv) (c) Percolation pit

(v) (c) Bituminous

(vi) (a) Both A and R are true and R is the correct explanation of A

(vii) (a) Sugarcane

(viii) (d) Rourkela

(ix) (a) Air transport because it is the fastest.

(x) (b) Recycling waste

4. (i) (a) Global warming/El Nino effects are the reason for the below normal rain in 2023.

(b) During June to September, India receives major amount of rainfall.

(ii) (a) **Punjab** Western disturbances originating in the Mediterranean region or Temperate cyclones

(b) **Tamil Nadu** North-East winter monsoon wind or retreating monsoon.

(iii) (a) Kerala gets rainfall from the summer monsoon much before Uttar Pradesh because Kerala lies in the South-West of the country where the South-West monsoon wind strikes first. The wind then advances to the North and reaches Uttar Pradesh.

(b) Visakhapatnam records a low annual range of temperature because Visakhapatnam has a coastal location and experiences the moderating influence of the sea.

(c) Winds are mostly offshore during the cold season because land loses heat fast and high pressure develops over it during the cold season. The surrounding seas remain warm and have low pressure during this time. Thus, winds blow from land to sea and are offshore.

(iv) (a) The annual range of temperature of station X is 10°C.

(b) April is the driest month.

(c) The wind that brings maximum rainfall to this station is retreating monsoon winds.

5. (i) (a) Bhangar and Khadar soil are been discussed in the above passage.

(b) The Khadar soil gets replenished every year and is hence more fertile.

(ii) (a) The possible causes of soil erosion in India due to human activities are deforestation and urbanisation.

(b) Crop rotation and contour ploughing are the two innovative techniques of agriculture that can help to prevent soil erosion.

(iii) (a) Red soil is formed by erosion and weathering of crystalline metamorphic and igneous rocks.

(b) Red soil is good for dry farming because it has a high iron content and good drainage, which helps retain moisture effectively in arid conditions.

(c) They are mostly found in parts of Odisha and Madhya Pradesh.

(iv) (a) Black soil has self-ploughing property because black soil hardens and cracks when dry which helps in aeration of the soil naturally.

(b) Laterite soil is not suitable for cultivation due to leaching, the essential minerals percolate down the soil profile making the top soil infertile.

(c) Alluvial soil is extensively found in the Northern Plains because the numerous rivers here bring large amounts of sediments and deposit them to form fertile plains.

6. (i) (a) He came across the Tidal Littoral forest.

(b) An area in India where this kind of vegetation is found is the delta of river Ganga in Sundarbans.

(ii) (a) Tropical Deciduous forests are commercially the most important forest belt in India because

(i) They supply high-quality hardwoods like teak and sal, which are crucial for furniture, construction and other industries.

(ii) They occur in pure stands making exploitation easier.

(b) Long and deep roots are typical characteristics of desert vegetation to draw water from deep underground as rainfall is scanty here.

(iii) The forest conservation is the need of the hour because

(a) **Biodiversity** Forests house 80% of terrestrial species, crucial for ecosystem balance.

(b) **Climate** Forests absorb CO_2, mitigating climate change.

(c) **Livelihoods** Forests support millions of people with food, medicine and shelter.

(iv) (a) Social forestry is the forest conservation method that involves the local community.

(b) Jhum cultivation is the primitive system of agriculture that had led to large scale destruction of the forest in the past.

(c) Reforestation is the process which involves planting two saplings for each tree that is felled.

7. (i) Irrigation is a need in India because

(a) Irrigation provides a reliable water supply, reducing reliance on unpredictable monsoon rains.

(b) It enables multiple cropping and higher crop yields, improving food security and farmers' incomes.

(ii) Inundation canals are floodwater canals that carry water only during the rainy season when the river floods. On the other hand, perennial canals carry water all year round as they have a weir or dam at the head to regulate the flow of water.

(iii) (a) A state in India where tube wells are commonly used is Punjab.

(b) The geographical condition that favour tubewell irrigation in Punjab are

(i) **High Water Table** Punjab has a high groundwater level, making it easier and cost-effective to access water through tube wells.

(ii) **Permeable Soil** Punjab has permeable alluvial soil, which allows easy drilling and efficient water absorption for irrigation.

(iv) (a) The rainwater harvesting is collection and storage of rainwater for future use.

(b) Two water harvesting practices followed in India are

(i) **Rooftop Rainwater Harvesting** A widespread practice across India where rainwater is collected from rooftops and stored in tanks or recharge pits for various uses such as drinking, irrigation and recharging groundwater.

(ii) **Stepwells (Baolis)** These structures in Gujarat and Rajasthan designed to store rainwater and provide a water source during dry periods.

8. (i) (a) Biogas generation can be achieved in every household of rural India primarily because of the abundance of organic waste available from agricultural residues, animal dung and kitchen waste, which are essential feedstocks for biogas production.

(b) Generation of Biogas energy proves to be a boom for Indian farmers due to the following reasons

(i) **Reduced Energy Costs** Biogas generation provides a renewable and cheaper alternative to traditional fuels like firewood and LPG, saving farmers money on energy expenses.

(ii) **Improved Soil Health** The by-product of biogas production, known as bio-slurry, is a nutrient-rich organic fertiliser that enhances soil fertility and crop yields, benefiting farmers economically.

(ii) (a) River Mahanadi

(b) Odisha is benefitted by Hirakud project.

(iii) (a) Iron ore can produce steel.

(b) Manganese is used to strengthen steel.

(c) Copper is found in Madhya Pradesh and Rajasthan

(iv) (a) Solar energy is being harnessed in the above picture.

(b) It is preferred over fossil fuels because it is a clean source of energy.

(c) India stands at an advantage in the production of solar energy due to the following reasons:

- **Abundant Sunlight** India's geographical location ensures ample solar radiation.
- **Supportive Policies** Government initiatives include subsidies and incentives for solar energy.
- **Cost Efficiency** Decreasing solar technology costs make it competitive with traditional energy sources

9. (i) Two agriculture reforms done by the government for betterment of the agriculture sector are

- **Crop Diversification Policies** Introducing policies to promote diversification of crops, reducing dependency on traditional crops and enhancing resilience against climate change.
- **Integrated Watershed Management** Implementing watershed management programs to improve water efficiency in agriculture, especially in regions prone to drought or water scarcity.

(ii) (a) **Rabi Crops** is sown in October or November and harvested in February or March.

On the other hand, **Kharif crops** is sown in May or June and harvested in September or October.

(b) Gujarat is the leading producer of groundnut in India.

(iii) (a) The soil found suitable for the growth of pulses is sandy loam soil. This type of soil provides good drainage and aeration, which are beneficial for the cultivation of pulses.

(b) Moong and Masoor are the two varieties of pulses grown in India.

(c) Pulses are the most popular food crop in India because

- It is a leguminous crop
- It can help to replenish the soil naturally.

(iv) (a) Cotton is grown by Rohan.

(b) Two climatic conditions suitable for cotton cultivation are

- **Warm Climate** Cotton thrives in warm temperatures, typically between 21°C to 30°C (70°F to 86°F), which promote optimal growth and development.
- **Moderate Rainfall** Cotton requires moderate but well-distributed rainfall during its growing season. Excessive rainfall or prolonged dry spells can adversely affect cotton yields

10. (i) The differences between small scale industries and large scale industries are

Small scale industries	**Large scale industries**
These require less capita l investment.	These require huge capital investment.
These industries employ less labour.	These industries employ more labour.

(ii) Cotton textile industries important for India's economy because:

- It gives us valuable foreign exchange
- It generates employment

(iii) (a) One reason for the growing popularity of the petrochemical industry in recent times is its durability.

(b) It is located close to oil refineries because

- To facilitates easy availability of raw materials
- To reduce transportation costs.

(c) Two petrochemical products are

- **Ethylene** Used in the production of plastics, fibers, and other industrial chemicals.
- **Propylene** Important for making plastics, synthetic fibers and various chemical products.

(iv) (a) Sugar production is gradually gaining importance in peninsular India because sugar plantations are well planned and scientifically managed.

(b) Indian silk products are becoming less popular in the international market because of the high price of Indian silk.

(c) The importance of the iron and steel industry will never decline because it is foundational to industrialisation, infrastructure development and essential sectors like construction and manufacturing.

11. (i) Two disadvantages of using waterways are

- It is a slow means of transport
- It can be affected by weather disturbances.

(ii) The Golden Quadrilateral improved India's economy in the following ways

- It has enhanced connectivity between major cities and industrial hubs.
- It has reduced transport costs and time.
- It has boosted trade and commerce across the country.

(iii) (a) The narrow gauge is mostly limited to hilly areas only.

(b) The organisation responsible for the maintenance of the National Highways of India is the National Highways Authority of India (NHAI).

(c) The inland waterway that connects Prayagraj (formerly Allahabad) to Haldia is National Waterway I (NW-1).

(iv) (a) At present times airports are being established even in smaller towns of India to encourage air travel for Indians as it saves time.

(b) Railways are well developed in the Northern states of India because of flat plain land.

(c) Helicopter services are crucial during emergencies because they can easily reach remote areas fast.

12. (i) (a) The impact of waste generation on surface water is that waste can contaminate surface water sources, leading to the spread of diseases and harming aquatic life.

(b) The impact of waste generation on the landscape is that waste can spoil the aesthetics of the landscape, leading to degradation of scenic beauty and potentially reducing property values.

(ii) Dumping is considered a harmful method of disposal because it leads to soil pollution and underground water pollution.

(iii) (a) Implementing proper segregation of waste and recycling would have helped in reducing health hazards in the above case.

(b) One measure that can be adopted in school to reduce waste is to promote the use of reusable water bottles and lunch boxes instead of single-use plastic items.

(c) One way in which domestic waste can be made useful is through composting organic waste to produce nutrient-rich compost for gardening and agriculture.

(iv) (a) Landfills are large areas in the outskirts of towns and cities where wastes are deposited in the ground and covered with Earth. The waste gradually decomposes, decreases in volume and gets converted to humus.

(b) Advantages of composting as a method of which disposal are

- **Reduces Landfill Waste** Composting diverts organic waste from landfills, decreasing environmental impact.
- **Produces Nutrient-rich Compost** Composting creates a valuable soil amendment that improves soil fertility and supports sustainable agriculture.

SAMPLE QUESTION PAPER
(UNSOLVED)
GEOGRAPHY X

General Instructions

Maximum Marks : 80

Time allowed : Two hours

Answers to this paper must be written on the answer sheet provided separately.

You will **not** be allowed to write during the first **15** minutes.

This time is to be spent in reading the question paper.

The time given at the head of this paper is the time allowed for writing the answers.

Part I is compulsory. All questions from Part I are to be attempted.

A total of **five** questions are to be attempted from **Part II**.

The intended marks for questions or parts of questions are given brackets ().

Part - I

(30 Marks)

Attempt all questions from this Part.

Question 1

Study the extract of the Survey of India Map Sheet No. G43S10 (Map 4 given at the end) Easting 47-57, Northing 24-34 and answer the following questions.

(i) Give six figure grid reference of

(a) Veterinary hospital in grid square 4924 **(2)**

(b) Brick Klin near Serua

(ii) (a) Calculate the length of N.H 168 from grid square 4925 to grid square 5222 in km. **(2)**

(b) What do the tiny curved black lines in grid square 4932 indicate?

(iii) (a) What kind of road connect Revdar to Warka and Selwara to Jolpur? **(2)**

(b) Give two reasons to show that the area in the map experiences seasonal rainfall.

(iv) (a) What could be the occupation of the people in the settlement of Revdar? **(2)**

(b) What does 3r in 5630 indicate?

(v) (a) What is the settlement pattern in grid square 5230? **(2)**

(b) Give four figure grid reference of the marble stone querries.

Question 2

On the outline map of India provided **(10)**

(i) Mark an area where red soil is found.

(ii) Mark and label a mountain pass in Himachal Pradesh.

(iii) Mark and label an important offshore oil field in Maharashtra.

(iv) Mark and name the largest lake in Kerala.

(v) Mark and label the Prime Meridian equivalent of India.

(vi) Mark and name one of India's largest coal fields in Jharkhand.

(vii) Mark and name the largest mangrove forests in the world.

(viii) Mark and label the state where Malwa plateau is primarily located.

(ix) Mark and label Aravalli range.

(x) Mark the city often known as the 'Silicon valley of India'.

Question 3

(i) Choose the correct answers to the questions from the given options. **(1)**

Assertion (A) The western coast of India receives heavy rainfall during the monsoon season.

Reason (R) The Western Ghats force the moisture-laden winds of the South-West monsoon to rise, causing orographic rainfall.

(a) Both (A) and (R) are true and (R) is the correct explanation for (A).
(b) Both (A) and (R) are true and (R) is not the correct explanation for (A).
(c) (A) is true and (R) is false.
(d) (A) is false and (R) is true.

(ii) Which of the following soils is formed due to weathering of ancient crystalline rocks? **(1)**

(a) Black soil
(b) Red soil
(c) Alluvial soil
(d) Peaty soil

(iii) The type of forest shown in the image below is found at high altitudes and consists of coniferous trees like Pine and Deodar. Identify the forest type **(1)**

(a) Tropical Evergreen Forest
(b) Tropical Deciduous Forest
(c) Montane Forest
(d) Mangrove Forest

(iv) Which method of irrigation is most suitable for regions with sandy soil and water scarcity? **(1)**

(a) Canal irrigation
(b) Drip irrigation
(c) Tank irrigation
(d) Perennial irrigation

(v) Jharia : Coal :: Kudremukh : .... **(1)**

(a) Bauxite (b) Iron Ore

(c) Limestone (d) Gold

(vi) Which of the following crops is grown using the 'Ratooning' method? **(1)**

(a) Wheat (b) Sugarcane

(c) Rice (d) Jute

(vii) Which industry is considered the sunrise industry in India? **(1)**

(a) Textile Industry (b) Information Technology Industry

(c) Cement Industry (d) Iron and Steel Industry

(viii) Which of the following is a major centre for India's shipbuilding industry? **(1)**

(a) Mumbai (b) Jaipur

(c) Lucknow (d) Bhopal

(ix) Which of the following is an advantage of pipelines as a mode of transport? **(1)**

(a) Highly flexible for carrying all types of goods (b) Most suitable for carrying liquid and gaseous materials

(c) Cheapest mode for passenger transport (d) Fastest mode of transport

(x) A farmer wants to improve soil fertility using natural methods. Which of the following waste materials should he use? **(1)**

(a) Broken glass and metal scraps (b) Plastic bags and wrappers

(c) Vegetable peels and animal dung (d) Old newspapers and cardboard

Part - II

(50 Marks)

Attempt any five questions from this Part.

Question 4

(i) The retreating monsoon season affects different parts of India in different ways. **(2)**

(a) Why does Tamil Nadu receive most of its rainfall during the retreating monsoon season?

(b) How does the retreating monsoon contribute to the formation of cyclones in the Bay of Bengal?

(ii) (a) Why does Delhi experience extreme summers and winters, while Mumbai has a moderate climate? **(2)**

(b) Name the factor responsible for this difference.

(iii) With reference to Figure A and Figure B given below, answer the questions that follow. **(3)**

South-West Monsoon

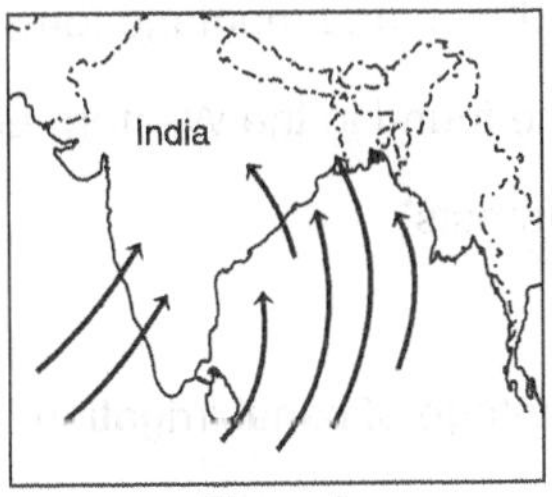

Figure A

North-East Monsoon

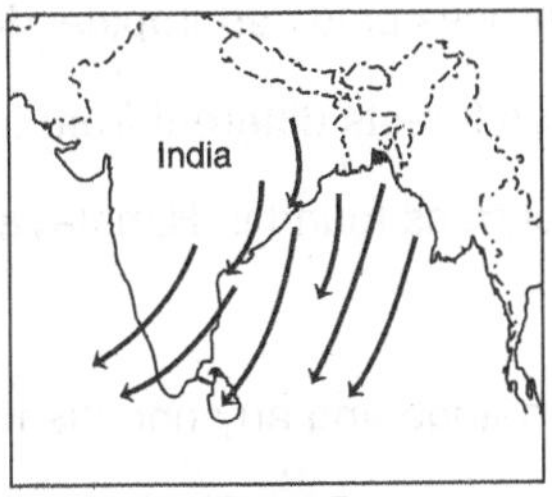

Figure B

(a) Which part of India receives the highest rainfall due to the winds shown in Figure B?

(b) Which Indian state benefits from the winds shown in Figure A?

(iv) Study the climate data of station X and answer the following questions **(3)**

Month	Jan	Feb	Mar	Apr	May	Jun	July	Aug	Sep	Oct	Nov	Dec
Temp (°C)	22.2	25.4	26.4	28.3	31.3	34.6	36.2	35.4	34.3	32.1	28.5	25.5
Rainfall (cm)	0.23	0.32	-	0.43	2.72	35.4	42.7	39.6	26.8	7.08	2.03	-

(a) Identify the wettest month based on the rainfall data.

(b) Which month receives the least rainfall?

(c) What is the total annual rainfall received by station X?

Question 5

(i) The Deccan Plateau is known for its rich soil, which is ideal for cotton cultivation. This region is a major contributor to India's cotton industry. **(2)**

(a) Name the soil type found predominantly in the Deccan Plateau.

(b) Mention two characteristics of this soil that make it suitable for cotton farming.

(ii) (a) How is alluvial soil classified based on its age? **(2)**

(b) Which type of alluvial soil is more fertile and why?

(iii) Give a geographical reason to explain each of the following **(3)**

(a) Farmers add lime to laterite soil before cultivation.

(b) Loamy soil is considered ideal for agriculture.

(c) Soil erosion is more common in deforested areas.

(iv) With reference to desert soil of India, answer the following questions **(3)**

(a) In which region is desert soil found?

(b) Why does desert soil have high salt content?

(c) Name one method used to improve the fertility of desert soil.

Question 6

(i) India has seen the highest rise in deforestation in the last 30 years, with a stark surge recorded between 2015 and 2020, according to a new report. *Source: Down To Earth* **(2)**

(a) Mention two major causes of deforestation in India.

(b) How does deforestation affect the climate?

(ii) Mention any two characteristics of tropical desert forests. **(2)**

(iii) State any three differences between tropical deciduous and montane forests. **(3)**

(iv) (a) Why are Himalayan forests different from those found in the Western Ghats? **(3)**

(b) Name two types of trees found in Himalayan forests.

Question 7

(i) Mention any one advantage and any one disadvantage of canal irrigation. **(2)**

(ii) Explain any two modern methods of irrigation. **(2)**

(iii) Give one reason to explain each of the following **(3)**

(a) Drip irrigation is suitable for arid and semi-arid regions.

(b) Tank irrigation is more popular in peninsular India.

(c) Groundwater depletion is a major issue in northwestern India.

(iv) Discuss any three structures used to recharge groundwater. **(3)**

Question 8

(i) Cheap electricity from renewable sources could provide 65 percent of the world's total electricity supply by 2030. *United Nations* **(2)**

(a) Name a renewable energy source that is widely used in rural India for cooking and lighting.

(b) Mention one advantage of using wind energy over thermal power.

(ii) (a) What is geothermal energy and where is it found in India? **(2)**

(b) State one limitation of using geothermal energy.

(iii) Give a reason for each of the following. **(3)**

(a) India has large reserves of coal but still imports petroleum.

(b) Nuclear energy is considered an efficient source of power.

(c) Limestone is an essential raw material for the cement industry.

(iv) **(3)**

(a) Name the primary fuel used in the power plants shown in the image.

(b) What is one major disadvantage of relying on this energy source?

(c) Name one thermal power plant in India.

Question 9

(i) Mention two climatic conditions that favour the cultivation of wheat. **(2)**

(ii) Give any two differences between intensive and extensive farming. **(2)**

(iii) Give one reason to explain each of the following **(3)**

(a) Sugarcane yield per hectare is higher in the southern states.

(b) Pulses are mostly grown in rotation with other crops.

(c) Ratoon cropping is becoming increasingly popular in India.

(iv) Explain the following **(3)**

(a) Shifting Cultivation (b) Rabi Crops (c) Terrace Farming

Question 10

(i) Mention two reasons why Maharashtra is a major center for the automobile industry. **(2)**

(ii) Gujarat a leading state in the petrochemical industry. Give two reasons to justify the statement. **(2)**

(iii) (a) Which city is known as the 'Manchester of South India' for its textile industry? **(3)**

(b) Mention any two factors that have contributed to the growth of the textile industry in this city.

(iv) Priya saw a factory emitting smoke and releasing wastewater into a nearby river. The factory produces cement, an essential material for construction. **(3)**

(a) Suggest one way this industry can reduce pollution.

(b) Name one raw material used in cement production.

Question 11

(i) Why is the development of expressways important for a country's economy? **(2)**

(ii) Mention any two problems faced by the Indian railway network. **(2)**

(iii) Name the following **(3)**

(a) The inland waterway that connects Allahabad and Haldia.

(b) The busiest port in India, located in Maharashtra.

(c) The longest national highway in India.

(iv) Give a reason for each of the following. **(3)**

(a) Road transport is more suitable for short distances than rail transport.

(b) Metro rail services are expanding rapidly in Indian cities.

(c) Coastal shipping is an important mode of transport for India.

Question 12

(i) (a) Why has there been a significant rise in plastic waste in urban areas? **(2)**

(b) Define composting.

(ii) Around 90% of Delhi residents don't know how to dispose of electronic waste, according to a 2016 study conducted by a non-governmental organisation Toxic Link. *Hindustan Times* **(2)**

As a responsible citizen, what ways will you suggest to your neighbours to manage E-waste effectively?

(iii) Identify the correct waste management practice for each situation **(3)**

(a) Converting vegetable peels and garden waste into compost.

(b) Carrying a cloth bag instead of using plastic bags.

(c) Donating old clothes instead of throwing them away.

(iv) Give a reason for the following statements **(3)**

(a) Burning of waste should be discouraged.

(b) Segregation of waste is important before disposal.

(c) Waste management is crucial for sustainable development.